From Tank Town To High Tech

SUNY Series in the Anthropology of Work
June C. Nash, Editor

From Tank Town To High Tech
The Clash of Community and Industrial Cycles

JUNE C. NASH

State University of New York Press

Published by
State University of New York Press, Albany

For information, address State University of New York
Press, State University Plaza, Albany, N.Y. 12246

Library of Congress Cataloging-in-Publication Data

Nash, June C., 1927–
    From tank town to high tech : the clash of community and industrial cycles
    June C. Nash
        p. cm. — (SUNY series in the anthropology of work)
    Bibliography: p.
    Includes index.
    ISBN 0-88706-938-X. ISBN 0-88706-939-8 (pbk.)
        1. Labor and laboring classes — Massachusetts — Pittsfield — History — 20th cen-
    tury. 2. Pittsfield (Mass.) — Economic conditions. 3. Pittsfield (Mass.) — Social conditions.
    4. General Electric Company — History — 20th century. I. Title. II. Series.
    HD8085.P653N37 1989
    330.9744'1 — dc19   88-15378
                                                                                    CIP

10 9 8 7 6 5 4 3 2 1

Contents

List of Tables

The last "tank" power transformer moves out of GE down North Street to its final destination in the Electric Power Research Institute. Photo by Joel Librizzi. Printed in *The Berkshire Eagle*, April 1989.

Acknowledgements

I am grateful to Max Kirsch for his assistance with the survey of workers from the International Union of Electric and Radio Workers Local 255 current and laid off list of members and with some of the other interviews with community members. His tact, insight and endurance contributed greatly to this study which will also be the basis for his Ph.D. thesis. My daughter, Laura, helped transcribe the many taped interviews, as did Leslie Gill and Elaine Holder. I have talked over the events recorded here with Kay Warren and Susan Bourque, who shared with us many of the cultural attractions that make the Berkshires ''a better place to live in,'' as the Chamber of Commerce says in its brochure to lure business. They inspired me to give form and meaning to these experiences when I might otherwise simply have relaxed and enjoyed them. Carol Greenhouse and Robert Asher brought their expertise on American culture to reading an earlier version that has helped considerably in the revision. An anonymous reader's careful critique has also contributed to greater clarity in the final version.

In the month that I spent at the Rockefeller Center in Bellagio, Italy, I was able to pull together the many thousands of pieces of information and recorded conversations that went into this book. I shall forever recall the gracious attentions of the senores Celli and the companionship of the scholars in residence during my stay. I am particularly grateful for the help of Ralph Wedgewood, who rescued me after a ''fatal error'' showed up on my computer screen.

This book owes much to Theresa, Vicky, Al, Carl, John, Dora, Alex, Nancy, Ed, Alice, Bus, and the many other Pittsfield natives who gave of their time and thoughts to enable me to write it. The fine reporting of local events in *The Berkshire Eagle* provided a daily cue as well as historical source to fieldwork. I was able to take advantage of the cooperative staff of the Pittsfield library, the newspaper archives and the excellent research facilities at Smith College and the University of Massachusetts at Amherst libraries.

I am grateful to my daughter, Laura, my son, Eric, and Mathew McCaslin for bringing their joyful presence to the quiet retreat in

Plainfield where I lived while working on the project. The book is dedicated to my mother, Mary Josephine Salloway Bousley, who spent her last summers listening to and joining in the conversations that became a part of it. It is also dedicated to my late husband, Herbert Menzel, who provided the intellectual stimulus to help me in writing the proposal and in working out a random sample of subjects. More importantly, he gave credibility to my entry into what anthropologists like to call "complex" society, helping with the wining and dining that provided the context in which those who had experienced Pittsfield's industrial process shared their thoughts with us. His insightful remarks upon reading the manuscript just before his death were of inestimable value. He brought clarity where there was confusion, and introduced force were it was merited.

Preface

I returned from my last field trip to Bolivia with the feeling that I had to do my next field work in my own country. It was 1971. The war in Vietnam was still going on and the moon landing had just been achieved. I had become so distanced from my native land that I could no longer answer the questions people in Third World countries asked North Americans. How could a nation that could send a spaceship to the moon endure poverty at home? Why do workers support the wars against their brothers and sisters in Third World countries? How do workers in the big corporations live? These were questions that Bolivian miners asked and to which I had no answer.

When I completed work on the materials that I had collected in Bolivia, I began to think of a project in the United States that would enable me to answer some of the questions posed by workers in the Third World. Like Anthony Wallace, who chose to write about Rockdale where he lived, I chose the industrial city of Pittsfield — twenty minutes by car from the Berkshire hilltown where we lived during the summer. There were many good reasons for the choice, besides its convenient location. It was host to a multinational corporation; General Electric had dominated the economic life of the community since 1903 when it bought out an owner-inventor's firm. The city had grown with the corporation, attracting immigrant labor in the early decades of the twentieth century and drawing on a national labor force in World War II. Like most U.S. corporations, General Electric began to restrict domestic production of consumer goods in the 1970s and 1980s, as the company expanded to low-wage areas throughout the world. At the same time, the corporation began restructuring the industry around the high-tech defense production favored by the corporation in these decades and around research and design in plastics. Defense production, which grew to a $250 million annual sales industry in the 1980s, was sharply curtailed in June 1988 when General Electric announced a proposed reduction of 900 jobs and $40 million cut in the $100 million payroll (*The Berkshire Eagle* June 5, 1988). A few smaller plants in Pittsfield manufacturing paper products, braid and machinery, survived from the early nineteenth-century industrialization. Some of

1

these, bought by conglomerates, were forced by central headquarters to close down during my field stay. Twenty small companies making plastic molds and products from injection molds had been organized by men trained at General Electric before they abandoned production and were the promise of future growth. The increase in service jobs employing the young and old cannot sustain the work force laid off at General Electric.

As a student at the University of Chicago, I was impressed with the lectures of William Lloyd Warner based on his studies in a New England industrial community. But, it requires a great deal of experience in other societies to view what is commonplace and "natural" in one's own culture as problematic. Sol Tax, another of my professors at the University of Chicago, put this in reverse perspective when he urged students to take very careful notes, particularly in the early days of field work when commonplace behaviors still strike one as peculiar. The shock of experiencing different ways of thinking and behaving wears off as one becomes accustomed to them. I followed this dictum in my work with the Maya of Guatemala, the Chiapas and the tin miners of Boliva. By the time I was ready to do work in my own culture, I felt that I had achieved the distance that enabled me to see rituals in daily routines and cultural patterns in pragmatic solutions. This study would focus on the impact of Pittsfield's industrial changes on the community and on families.

My fieldwork began formally in 1982 when I received grants from the National Science Foundation and the National Endowment for the Humanities. I had already met some of the women and men who organized the labor movement at meetings of the retirees club, and I had done preliminary interviews with people on the development committees, in women's organizations and in the peace movement. I also interviewed spokespersons for General Electric, along with owners and managers of smaller corporations and companies. Interviews focusing on the work histories of 100 workers on the International Union of Electrical Workers (IUE) active and laid-off lists broadened our network of participants. May Kirsch assisted me in these and some of the other interviews in 1982.

The focus of this book is on the workers in these industrial organizations and it looks at how the culture that they construct and reproduce in their daily lives is adapted to, and in turn affects, the operation of the global corporation in their community. The trade unions that for a brief period in the thirties presented an alternative pattern for structuring industrial relations reached an accommodation in the post-World War II period that gave the corporations the initiative to organize production. Today's visionaries of a new pattern are not yet recognized in leadership roles either in the corporation or in unions. Outside the institutionalized spaces in which corporate hegemony

Author Discusses Research with Visitor in Front of Mural
Painted in the 1970's Recession on North Street.

operates, they work in the movements concerned with women's rights, peace activism, and the environment. Their voices may yet prevail as people lose faith in the military buildup that sustains an otherwise stagnating economy.

The past achievements of the labor movement were coopted into what became corporate hegemonic control. My analysis of corporate hegemony differs somewhat from that of Gramsci, who portrayed the dimensions of corporate hegemony when it was being forged by Ford in the twenties, in stressing the worker's initiative in developing the institutions that made welfare capitalism work. Gramsci attributes that leadership to the corporate managers themselves. The men of vision in the corporations, such as Owen D. Young and Gerard Swope of General Electric, were informed by the demands made by workers who participated in the labor struggles of the turn of the century. As I see it, the strength of these men, women, and what they imparted to the corporate leaders and, through their input, to the government structures that attempted to guide the economic destiny of the nation, was inspired by the workers' vision of their future within capitalism. The industrial unions organized by workers introduced some of the basic terms of corporate organization through collective bargaining: pension, vacations with pay, medical insurance and other benefits that have stabilized the economy. These workers, who built General Electric in its periods of greatest growth in the twenties and during World War II, taught me much of what I have learned about those periods.

I brought to my field work in Pittsfield an interest in the relationship between consciousness and economic relations of production that I explored in Bolivian tin mining communities. Most foreign observers are struck by the lack of class consciousness and the absence of working-class political parties in the United States. Some attribute this to "false consciousness," assuming that the identification of workers' interests with those of the corporation is based on a failure by the workers to perceive their own goals as antagonistic. The implicit economic determinism in this view is challenged when we consider the multiplicity of cultural factors that condition the relations between classes. Within three or four generations, immigrants who came to work on the highway and construction gangs and in the factories have risen to the top of those institutions. They have experienced in their own lives and their children's the opportunities that they forged for themselves. The stigma associated with migration has turned to pride in their achievements. Some of the cultural factors they brought have become a part of the plant and the community that hosted it. Italians, who could not get a job in General Electric until World War I, were able to get a bocce ball court in the General Electric Athletic Association, and the company brought in carloads of grapes for them to make wine in the fall. Baseball teams formed by workers were sponsored by the company that for a time gave preferential hiring to good ball players. These after-work pursuits enhanced the esprit de corps on the job. In times of tension they provided a context to discuss common problems and plan collective action. Ethnic and kinship ties were extended into work relations as employees found jobs for family and friends in the shop where they worked. These ties strengthened their commitment to the corporation and to the wider society.

In the current period of deindustrialization so incisively analyzed by Barry Bluestone and Bennet Harrison (1982) this stability, which was based on the gains made by industrial workers in the large corporations, is threatened. The loss of blue-collar jobs combined with the attack on federal human resources programs during the Reagan period have eroded the preferred position of core industrial workers. Pittsfield is one of many U.S. cities that has experienced the impact of these changes in ways that threaten corporate hegemony. The failure of the corporation to maintain their side of the bargain—secure jobs and advancement to higher positions for workers and their children—nullifies the legitimacy of corporate managerial control of the economy and the social arrangements to support it. The layoffs of the young active work force are not matched by the influx of professionals and technicians who have been hired in the expanded ordnance division or plastics technology center at General Electric. Jobs in the expanded tourist industry in the Berkshires offer low pay and lack most of the benefits provided by the corporation. The Pittsfield city council and development committee build industrial parks and give free land and tax deferments in an effort to attract industries, much as Melanesian cargo cults built quays and landing fields to attract the wealth of supply ships and planes that abandoned their ports in the Pacific Islands when the wars were over. As developers try to remodel the town to fit the image of a quaint New England industrial city, installing wrought iron benches in parks on the main street and building "saltboxes" and "colonials" in new residential areas, the Salvation Army and the churches try to cope with the rising number of homeless individuals and families. How the citizens of this community respond to this major restructuring of Pittsfield's industries is the subject of this book. Since a similar process is happening in many industrial cities throughout the United States, their experience is an important base for assessing future developments.

My field work ended in November 1986 when General Electric announced the closing of the power transformer division that had been the mainstay of the local plant. Although the corporation had been "downsizing" its electrical machinery plant in Pittsfield, it still came as a surprise to workers attending a district council meeting of the International Union of Electrical, Radio and Machine Workers (IUE) in the local Hilton Hotel that the announcement was coupled with a statement of the decision to open a joint operation with Westinghouse to produce power transformers in Canada. The depth of the penetration of corporation hegemonic ideology was expressed by a delegate from the Lynn, MA plant who stated, "GE is climbing into bed with the competition and leaving us bareassed out in the cold!" Workers objected not so much to the arbitrary control of investments by corporations that were not held accountable to the community, as to the failure to live up to their own code of competitive free enterprise within national boundaries.

Yet the discourse between employees and an ever more distant management is widening and the corporation spokespeople no longer attempt to overcome the sense that "things are out of whack", as one retiree put it. At a time when General Electric leaders are talking about "growth through globalization" (John F. Welch, Jr. Chairman and Chief Executive Officer of General Electric, message "To our shareholders," *GE 1987 Annual Report,* Fairfield Ct. 1988) and calling for a "strong, lean machine," (Welch, quoted in Mark Potts' special to the *Washington Post,* reprinted in *The Berkshire Eagle* May 29, 1988:D1) union leaders in General Electric plants throughout the country are demanding job security, pensions, and benefits "to enable workers to live in their communities," (Lewis C. Cuyler, *The Berkshire Eagle* June 1, 1988) as they entered negotiations for a three-year contract.

Chapter 1

Community and Corporate Hegemony

A glossy color brochure printed by the Berkshire County Development Corporation announced the advantages of bringing your business to the Berkshires. Color photos of the lakes, residences surrounded by well-kept lawns, meadows with sheep grazing on them, golf courses and ski slopes call attention to "...a unique combination of business and personal environments which represents a place that's better for your business, better for your family, better for your employees and better for you...we want you and your business here."

The features that make Berkshire County better are specified: an available labor force ever since Turner and Cook Inc. had a buggy whip business in 1796 and Crane and Company Inc. began to make paper in 1801; workers in the forefront of developments in plastics, paper manufacturing, machinery, structural steel and pre-cast concrete, industrial threads, textiles, electronic components; analysis and manufacture of instruments for pollution control; a low crime rate, parks, hospitals, and public schools, a community college, sponsored athletic programs. It is, the authors conclude, a good place to live, offering a choice of lifestyles and substantial financial resources in the many banks servicing the business community. A slide show produced by the Central Berkshire Chamber of Commerce amplifies what this variety of lifestyles includes, calling attention to the quiet, crime-free streets, fine colleges and universities, Tanglewood and other cultural institutions, as well as sports and recreational facilities. Picture postcards showing skiers, a candlelight "business dinner" at Tanglewood and tree-lined highways are sent out to prospective enterprises. The message on the reverse side, "If quality of life is important to you — or your employees — you may find a move to Pittsfield rewarding," is that of the general manager of the local plant of General Electric.

The campaign exemplifies a response of communities throughout the United States as they attempt to woo new high-tech industries to overcome the loss of jobs in smokestack industries and the decline in local tax revenue. It stems from the logic of intensifying salesmanship when there is a decline in prosperity. In the present crisis of U.S.

capitalism, corporations are increasing sales promotion and buying out smaller firms in the U.S. while investing overseas in production facilities to compete in the new international order. At the same time, communities are seeking to sell themselves to prospective employers rather than adapting new ownership and control mechanism. The strength of the industrial system that once rested on competitive expansion and production is vitiated as large corporations disinvest in productive facilities at home.

The thrust of the campaign is to promote a culturally advanced area with "a blend of cosmopolitan sophistication and rural beauty." Descriptively the text is accurate. There is an excellent infrastructure, with financial institutions, rail lines, water reservoirs, airport and roads, though the city lacks a bypass connecting with the major highways that would link industries with Boston and Albany markets. The educational and recreational facilities are so good that people use these facilities in preference to private schools or resorts in other areas, even when they could afford such choices. This infrastructure was put in place by nineteenth-century industrial and community leaders. It is now being advertised to lure new high-technology industries to replace those that have been removed to the south and overseas throughout the twentieth century.

The city of Pittsfield, where I had chosen to study the impact of industry on community, encompasses much more than the features emphasized by the promotional material. It is a living museum of industries that go back to the eighteenth century, when water mills facilitated but did not displace domestic production by the pioneer householders. Elegant red brick factories on the preferred water sites of the many rivers and brooks now house small injection mold and mold-making concerns. General Electric Company purchased the Stanley Electric Company, a locally organized electrical machinery company, in 1903. It still uses some of the older buildings of the Stanley works situated on the banks of Silver Lake. People say that the lake reflects even the faintest glimmer of the moon because of the accumulated metals and chemicals cast out by successions of mills, forges, tanneries and factories that were located there. The last industry to occupy this site was the General Electric gynal plastics operation which was closed down in December 1982. One of the workers that we interviewed on his last day of work spoke bitterly of the abrupt layoff as General Electric's last Christmas present.

Farther east is the main building for the Power Transformer Division, which at one time employed ten thousand workers but by 1986 employed less than 2,000. In November 1986 General Electric announced that it would stop production of power transformers, laying off 1,300 workers and retaining only 600 in bushings and arrestors, and in 1988 bulldozers were removing the structure. Ordnance Systems, where General Electric produces defense contracts, has gradually taken up space in the remaining facilities formerly occupied by Power Transformer. Across the street at the extreme end of the employees parking lot is a huge smoke stack reminiscent of the old industries that were replaced by the advent of electrical machinery. This is where the company is burning off polychlorinated biphenyls, once used in pyranol, the insulant for power transformers, that have accumulated on the site or have been shipped in from other General Electric plants. One of the few thermal oxidizers in the country approved by the Environmental Protection Agency, this has become a specialization of the local plant.

If we turn left off East Street beyond the main building that housed power transformers and travel north on Plastics Avenue (formerly called Ceramics Avenue), we come to what appears to be the future of the corporation and the community. With vaulted arches encased in a polished sheen of lexan over a brick base, this space-age building was constructed in 1984 to provide offices and laboratories for a multinational venture General Electric has planned for research and design in plastics. Built on the curve of the Housatonic River where a Mohegan Indian village was settled before white encroachment, the Massachusetts State Historical Preservation Society decided against investigating the excavation site because it was mostly landfill shipped in from other General Electric sties and considered to be potentially hazardous. The new facility employs 700, for the most part highly skilled and educated engineers, designers and managers, and despite high sales in the first few years of its development, it is not expected to increase employment by more than 30 percent, since there will be no production work on the site. Some test units will be produced in one or another of the twenty small plastics firms in the area, many of them started by former General Electric technicians when mold and injection plastic production was phased out by the corporation.

The growth of Stanley Electric Company, formed in 1887, that began to produce alternate current power generators in 1890, transformed Pittsfield from a declining textile mill town like its neighbors to a thriving industrial city. When General Electric bought out the local plant in 1903, production was expanded until it employed over 6,000 workers by World War I. The growth of the firm ensured the growth of the town. By 1929 when GE had its best year, the population had reached almost fifty thousand, more than twice Pittsfield's size when General Electric bought the plant. During the peak production year of World War II, when the plant employed twelve thousand, the population of the city reached 53,560, more than two-and-a-half times its size in 1900. The population peakwas reached in the 1970 census, which recorded over 57,000 citizens.

The growth of the city in the early decades of the twentieth century was marked by the proliferation of many distinct neighborhoods reflecting the diversified work force drawn from throughout the world. Many of the Polish and French-Canadian immigrants, who were drawn by the textile mills, and Italian workers, who worked on the road and construction crews, eventually found jobs in the General Electric plant.

The prosperity of the city was increasingly based on activity at the plant, which employed at times up to three-quarters of the work force. When General Electric has a cold, people say, the city gets pneumonia. Yet there are few laws, regulations or even plans that try to insure a stable level of employment. Town officials, local businessmen and the workers accept General Electric's statements as to what their market pressures are and try to work their lives around the cycles of production these pressures create. The problems faced by Pittsfield city officials "reflect national trends far beyond their control," as a local newspaper reporter commented when the new mayor was criticized for her handling of layoffs in Ordnance and other firms, yet these developments become major issues in local elections (Anthony Flint in *The Berkshire Eagle* June 5, 1988).

This consensus between workers and the corporation characterized relations in the community, even with severe attrition of the production work force in the Power Transformer Division after the mid-seventies and particularly after 1982. Finally the General Electric Company announced on November 22, 1986 that the entire division would be closed. Over half of the two thousand workers still working in the plant would be laid off in 1987, and the company could not promise that the remaining workers would continue to be employed making arrestors and bushings.

The announcement came almost one hundred years after William Stanley formed the original company in 1890. It was not entirely a surprise, since the Power Transformer Division has laid off over 3,000 workers since 1974. The attrition of blue-collar employment that is concomitant with the shift from power transfomer to ordnance production has split generations, as children leave the city to find jobs elsewhere. The gap between a highly-paid technical staff and an unemployed or marginally-employed working class is growing as jobs for production workers in the corporation decrease.

What is happening in Pittsfield is happening throughout the industrial northeast and midwest as the restructuring of American industry proceeds. This book is about the impact of these changes in employment opportunities and in the redistribution of profits on community and family. The core of the problem is the cultural construction of corporate hegemony and how that is affected by the current conversion from consumer-production industries to high-technology defense production and research and design. By corporate hegemony I mean the leadership by the great corporations that took shape at the turn of the twentieth century in setting the agenda for industrial organization. I shall argue that this leadership was effected not only by the corporation's cooptation of workers' struggles, but also by government mediation forcing private capital to yield some of its surpluses through taxation, minimum-wage laws, unemployment compensation and other rights won by the labor movement. These gains often served to contain the labor movement within the parameters of private capitalist accumulation.

In the present climate of government deregulation and corporate disinvestment I address some of the prevalent questions that arise in communities experiencing the restructuring of industry: How do people respond to these changes behaviorally and in their own planning? How have smaller industries and businesses adapted to the transformation in the large corporation that has dominated the local economy? How have municipal, county and state officials adapted their strategies to counter economic decline and the disruption caused by unemployment and growing wealth differences? Is hegemonic control weakening with the breakdown of the corporate side of the ledger in the social contract — jobs and good wages for blue-color workers?

The Construction of Corporate Hegemony

Hegemony is, in Gramsci's (Williams 1960: 587) terms:

> ...an order in which a certain way of life and thought is dominant, in which one concept of reality is diffused throughout society in all its institutional and private manifestations, informing with its spirit all taste, morality, customs, religious and political principles, and all social relations, particularly in their intellectual and moral connotations.

Hegemonic control rests on persuasion as well as force, gaining consensus through concessions. In the United States the social contract between labor and corporations was based on an accord that ensured labor peace and a minimum of political activity in return for well-paid jobs for the primary sector of the work force. Priority given to male white workers reinforced the terms of the accord with a lower-paid female and black work force pulled into or expelled from the labor market in response to economic cycles. When Gramsci (1973:285) analyzed American corporate hegemony fifty years ago he noted that:

> ...it was relatively easy to rationalise production and labour by a skillful combination of force (destruction of working class trade unionism on a territorial basis) and persuasion (high wages, various

social benefits, extremely subtle ideological and political propaganda) and thus succeed in making the whole life of the nation revolve around production. Hegemony here is born in the factory and requires for its exercise only a minute quantity of professional, political, and ideological intermediaries.

While some aspects of this control system have changed in the last half century, particularly those related to the exercise of state repressive measures, others have been enhanced over the years.

The construction and maintenance of hegemony is increasingly based on inputs from labor and professionals as well as corporate managers. What changed the picture was the labor struggles of the thirties. The Wagner Act put the sanction of the federal government behind the right of workers to form autonomous trade union organizations and the National Labor Relations Board provided the legal machinery to ensure its enactment. These changes affecting the workplace were combined with opening up of educational opportunities in state-supported schools and the entry of working-class children into technical and managerial positions. Social Security legislation passed in 1935 lessened the dependency of retired workers on adult children, and the Fair Labor Standards Act eliminated the competition between generations by setting minimum wages and limiting the entry of children into the labor force. Unemployment compensation relieved workers of the necessity of taking just any job available, regardless of their training and level of expertise. Corporate hegemony works in America, as Stuart Hall and Tony Jefferson (1983:39) indicate it does in Great Britain, "by inserting the subordinate class into the key institutions and structures which support the power and social authority of the dominant order."

The fruits of the organization of the industrial unions in the 1930s were not fully realized until after World War II because of the war-time freeze on wages and the no-strike pledge. Following the war, the wave of strikes spread from auto and steel workers to the electrical machinery industry. Nationally organized trade unions confronted nationally integrated industries. The ethnic divisions and some of the racial divisions that split labor in the pre-war years were overcome by the patriotic commitment of second-generation Americans in the war effort. Wearing uniforms on the picket lines, young veterans let the managers of the corporation, who were often recruited from out of the city and out of state, know that they were the natives.

The value system, or ideology, that sustained corporate hegemony emphasizes economic rationality, individualism, competition, mobility and equal opportunity. The principle mode of dialogue between management and employees is cast in terms related to the market. Survival of industry is accepted as a responsiblity of labor and community leaders as well as management in order to maintain a competitive position in a world market. In return, the corporation is expected to stabilize employment levels and redistribute some of the profits through the United Way Fund and taxes.

These terms were accepted by labor and continue to be the basis of their discourse. The corporation, however, has set new conditions that call for the reduction of taxes while disinvesting in U.S. plants, raising productivity of workers while keeping wages "competitive" with other areas throughout the world and reducing the production work force through automation. During the Reagan administration, corporate leaders found an ally in their attack on government mediation in the interest of the poor and regulation of the environment. The social contract is threatened as the balance between community and corporate power is weakened by the ability of corporations to shift production to other sites in the U.S. and overseas.

The values that gave life and meaning to corporate hegemony are homologous to those in the family and community that often provided models for relations in production. The unity of the family is predicated on a a male breadwinner and a single-worker household. When women entered the work force, it was considered a temporary expedient to pay for "extras" like vacations and dining out, but as it went on, women's wages went more frequently for lunches for the kids, clothing, and other basic maintenance costs. In business, family, sports and community affairs of Pittsfield, the striving toward precision, technical know-how and one-ups-manship defined the behavior that was exhibited, applauded and emulated. These qualities are manifested in the pruned hedges, mowed lawns, polished and tuned automobiles. Norman Rockwell is the preferred artist and attention to detail is the criterion for appreciation of artistic products. Sports competitions provide a universal meeting place for management and workers where they project a universalized form of competition in games involving professionals or their own children. The downtown shopping area has four sports stores that have continued in business where three apparel stores closed. The town's only bag lady wore a backpack. The best praise one can offer of a game, a business or an academic program in the community college is that it is "competitive."

Equal opportunity and upward mobility are important validations for corporate hegemony. And if mobility is often translated into horizontal geographical movement, or if certain minorities never entered the circuits of mobility, that is blamed on individual failure or natural conditions. So long as one could assume equal opportunity, each and every individual is expected to maximize his or her own potential.

These values continue to be important reference points for judging individual behavior, even while they are challenged by the changing terms of hegemonic control. Critics of the system are suspected of being communists or foreigners, although there is more discourse permitted since the revolt against the Vietnam War and there is protest against the government's policies in Central America and the buildup of armaments. This discourse is more tolerated if, as a *Berkshire Weekend Sampler* article on peace activists noted, the people go jogging, garden, play tennis and concern themselves with their family responsibilities while engaging in political activities.

The working of corporate hegemony can be seen in the rules that govern behavior in a community such as Pittsfield, where the General Electric plant dominates economic life. First and paramount is the assumption of leadership by management of any initiatives that stem from the base and appear to have a broad support. Second is the containment of political activism in a cold war policy that identifies criticism of the system with communism. Finally these strategies are grounded in generally accepted principles that are part of the "American" way of doing things. Family, that gives purpose and goals to daily toil; patriotism, that responds to the desire to reciprocate in the nation where one has received greater rewards for labor than in countries of origin; community spirit, that appeals to the needs of those less fortunate than the employed work force; freedom, that permits the individual to maximize his/her life potential — all of these reference points are coopted by the corporation as they hold "family days" to celebrate the anniversary of the firm's presence in the city, as they promote the defense industry with displays of the latest products with which they are "meeting the challenge" of Soviet aggression, and as they assist cultural and welfare organizations in their contributions of deductions from workers' paychecks to the United Way Good Neighbor Fund and in voluntary service by managers on the boards of many social service agencies.

Hegemonic control is found in all societies where unequal social relations are successfully reproduced without the constant use of force. The existing power structure is able to incorporate threatening elements in such a way that the configuration of cultural traits is not disturbed. This requires an appeal to central values taken as axiomatic in the society. The fact that these axioms may have been the battle cry of earlier days is not considered, as school children repeat the words of the Declaration of Independence, "We hold these truths to be self-evident, that all men are created equal, that they are endowed by their Creator with certain unalienable Rights, that among these are Life,

Liberty and the pursuit of Happiness.'' The corporation relates to these truths as they "Make good things for living," the advertising slogan for their production.

The vehicle for hegemonic control is found in the language of business that permeates all facets of life. Social workers talk about "marketing a product" in making out grants for the care of elderly, just as salesmen do in the corporation. A young administrator of a Pittsfield medical center, described as having "an entrepreneurial mind set" by the reporter of the local press, talked of his attempts to "downsize" the staff at the same time that he expanded the hospital's "market share." Educators in the schools and community college are expected to prepare their students for the labor market and are criticized when they deviate from that task. Softball, once considered a girls' game, is now considered "competitive." Artists and performers are incorporated in cultural promotions attracting not only tourists but also highly-skilled professionals, engineers and managers for the corporations that are based in Pittsfield. Art is at the service of business, and when the development committee and Chamber of Commerce cosponsored a week of cultural events called "Artabout" it was expected to prove cost effective in stimulating commercial activity in the downtown shopping area while reinforcing an image of Pittsfield's potential as a corporate industrial headquarters. When it failed to meet this criterion, it was discontinued.

The success of hegemonic control depends upon the ability of the power elite to respond to new interest groups as they make claims on the society. Although these claimants may issue from outside the workplace, and their claims may have little to do with the "class struggle," the ability of the society to respond to them strengthens the economic system. Successful incorporation of each contingent is often marked in ceremonial events that publicize the transformation from outsider to participant. In Pittsfield, parades on patriotic holidays provide the staging for public entry into the mainstream. Vietnam veterans, who had borne the burden for an unpopular war, marched in camouflage uniforms and green berets first in the Memorial Day parade in 1983 and then in the Fourth of July parade. In subsequent years, they rejected their isolation and found an accepted position in the city and in the job market where they had at one time been discriminated against. The handicapped appeared in parades in the 1980s, rolling along in their wheel chairs and proclaiming their victories in basketball games and marathons that were once beyond their dreams. The Council on Aging, a creation of the seventies, now regularly supplies a float with "Senior Citizens" dressed in period gowns that vie for attention with the carnival and winter sports queens much their juniors. A special education program begun in the city schools in the eighties brought out children with learning problems and neurological disorders who would formerly have shunned public occasions. Even cancer, with its growing incidence in a population exposed to industrial toxic wastes, was incorporated in the parade as nurses in white shorts carried yellow balloons and a sign announcing the Berkshire Medical Center's new cancer unit.

These cohorts have only recently become participants in the public arena, but their entry into spaces that were once reserved for the young and able-bodied confirms for many the rightfulness of existing authority. The ways in which society responds to them are in no way determined by economic processes, but their successful incorporation influences the position of those in control of the major economic enterprises and ultimately affects the survival of the system.

Rosenzweig (1983:8 et seq) emphasizes the ethnic working-class presence made visible in the Fourth of July parade in the latter decades of the nineteenth century and the early decades of the twentieth century in the industrial city of Worcester, Massachusetts. In Pittsfield seventy-five years later, the event epitomizes the integration of the population with traditions that reveal the talent for incorporating new cultural elements in a way that strengthen corporate hegemony.

The Place of Pittsfield in the Incorporation of American Society

The processes set in motion by industrialization have resulted in distinct profiles of industrial commmunities analyzed at different times and in different places. Small competitive firms in the early industrialization of towns like Rockdale, Pennsylvania show the importance of ideological hegemony based on Christian principles that fostered paternalistic control of the work force. In those years, patriarchal relations in the family were sustained as whole families moved into the factory and the father received the wages of his wife and children whose work he supervised (Wallace 1978). Intimate relations of friendship and kin reinforced the ties among the entrepreneurs that ensured their leadership in the community.

Hareven's (1982) interviews with former workers of the Amoskeag Company, combined with study of plant records from the turn of the century to its closing in the thirties, give us a later view of the textile industry when it had reached maturity as a large corporation employing thousands of workers. The deterioration of paternalistic ties between management and labor as the corporation could no longer provide abundant numbers of jobs was signaled by a strike that led to disinvestment by the corporate managers in the thirties.

Both these studies show the impact of changes in the world capitalistic system affecting the prices of raw materials, the innovation of technology and the rise and fall of population in the towns. Wallace saw that "small communities, no matter how primitive, are never really isolated, and in the case of a nineteenth century cotton-manufacturing town, its significant environment was, literally, the entire world, for the manufacturers, and through them the workers responded directly to economic and political events occurring in the lower Delaware Valley, in the United States as a whole, and even in India, China, Africa, and of course Europe." (Wallace 1978:xv–vi). The Amoskeag plant was the largest textile factory in the world in the early twentieth century when it employed 17,000 workers (Hareven 1978).

Pittsfield contributed products to world trade from the early days of its settlement when it sold hides and beef to British shippers to the Caribbean. It became a world distributor of electrical machinery and armaments when General Electric bought the Stanley plant. These developments are the theme of chapters 2 and 3. Pittsfield's greatest growth began when the textile cities began to decline as the U.S. entered the twentieth century electronic age.

Cumbler's (1979) emphasis on the significance of culture in the formulation of class consciousness in his study of Lynn and Fall River is a recurrent theme in this book as well. Cumbler maintains that "the viability of the working class institutions affected the ability of the community to hold itself together over time, to maintain class solidarity, and to sustain collective action among its members."

These same institutions provided the basis for accommodation to corporate hegemony as General Electric became the principle employer in Pittsfield as well as Lynn. The entry of General Electric in Pittsfield occurred much as Cumbler describes its entry into Lynn. A local shoe manufacturer purchased the American Electrical Company in Bridgeport, Connecticut and brought it to Lynn in 1883, just a few years before the formation of the Stanley Electric Company, with money from local textile manufacturers, in Pittsfield. General Electric bought the Lynn company in 1887 and followed this with the purchase of the Stanley Electric Company in Pittsfield in 1903. By 1910 the Lynn General Electric plant employed 10,000 workers, almost as many as were employed in the shoe industry. The Pittsfield plant employed about 6,000 at that time. The new form of industrial trade unionism led by the United Electrical workers succeeded in establishing a bargaining unit in the Lynn General Electric plant in 1937, three years before Pittsfield workers gained a contract.

Comparing the labor process in the shoe and electrical machinery industries, Cumbler (1979) concludes that, "in fighting a sophisticated and remote enemy, Lynn workers had joined with other electrical workers in other plants in other parts of the country [to build] a powerful and highly centralized labor institution to combat a powerful and highly centralized corporation in an increasingly complex and formalized world of labor-management relations." Despite the overtly class-conscious and militant position of the UE, the bureaucratic regulations introduced in management-union relations strengthened a new form of corporate hegemony. The contract negotiated by the unions and company labor relations managers specified the conditions and payment of work along with the prerogatives of management in control over the workplace. As workers were incorporated as union members in the work site, class antagonism was transformed through bureaucratic regulations governing relations in production. Union leaders were named to community boards along with company managers and they became an important voice in public life beyond the factory. This process is described in chapters 4, 5 and 10.

Aspects of the labor control system developed in Pittsfield along lines described in other community studies. The Lynds' study of Middletown (1929; 1965) encompassed the years in the twenties and thirties when technological control by management in the form of the assembly line set the pace of work (Gordon, Edwards and Reich 1982). They show how the debasement of the task structure (Braverman 1974), by which skills were reduced with the minute division of tasks, affected the labor force at home as well as at work. At the time of their study, factory workers in Middletown had not yet gained recognition of a bargaining unit, and the lack of seniority meant that older workers were at a competitive disadvantage with younger workers, even their own children.

The Lynds' documentation of the breakdown of skill hierarchies can also be seen in the study of Yankee City by Wiliam Lloyd Warner and associates (Warner and Low 1937; Warner and Lunt 1941, 1942; Warner and Srole 1945. This process affected female sex-segregated jobs assembling electrical appliances in the Pittsfield plant. Most of these jobs were transferred to the south or overseas by the sixties.

The absorption of owner-managed firms in decentralized corporations attended the decline of paternalistic relations between owners and employees in all of the communities studied. This occurred not only in General Electric, but in the paper and plastics industries in Pittsfield, as will be shown in Chaper 6. Those few firms that survived from the nineteenth century had been swallowed up by conglomerates and most of them were being closed in the last year of the study.

These case studies of industrial communities provide a matrix for critiquing the theoretical analyses of the debasement of the labor force (Braverman 1974) and its segmentation into a "primary" and "secondary" labor force (Doeringer and Piore 1971), and the elaboration of a segmented labor policy to divide workers (Gordon, Edward and Reich 1982). The political, social and cultural contextualization found in the holistic studies of industrial communities enables one to assess the dialectic of labor proccesses in relation to the wider society. Divisions based on ethnic and racial lines are often attributed to managerial and employer strategies to divide the working class. Yet studies of industrial communities, notably that of William Kornblum (1974), show how these divisions are generated within the working-class neighborhoods, as the precarious security workers struggle to achieve is based on exclusion, particularly of blacks and foreign workers. The positive aspects of identification as a distinctive group are counterbalanced by the negative consequences in undermining class solidarity as each ethnic and racial group negotiates a position in the political and economic power structure.

In Pittsfield successive waves of English, Irish, German, French Canadian, Polish, Italian, Greek and recently Hispanics and Asians have found a source of defense in family and neighborhood structures that enable them to deploy their members in a mix of industrial settings that minimize risks through diversity. The very paucity of blacks may be a result of the success of these other groups in controlling their niche in the industrial context. Since World War II, ethnicity, except in the case of a few Hispanics, has served more as an arena for cultural and social self-realization than as a defensive barrier. People hire others to dance their ethnic dances or cater their special foods in ethnic fairs and celebrations. Americans have become consumers of their own cultural roots, as I try to show in Chapter 7, on the commercial life of the community, and Chapter 9, on family life.

Holistic studies of communities also allow us to see how, in their leisure pursuits, workers maintain alternative values from those that prevail in the work place. Rosenzweig (1983:223) shows how Worcester's working class in their leisure pursuits call into question any thesis of cultural consensus. Many of the workers in the Pittsfield General Electric plant carry out elaborate projects in the home that redeem their own sense of skill and proficiency. In their family life, discussed in Chapter 9, workers express the individuality and autonomy that are often denied on the job.

The studies that concentrate on the labor process divorced from the wider society tend to overemphasize the exclusive control of employers and neglect the strategies of workers in shaping the labor process. Burawoy (1980) sees the workers' entry only as passive consent, whereas workers themselves express a much more active role in defining the organization of work to those analysts such as Halle (1984) who participated with groups both on and off the job. Similarly Kusterer (1978) and Rosen (1987) counter the passive image of a debased labor force that Braverman develops in *Labor and Monopoly Capital*.

Another advantage of holistic studies of industrial communities is that we can perceive the different goals and strategies of firms that operate in competitive markets and those in the monopoly sector. These are issues that I raise in chapters 1 and 2 on nineteenth century industries and the early decades of General Electric, as well as in Chapter 6 on competitive capitalist firms that persist. Historically, the greater margin of profitability in the latter made it possible for large corporations with relatively secure markets for their products to accommodate to the industrial unions. Smaller competitive firms responded by fleeing to non-unionized areas. The gains in the monopoly sector reinforced the divisions in the working class related to primary and secondary work force. When this segmentation followed gender and racial or ethnic lines as it tended to do in Pittsfield with women, blacks or other discriminated groups in the small competitive firms and white men in monopoly industry, it enabled competitive capitalist firms to remain in the same community. This complementarity between monopolistic and competitive firms in the same community is recognized by employers and maximized by unions that concentrated organization in the major firms.

The clash is among monopoly capitalistic firms that, in the first half of the twentieth century, prevented other large employers from entering the cities where they had large plants. This is recorded in Lynn (Cumbler 1979), and it is asserted by union leaders in the General Electric plant in Pittsfield. The community relations managers in the Pittsfield plant confirmed this in assuring me that it no longer exists. "We no longer want to be the big fella on on the block," one relations director put it. Management now prefers a diversified economic base in the communities in which it operates. They have relocated rapidly expanding departments from their larger plants to other sites in order to limit their presence in any one community (Wichman 1969:24). Some of the issues concerning firm size in relation to other industries are touched on in chapters 4, 6 and 7.

The dilemmas faced by the city government in the "downsizing" of the firm challenge the social contract put in place during its growth years. The solutions of developers are posed in almost mercantile captialist terms as they try to "sell" the town to wayward industries, offering giveaways and tax rebates that put city governance in the realm of shoping mall hawkers discussed in Chapter 7. The growth of the high-tech defense wing of Ordnance deflected the shock waves of the layoffs, overcoming the negative reaction to producing weapons of destruction by offering compensatory jobs as shown in Chapter 8. Yet even in this division, rumors of layoffs began to circulate in May 1988 and these were confirmed by a company announcement on May 18 that there would be significant reductions in the next 18 months with layoffs of an estimated 900 employees and a cutback of $40 million in payroll. Pittsfield residents wrestle with the dubious distinction of being the number eight priority target in case of a nuclear raid, at the same time that they are concerned with the threatened loss of the corporation if they do not accede to the corporation's plan.

The threat of shutdown has always been a means of controlling labor. Studies of communities where the major employer did shut down the plant reveal the devastating effect. We have as a baseline for understanding the impact in Clague and Couper's *After the Shutdown* and Jahoda, Lazarsfeld and Zeisel's *Marienthal: The Sociography of an Unemployed Community* (1971; first published in 1933). Shutdowns resulting from technological change have been studied in iron-mining communities (Landis 1934), automobile (Carr and Stermer 1952) and steel (Walker 1950). Recent studies of the effect of a plant shutdown on a community, including Leonard P. Adams and Robert Aronson, *Workers and Industrial Change* (1977) and Hareven's *Amoskeag* (Hareven 1978; 1982), provide convincing evidence of the interdependence of community and industry. In contrast to U.S. towns, where social protest failed to result in government action except to bail out the corporation, as in the case of Chrysler, Zalch and Berger (1978:845) found a great deal of protest mobilized in France and England with the governments of those countries intervening to assist in the formation of nationalized enterprises or cooperatives managed by workers. Large corporations with many branches throughout the country and the world simply shift production to satellite plants (Drucker 1953; Wichman 1969). Bluestone and Harrison (1982) provide a summary and analysis of these policies on the control of labor in the U.S..

Pittsfield illustrates a new process that is emerging in the old "deindustrializing" sectors of the United States economy. My initial plan in this study was to observe the effects of deindustrialization on the community, since it was clear from the beginning of the eighties that Power Transformer was experiencing attrition that might result in a shutdown. The restructuring of the plant around Ordnance Systems occurred with the Reagan administration and the decision by John F. Welch, chairman of the board of General Electric, to gear production to those contracts. This has changed the focus of this study to an analysis of the transforamtion from mass production industry to new high technology engagement in defense contracts. Simultaneously there has been a shift from production work to jobs in the service sector. Pittsfield is part of the Berkshire County tourist area, where the number of service and retail jobs has increased 18 percent over the last five years. The corporation employs one in five active members of the work force even after massive layoffs, in 1988. The loss of blue-collar jobs is not compensated by the increase in technical and professional workers, and service jobs that pay on the average of four to nine dollars an hour, only half that paid in the General Electric Company, are unable to attract a work force that will fill the demand. As a result, there has been a steady decline in population as younger workers have left the city to seek production jobs elsewhere and a change in the lifestyle and buying habits of an increasingly polarized class structure.

This is the problem setting that gives urgency to the study. The core of the thesis developed here is that labor's alliance with the state mediates the class struggle in such a way that labor's victories have reinforced corporate hegemony. The curtailment of this mediation in the 1980s threatens the survival of the corporation as well as the communities involved. This is dealt with in Chapter 10 with the use of a redistributive model that I shall introduce here.

Redistributive Strategies

The consensus sustaining corporate hegemony draws upon institutions that redistribute wealth accumulated at the source of production. Redistribution, following Polanyi's (1947) model, requires a central pooling of resources controlled by individuals or groups whose political power is strengthened in the process of allocating shares to a wider polity. In his original model, Polanyi emphasized the evolution of exchange relations from simple exchange to market practices, with redistribution a means of legitimizing and strengthening the political position of patriarchal households in societies such as the Hebrew, Greek and Roman states. His collaborative work with Arensberg and Pearson (1957:253 et seq.) links redistributive processes with legitimization of authority, persisting in the modern welfare state. There they coexist uneasily with market mechanisms of exchange as government agencies at national, state and local levels try to overcome the inequities resulting from capital accumulation. The structure of redistribution gives vitality to the myths of equal opportunity, of mobility and of justice. (I use myth in the anthropological sense, not as a pejorative category but as the charter governing social behavior.) So important are these counterweights to centralization of economic power and polarization of wealth that the current attack on welfare provisions might threaten the corporate hegemony central to the capitalist ontrol system.

A redistributive model of the evolution of custom and law must consider the coordinates of time, place and role relationships operating in each institutional context. Redistribution involves people in a chain of interactions that relate to corporate group structures that persist beyond the life of any individual and may be independent of the dyadic ties existing between any members. The time horizon often involves several generations, in the case of families, and spans a century in the case of corporations (Gluckman 1968). Yet government agencies that intervene in these structures operate on annual budgets within the four-year presidential terms, where priorities are set in response to a changing political ideology. The difficulty in coordinating these differently timed institutions can defeat long-term goals, usually in such a way as to disfavor the weaker member.

Differential degrees of commitment to space also create problems of coordination for a work force, and community. Automated technology and integrated production have increased the mobility of firms, enabling them to set up production sites in remote places and dismantle them with less cost and disruption of corporation schedules than formerly. Tax laws favoring investment in new sites and in new technology exacerbate this tendency toward mobility. Workers tied by family, mortgages and cultural preferences to specific areas and communities are the victims of this new mobility. The threat by corporations to move is a powerful means of reducing claims for returns to workers in the form of wages and to communities in the form of taxes, thus upsetting the redistributive mechanisms won over decades.

The disparity in time and space commitments of corporations, communities and families makes the coordination of social planning ever more difficult. Added to this are differentiated goals of segments of the population. The allocation of roles in production is locked into a segmented labor market with stereotypes related to gender, age and ethnicity channelling people into differentially compensated jobs that vary in a status hierarchy. While the mystique of modernization theory asserted the shift from particularistic to universalistic criteria guiding the allocation of these roles, empirical studies[1] indicate that education and skill are not attuned to rewards. The labor market is shaped by class, ethnic and gender dominance hierarchies in the wider society. These segmented markets control entry through corporate group structures in trade unions and professional societies with disparate and often conflicting goals.[2]

The holistic view offered here may enable us to evaluate the relative effectiveness of measures affecting the redistribution of the social product. I have chosen to look at such processes in the special arenas in which this occurs — the workplace, or site of production (Chapters 4, 5, 6); the household and family, or site of social and biological reproduction (Chapter 9); and the public and private agencies that intervene to strike a balance (Chapter 10). This artificial separation for analytical purposes will be followed by an integrative view of the community (Chapter 11). The ''commoditization of social relations '' in the Marxist sense of transforming interpersonal and intersocietal modes into cash relations that occurs as exchange relations develop, is treated in Chapter 7. How the government enters into and transforms redistributive patterns through expenditures for defense production is central to the restructuring of industry in Pittsfield as well as in many other American cities. This issue is examined in the context of accommodation to the military-industrial complex (Chapter 8).

This extension of the redistributive model from government mediation to the sites of production and the family is contrary to usual practice. I find it useful because it introduces the notion of the politics governing the wage structure and the allocation of roles in the family. Polanyi would have considered wages in modern capitalist society to be regulated by the market, and this is accepted practice in neoclassical economic theory. The Marxist distinction of surplus value — that amount created by workers over and above the wage as the basis for the extraction of profit — highlights the political interplay, which I call redistribution. Polanyi (1947) also explicitly excluded households and family from the redistributive model as based on a different dynamic. Yet families also operate in a political setting, where dominance and control are related to the economic redistribution that takes place in production and to ideologies of partriarchy and female dependence that constrain gender behavior. Differential wages promote and maintain female subordination in marital relations, in which women may even suffer abuse in order to retain access to the greater economic rewards that men control. Westwood's (1985) study of women workers in a British garment factory illustrates graphically the daily reinforcement of subordination on the job and at home, a theme that Rosen (1987) reiterates in her study of Cambridge, Massachusetts workers.

The fiction contained in marginal productivity theory that wages are direct payments for each individual worker's contribution to production conceals the political process of redistribution.[3] Manager/owners pool returns from production and disburse it to a wide variety of personnel; only a small portion of it goes to direct producers. Trade unions and state agencies intervene in those decisions to set the amount of wages and benefits, as well as the allocations to different segments of the labor force. This intervention, in Galbraith's phrasing of mainstream economic theory, "is to replace the determination of wages by the market with a process of negotiation which protects the individual union member from the market." (Galbraith and McCracken 1983:31). The state, in turn, serves "to temper market with price supports, minimum wage legislation, unemployment compensation, and old age pensions." (ibid. 1983:31).

The issue I shall raise is how market forces operate in the context of a particular community to set wages. I shall argue that even before the introduction of unions and government regulations, the supply of and demand for labor was a politically manipulated equation. The actual amount given as wages is also defined in a socio-political field. Differential scales of payments for men and women always existed in large industrial establishments and cannot be explained in market terms. Both the unions and corporate managers have tried to manipulate the supply of labor; the unions by limiting access to jobs and the managers by encourging immigration at an earlier time in history, restricting entry of large employers to those communiteis where they have established plants, or currently, moving production abroad (Doeringer and Piore 1971). Their actions are largely contained in the monopoly sector of capitalist enterprise, where large profit margins and longer time horizons enable them to extend the political range of their struggle. General Electric used its influence in the past to discourage several large employers from entering Pittsfield.[4] Even now when they are planning massive layoffs they are open to development plans that call for low-paid service jobs, but they are not amenable to an increase in production in their plant or the entry of large-scale industry. The structure of "satellite plants" (Drucker 1953) enabled General Electric to regulate the demand for labor within their own enterprise. Another technique that is becoming increasingly important in the local plant is outside "sourcing" of many parts of production to avoid hiring a labor force that can put demands on the firm. This means that the corporation buys parts or contracts assembly operations in smaller firms where workers are paid less. Labor unions, on the other hand, are losing the control they once held over the labor force because of waning membership rolls, a failure to extend organization to smaller competitive firms during periods of high employment and lack of political influence on government to curb the power of corporations.

The fact that competitive marginal capitalist firms persist and employ a less favored "secondary" work force changes the nature of this struggle. Alliances are made between representatives of management and workers in the interest of protecting the vested interests of each. Thus redistribution in the form of wages, salaries and profits differs according to the type of enterprise as well as the category of work. The strength of the claims for better working conditions and higher wages that workers can make on the firm is related to the cultural and social characteristics of the work force as much as it is to the specific contribution in production. Symbiotic ties relate workers and managers in competitive capitalist firms with those in the monopoly sector in ways that affect their engagement in the political struggle for redistributive gains. Some of the competitive firms prefer hiring the wives of General Electric workers. Though they earn far less money, they are said to prefer the more flexible schedules that give them latitude for their major responsibilities in the home. The very fact that many of these firms have fluctuating production schedules and frequent layoffs means that these women can catch up on their housework.[5] The complementarity of these enterprises, that are differentially integrated in the world capitalist system, reinforces corporate hegemony.

The integration of the system is also related to a process of redistribution that occurs in the household when the primary work force male, enjoying the higher pay and benefits of work in the monopoly sector, brings the higher rewards he enjoys back into the family, pooling this with whatever income the lower-paid women earn. In the pooling of these resources, the greater earning power of the men is recognized and reinforces patriarchy in the home. The differential in pay is so pervasive that when women earn higher incomes the marriage is threatened. The gender-segmented labor market has provided a powerful reinforcement to corporate hegemony, recognized in the preferential hiring and retention of male heads-of-household in this General Electric Company during the depression, and the replacement of women with men following the war.[6]

With the increasing number of female-headed families, (they constituted 30 percent of the total number of families in 1980, as compared with one-quarter in 1970, according to the U.S. Bureau of the Census) the complementarity of male/primary, female/secondary employee is beginning to break down as more and more women become committed to full-time employment. Women working in the smaller firms recognize that they can not make their wages cover the costs of raising a family. As a result, female heads of families are more demanding: the longest strike in Pittsfield's history was carried out by women workers in a garment factory. State mediation may, indeed, accelerate the formation of female-headed families since it offers an alternative to intolerable domestic situations, but it does not explain the breakdown in the conditions which support nuclear families. The answer to this lies in the complex interworking of a fluctuating production cycle with layoffs and changes in real income combined with changing expectations in careers and lifestyles.

The differential and often contradictory impact of state regulations can be seen more clearly within a community. Pittsfield has experienced the rise and decline of textile and electrical machinery manufacturing. The city has weathered all of the major changes affecting corporate capitalism since the turn of the century when General Electric Company bought the William Stanley Company, and produced the first alternating current electrical generator. It became the principle employer in a city that grew with the expansion of electrical machinery production during World War I and the 1920s. It experienced the rise of industrial trade unions in the late thirties and participated in the post–World War II strikes. It suffered the loss of many production jobs that went to the plants opened up by General Electric in the south during the fifties. Smaller competitive capitalist firms have been swallowed up by conglomerates and many more production jobs employing women workers were lost as these conglomerates transferred such operations to other sites. In the recession of the seventies, many layoffs occurred in the Power Transformer Division, and fewer than half of those workers found jobs in the expanding defense activities, with their contracts for the Polaris Missile, naval balistics missiles and the automatic gear shift for the Bradley fighting vehicle. A major shift in population came about, as over 9,000 people, more than one-tenth of the population, left town. By the end of 1985, the population had dropped below 50,000, threatening the city's eligibility for block grants for cities above this benchmark if the drop persists in the 1990 census.

This high outward migration, the growing incidence of alcoholism and divorce and 21.6 per thousand infant mortality rate in the first four weeks of life for Southern Berkshire County in the five year period 1979 to 1983 (comparable to that of many impoverished Third World countries) — these are the measurable signs of the personal and social costs involved in capitalist crises. As yet, the crisis is contained within the parameters of corporate hegemony. Union leaders complained about the loss of blue-collar jobs, but their call for new product lines was drowned in the promise to rehire laid-off workers in the growing Ordnance Division. Only one state representative has picked up the claim for jobs to replace those lost in Power Transformer. Most national representatives are tied in to defense production, releasing announcements of new contracts from their offices as a way of claiming a share in the credit. As defense orders decreased in 1988 the forecast for the Ordnance Division began to sound like that for the power transformer division in the early 1980s. The mayor, urban planners, the Chamber of Commerce and state representatives are busy campaigning to ''sell'' the community to enterprising businesses or industries that fit the new high-tech low-pollution image that they are developing.

A new kind of redistribution is occurring, one that draws wealth through taxation of those enterprises and residents that have remained in the declining industrial states while giving substantial tax writeoffs to investments in new commercial and industrial ventures. If the resulting discrepancy persists at the expense of other mechanisms for overcoming the increasing wealth differences, the mythic structure of equal opportunity and mobility that sustains the social contract with corporations may be destroyed and with it the validation of corporate hegemony. The book identifies the supports for that structure and the stresses that tend to undermine them; it does not try to answer the question as to whether a new balance will be struck.

Chapter 2

Industrialization and Urban Growth

Like many of the towns in western Massachusetts, Pittsfield was developed by a private corporation of owners who sold lots to prospective settlers in the mid-eighteenth century. The Mohegans had hunted and made settlements in the area which they called Pontoosuc, haunt of the winter deer (Smith 1869:16). They allied themselves with the settlers in the battle against the Pequots and Narragansetts. The settlement was incorporated as a town in 1761, and by 1774 most of the sixty lots were sold and a population of 1500 whites and 300 Indians lived there (Smith 1869:97).

The Park that Surrounded the Elm Became the Focal Point
for Civic and Religious Buildings in the Eighteenth Century.

Most of the settlers were subsistence farmers and selectmen were told to "warn out" paupers and vagabonds. In addition to growing Indian corn, flax, barley, oats, hay, buckwheat, wheat, apples, potatoes, pumpkins, squashes, turnips, beans, peas and cucumbers, the settlers raised cattle, sheep and swine. The first export industry grew out of these pastoral activities, with horses and mules bred for the West Indies and beef and hides sold to commercial packers outside of the region. At the turn of the century, all of the people cultivated the land, even if they had other occupations. The clergyman himself grew crops for his own needs, and self-sufficiency in food, clothing, and shelter was the norm.

Early Industries

The very isolation of the area promoted infant industries. Cut off by mountain ranges from the Hudson River on the west and the Connecticut River on the east, these Berkshire towns developed their own local mills and urged "non-consumption of British manufactures" at the Stockbridge Convention in 1774. This patriotic zeal in the face of the struggle for independence was an important ideological support for entrepreneurial advances. Patriotism remained linked to industry, and after the Revolutionary War many of those who received water privileges were veterans. Zenas Crane's exhortation to "Americans! Encourage your own Manufactories, and they will improve; Ladies, Save your Rags," when he set up his paper mill in 1800 reflected the spirit of the age.

Water Resources

If it were not for the mills that used the abundant and rapidly flowing streams for energy, many of the farmers would have joined the migrants to New York and Ohio in search of better land. Grist mills, fulling mills, saw mills, iron forges and even a linseed oil mill were built along the Housatonic River and its tributaries in the eighteenth century.

The material base for nascent industries was the abundant supply of water power, the first natural resource controlled by the communities in the Berkshires with legislation as early as 1726 (Smith 1946). The limited labor supply put a high priority on mills, and in order to lure millers, towns granted riparian rights far upstream and even provided free labor in setting up the mill (Hunter 1979:30-37). At the very time that Boulton and Watt were beginning to apply steam engines to their hardware factory in England in 1776, Berkshire millers were damming the lakes and river. Because of the superior reserves in glacial lakes and ponds and the great drop in the flow of the major waterway, the Housatonic River, from altitudes of 1000 feet in Pittsfield to 600 feet

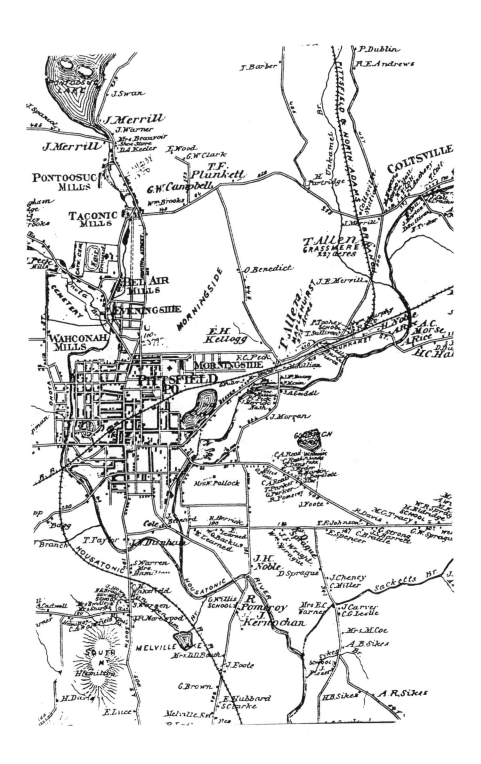

in Canaan, Connecticut, mill owners continued to rely on water power into the 1860's and 1870s, when English mills had long since abandoned it in favor of steam. Water powered mills in the United States permitted the increase in size and concentration of industries that is associated with the industrial revolution and steam power in Great Britain (Hunter 1979). The lower operating costs — Hunter (1979:217) estimates that the cost of water power was $25 per horsepower per year and that the lower initial costs of preparing water sluices and wheels made entry into factory ownership more accessible. This diminished the gap between entrepreneurs and operatives, some of whom became partners with their employers. Possibly of even greater inportance was the fact that factories based on water power are more committed to geographic locales. It was electrical energy, not steam power, that transformed industrial development in the United States.

Founded at the confluence of the east and west branches of the Housatonic River, and with six glacial lakes and ponds for backup supplies of water, Pittsfield had even greater access to water power than its neighbors. Six iron forges making anchors, ploughshares and nails were built between 1767 and 1800. The town retained a certain amount of control over water privileges, demanding good services for the "Proprietors" (settlers who bought lots) on penalty of losing leases and purchases of dam sites. In 1763, William Brattle was "privileged to set up lengthwise in the road against his house, a malt-house eighteen feet wide, and keep it there as long as he made good malt." With this malt, local inhabitants brewed their own ale. Deacon Crofoot was given a dam privilege at the Elm Street overpass of the West Housatonic River, but he was warned that it was contingent on his "accommodating the proprietors with good grinding and bolting." The public nature of the trust was apparent in that, upon his death, his heirs were "relieved from their obligation to keep the mills in good repair" and the privilege and neighboring land passed into the hands of an Ebenezer White (Smith 1869:140-1). The street where Crowfoot's mill stood still bears his name.

Regional historians and poets wrote eloquently of the lakes and rivers that provided the energy for the nascent industries. Formed by the springs and rivulets that rush down from the Taconic mountains to the west, the Hoosacs to the east and the commanding Mount Greylock to the north, the many branches of the Housatonic River inspired Oliver Wendell Holmes to write of its "silver-braided rills/ Fling their unclasping bracelets from the hills,/ Till, in one gleam, beneath the forest's wings/ Melts the white glitter of a hundred springs." A local historian, J. E. A. Smith (1869) saw, "On every side the exquisite curves of this graceful stream and the slender thread of its innumerable tributaries, embroider the rich green of the meadows and the more sombre verdure of the uplands; while not far away, although not all visible, sparkle the bright waters of six beautiful lakelets...."

The "emotion of sublimity" that pervaded Smith as he wrote these lines did not cause him to overlook the utilitarian value of the energy source, nor did he underplay the problems of contaimination. The waters of these rivers and lakes, swollen by dams, and channeled into the early grist and saw mills, tanneries and later textile factories, became glutted with wastes that destroyed the abundance of fish. But he relates this with that mixture of awe and respect that marked his generation as they looked forward to progress and plenty brought by industrialization:

> *The waters pent up with this costly economy as well as those which in the free streams trip with rippling laughter to their tasks, are made to do giant's work before they escape out of the country.*

On the banks of each brook, pond, river and lake one sees signs of nineteenth-century industry in renovated mills, abandoned factories or former manufacturing plants now used as warehouses. The succession of water mills followed by water-powered industrial factories occurred on all the branches of the river that meanders 167 miles down to Long Island Sound. On the main and western branches of the Housatonic River, saw and grist mills were followed by iron forges, fulling and dyeing works, and, by the time of the War of 1812, spinning and weaving factories. A paper mill begun in 1801 by Zenas Crane on the west branch of the Housatonic was followed by competitors. All these except for the Crane plant have left the field.

The importance of water privileges was so great that it would not be an exaggeration to say that success of a business venture depended directly on control over that resource. The succession of larger and larger mills on each of these water privileges involved an evolution in manufacturing processes. From simple suppliers of the elements that assisted household production of basic necessities by tanning, fulling and dyeing or milling of grain, factories became independent producers for distant markets. During the period of maximum growth of water powered industries from 1820 to 1831 when the productive capacity increased six-fold in cotton mills, American water law was reformulated to suit the needs of industrial development (Horowitz 1977:46-49).

Judges interpreted the traditional rights of property to entitle owners to exclude competitors, and the public character of mills gave way to private ownership.

Abundant and Rapid Flowing Water Remained an Important Energy Source Late into the Nineteenth Century and is Still an Important Resource for Paper Manufacturers.

These changes were not, as in the case of England's industrialization, the result of steam power. Pittsfield, like the industrialized towns of Florence, Williamstown and Haydenville on the Mill River and Lowell, Haverhill and Lawrence on the Merrimac, relied on water power (Hunter 1979:180) up to the middle of the nineteenth century. Even as late as the 1860s, new mills were erected on old mill sites in order to acquire the water privilege. The Pittsfield Woolen Company, for example, bought the water privileges of two sites on the west branch of the Housatonic in 1852 and operated there for a decade. In 1895 the Massachusetts Census of Manufacturers reported 41 percent of the horse power in use as generated by water mills. This contrasts with other parts of the country where water power was not as strong. Rockdale's earliest steam engine was, according to Anthony Wallace (1978), installed in 1837. Despite this modernization, the textile mills in Rockdale could not compete, whereas Pittsfield's mills, using water and steam power, stayed in business into the twentieth century. Nationally the decline in water power was rapid after the Civil War. Hunter (1979:400) figures that steam power comprised 96 percent of the increased in capacity in manufacturing from 2.4 million to 6 million yards in the period 1869 to 1889.

Woolen and Cotton Textile Companies

We can follow the process of the organization of an industry and the regulation of the market by looking at the case of the early manufacturers of woolen and cotton cloth. One of the first industries to attain independent stature, the textile industry was the principle activity of the city until the 1870s.

The woolen textile industry grew out of the fulling and dyeing mills of the eighteenth century. Arthur Scholfield is credited with devleoping the first textile machinery in the Berkshires. The son of a Yorkshire clothier, he built his first fulling and dyeing mill in 1800 on the banks of the West Housatonic where it passes under a bridge of the street bearing the river's name. There he constructed a carding machine based on his memory of those he knew in England. An advertizement announcing the event appeared in the *Pittsfield Sun:*

> Arthur Scholfield respectfully informs the inhabitants of Pittsfield and the neighboring towns, that he has a carding machine half a mile west of the meeting house where they may have their wool carded into rolls, for 12½ cents a pound (mixed 15½ cents per pound). If they find the grease, and pick and grease it, it will be 10 cents a pound and 12½ mixed. They are requested to send their wool in sheets, as they will serve to bind up the rolls when done. Also a small assortment of woolens is for sale. (Smith 1876:166)

With this modest entry, Scholfield introduced wool manufacturing as an adjunct to household production. When housewives tried it and found they could spin two times as much with the carded rolls, his success was assured. In 1806 he began to make carding machines for sale. Some of his machinery was used by the Pittsfield Woolen and Cotton factory, incorporated in 1809 by Lemuel Pomeroy and other shareholders. The wool was supplied by Elkanah Watson, who brought merino sheep to the city in 1807. Other companies entered the field with the onset of the War of 1812. The Housatonic Manufacturing Company, formed in 1810, accepted raw wool, flax, firewood and soap in exchange for any of their woolen goods, with the exception of those using indigo blue (Willison 1957:41). Root and Campbell set up their woolen mill the same year, and the following year Stearns and Barker organized another woolen company. At the Berkshire Agricultural Society for the Promotion of Agriculture and Domestic Manufacturies in 1811, rolls of broadcloth, cotton duck and blankets were displayed along with nails, anchors and leather goods.

These early manufactures created interests diverse from those of the rest of the state, which was tied in with commerce with England. The support of the War of 1812 brought orders for blankets, uniforms and sails to industries in western Massachusetts. Elkanah Watson boasted at the Ladies Cloth Show of the Agricultural Society in January 1813, that the President of the United States and the President's frigate were clothed from Pittsfield woolen and duck looms (Smith 1876:467). In addition to his interest in the textile industry, Lemuel Pomeroy also had an iron forge where muskets were made for the U.S. Army. Plunkett's iron forge also benefitted from war orders. Smith (1976:196) soliloquized without a trace of irony, "The love of country and the hope of gain thus operated reciprocally upon each other, and harmoniously together in the encouragement of manufactures".

At the end of the war in 1814, the factories lost the U.S. Army orders. At the same time, they were flooded with British fabrics which were cheaper and sometimes of superior manufacture. Henry Shaw, a representative from the Berkshires in Congress and a resident of the nearby town of Lanesboro, led the battle for a tariff law and succeeded in getting it passed in 1824. He immediately set out to prove its effectiveness by forming the Pontoosuc Woolen Manufacturing Company, with himself as president. The company had the best water privilege in town, at the drop from Pontoosuc Lake into the main branch of the Housatonic, and it was to last until the 1930s. When the Wyandotte mills rented the site in 1933 they used a steam engine fired by coal. The firm employed forty men and sixty girls as operators, an unusual disproportion of women in those days. They produced plain broadcloths and satinets in the first decade, then commenced the production of "drab carriage cloths" until 1860, when they produced the Balmoral skirts that were famed throughout the country (*First Gazeteer* 1885:291). This entry into a national market attracted other producers in the area.

The tariffs encouraged new factories and the expansion of old firms. When Stearns's sons took over the business, they built on a water privilege with a twenty-two foot drop and added another set of machinery to run broadcloth. They quadrupled the machinery in 1852 and added a finishing mill. A further expansion in 1866 was made possible by their incorporation with their employees and a commission-

The Pontoosuc Woolen Manufacturing Company Controlled
the Best Water Privilege in Pittsfield. Built for the Ages, it
is Still Being Leased to Small Plastics Manufacturing Firms.
(Photo by June Nash.)

house in New York. The village that grew up around this factory
included an office, a store and thirty cottages for operatives, all on forty-
five acres of land (Smith 1876:495).

Following in the tracks of the Stearns brothers were the Barker
brothers. An employee of the Stearns, one of the brothers bought the
1811 mill of the Stearns's in 1865 and founded, with his brothers, the
village of Lower Barkerville, with two stone factories holding eight sets
of machinery, a wooden weaving shop and wool house, two stores
and a large number of dwelling-houses on seventy acres. In 1882 the
brothers took over and developed another of Stearns's factories in
Barkerville. The success stories of these operatives-turned-employers
was probably unmatched in England at that time, when concentration
of captial was far more advanced.

The factors limiting entry into industry in England were the capital
costs for steam engines and the energy costs to run them. In New
England, the control over water privileges also resulted in some
exclusion. When conflict erupted among owners of privileges on the
same river in the early decades of factory production, it usually ended

with the bankruptcy of one who was cut off from the headwaters. In 1832, a Mr. E. M. Bissell, who put in a four-story brick factory between the Taconic and Wahconah mills situated on the main water privilege out of Pontoosuc Lake, was unable to continue in operation when the upstream mill owner put in a mudsill-dam that, according to Smith (1876:499), left the Bissell mill without water. Smith discretely fails to mention the name of the upstream owner, but since he places the Bissell factory midway between the Taconic and Wahconah mills, with Robert Pomeroy, one of the partners of the Taconic mills, above controlling the headwaters, it is not hard to guess who did it. Twenty years later, Robert Pomeroy and Edwin Clapp, possibly kin to the Thaddeus Clapp who was a shareholder and factory manager from 1826-1860 in the Pontoosuc Woolen Mills, bought the Bissell mill and formed the Pittsfield Woolen Company. With the water privilege next above combined with the old, they obtained a fall of twenty-six feet.

The woolen textile industry reached its apogee in the decade of the 1860s. The census of manufacturers in 1869 listed eleven woolen manufacturers, a cotton factory for cloth and another for warps used in satinette. The woolen mills alone employed 1308 hands and produced over four million dollars of value annually. Reverend Thomas Allen's prediction in 1810 that Pittsfield was destined to become a successful manufacturing town because of its abundant water supply was realized by the middle of the century. It was not, then, an exaggeration for Smith to state that, "Mainly by their aid, manufactures have come to be the chief source of its material prosperity; so that 17 millions of the 24 millions returned as the value of its industrial products in 1865, were derived from that source." (Smith 1876:502).

The Growth Of Industry And The City

Pittsfield's growth as a city is linked to the development of these early industries. As early as 1800 it was the most populous town in the Berkshires, with a population of 2261, closely followed by Williamstown with 2096, Sheffield with 2050 and at last nine other towns ranking above a thousand population in Berkshire County (Smith 1876:20). In midcentury, the city was more a congeries of villages surrounding each major manufacturing site than a unified city. The First Gazetteer, Berkshire County, Massachusetts (1885) listed Pontoosuc, the village around the company that Henry Shaw had founded and that had passed through several owners to J. Dwight Francis; Taconic Village, neighboring this and surrounding the Taconic mills;

The Mills in the Mid-Nineteenth Century were the Center of Villages that included the Houses of the Workers and Owners, Stores, and Occasionally a Church. (Photo from Beer's Atlas of Berkshire County, 1876, Reissued 1977 by George G. Francis. Great Barrington, MA: The Berkshire Courier.)

Bel Air, that had taken over Pomeroy's Pittsfield Woolen Company that occupied the mill site of the unfortunate Mr. Bissell; Wahconah, the flouring mill owned by Mr. Goodrich; Shaker Village, with its flouring mill and mine; Coltsville, where there was a paper factory founded by Colt and later purchased by Crane; and the villages along the West Housatonic, where Stearnsville, Lower Barkerville and Barkerville were situated. Each village revolved around the hub of the factory of the same name, with the "center village," or main downtown area, focused just south of the Wahconah mills. By 1875 the city outstripped its neighbors more than five times, with a population of 12,267.

While textile production was the chief industry, there were a wide variety of other manufacturers producing paper, metal holloware, saddles, harnesses, railroad cars, coaches, chaises, wagons and buggy whips. Hat manufacturing and tanning persisted, shoe manufacturing was introduced in the last quarter of the nineteenth century, and there were increasing numbers of seamstresses, usually self-employed or working in small shops. Small, self-sufficient farmers were still an important part of the economy, and large farms producing sheep and cattle provided some of the basic raw materials for the factories. Paper manufacturing persisted, with Crane buying out other companies as he expanded his production to include government bills.

In the first century of industrialization, from the early mills of 1765 until the centennial of the town's settlement, there was a growing perfection of water mill technology but little innovation in machinery. Some of the skills that went with the millwrights' arts began to spill over into more complex technology in the mid-nineteenth century (Hunter 1979). The larger factories of the midcentury used the same hydraulic system of dams, millponds, races and wheels, but there was much greater effort involved in gaining a higher head of water and greater reserve of water. The energy was conveyed to the looms through shafting, pulleys and belting that created a great deal of noise and confusion. Steam engines were increasing in number and power in the decade 1885 to 1895, but water wheels were also still being applied, as the following table shows.

Table 2–1

Mechanical and Motive Power in Use in Pittsfield, 1885–1895

	Horsepower units		
	1885	1895	Increase
Steam engines	1,374	1,846	+468½
Water wheels	950	1,356	+406
Electric motors		53	+ 53
Other power		2	+ 2

Source: Massachusetts Census of Manufacturers 1895

The 2 percent drop in percentage of energy from water power during the decade from 1885 to 1895 was a result of increase in electrical energy, not steam power.

Much of the innovation took place in the field of finance and politics. The formation of companies and even corporations took shape within kinship and friendship networks. The corporation with shareholders proved to be as significant an invention as the spinning jenny, yet in the first half of the nineteenth century, it was not the preferred means of financing business. Those who resorted to it of necessity tried, at a later stage to buy out their co-investors to form family companies. This was the case with Lemuel Pomeroy, who bought out his shareholders when he emerged as the richest man in town after the War of 1812 and renamed the company Pomeroy and Sons. Heirs of Pomeroy and Plunkett invested their gains from industry in the Berkshire Life Insurance Company formed in 1851 that amassed capital for new ventures in the electrical industry.

The impact of corporate power was forseen by James Bryce, who wrote in *The American Commonwealth* (cited in Tarbell 1927:1):

> The power of groups of men organized by incorporation as joint stock companies or of small knots of rich men acting in combination, has developed with unexpected strength in unexpected ways, overshadowing individuals and even communities, and showing that the very freedom which men sought to secure by law when they were threatened with the violence of potentates may, under the shelter of the law, ripen into a new form of tyranny.

A Century Of Progress

These early industrialists provided the communication and transportation system that opened wider markets for them at the same time that it made them more vulnerable to competition. Lemuel Pomeroy was one of the eight "judicious and cautious citizens" (Smith 1876) who obtained a charter for the Pontoosuc Turnpike Company that completed the first highway from Springfield to Pittsfield in 1829. In 1838 he joined S. M. McKay and T. A. Gould to incorporate a railroad line from West Stockbridge to the New York border, and with M.R. Lanckton and R. Campbell for the West Stockbridge to Pittsfield line. Construction provided jobs for 1,000 laborers, many of them Irish immigrants. They came with their wives and families, living in shanty towns while the work went on. On October 4, 1841, the first railroad train arrived in Pittsfield.

The transportation system connecting Pittsfield with the western and eastern ports and markets provided the stimulus to business that the leaders had envisioned. Smith (1876:542) summarizes this with his usual acumen:

> During the four years it had been in the course of construction, the money expended by contractors and workmen, and the market provided produce and labor, had given a great impetus to the business of Pittsfield, and had materially increased its population and capital. The communication opened with the great market centers, also materially increased the value of the manufacturing establishments, and of the water privileges upon which others might be establised. Every species of property in the town, including men's property in themselves, felt the beneficial effects of the railroad, even before it was opened.

The *Berkshire County Whig* (May 4, 1841) commenting on the arrival
of the first train, stated, "The village feels sensibly the great influence.
The smith, the carpenter, the joiner, the mason, the merchant, the
tailor, the coachmaker, drayman, and hackman, are all alive with busy
employment."

Smith's phrasing, "every species of property in the town, including
men's property in themsleves," captures the spirit of capitalist development in which all social relations were becoming alienated as com-
modities and evaluated in those terms. In the nineteenth century, social
historians could still be lyrical about progress made in terms of commerce and industry.

Pittsfield had a good deal to celebrate on the occasion of the
Berkshire Jubilee on August 23, 1844. Dr. William Allen (1845) read
a poem in praise of work and industry:

> Poor listless man of indolent repose
> Of unknit frame and mind of feeble might
> Come, taste the good, which industry bestows,
> And work out health, and power, and sweet delight.
>
> Tis toil, that braces both the frame and mind,
> In wrestling with the wind the tree grows strong.
> Manteled with green the stagnant pool we find
> But pure the streams, which murmuring rush along.

The speakers, who in Birdsall's (1959: 319–321) cultural history of the
Berkshires, "hailed New England as a vast character factory of
immigrants," failed to note some of the negative effects of industrialization that were already appearing.

The growing eminence of Pittsfield in the western part of the state
was recognized in its being named the shire for the county seat in 1867.
A courthouse was added to the public buildings situated on the
commons, and a jail was built not far from the intersection of the main
streets. The importance of the city as a business and financial center
was marked by the construction of a four-storied building by the
Berkshire Life Insurance Company that same year. The building, which
still stands at the intersection of North, South, East and West Streets
on the park, provided a locus for three banking houses, government
offices and the post office, in addition to offices for the Berkshire Life
Insurance Company. Smith called it "one of the most perfect business
structures in the country" in his first volume, written a year after it
was completed (Smith 1869:38). The building is a monument to the

ability of these local entrepreneurs to accumulate capital and reproduce social institutions at an even larger scale. Another imposing structure on the park, the Berkshire Atheneum, constructed in 1874, epitomized the educational and cultural concerns of the citizens (*First Gazetteer* 1885:287). Industrial and financial leaders of the city served on its board, forming an elite social group that set the agenda for investment and the future accumulation of capital.

These buildings clustered around the park symbolized the progress that had been made in the century since the city was established in 1761. The prosperity of the mills enabled the population to quadruple to over 12,000 people. It ushered in the new immigrant populations and the wealth differences that augmented class distinctions that were exacerbated in the century to follow.

Capital And Class Distinctions

Retrospectively, the decade of the 1860s can be seen as a watershed between locally controlled industry that evolved with English and Irish labor and capital generated in local industries and more highly capitalized ventures that attracted immigrants from Canada, Italy and Eastern Europe. Farmers survived alongside the burgeoning industrial villages. Small shops employing a few dozen men turned out locomotives, machinery, railroad cars and boilers at the same time that textile firms employed over 1200 men and women in the mills (*Branches of Industry in Massachusetts for the Year ending May 1, 1865;* 1866). Sheep and cattle were still pastured in the outlying fields and farms.

Wealth differences existed in this first century, but the owners of the mills built their imposing residences near the row houses that housed the workers, and it was with donations from their fortunes that cultural institutions such as the Atheneum were built and maintained. Washington Gladden (1897) talked of the ''uncompromising radicalism'' of the area, where the sense of equality persisted:

> Nothing had yet occurred to disturb the sense of equality which characterized all social relations. I have attended an evening party in one of those new fine houses at which were present not only capitalists and merchants and professional people, but working mechanics and clerks and operatives in the mill of which the host was the owner. That class consciousness which some of our industrial leaders show would have been wholly inconceivable to the people of this New England town forty years ago.

Gladden captured only one facet of class relations at the evening party he attended, yet it gives us an insight into the relations of at least a segment of the work force in production in the midcentury. The segmentation of the work force, with a preferentially-treated core of workers with life-long service distinguished from transient casual workers,[1] seems to have been well developed by that time. Smith (1876:479) complimented Pomeroy on his superior management of his mills: "A peculiarity in the management of the Pomeroy Mills, which they share with that of other old Pittsfield factories, is the long retention of faithful employees." He cited the case of Solomon Wilson, superintendent for fifty years; Jack Moulthrop, a spinner for forty years; four finishers who each worked forty years; and Wesley Hansen, a fuller for thirty-five years. These long-time employees were not only all male, but apparently of Anglo Saxon origin. Girls and women were employed in the textile mills, at least after the 1824 tariff laws. Smith (1876:488) notes that there were forty men and 670 girls employed in the Pontoosuc Woolen Manufacturing Company in 1825, and in the census of industry of 1865 (*Branches of Industry in Massachusetts for the Year Ending May 1, 1985:* 1866) the proportion of female to male workers in the two cotton mills was eighty to seventy, in the ten woolen mills 415 to 531 and in the fourteen mills making balmoral skirts, 146 to 215, in the eight garment and hat manufacturies twenty-six to nineteen and in paper manufacturing twelve to eight. Their tasks were distinct and often segregated in space. Women worked in the spinning section of the wool manufacturies, although they were included among weavers in the cotton factories where their numbers prevailed.[2] In the paper factory they worked in the rag room.

The "egalitarian" nature of class relations that Gladden noted referred to a limited core of preferentially-treated key workers and foreman in a setting in which there was growing differentiation in the work force. Only three years after Gladden published his comments, the workers of North Adams went on strike and joined the Knights of Saint Crispin labor union. The manager was sent to California to "buy" a trainload of Chinese and when they arrived an angry crowd met them at the depot, along with the factory manager and an armed constable. Strikers threatened violence if the "yellow-skinned heathens set foot on the ground," but they were let through (Federal Writers' Project 1939:22). Despite this unhappy encounter upon arrival, those Chinese who remained were, within a generation, integrated in the community and running small business enterprises.

If the decade of the 1860s was the zenith of early industrialization and the textile mills, the following decade was its nadir. The recession in the textile industry affected the North Adams mills more severly than those in Pittsfield. This may have been due to the greater labor movement in the former city. The Taconic mills closed down from 1873 to 1880, but at Barkerville and Pomeroy's mills only some of the sets of cards were idle (Boltwood 1916:27).

It was during the decade of the seventies that labor unrest, combined with the decline of old mills, stimulated the capital investments that changed the labor process. The consolidation of capital holdings and the increase in capital-intensive production broke whatever remained of the intimate relations between management and workers. The Pittsfield Woolen Company updated its buildings and machinery after a fire in 1861. The owners were in a position to buy out the Bel Aire Manufacturing Company and replace their old buildings and machinery with new, more sophisticated cards and looms. There were fewer women and girls employed in the new mills, with only one-quarter to one-fifth of the work force of about 150 being female (Smith 1876:499; 500). This seems to have been a response to the technical innovations that were deskilling the work process and reducing the number of the jobs that women had held. New woolen companies were formed, with the S. N. and C. Russell Manufacturing Company in 1886 and W. E. Tillotson Manufacturing Company in 1889 coming into being at a time when the older companies were in decline (Willison 1957:75). Their work force of 800 to 900 workers was twice the number employed in earlier mills. The A. H. Rice Company began production of silk braid in 1887, using new complex machinery to turn out specialty products. Machine shops owned by William Clark and Company came under the ownership of E. D. Jones who later became a producer of manufacturing machinery, some of which was sold to Crane's expanding industry. This company attracted a core of metal workers that expanded the skilled labor force.

New industries proliferated in the seventies and eighties. The Pittsfield Shoe Company vied with the Cheshire Shoe Company; the Terry Clock Company went into production of a device for telephone signals and then was reorganized under Russell and Jones. The paper mill built in 1863 by Thomas Colt was bought out, first by the Chalmers brothers and then by Crane and Company in 1879.

The ferment in industry signaled the expansive potential of the more capital-intensive industrialization that was succeeding the old. It provided the fertile base for the next advance, into the electrical machinery business. In the decade from 1865 to 1875 the population grew from 9,679 to 12,267, despite the depression in some industries. The new industries, including machinery and shoe manufacture, were attracting a more highly skilled labor force, affecting the ethnic and class composition of the city. In the decade of the nineties, Italians, Poles and French Canadians swelled the ranks of Catholic congregations. In 1897, Mullany (1924:52-3) noted that "no Poles were known" but by the time she wrote the second volume of Catholic Pittsfield in 1924 there were 1500 settled in the North End. The last wave of immigrants came in 1913.

New churches were added as immigrants settled permanently in the city. St. Joseph's was the first Catholic church of the diocese, built in 1844 with money donated from the leading industrial entrepreneurs, usually of the Protestant faith, for the spiritual uplifting of their Irish workers. The new churches were related to ethnically segregated parishes: Notre Dame built in 1867 was French Canadian; Mt. Carmel built in 1903 was Italian (Willison 1957).

The growth of these churches and their related ethnic populations inspired Katherine F. Mullany (1924: vii) to write:

> The increase of the Catholic population has been marvelous, but this book shows that the Church building by this people has been still more wonderful, considering that they were chiefly laborers of small income....Fifty years ago they were laborers only; now they are in all the professions, in every line of business; teachers in the schools, filling city offices, clergymen in the churches, and doing well in every walk and place.

Her description of the Italians who were arriving at the turn of the century gives one an insight into why the newly-arrived Catholics went to great pains to build their own churches:

> They were a wandering tribe of people in those days...going wherever work invited. They were content to camp in open fields or deserted buildings on the outskirts of the city, cooking for themselves, gypsy fashion; sleeping on hay or rough blankets spread upon the ground after their day's hard work in ditches, or climbing ladders under the burden of mortar boards, and the heat of boiling sun rays.
>
> We all remember them flocking into town with their household belongings draped upon their backs, and all their other earthly goods in the roped black boxes carried in their hands; a nomad race, despised and suspected.
>
> They brought with them habits of settling disputes that have prevailed in their country for ages — as the code of honor, and these horrified us, naturally. They wrangled among themselves, and knives were in evidence at once — sometimes with fatal results —

but not often. The wounded, however, barely escaped death, more frequently than we like to relate. This vengeful characteristic of quick-tempered Sicilian who formed the majority of these laborers gangs, make them a dreaded people everywhere, which is but natural....

But Mullany continues in a more charitable tone:

But to condemn the Italians as a race because of this dominant fault of one Island, is a mistake in judgement to say nothing of charity ....Some of the gentlest, most law-abiding Italian men that I know — and there are many — are from Sicily.

Her observations on the Polish population were more tempered, and she found them a "sturdy race, vigorous, energetic, thrifty, and generous in support of the church," but they too were "inclined to disputes owing to centuries of fighting blood that runs in their veins."

The immigration of Polish workers was sponsored by the Berkshire Woolen Company, the Taconic Mills and the Russell Mills in the decade from 1890 to 1900. Their first distinctively Polish settlement was a tract developed by the mill owners and located between the textile mills on the northwest side of town. Workers moved from scattered residences throughout the city to settle there in 1913. The owners of the textile mills maintained a paternalistic relationship with the Polish immigrants. The president of the Berkshire Woolen mill suggested the organization of a Polish Citizen's Club in 1913, and in 1914 the president of the Taconic Textile mills donated land for the construction of the Polish Falcons Club. Sports were a strong emphasis of the clubs, and after attending a gym exhibit the presidents of the Berkshire Woolen Company, Taconic and Russell Mills offered an interest free loan to the Falcons (Clowes 1981). It was not until the First World War that Polish workers were hired by the General Electric Company.

One can be sure that Ms. Mullany's observations reflected the temper of the times, as townspeople saw the influx of successive waves of people who threatened their precarious positions in the employment rolls. Churches and social clubs enabled the newcomers to their own place in the society. The extraordinary feature of the town was its ability to absorb these people, as past generations had themselves been absorbed, despite the racial and ethnic prejudice that distorted their view. An expanding economy permitted the new populations to find their own position in the new nation.

Aiding and abetting the industrialists, who were the agents of their incorporation, were banks and insurance companies. The first bank chartered in 1806 failed because of the embezzlement of $200,000. This was followed by the Agricultural Bank chartered in 1818 with Root, Campbell, Pomeroy, Colt, Bissell, Allen and others familiar in the early fraternity of industrialists as well as a few outsiders as corporate shareholders of the capital fixed at $100,000. The Berkshire County Savings Bank was incorporated in 1846 with some of the same shareholders, especially notable being Thomas A. Gold who figured prominently in the first bank and Plunkett, Clapp, Peck and Russell, all of whom were local industrialists except for Gold. The Pittsfield Bank was organized in 1853, with some of the same shareholders including Pomeroy, Colt and Barker. It was reorganized in 1865 with a capital of $1,000,000., almost ten times the original capital. The institutional process for the accumulation of profits at an even larger scale was carried out by local industrialists themselves. The Berkshire Mutual Fire Insurance established in 1835 and the Berkshire Life Insurance, whose first president was a descendant of the Plunkett iron forge owners, provided the sense of security needed to maintain stable production. The remarkable frequency of fires in the mills and factories raised the question of arson as a way of gaining capital in cyclical changes.

These transformations in the industrial base and the population of the city preceded and ushered in the new industrial age of electrical machinery. The abundant water resources were no longer the attraction for industry in the new era, but in the century of industrial development based on water power, the infrastructure for twentieth-century industrialization was laid. Pittsfield was tied by highways and railroads to markets in the east, west and south. Local banks could provide capitalization for the new industries based on electricity. Schools, often named after the successful financiers and industrialists of the age — Pomeroy, Plunkett and Crane — provided an educated labor force. The machine shops, especially in the advanced factory of E. D. Jones, attracted and held a highly skilled labor force needed in all the manufactures that required more and more complex and sophisticated machinery to maintain a competitive position. The sons of industrialists entered into banking and insurance businesses, and some, like William R. Plunkett who was president of the Berkshire Life Insurance Company, treasurer of the Pittsfield Coal and Gas Company, and president of the Pontoosuc Woolen Manufacturing Company, provided linkages among the most important enterprises. The new financial institutions were an index to the city's growing importance as a commercial and industrial center, and they in turn stimulated development in both arenas. As the shire seat, Pittsfield attracted the attention of politicians and in turn was able to influence government investment. By 1895 there were 200 private firms and twenty-one corporations listed in the Massachusetts Census of Manufactures.

The industrialists of this first century were creatively involved in the companies they sponsored and in the "villages" that grew around them. Some, like Arthur Scholfield, served as culture brokers, bringing the knowledge gained from British industries to the area. Because of their intimate knowledge and close participation in the production process, many of them invented and applied new processes. They risked their own fortunes on ventures that were often destroyed by fire or collapsed because of changes in the market. The very fact that they were tied to the locality by the rights to water privilege and the fixed capital assets they held in the community made them more responsive to the people among whom they lived.

Along with other technological inventions in this age, the act of incorporation was one of the greatest innovations of the time, though it was not recognized as such early in the century. It was applied by Pomeroy and other shareholders in the Pittsfield Wool and Cotton factory in 1814, and it provided the capital for the formation of the banks and insurance companies in the second half of the century. The greater flexibility in operation and the increased potential for the accumulation of capital laid the basis for the larger and more heavily capitalized enterprises of the succeeding century.

Characteristic of these early industries was their ability to respond to a fluctuating market, although from the very early years, they were tied to the national and world markets. Prior to the Revolutionary War, Pittsfield supplied raw materials to other colonies of Great Britain in the western hemisphere. During and after the War of 1812 the city and region contributed to and promoted the growth of a national market. Political ties to government spending agencies, developed during the wars of the nineteenth century, were an important precedent for industrial growth in the electrical machinery industry of the twentieth century.

By 1895, Pittsfield had a diversified industrial base. There were manufacturers of carriages, boots and shoes, boxes, clocks, drugs, furniture, liquors, beverages, machinery for agriculture and paper plants, paper goods factories, scientific instruments and wooden implements. These small-scale industries were complemented by larger industrial establishments manufacturing woolen, silk and cotton textiles. The electrical machinery industry was already the fastest growing and there were four such manufacturers. Only twenty-six of the enterprises in the 1895 census were corporations; the remaining 207 were private companies. Steam boilers, of which sixty were listed in the 1895 census, prevailed in motive power, with nineteen water wheels still operating and seven electrical engines. The work force consisted of 4,359 men and 2,280 women and with 901 men and 164 women listed as unemployed. Men earned an averge of $436 a year, but women earned far less.[3] Manufacturers represented 96 percent of the gross production in the city with a scant 4 percent coming from agriculture and .03 percent from fishing (Carnegie and Hill n.d.).

The future looked rosy at the turn of the century. However, William Cullen Bryant, on a visit to Stockbridge, envisioned what Indians might see of the use their land was being put to, in his poem *An Indian at the Burial Place of his Father;*

> Before these fields were shorn and tilled
> Full to the brim our rivers flowed;
> The melody of waters filled
> The fresh and boundless wood;
> And torrents dashed and rivulets played,
> And fountains spouted in the shade.

to be replaced by

> The springs, silent in the sun,
> The rivers, by the blackened shore,
> With lessening current run.
> The realm our tribes are crushed to get
> May be a barren desert yet.

Chapter 3

General Electric Company and the Incorporation of American Society

The rise of industrial corporations in the nineteenth century transformed the American economy and with it the way of life. With the development of a railroad network throughout the United States and the spread of a communications system linking major centers, a mass market was created to sustain demand for the increasing factory production. Trachtenberg (1982) documents the incorporation of American culture from the middle of the nineteenth century when railroads used corporations as a means of integrating capital and the productive forces to link a vast network of passenger and freight lines, to the early decades of the twentieth century when corporations became the preeminent organizing force in American life. The expansion of the industrial system "brought about changes in cultural perceptions and the emergency of a more tightly structured society with new hierarchies of control" (Trachtenberg 1982:3).

Pittsfield had seen small corporate ventures in the early nineteenth century replaced by large manufacturing companies as some of the prominent families accumulated the capital to buy out their shareholders. The reversal to corporate forms was on a scale that could never have been imagined by the financiers and manufacturers who advanced the capital for the formation of what was to become part of one of the largest corporations in the country. Economic and social crises in the twentieth century were resolved in ways that reinforced the capitalist control of major institutions in the community. The events during the first half of the century that precipitated the crises were World War I, the Depression and World War II. The resolution of each of these crises came with the incorporation of some of workers' demands that ensured a position for them within a structure dominated by capital. As a result of the strikes in World War I, workers gained a voice in the corporation, albeit controlled and channeled through company unions. Responding to some of their demands in "Welfare Capitalist" programs, the corporations strengthened their own positions. The high unemployment and labor surpluses during the Depression enabled

51

them to reverse some of the concessions made in the previous decade until they were countered by independent unions sanctioned by the National Labor Relations Act. The confrontation of nationally integrated unions with nationally integrated corporations culminated in the post World War II strikes. This set the stage for new corporate strategies to break union solidarity and counteract the strength of organized labor through decentralization and dispersal of plants in the south. By the time unions regrouped their forces in the sixties to counter the corporation in the 1969 strike, General Electric and other large corporations had accelerated the move overseas of many of their production sites.

The incorporation of business enterprises in larger units gave some stability to the market even though it augmented fluctuations in the economy. Workers and their families became more dependent on fewer sources of employment. Communities lost their autonomy as the tax base and industrial activity was restricted to a limited number of firms. Yet despite the growing dependence of communities on employment in corporations, there was attrition of the public character of corporate entities that had begun in the nineteenth century. As corporations began to integrate their position in a world system, they were able to evade whatever controls communities and nations tried to exert over them.

Pittsfield was an epicenter in the developments that transformed American society in the late nineteenth century up to the middle of the twentieth century, yet the citizens experienced all of the waves resulting from the restructuring of industries around corporations. The response of community and families to the transformations resulting from decisions made far beyond their boundaries is indicative of the power and pervasiveness of these evolving corporate structures. In this chapter I shall analyze the struggles in which workers forged their own positions within the corporation up until the last great strike in 1969. Chapter 5 describes how those relations emerged in daily life.

Development Of The Electrical Machinery Industry

The Growth of Oligopolies

The superficial reason for the transformation was the shift from water power backed up by steam engines to electrical machinery. Underlying this were the changes brought about by preceding decades of industrialization: rapid urban growth, the integration of a national market opened up by railroad transporation and by the breakdown of state and local restrictions to the movement of goods and the availability of a skilled and disciplined labor force brought in by the nineteenth century industrialists. These earlier changes promoted technological innovation and became the basis for ever-greater capital investments.

Growth in the electrical machinery industry depended on a large and growing market for consumer goods as well as industrial power. The U.S. economy met these qualifications in the late nineteenth century. The relative homogeneity of the market for equipment for the transmission of electrical current, for trolley transportation, and for industrial dynamos and generators enabled the engineer entrepreneurs who promoted the industry to plan the production facilities that could produce such gigantic units (Passer 1953:1–4; Walton and Cleveland 1964:16). All of this required an unsurpassed level of capital expenditure.

Production for such a market required a more dynamic view of supply and demand functions than classical or even neo-classical economic analysis permitted. An increase in the supply of current permitted greater consumption of electrical products. This consumption in turn stimulated the generation of more power, expanding the market for turbine generators and transmission equipment. Ralph Cordiner, president of General Electric in the 1950s, summed up the market outlook, that had motivated production as follows (cited in Greenwood 1974:15):

> A turbine generator installed in a power station makes possible the sale of more lamps, appliances, motors, and other uses of power. And as more people buy lamps, appliances and so on, they create the need for another turbine generator and more transmission equipment. Thus, each new use of electricity accelerates the turn of the circle — creating a bigger potential market for GE products, not only in end-use equipment, but in equipment to produce, transmit, and distribute electric power.

These characteristics of the market promoted two strategies in the corporation: (1) oligopolistic control of the market shared by the two giants, General Electric and Westinghouse; and (2) promotion of consumer markets for domestic and industrial gadgets that required electrical energy (Greenwood 1974:15; Passer 1953:4). General Electric and Westinghouse evolved in a series of mergers in the 1880s and by the last decade of the nineteenth century, these two companies had ninety percent of the business. The first electrical trade association was organized in 1905 "in the interest of stabilizing market shares and furthering the interest of manufacturers" (Walton and Cleveland 1964:204).

The second strategy, of promoting consumer demand, became more evident in the 1920s under Gerard Swope's leadership. Along with Owen D. Young, he developed the consumer product market to promote consumption of electrical machinery. He advancecd workers' insurance and other means of ensuring stable consumption with pensions, unemployment insurance and credit associations that enabled workers to buy the products they made.

The first half century of the life of the General Electric Company was a period of expansion during which the control that could be exercised through the corporation was continuously perfected. By means of the corporation, a perpetual succession of individuals acted in behalf of the corporation without being accountable to the civil government. Thus while the power and wealth controlled by corporations such as General Electric grew (see Table 3–1) their responsibility to the public was not expanded (Kuhn and Berg 1968).

The corporate basis for worker organizations was, however, explicitly denied. In 1835 a union of shoe makers was found legal, but shortly thereafter in 1842, Chief Justice Lemuel Shaw of Massachusetts found workers' combinations to raise their wages illegal. He reasoned that, since workmen owned no property at their place of work, they had no claim for protection (Kuhn and Berg 1968:16). This imbalance continued until the National Labor Relations Act was passed in 1936.

Table 3–1

Growth in General Electric by Number of Shareholders, Employees and Manufacturing Facilities

Year	No. of Shareholders	No. of Employees	No. of Plants
1892	3,272	10,000	3
1900	3,170	12,000	4
1910	9,486	36,200	13
1920	17,338	81,977	54
1930	83,958	73,380	33
1935	185,975	63,048	47
1940	211,622	85,746	54
1943	226,386	184,445	76
1945	238,975	161,822	108
1950	249,530	183,800	117

Source: The Electrical Industry in Pittsfield

Local Developments in the Electrical Machinery Industry

These developments in the industry nationally were reflected in Pittsfield. The transformation from water power and steam engines to electrical energy already experienced in Schenectady, Lynn and Pittsburgh was beginning to be felt in Pittsfield during the 1880s. A young inventor-engineer working for Westinghouse, William Stanley, triggered the venture into maufacturing electrical machinery. When he failed to convince his employer of the superior efficiency of alternating current in power generation, he left Pittsburgh in 1885 to go to Great Barrington, where the clear air was better for his health. There he set up a laboratory where he invented and applied the first polyphase alternating current generator in a lighting system for the town in 1887. That year he became president of the Pittsfield Illuminating companies that allied with the Robbins and Gamwell plant in 1890 to form the Pittsfield Electric Company. During that year he worked with Pittsfield financiers to organize the Stanley Company, assembling twenty-seven subscribers to raise $25,000. Among the shareholders were descendants of nineteenth century industrialists. William R. Plunkett, whose predecessors had started the first forge for muskets and who was president of the Berkshire Life Insurance Company and

STANLEY WORKS, PITTSFIELD, MASS.

The Stanley Electric Company was Well Established when General Electric Purchased the Plant in 1903.

of the Pittsfield Gas Works, was prominant among them along with Charles Atwater, who had worked in Pomeroy's mills and served as president of that company. The shareholders celebrated the organization of the new company in a building on the site of the Merrick Tavern where the first textile corporation was organized in 1809 (Boltwood 1916:263). The Stanley company took possession of the first building purchased for production in Pittsfield on January 1, 1981, with sixteen employees producing light transformers (Boltwood 1916: 259 et seq.)

In this first electrical machinery plant in Pittsfield, Stanley worked with a former associate from Westinghouse, John H. Kelman, and with Cummings C. Chesney, who had worked with him in Great Barrington. The enormous growth of the company can be seen in Table 3-2: capital investment increased twelve-fold in the first five years, and the work force multiplied a hundred-fold.

Table 3-2

Growth of the Electrical Machinery Industry in Pittsfield

Year	Capital	Employees	Gross Earnings	Profit	Corporate Ownership
1890	25,000	16		1891-1895	Stanley Electric Manufacturing Co.
1891	50,000	300			
1893	200,000	300	7,500	/	William Stanley Co.
1894	300,000				
1896	500,000				
1897	402,000		300,000		
1899	1,000,000	500			
1901		1,200	1,500,000		Backing of Roebling
1903	4,000,000	1,700			General Electric Co. bought out, retaining name
1906	+ 280,000		1,500,00		
1907	+ 300,000				General Electric Co., Inc

Source: Boltwood 1916 and newspaper accounts from the archives of the *Berkshire Eagle*.

Despite this success, or perhaps because of it, Stanley Company could not retain its autonomy. The need for ever-higher levels of capitalization combined with pressure from Westinghouse, which brought patent suits against Stanley in connection with its financing of his Great Barrington laboratory, forced the firm to sell the growing company to Ferdinand W. Roebling of Trenton, New Jersey.

Stanley clearly did not want to get out of his thriving business. Passer (1953:308) quotes him as saying that "'One of the high officials of the Westinghouse Company made a visit to our principal banks at Pittsfield at which he stated that they were going to 'drive me out of business no matter how much it would cost' and advised them 'not to loan the company or myself any money as they would certainly wreck us.'" In 1897 the $80,000 in capital stock voted by the board was not subscribed and the company managers turned to Roebling who was connected to the Morgan interests. The company expanded to 1,200 operatives turning out $1,500,000 (Boltwood 1916:27).

Westinghouse succeeded in their patent suit against Stanley in 1903, the very year that General Electric purchased the company. Just five years earlier, General Electric had attacked Walker and Lorain in Cleveland with patent suits that forced the sale of that company, which went to Westinghouse (Passer 1953:331-333). Stanley remained in nominal leadership of the firm that continued to bear his name until 1907, when it was changed to General Electric. (Some of my older informants, those in their sixties and over, still refer to the company as the Stanley Works.) Stanley's comanager in the early company, Cummings Chesney, became the plant manager and figured prominently in the first strike in 1916 (infra., p.62 et seq.). Stanley set as a condition for the sale that all of the employees be retained (personal communication, Ann Kohn).

General Electric Company, which had already incorporated the Edison Electric Company in Menlo Park, New Jersey in 1878, the Schenectady plant in 1886 and the Thompson-Houston Company in Lynn, Massachusetts in 1883, was concerned with the growing competition for their direct current power generators from the Stanley Electric Company. When they purchased the company in 1903, Pittsfield's citizens feared that it would be shut down. The local newspaper (*The Berkshire Eagle* February 12, 1903) reported the transaction:

> A deal looking to the transfer of the Stanley Electric Manufacturing Company of this city, to a syndicate of New York capitalists, who, it is said, are friendly to the General Electric Co., has been carried through; notice to that effect will be issued to Stanley shareholders in a few days. The terms at which the stocks will be unloaded will be set at about $125 a share. The plant, which employs about 1000 hands, is to be enlarged. Young men were to be trained on larger work.

The contract, signed on Tuesday, February 10, 1903, was followed by an increase of one million added to the existing three million dollar capitalization. The article went on to evaluate the deal:

The Stanley Company is backed by powerful financial interests, and it is believed that the main object of the General Electric Company in acquiring control of the property was to remove what might have eventually developed into a formidable competitor. Then, again, the enormous business of the General Electric Company closed with a net gain of 3⅝ths points, crossing $200.

The question as to whether the plant would continue in operation was resolved shortly after the purchase when the Edison Company of New York awarded the Stanley Company a contract for fourteen large rotary converters and forty-two static transformers.

The Federal Writers' Project of the Works Progress Administration for Massachusetts (1938:79) attributes the transformation of the city of Pittsfield in the first decade of the twentieth century to the presence of General Electric stating:

The entire complexion of the city was altered by the establishment in 1907[i] of the huge General Electric Company northeast of the Park past Silver Lake. As soon as it was opened, the city's early isolation was shattered by the new needs and technique of industry.

While it is true that the city doubled in size from 22,000 in 1900 to 50,000 in 1930, its isolation had already been shattered before the mid-nineteenth century. Many foreign born workers came in during the last decade of the nineteenth century to work in the textile mills (Chapter 2). The transportation and communication systems as well as insurance companies were well established and several banks served the business community beyond the city limits. The infra-structure that had been put together so laboriously was a legacy that came without claims on the corporation for mutual responsibility. The electrical industry itself was well developed, with a trained work force of 1,000 and a proven product with sales throughout the country. This was the inheritance that General Electric acquired along with its purchase of Stanley Electric Company.

From the beginning, the General Electric Company threatened to close down the local plant. The proven efficiency of the alternating current generator in carrying higher voltage capacity over longer distances at lower cost persuaded the management to keep the plant open. In the decade after the purchase, General Electric invested a million dollars in plant and equipment.

Developments In The Labor Process

The incorporation of the work force into the corporation falls into three periods marking shifts in corporate policies as well as changes in worker organization. The major events setting the context for these organizational changes — World War I, the Depression and World War II — made drastic changes in the numbers of the employed work force and the gender and economic composition of the workers. During World War I, the Polish and Italian workers became foremen and hired workers from their ethnic group. Women lost many of the jobs they had during the 1920s as these divisions were sent elsewhere. The remaining production of electrical machinery employed a predominantly male work force, distinguishing the Pittsfield plant from other General Electric plants where consumer appliances were produced. This trend was exacerbated in the Depression with General Electric's personnel retention policy based on number of family dependents. The trend was reversed in 1941 by the advent of the war when the percentage of female employees increased from 20 to 30 percent of the work force as men were drawn into the armed forces.

The tensions and contradictions incumbent on these events provoked major conflicts in which relations in production were fundamentally altered. The 1916 strike raised the spectre of worker organization that provoked General Electric to recognize workers' councils in a kind of company unionism. During the Depression, the National Labor Relations Act introduced government sanctions that gave autonomous labor union organizations a new strength. During World War II the government established new base lines for negotiation that ushered in an even greater bureaucratization of the labor process with wages hinged to cost of living increases and productivity.

These national changes can be appreciated in the life stories of the men and women involved in them recounted in this chapter. The transformation in the hegemonic alliance that was established in this period in the post–World War II period is recounted in Chapter 5.

Labor Immigration

The rapid expansion of the firm and the large-scale construction prompted by residential and industrial growth succeeded in attracting many of the newly-arriving immigrants from east coast cities. A member of the second generation of a four-generation GE family, whom I shall call John Leonardi, reminisced about his father's experience in coming to Pittsfield in 1913:

We come from the bottom of Italy between Rome and Naples where, my mother said, I was born in the shadow of the Benedictine monastery. Conditions in that country, according to what she tells me, were bad. It was an agricultural place, and if you didn't have a little plot of ground to live off of you didn't eat very well. You had your own sheep, and livestock, and if someone was rich and really lucky, they had a cow. He was able to borrow and scrounge and beg the money to get here.... When he first came over, he worked in Beverly, Mass. You come from there? It was a rich man's playground, so to speak. The big estates. Well, he worked on one of those estates for about a year. The Leonardis were a tremendous clan. They spread to Beverly because the work was there. And one went back to Italy and said that there were jobs. My father left the family — that was me; they had two other children and they both died — and he left in the month of May. So I never knew him until he returned. And he came to work in Beverly on that estate. There were about twenty or thirty gardeners at that time. Then he came to Pittsfield, because he had friends that migrated here. He liked the environment and the pay was good. He got work shortly after as a laborer and then he got a job in the Stanley Company in 1908 working as a truck driver's helper. At that time, the management sold groceries in the company store, only to employees. They were using electric trucks to make deliveries to the families. They were huge things and they were able to carry a tremendous amount of payload. Hard tires, they were, not pneumatic, and of course they were hard riding and hard working.

It wasn't until after World War I that Italians were hired inside the General Electric Company. "They didn't call it discrimination then. It was known as, well, you were too old, or you didn't comb your hair straight, or you weren't Irish. But when a construction gang went in to do a job in the GE, the contractor made sure he hired all Italians," John added.

Few immigrants of any nationality other than Irish and German were regularly employed in General Electric Company until World War I. The French, Poles, Germans, Jews, Armenians, Greeks, Lithuanians and Negroes drawn to Pittsfield to work on the construction gangs and in service jobs or trucking in supplies for the company store, like John's father, were employed for the first time in the GE plant during World War I, when the work force increased from 5,300 in April of 1916 to 7,500 in December of that year (Willison 1957:90).

The city was becoming dependent on General Electric as the principle employer, although the woolen mills continued in operation, changing ownership in response to market fluctuations. The Pontoosuc

Italian Immigrants Formed the Italian American
Foundation Soon After Their Arrival.

Woolen Company, the Berkshire Woolen Mill, the S. N. and C. Russell
Manufacturing Company, W. E. Tillotson Manufacturing Company
and Pecks Upper and Lower mills were still in operation, along with
Rice Silk Company. E. D. Jones added to the their machine tool workers
during the war. Even before the U.S. government entered the war,
the increase in demand, as European countries bought guns, ammuni-
tion and food as well as woolen uniforms and blankets, stimulated
production and the demand for labor. Women were hired in the
General Electric Company to run machinery for the first time. They
ran punch presses, lathes, drills, milling, wire-covering and winding
machines (Willison 1957:439).

World War I

The increase in demand for American products led to increases in
prices, and workers began to protest the rising cost of living and the
decreasing value of their wages. Labor conflicts were frequent in Pittsfield, as they were in other industrial cities. Spinners, organized by
fourteen craft unions, had a two-month strike in July and August 1916
in which 1,156 workers in the woolen mills participated. Inspired by

the textile workers' gains of a 5 percent wage increase and a fifty hour week, General Electric workers called for similar gains. When the management refused to hear them, a strike was called and 4,800 of the 6,000 workers employed in the plant, 600 of them women workers, walked out.

I first heard about the strike from retired workers at a meeting in the IUE union hall. One recalled the police repression:

> I remember I was standing on Kellogg and Parker Street and Maggie Malloy, she worked in the plant, sassed these big six-by-six cops that was pounding everyone, and they beat her. She was standing right there on her own property and they beat her. My brother went out and beat up the cops. And GE blacklisted him for the rest of his life...The GE would beat people right in public, right over on our lawn. They used to bring in these metropolitan cops from Boston. They wore these helmets, hats like bobbies.

Piqued by the story, I checked the archives of the local newspaper. The pending strike was reported in *The Berkshire Eagle* on August 26, 1916, the same day that a national railroad strike was said to be "paralyzing the country's transportation system" and "crippling the allied war effort." Labor officials from seven unions that had members who worked in the firm, including machinists, patternmakers, metal workers and electrical workers, arrived in town. Although 3,600 of the 6,000 workers in the plant were union members, the company did not recognize any bargaining representatives.

The union representatives failed to get an audience with Cummings C. Chesney, the local manager, who was accused of trying to "parcel out" work to the Lynn plant, with the intent of a lockout in Pittsfield if a strike were called (*The Berkshire Eagle* August 29, 1916). The reasons given for the strike, set for Labor Day, September 2, were the failure of General Electric management to consult with workers, and firing those who joined unions. The cooperating unions requested wage increases of 10 percent to make up for shortening hours from fifty-five to fifty-two and a half a week. The Schenectady General Electric plant, where 20,000 people were employed, had just accepted a reduction of hours to fifty-two and a half with a 5 percent increase in wages. Settlement with this plant early in the game reduced the chances of integrated action by workers of the same corporation in all their sites.

On September 2, 80 percent of the 6,000 workers quit, and 2,176 of them took part in a parade leading up to a protest meeting on the commons. No disorders were reported and neither municipal nor special policemen had anything to do, as crowds up to "hundreds" reportedly cheered the marchers, who went from the plant up to Park Square where some of the labor organizers gave speeches. The reporter noted that, "Men were smoking and girls were laughing, but older women had serious expressions as they assembled at Kellogg Street." The speakers congratulated the men and women for their courage. Bugniazey of the Electrical Workers discounted claims of disunity in the plant, saying that the strike included not only the unskilled, but also machinists getting $15 to $24 a week. Another speaker derided Chesney for leaving town and refusing to speak to the workers. "When the presidents of large companies and of the General Electric Board of Directors have agreed to hear us, and a local head has the arrogance to refuse," he declared, "the methods in the local plant are only a form of slavery" (*The Berkshire Eagle* September 2, 1916).

Systematic picketing was reported in the following week, with only 300 workers, including tool and die makers, engineers and firemen reporting to work. Although not yet organized, these technicians were reported in sympathy with the strike (*The Berkshire Eagle* September 5, 1916).

In the power play that ensued, each side tried to mobilize wider support in the community and the state. The labor committee headed by the International Association of Machinists tried to gain the support of other General Electrical plants in a sympathy strike, a principle endorsed by the 5,500 union members in the Schenectady plant in the early part of the strike. However the fact that the company had settled the Schenectady contract added to management's insistence that each plant of the General Electric Corporation "is handled as an independent unit" (*The Berkshire Eagle* September 5, 1916). This negated unified action. The union did secure the endorsement of the Massachusetts State Federation of Labor, but the company ignored the attempts by the state conciliation board to bring about negotiation. The corporation organized the Berkshire Manufacturers' association headed by Chesney, with the stated aim of "defending the American principle of the open shop" (Willison 1957:95). Throughout the strike, Chesney refused to have an audience with the union leaders, even when the respected president and owner of the neighboring Crane paper company tried to intercede. Chesney stuck to his original offer of a 5 percent increase with some individual adjustments to bring wages up to a "fair market price." The agreement to shorten hours from fifty-five to fifty-two and a half without an hourly wage increase also remained fixed.

With negotiations deadlocked, the company was reported to be hiring "foreign" workers as strikebreakers. One of the retirees whom

I met in the union hall recalled that when he was on his way to work mowing lawns during that strike he saw Negroes walking down to the plant gate. He was told that they were among the strikebreakers. This was not reported in the local paper. What the press did report (*The Berkshire Eagle* September 22, 1916) was "an exchange of shots" between police officers and "strike sympathizers" attempting "to rush the foreigners."

The corporation backed its strategy with force. A group of private "detectives" first reported at the plant on September 8. They were joined by a cohort of fifty-two Boston Metropolitan Park Police, ordered by Police Chief Sullivan to back up the local police under his command. This provoked the anger of local citizens, who were footing the bill of $400. a day for the police. They drew up a petition with 500 signatures asking that the city council hold a public hearing on the matter of "police harassment of property owners." In these New England communities, "taxpayers" and "property owners" are categories that supercede "class" and "occupation," since city officials and services are supported by property taxes.

As the strike wore on in the month of September, a division between machinists and assembly line workers appeared to be emerging. The International Association of Machinists' president commented that their workers were in high demand and could get jobs elsewhere (*The Berkshire Eagle* September 22, 1916). Although some other jobs, such as that of winders, were very skilled, workers could not transfer their skills from electrical machinery to any other industry and so were limited in their bargaining power. The only hope for settlement was a sympathy strike at the Schenectady plant, and when this failed, the strike dissolved. On October 2, the union agreed to the original GE offer. The only concession by the company was an agreement to hear grievances presented by a committee made up of one representative for 200 workers chosen by the workers themselves, but not a union representative.

Both sides claimed a victory, the union asserting that it had accomplished what it had set out to do in demonstrating its ability to coordinate a walkout of nearly 5,000 workers, with the concrete gain of shop representation. The company claimed that it had won because it had not moved from the original wage offer and had not accepted union representation. The only concrete concession on the part of the company was that striking workers would not be discriminated against when they returned to work (Willison 1957: 94-95). Since the firm was hiring at a rapid rate, this concession was in fact a necessity. By December, employment was up to 7,500, and in that month General

Electric gave a 10 percent bonus to all workers making less than $2,500. a year. The Rice Silk Mills and other companies followed. Company schemes to "make steady workers" (George M. Ripley, public relations officer for GE quoted in Montgomery [1987:439]) proliferated as mutual benefit associations, safety committees, apprentice schools, women's clubs and engineers' societies were instituted. As Montgomery (1987:455) notes, these years of labor militancy were the productive ones for corporate reform policies.

The outstanding feature of this strike was the moderation of the union demands — always referred to as requests — and the apparently unchecked power of the corporation. Management could ignore the Massachusetts State Conciliation Board and use public funds and police to protect the strikebreakers brought in at the taxpayers' expense. The greater integration of the company, which had several different plants to which it could shift production enabled management to hold out against labor, which could not gain the support even of workers in the neighboring plant in Schenectady (Nash 1984).

The hostility against management simmered until it again came to a boiling point in May, 1918 when six thousand workers called a strike. With the intervention of the National War Labor Board, the workers were awarded a minimum wage for unskilled and semiskilled workers, equal pay for equal work regardless of sex, abolition of the individual contract, and a substantial general wage increase (Montgomery 1987:443). In the following months, delegates from General Electric plants throughout the country met in Erie to discuss formation of a national federation. As soon as the war was over, Pittsfield General Electric managment retaliated, dismissing 262 of the leaders in the movement (Montgomery 1987:448-9).

Welfare Capitalism

Following the war, the electrical machinery industry experienced its highest growth period when the number of production workers went from 241,000 in 1919 to 343,000 in 1929 (Montgomery 1987). In Pittsfield, the work force rose to a thousand more employees than in the peak war years, reaching 8,050 in 1929. The plant produced orders for transformers in the south and overseas (Willison 1957:39-40).

In this era of general prosperity, the repressive period in labor relations was relaxed. In the ideology of "Welfare Capitalism" labor and capital were declared partners in a common enterprise where conflict was reduced, work was "zestful" and democratically organized. Profit-sharing and worker ownership of stocks were extended, along with self-help and other lines of advancement for workers (Herman 1981 :253).

The General Electric Company did not, however, recognize any independent unions as bargaining agents for the workers. Instead they had company-sponsored unions, called Workers' Councils, that negotiated a pension and wage that was slightly higher than the average for industrial workers in the state. Sam who came from Barry, Vermont to work in GE in the 1920s spoke about this period in the company's history:

> The GE had a good man once upon a time, Gerard Swope. He wanted a union in the GE, not what we have now, our own sort of union, but he wanted a union so that he could negotiate with the workers, give them some benefits, and he'd have better working relationships. It was a miserable little pension, but he started the pension system on his own. He was quite progressive.... Other countries in Europe were way ahead of us on pensions. For many years we had nothing until we had a terrible depression and they had to do something. But it was only common sense, and Gerard Swope, they say he was Jewish, which probably account for intelligence on his part [laughed]. At that time, GE was a progressive company as compared to the rest.

As Sam makes clear in his comment on his ''common sense,'' Swope's interest in expanding consumer sales prompted his encouragement of stabilized incomes throughout the life of the employee. This included pension plans, workmen's compensation, life insurance, mutual disability and other employee benefits.

Despite these advances, favoritism and personal ties to foremen and supervisors were foremost in deciding who was to be laid off or promoted. Most workers felt they had to give their foremen a gift at Christmas, and throughout the year they gave offerings from their gardens or firewood they had collected. Management set up its own priority system to determine who was the last to be laid off. This was based on the number of dependents for each male worker. As one former shop steward told me, this increased management prerogative, since the men with the largest number of dependents were at the peak of their productive power. As dependents dwindled when children left home, so did the strength of the workers, and they were faced with being laid off before they acquired a pension.

Segmented Work Force

A work force segmented by gender and ethnicity in the wider community was channeled into jobs classified as skilled, unskilled or requiring greater strength and training. The allocation of workers to jobs differentiated in wages and stability of employment was not a simple management preogative. Workers came with expectations and priorities that they sought to realize in the workplace. Foremen, recruited from among the ranks of workers until World War II, became the gatekeepers in applying discriminatory criteria derived from their own ethnic and gender origins.

Vicky was Forced to Abandon Her Village During World War I and Flee with Her Parents to France and Later to the U.S.

Women were being hired in ever greater numbers during the twenties. Vicky migrated with her family from Lake Garda in the northern part of Italy in 1918 and started work in the cotton mills in North Adams in 1923, when she was 15 years old. As soon as she was 16 she applied for work in the GE. The management did not accept younger applicants since they were required to continue schooling part time. She spoke of these times:

> When I started in the GE in 1924, we were working forty-eight hours a week and I was getting twelve dollars — twenty-five cents an hour — that's what I started out with. But I felt like a millionaire. Well, twelve dollars was not much money today, but then — I mean we didn't have the things we've got today, naturally. We didn't have no radio, we didn't have no washing machine, we didn't have

no T.V., no car or anything like that. But with twelve dollars, you made it if you were really thrifty and saved one dollar a week. You felt like you were saving something, and today they get that in an hour! Some get more than that in an hour. [But you could buy more.] Oh, yes, things were very different. I used to get a loaf of bread for five cents and things like that. Very, very different. Even in the GE from when I started, to when I left, things were very different. But personally I think things are better off now. They've got a lot more benefits than we had when we first started. There was no such thing as unemployment [compensation], pensions, medicare — we had nothing. Maybe just a little bit of insurance that the company gave.

I started out in, like I said, what they used to call the Porcelain Plant. It was out on Ceramic Avenue, where they have the plastics now. In fact, the old building is still standing there. I was living in North Adams when I got the job and I used to have to commute... There was a train that specially came down in the morning, whistle was loud coming down, and then it picked us back up at night and took us all back to North Adams. You bought your ticket by the month.

I started off there, and after that I went to — oh, wait a minute, in between I got married. That was in 1924. But I was only out of work a month. I went back to work, and I went in what they call radio base. It was in Building 35. They used to make bases for radio tubes. Oh, it was quite a business at the time. There was over 800 women working in one department. I was with that department for many years, and then it went out. I did just about everything. I worked on the drill press most of the time, but there was all kinds of jobs. Just factory work, you know.

Vicky worked on piece-work rates, and because she was a steady worker, she "managed to do fairly well, no complaints." Then the radio base went out and she was transferred to fan motors in Building 26. When that department was transferred elsewhere, she was sent "to just about every department." She tried to keep up with schooling but found it too hard after her marriage. She tried out a job in the office and worked there six months and found out she "didn't like it a bit." She requested a return to her production job. "I was more used to it," she said, "and I mean, we're not all suited for the same thing." Vicky's daughter was born in 1928 when she still had jobs "galore." The corporation reached its highest pre–World War II production in that year with the rapid spread of electrical energy throughout the nation. The consumer market for kitchen appliances expanded the field in which many women were employed, and there were 8,050 in the Pittsfield plant. Vicki was out only two months without pay:

> I was working, but I did ask for two months' leave of absence, and I got the leave and that's it. There was no maternity, you didn't get nothing. Not like they do now — they pay for the hospital and everything. Things are a lot better now than they were then. I went back to work when she was two months old. My mother took care of her. I was living at the time where my mother lived next door. It was across from Silver Lake. It's not there any more. They got high power tension lines there now.... I always walked to work.

A great deal has been written about the "Welfare Capitalism" period of the twenties when Gerard Swope, following the lead taken in the Ford Company and General Motors, introduced pensions, vacation and job security. Patriarchal premises extended to these benefits, and women workers, Schatz (1983:21) points out, "rarely acquired enough seniority to obtain vacations and pensions." They were also excluded from the life insurance plans. Judging from Vicky's experience, women's position in the work force continued to be vulnerable since they lacked the security of seniority that the core privileged workers garnered in these years of high employment. The Depression revealed the ephemeral nature of these benefits.

The Depression

The prosperity of the twenties forestalled the impact of the Depression until 1930 because of the many orders on hand. Nationally the industry suffered a 75 percent cut in production during the Depression, and forty-seven of every 100 jobs were eliminated. Employment in the Pittsfield General Electric Company went down from 8,000 in 1929 to 2,300 in 1934 and unemployment rose. Over 1,300 people were listed as unemployed in 1930. Public relief payments of $101,500. paid out in 1930 rose to $655,840. in 1933. In 1934, when 1,500 families were on relief — one-tenth of those in Pittsfield — relief payments rose to a million and a half (Willison 1957:1745). Foreclosures on homes were on an increase and soup kitchens were barely able to keep up with the influx of hungry people. Sam, the winder whom I quoted above, told me about his experience when he was working in General Electric in 1929:

> '29 was a pretty good year here. Then they lost that big contract, I think it was for Seagram's. They had an order for a big transformer

and they already started it when all of a sudden, everything stopped. That's what killed everyone. You know what they did when there came the Depression? They hired some help in 1929 and they were the people they kept. They laid off guys with fifteen or eighteen years, and gave work to guys with one year service. And you know why they did that? On account of the pension. You see, they wouldn't have to pay the pension. In fact, where I was rooming, the man I used to room with, the people who owned the house, he was a foreman, and during the Depression, they kicked him out. He was transferred from Schenectady, but then they told him he was done and that he wasn't old enough for a pension. That's what they were doing during those days, they were giving these guys a cash settlement....

I lost two years, six months and twelve days during the Depression. I picked up odd jobs. I couldn't get on the WPA because I was single. When I went back to work after being laid off, I got less money. I started at fifty-five cents an hour, and I had been getting sixty cents. And then you'd work — my God, you'd work for a year and they'd never give you a raise, but if you asked them for a raise, you know what they'd give you? A penny an hour, and it would take you six months to get it, you know, before they'd put it in your pay check.

Sam lived only a fifteen minute walk from work, so he had no transportation costs and he paid only three dollars a week for his room. He would get five dollars worth of meal tickets to eat in a nearby restaurant. But he rarely worked a full forty-eight hour week until the upswing in 1935. The company adopted a plan of giving no less than one-half of a full-time salary to laid off workers. Bus, who began his career as a winder in the GE in 1929, told me about that period.

In the GE, from 1929 until after 1936 began, we went to work, but we worked only one day every two weeks. But we got fifteen dollars a week. They assessed the salaried workers one percent of their earnings in order to pay the people up to fifteen a week. So this went on until 1932, and we got laid off outright. From that point on, for six months, we collected fifteen dollars. And after that they gave us food over at the store. I used to give it to my mother towards my board.

Company policy that discriminated against older workers during the Depression also discriminated against women. Even those women who were single heads of families or whose husbands were not working were not favored in the lay-off policies even when they had dependents. Vicky was laid off during the depression because of this policy even though she had worked steadily after the birth of her child during the twenties when times were good.

> And then I was laid off cause I was married. It was the time in the GE that they laid all the married women off. It made no difference whether your husband was working or not, but mine happened not to be. But as far as GE was concerned, that was the rule. If you returned to the factory within one year, you would get your service back, but if you didn't return before the year was up, you lost all your service. That's what happened to me. I was laid off, and I didn't get called back until about two years later.

Difficult as things were for GE workers on layoff, those who were forced to live from day to day seeking part time jobs faced even greater uncertainty. Alex was twenty-five years old in 1933. His father and mother arrived in America in 1916 with four children and the family had doubled in size by the time of the 1929 crash. His grandson interviewed him about the time of the Depression when he was looking for work:

> People today would not understand what the Depression was from '29 on. There was a bad stock market crash and everyone suffered for it. And to go out and strive and support your family was no easy task. You went from street to street, from location to location, from manufacturer to manufacturer looking for an hour's pay, four hour's pay, or a day's pay. If you were fortunate enough, you might get three day's pay. The wages were forty cents an hour, forty-five cents an hour and the government was paying fifty cents an hour. But every time that you attempted to go out and seek work to support your family, you were not that successful. So on one of these trips one morning, I started out and I got to three different places. And after I exhausted my possible spots for employment, I returned to Main Street and I encountered the local officer, Al Morano. And he says to me, "Alex, are you not working today?" "Naw, I couldn't find anything today, Al. They just didn't have anything." And he says, "Do you want to shovel a little snow?" And I says, "Yeah, sure. I'll shovel anything." So he took me to Engstrom's drug store on North Street, close to Union, and he asked Engstrom if his sidewalk needed shoveling. And he says, "I've got a man who'll shovel it for you." He says, "Surely," and he handed me the snow shovel. So I go out to the sidewalk. It was not that long, but very deep, eighteen feet deep by perhaps twelve to fourteen feet wide. And when I got through chopping the ice and shoveling the snow I brought the shovel back into Mr. Engstrom and he says, "You all through, young man?" I says, "I am," and

I laid the shovel down and he handed me fifteen cents. And I says, "Thank you, sir." I walked out of Mr. Engstrom's store and started walking down North Street on my way home to Robbins Avenue and I says to myself, "This is not much, but it will buy a loaf of bread." Bread was twelve cents a loaf, which was better than nothing at all.

Alex's story is a graphic description of what it meant to be without prospects of work. His acceptance of the owner's terms for the employment, far from illustrating the operation of the market, shows that in times of high unemployment, with all the power on the side of the employer, the market transaction is one-sided. Workers were unable to exercise choice and could not refuse even the lowest terms. Later on in the Depression he rejected a job breaking up auto bodies for twenty-five cents an hour, half the going rate. But much later on in life he felt that it had been foolish thing to do:

Twenty-five cents an hour! Hungry, young, foolish! This is among the things that you can think of that you have done lots of time, gone out to work and Lord knows what would happen. You didn't care about what happened if you brought a dollar in the house to buy bread for the family.

During the Depression, the behavior of employers as well as that of employees was rationalized in terms of support for the family, and this reinforced General Electric's policy giving preference to men with families when they were laying off workers. People competed desperately for the few jobs that were available, only to be exploited by miserable wages.

Those who were able to find jobs often had to take on more than one job because the pay was too little to support a family. John Leonardi, who described his family's entry to the U.S. in search of work, started work in General Electric at the age of fourteen earning $5.50 a week as an office boy. He had to help support the family since his father was unable to work because of a job-related injury. He quit when he found other work that paid better, but it meant working around the clock.

In 1933 I was driving a taxi, because that was the only job available to me; a friend of mine was boss man of the Yellow Cab Co., and I could drive, had a license — I was a fair driver, you know. And that job paid off in commission only. You might have made a dollar and a half a day, but if you made three dollars a day, you made a tremendous amount of money. It was the Depression. I graduated from high school, but at that time it didn't matter too much. Oh, I've seen college graduates who couldn't get a job in what they studied, so they worked whatever they could get.

Well, I got married in 1933, and I decided I was going to put my nose to the grindstone, and I had five jobs. Now ninety hours a week was a kind of short week. I drove a taxi, I worked on WPA as a laborer, three more days as a truckdriver, and then I had a little business on the side. I cleaned beer coils and taps for a quarter. I had a little machine we put together. Then the other job was tending bar for Dave Shay, the fighter. I tended bar for him nights and I used to make a pretty fair wage. There wasn't any one place paying me much, but the many places paying me accumulated. I used to get up at five in the morning and get home at eleven at night. And we needed it because my wife was sick and had a few problems. Never got ahead, but never fell back either.

Finally John got a regular job at the GE in 1936, starting out at forty-five cents an hour. "That was a let-down from what I was making previously — I was making $19.50 a week as against $70. up to $90. dollars before — but it was an eight-to-five job, Monday through Friday, and that was it. But I still did the other jobs anyway because there was Saturday, Sundays, and nights which supplemented the income." His wife, Dora, worked at the General Electric before her marriage making radio bases and earning $18.50, but the job lasted only a year and a half since the management "sent that production elsewhere."

Dora's sister, Nelly, had the same sense of satisfaction in gaining employment at the GE that her brother-in-law did. In comparison with the work in small commercial enterprises in the city, it represented a real advance:

> Before I went into GE, I worked in the laundry. There was my sister, myself, Dora's husband, my brother Joey, and my mother worked there. Yeah, twenty-five cents an hour. Oh, boy, that was a sweatshop. That was really a sweatshop. We used to work sixteen hours a day. And the boss used to stand like this [took posture with legs spread apart, arms folded over the chest] at the top of the stairs and watch you. If you went in the bathroom and stayed too long, he sent in somebody after you. Twenty-five cents an hour! I worked nine years that way. And I used to say, "Oh, if I could only get into the General Electric, I'd make sixteen dollars a week. I'd be a millionnaire!

The breakdown of the market during the Depression set in motion contradictory currents in the community. The search for a livelihood brought a sense of accomplishment to those who were forced to take low-paid, unskilled jobs. The shared misery turned people inwards, to the family and community, when the money for diversions, a car or even gas was lacking. A subsistence economy flourished as the household took over many productive activities that had recently been part of the market economy. Most families had gardens and women preserved vegetables for year-round supplies. Men could still find enough wild life in the hills to go hunting and the rivers still had some fish that had survived the first century of industrialization. Labor exchanges overcame the lack of cash as the market nexus collapsed. A wild turkey or rabbit would be given to a neighbor who helped patch the roof or filed a saw. The knowledge and skills that enabled people to respond to the crisis were still available to this first generation of immigrants who had come from the rural villages and provincial towns of Italy, Poland, Greece or Canada and were not totally dependent on wage work.

During the Depression, Bus lived with his parents in Morningside, where people still had gardens:

All those people up in the hill had to have cows, had to have chickens, they had to have a garden, a big garden. I used to love to live there. No matter where I went, it was great.

His wife, Susan, commented on the difference it had made to be a girl during the Depression:

He never really felt the Depression. It didn't bother him as much as it bothered me. ["Nope!" he agreed, "because everyone was good to us."] Well, we never had what he had. He could go around because he was a boy, a male, and he could get free services, like a haircut or somebody taking him into the restaurant. There was no such thing in our home. I was the oldest of seven children. My father was out of work maybe at the time, and he drove a milk wagon and delivered milk from our cows. We helped deliver the milk and we ate from our own gardens, but there was no money coming in. People didn't have money to pay the milk bill. So we felt it much more than he did. For a boy, he could get along with just a jacket and shirt and pants, but for a girl it was very hard. We knew poverty. We went without everything.

Boys had greater freedom to enter in to the casual labor that was available, but was not accessible for girls who were concerned about their reputations. Bus would hang around with other youths at the garage of a hauler, and when a job came in they were off in a moment. The barber would give them a haircut free, a restaurant owner might ask them to wait on tables and they would get food. "He [the owner] would tell us," Bus said, "Try to get some money if you can, and if you can't, don't worry about it.' This is the way we lived on Morningside."

The internal labor market — hiring done on the basis of contacts, usually kinsmen, friends and neighbors — operated even more rigorously during the Depression when jobs were scarce. When you didn't have direct contacts with the foreman, you needed a gift to accompany your request for a job. Al, who later became business agent for the IUE local, told me about his problem coming from a poor family which had limited entry into this market:

When I first hit the labor market when I was a kid — of course we used to go to work at fourteen, all we had to do was to get a slip from the school, and we used to have to go to vocational school half a day a week — but I went out searching for work. And I remember the textile mills used to be here in Pittsfield and in Adams. And if you were a family that was well off and your mother and father had a big garden and had some wine bottles down in the cellar, you could bring this to the foreman, you know, 'cause there was no employment office. All you had to do was to know the name of a foreman. I remember the mill down here off Pontoosuc Lake and there was these steel stairs, fire escapes, that we used to climb up, and we'd say to one of the employees near the door, "Where's the boss?" "He's down the other end." "Well get him down this end." And he'd come up and "What can I do for you?" "We were looking for a job, and we would do anything, anything for you." "Had no work, right?" And right behind us, here comes this big basket of fruit, and bottles of wine. "Go right to work!" This happened in the GE too, by the way. So all they did was go to the foreman and put some stuff in his pantry, and then he would go to the guy in the employment office, "I know a guy by the name of Al Litano. Give him a a job. Good worker, know him personally."

What happened to me, I went to North Adams in 1933–34. I'd go down and stand on the line for six months, the GE employment line. And they'd come out and they'd go, "You, you, — " or something like that. Finally I got disgusted. I said, "I don't want this, I want to work as a laborer." By luck I got a job with a contractor and we finished the job in Pittsfield, and then we went to North Adams. And while I was working in North Adams, I got a letter from General Electric to go to work. So I used to come home weekends, and my mother says, "Hey, this is a big thing, you know. Why don't you go work for the GE?" And I says, "Ma, I'm working already. I can't quit this guy now. He was so good to me."

"But you're going to make more money." I said, "Ma, I can't quit this guy. I gotta work for this guy till the job finishes up." Then I says, "OK, if they want to hire me after I get through with this guy." "Fine," she says, "You're crazy. Go to work!"

Even before Al started working this job, he had always contributed to the household by selling papers and distributing bootleg liquor. The Mafia had an affirmative action hiring policy that always took care of widows, like Al's mother, and others who couldn't get jobs. This was especially effective in Lakewood, a tightly-knit Italian community just south of the General Electric. Most families urged their children to get into the GE. Al recollected, "And if I had gone in in 1934, you figure, I'd have had about 40 years' service now." Al's account reveals the workers' strategies of developing personal ties to overcome the uncertainties of employment.

General Electric took full advantage of the devastated position of labor during the Depression. Yet despite the extremely low wages and uncertainties in employment, a job at General Electric was still considered the best opportunity in a lifetime, and anyone who turned it down was considered to be very foolhardy. This marginal advantage meant that it was not General Electric workers, but the textile workers that tested out the labor legislation of the New Deal.

New Deal Legislation and the Rise of Unions

During Franklin Delano Roosevelt's first term in office, the passage of the National Labor Relations Act in 1934 guaranteed workers the right to organize and bargain collectively through representation of their own choosing. A nationwide textile strike that year called for improved wages and working conditions, testing the new legislation. North Adams textile mills supported the strike and sent representatives to Pittsfield, but Police Chief Sullivan, who had been in command of the police during the 1916 strike at the Pittsfield General Electric plant, sent them back (Willison 1957:177).

The ferment of organizing did not stop with this initial setback. In Pittsfield, workers in the competitive sector of industry were more active than those in the General Electric Company. The marginal advantages GE employees enjoyed because of Swope's welfare capitalist policies minimized active organization, although discontent was rampant. Workers in the Berkshire Woolen Mill and the Wyandotte Worsted Mill, which had taken over the Pontoosuc Woolen Mill in 1930, joined the protest over wages and hours. The first Congress of Industrial Organization (CIO) Union in Pittsfield was organized by workers at the Lichtman Tanning Corporation in 1937 (Willison 1957:- 134). They were earning $8. a week, while General Electric workers were earning $12. to $15. General Electric employees did not test the new legislation guaranteeing the right to collective bargaining until after 1937 when these rights were assured by the favorable decision of the United States Steel Company signing a contract with steel workers.

By 1935 conditions in the national economy were improving. General Electric had a contract to build a transformer for the Colorado Boulder Dam. Tourism in the Berkshires was growing, with the establishment of Tanglewood in Lenox in 1934 and some spillover of construction and service jobs into Pittfield. Ski trains brought in vacationers during the slow winter months. There was a drop in the number of families on relief. Eaton Paper company and the textile mills began hiring again and recovery seemed assured in 1936. The payroll of Pittsfield's twenty-two plants rose to $193,000., up from $132,000. in the previous year. Public works projects in Pittsfield employed most of the construction workers and laborers, building the state police barracks and installing bridges and dams.

However, in 1837, Roosevelt cut back on the Public Works Administration's funding, as well as on WPA, CCC and other federally-sponsored projects. The impact was severe, forcing welfare costs back up to their 1935 level. Most of the workers I talked with who worked during that time felt that Roosevelt had responded to big capital interests.

Several workers who were laid off during the 1936 recession emphasized that it was the workers with more years of service and higher pay who were more likely to be laid off. It was the arbitrary exercise of power by the company and uncertainties in work and wages that motivated workers to support an independent union when it was safe to do so.

In 1939 organizers arrived from Schenectady, where the United Electrical and Radio Workers (UE) of the Congress of Industrial Organization had organized a local in 1936. One worker who helped organize the Pittsfield plant recalled this period:

> When the union started coming in, foremen were told to advise men not to join. First some organizers came over from Schenectady. With the threat of having a union in Pittsfield after Schenectady was already organized, GE offered nine cents an hour increase.

Organizing an independent industrial union when Swope was president involved an adroit strategy to convince workers that they had something to gain other than what the Workers' Councils offered. A machine tool maker, Carl, spoke of the same period:

> Swope encourage the company to unionize, not exactly a company union, but working in harmony with the company. Yes, he was a bit of an idealist within the context of the system. Anyway, Schenectady was organized and they sent individuals over to see us. We'd meet with them at night. We had this Colts Club which at that time was almost a wilderness, just a crossroads with billboards and whatnot. And we'd sit and camp behind a billboard and talk. So we did use secrecy at first. There was one who was very outspoken in the shop even at that time, when they were threatening those who were organizing the men. That was Bus. He felt very secure because he was a super winder.

I interviewed Bus in the union hall, where he was preparing for a meeting of the retirees. He confirmed what I had heard of his starting the union in the Pittsfield GE:

> I know about the organization of this union because I was one of the first to get in. I did come in right in the beginning because they (UE organizers) kept after me because they knew that I wanted a union. I'd say we started around 1934 or 5. It was just when the Wagner Act came in. I think it was during the change of contract with the company in 1933. I used to wind things no one else in the company could wind. I went in there and did the dirtiest job in the shop that no other man would do and go back and work in the winding room.... When they found out that I was one of the seven or eight guys that was going to be the directory, the organizer that came in the shop at noon signed all us winders. Then the manager called us together and said, "You know, you've been having it pretty good. Anything you ever wanted you got." And I says, "As one man, I used to get it, but wait till you see me with 5,000 people behind me. Then it will be a lot different. I'll be able to talk a lot tougher than I can now."

Because of his preferred position in the winding room, Bus had negotiated for himself a contract of eighty cents an hour minimum and thirty-six hours a week. He was kept on when most men in the shop were laid off. Bus elaborated on how he achieved that position:

> I told you, an old timer taught me how to wind. There was some things he knew, and he told me, "Don't you dare tell anybody else." So there were freak jobs that used to come through that place, and like winding a wire 425.0–5. You have to picture that. That's

about that wide and that thick. And you had to keep that thing standing up. I don't think there's a man there today that can do it. A broad wire with a very thin base. There were as much as 8 or 900 turns on one layer. The man who taught me to do that was one of my best buddies. He used to say, "Jesus, you're the only guy I ever seen stand up to supervision!" They used to tell us that you couldn't, you're not supposed to talk to them. You're supposed to sit at that machine and work all the time. Hell, I would take a walk by myself. I did a lot of things in the General Electric. Like when they would call up the grievance committee and say, "Rodger's walking around again." And the foreman would say, "There's something wrong with the job again. He just fires his tools to one side and gets his hat and coat if it's wintertime, or if it's summer time he takes off. And I don't say nothing to him because when he comes back, that coil's going to come together." They told me at the end of the first year that I'd never be a winder. They were going to get rid of me, but my inspector said, "Boy, leave that guy alone. He's going to make some winder. Don't you dare take and tell him he's going too slow. He's learning it right." And old Hart, when they wanted him to teach someone, he said, "There's only one guy I want to teach, and that's that feller right there next to me." Course that's when I really learned something.

Workers like Bus who started organizing the union in the early 1930s usually had superior skills that made them less dispensible, since the men who signed up for them were often fired as soon as it was discovered. The foremen were advised to warn men that they would lose their jobs if they did that. In 1939 the UE organizers again came over from Schenectady and Sam told me about how they went about organizing the welders in the General Electric.

It was through the winter months. I remember very well and we were going around to the different houses, different people that we knew and we'd ask them if they wanted to sign up. And then when we figured we had enough cards, we had the election to ask for bargaining rights. It didn't bother me to go around asking people to sign up because by then you had the Wagner Act. You had the right to organize and they couldn't fire you. Oh, I was out every night in the week. Oh, my wife, she got tired of it after a while. I'm surprised she didn't move out. I was out every night in the week. 'Cause I knew a lot of people in the shop.

Well, we got some good responses, and we go some pretty rotten ones. We got a lot of people told us to get out. Oh, yes, they were afraid because the boss was saying not to organize and that scared them off. And you'd be surprised at some of the wives. The men would want to sign, but the wives wouldn't let them.

I asked Sam, "Why weren't you afraid?"

Well, up in Barry, they were organized up there. I was brought up on unions. (Sam was a stonecutter from Barry, Vermont before coming to GE.) I remember when my dad used to go out on strike. And in them days you used to run the groceries up, and when you were back at work you used to pay up. [You couldn't do that with the chain groceries.] Course in them days you had all family groceries. And people paid their bills. They felt guilty if they didn't pay 'em.

The fact that Sam came from a union background gave him the courage to start organizing when others were still afraid. It was not only the family background, but the faith in community that was still kept alive with the extension of credit and neighborly support. Each worker tried to involve others in his own network:

We used to try to get meetings with the organizer. We'd get different guys in different departments to try to organize their department, the tool room, the machine shop, and over in the winding department and in maintenance, you know, all of 'em. And we'd try to get a key man in that department. Someone who was pretty popular in the department.

Popularity is a measure of the ability to manage key cultural symbols. Here it meant conforming to ideals up to a point, and knowing where one could take liberties with them. Bus, like Sam, was one who could conform to basic standards at the same time that he could oppose the written and unwritten codes of behavior in the shop. The mere fact that he challenged them gave him greater popularity.

Wages moved up rapidly as the company tried to combat the union wave. When they started organizing, workers were getting fifty-five cents an hour. By 1939 they had moved up to ninety-eight cents an hour. Sam commented:

That goes to show you that they didn't want us to organize. Before that, you'd ask the boss for a raise and it took six months to a year to get a penny. Then all during the war we got a dollar twenty-three an hour.

General Electric began to call back some of the laid-off workers in 1939. Bertha E. Prew recalled that year in an article published in *Berkshire History* (Spring 1983):

> In mid-1939, my husband was again one of GE's 4,500 workers and we recklessly traded in the black 1930 Model A Ford for a spiffy 1935 gray one with a trunk, no less. In October of 1939 we plunged again, this time buying a house in Hinsdale, a bargain at $1,900, with wide floor boards, a pantry and large rooms. We bought it with a Home Owners Loan Corporation mortgage and a lot of courage, as every room had plaster missing from walls and ceiling. Paint peeled everywhere. The cellar stairs had been used as kindling to start the old monster of a coal furnace, squatting in the dark stone-walled cellar. So, while Poland was falling and Britain was desperately trying to hang on, we were scraping and painting and papering, all the time under a cloud of anxiety. We didn't know then that bombs would not fall on Massachusetts.

Mrs. Prew recalled going to New York in 1940 to see the World's Fair, along with 4,000 Pittsfield General Electric employees and family members in a four-section train of forty-nine cars. They heard President Charles Wilson of the General Electric announce plans for the $1,500,000. plastics plant to be built on Plastics Avenue in Pittsfield. By the end of the 1941, 10,000 workers were employed.

General Electric Goes to War

It was World War II that pulled the U.S. economy out of the recession of 1937. When war was declared on December 7, 1941, General Electric had fifty-four plants with twenty-nine million square feet of floor space. During the war, from 1940 to 1945, the company built fifty-four new major plants bringing the total number to one hundred and eight with forty-one million square feet. Half of the investment came from General Electric Company's own sources and another 158 million from the defense plant corporation funded by the U.S. government. The Pittsfield Plant gained an eight million dollar building for Ordnance and a $1,500,000. building for Plastics with a $325,000. addition to Power Transformer. Three shifts went into production to produce tubes for bazookas, radar systems, gun directors and plastic housings and control buttons. Transformer production reached the highest point in history with orders for the domestic and foreign market, including the Union of Soviet Socialist Republics.

The most dramatic change in the labor force was the employment of women in other than routine assembly jobs. The proportion of women employees in the industry went from 20 percent in 1940 to 40 percent in 1944. Hundreds of women were trained for drafting work and machine operation. College graduates in mathematics and physics were for the first time assigned to engineering jobs (Miller 1948:237) as they replaced 50,000 employees who had gone into the service and filled new vacancies. Employment rose from 76,000 to 175,000. Although many of the employees were new recruits, production increased by 85 percent in the first year of the war and by 1944 was two-and-a-half times the 1940 figure (Miller 1948:180).

Miller (1948:237–238) saw the quick response of women to the new job opportunities as motivated by their primary role in the household. He cites a "gray-haired woman who ran a lathe at the Pittsfield works" as saying, "I've decided that my place is at a machine where I can do something to help. I worked in a machine shop in the last war. My son is missing in action somewhere in the Pacific, and I'd do anything to help now." The company certainly benefitted from the claims of partriotism, but there were pressing economic issues too that drove women into the work force. Bertha attests to this with her statement in the Berkshire Historical Society's newsletter:

> 1940 turned out to be a difficult year. The war in Europe went badly with Dunkirk in May and the fall of Paris in June. In my own life there was the sudden death of my husband in August and the birth of my daughter in September.

She commented on Charles Wilson of GE's announcement in October that there would be a new $1,500,000. plastics plant:

> This news was heartening to me, as I knew that sooner or later I must get a job. It indicated returning economic health, as did the local construction trade's completion of 119 single houses. Also the Wyandotte Mill in Pittsfield had been awarded a government contract for 250,000 blankets. The Pittsfield Chamber of Commerce hailed the year's employment figures as the highest since 1917.
>
> Still, there seemed to be no pressure building to hire women for factory work in Pittsfield, no matter how Rosie the Riveter flourished in the big California aircraft factories.... The war was out there somewhere, a series of disasters we tried to follow on large wall maps put out by the United Press, available at *The Eagle* for fifteen cents. As boundaries of countries and places and names changed, we listened to the news on the radio and gave send-off parties for departing servicemen, but we also laughed at "Boots and Her Buddies" on the comic page and started our gardens and sent the children off to school as always.

Just a few days before Pearl Harbor, a group of Hinsdale women, my sister-in-law among them, became the first county women to get instruction as a unit of the newly formed Women's Defense Motor Corps. This was just one link in a large Civil Defense network being put together all over the country. When the Japanese struck Pearl Harbor, suddenly all kinds of plans solidified. Rescue teams, repair groups, ham radio operator groups and Red Cross classes were organized. Seven thousand county air raid wardens had ID photos taken. The Recruiting Office announced that it would stay open 24 hours a day.

With 800 men from Pittsfield in the armed forces, at the time of Pearl Harbor women were called upon by the War Manpower Commission to enter the work force. By the end of 1942, 3,500 men were in the service. Mrs. Prew began to work six days a week in the General Electric:

When I was hired, I was a typical housewife-turned-war-worker. I had no work experience. I had no idea what "Load Ration" (the department she worked in) meant or what I would be expected to do. I'd been fingerprinted, presumably checked for subversive tendencies, issued an ID badge and hired, along with dozens of other green housewives of all ages and backgrounds. My group was trained to make "cables." This involved placing gray, cloth-covered wires on a large varnished pine table, hooking the wires'; terminal circlets to pegs in a precise pattern, then "lacing" the whole together with stout waxed cord. Wearing gloves, we stood in one spot all day, making cables for the Manhattan Project, a rigidly inspected government undertaking of top priority, and we learned after the war, ultimately responsible for the destruction of Hiroshima and Nagasaki. I still feel that I earned my $36.00 a week.

Mrs. Prew's account of her job differs considerably from Miller's (1948) patronizing attitude about women workers: "Some former beauty-shop workers," he exudes, "found that dexterity developed in curling hair was valuable training for delicate assembly operations." He forgot the highly skilled machine operators like Vicky, who had been pushed out of the jobs they held in the prosperous twenties when the Depression came on. Vicky was called back to GE in 1941, just before the United States entered the war.

When I did go back, I shall never forget it because I went to the employment office asking for the job, and he told me he couldn't hire me because I was married. But he said to me "If you go to

Victory School — they had a Victory School where they sent a lot of women to learn the machines — if you go to Victory School, when you graduate we will be able to hire you." I said, "If you guarantee me you will unmarry me I will go to school, but I don't need to go to school," and I didn't because I had run all of their machines before. Anyhow, I talked myself into it, and he said, "Go down to see Mr. Morgan and if he says it's okay, you got a job." So I went down to see him. "Just give me the machine and I'll show you whether I can run it or not." I knew I could. Before the war, only the boys were sent to the school to learn the machines, before there were a lot of openings. That was why they had these "Victory Schools" to teach the women how to run the machines, but I had already done that in the GE previously. Well, anyhow, I got rehired, and I worked all through the war on the screw machine. And then, of course, when the boys got back they got their jobs back. They put the boys back on the machines. There were no women running them. There may have been a few out in the east side but they transferred them somewhere else.

When war was declared on December 7, 1941, the new union signed a no-strike pledge and wages were frozen for the duration. Workers were aware that the appeal to patriotism was a false plea aimed at a true sentiment. They were committed to the war effort in part because their relatives and friends were fighting at the front. At the same time, they were aware that the company was making profits. Carl was explicit about the specious nature of the appeal:

They [GE] built a plant that they called Ordnance and got their first big contract in 1941. So they were doing war work and we had a pledge signed by UE Leadership that they would never strike during the war. Which meant that, with the company making profits doubling and tripling during the war, we demanded a good size raise. In fact we demanded eighteen cents an hour and more. Course we made thirty at the end of the war, but other companies were getting eighteen cents, eighteen and a half cents, which was a lot of money at that time. The average pay was about ninety cents to one dollar an hour, and one dollar twenty-five an hour. The union wanted a straight across-the-board rate; the company wanted percentage raises, to keep what they called a differential. But the union stand was that the sweeper also had a family to raise, and he had to pay just as much for a loaf of bread. So we did get the eighteen cents, and very often we just got the straight across-the-board raise.

The raise was based on cost-of-living increases which could be objectively determined by Bureau of Labor Statistics indices. This government-initiated plan became an increasingly important part of negotiations after the war. The straight across-the-board application of the raise, rather than percentage increases based on previous wage, was a continuing issue that resulted in the breakaway of some salaried employees from the union after the war.

I was curious to know what the real effect of the no-strike pledge meant during wartime and so I asked Carl whether the workers were still able to get concessions during negotiations. He replied that there were very few small concessions on contract language. As he explained, contract language is an expression that covers almost everything except wages — seniority, rights and how things are going to be handled, whether by arbitration or not.

At the same time that workers were restricted to limited wage increases that failed to keep up with inflation, supervisors were given pay raises. Bus pointed to this contradiction in the GE's claims of trying to hold down inflation in the war effort:

> The General Electric comes in and they sit down at the negotiation table. "We'd like to inform you that your government, (your government!), has just put in a graduated income tax. That is going to hurt us. We've got to take and increase all of the pay of our people from the superintendents on up to the top and increase all of their salaries so that they get what we want them to get after they pay their taxes." And they got substantial increases. Then they come away and they pull the best one yet. "We're going to stop using the book value of a shared stock," — in them days, it was around 21 percent of the sales dollar; it's just like the supermarket — "We only make one penny on a sales dollar." But how many sales dollars goes through that chain supermarket in one year? Nobody ever tells us what was their gross business so you could figure out what one percent equals, how much money have they got invested compared to how much they get comin in.
> That always outnumbers the investment.

Post World War II Reconstruction

Following V. J. Day on August 14, 1945, the long-suppressed drive by labor to catch up with inflation went into operation. On December 14, 1945, UE locals throughout the country voted on whether to go out on strike. The strike vote was 86,229 for and 17,225 against, or 5 to 1, nationally, and in Pittsfield it was 4.6 to 1 in favor. In January 1946, an industry-wide strike was declared by the UE. All the trade unions in the city of Pittsfield, including the Journeymen Barbers International Union, came to the support of the strikers and contributed funds. Two hundred thousand United Electric members set up picket lines across the nation in General Electric, Westinghouse and General Motors electrical division plants. A week later, 800,000 steel workers shut down steel plants, revealing the unprecedented scope of the organiztion of workers (Matles and Higgins 1974:140). Strikers encountered support from local police, farmers, congressmen and the mayors of over a dozen cities in which General Electric was the biggest employer. Fifty-five U.S. senators and congressmen made a special public statement, declaring, "UE strikers deserve full moral and financial support in their grim struggle for a substantial wage increase and for a decent American standard of living." In nearby Lynn, Massachusetts, merchants contributed $3,000 the first day of the strike, and the town community fund gave help to needy cases. The mayor of Bloomfield, New Jersey, where a large Westinghouse plant was located, addressed a town rally in support of the workers, saying that the strike of Westinghouse workers was just, and he joined the picketline with the mayor of Winfield, New Jersey.

In Pittsfield, picketing began on January 15 with 600 people in the line at the height of the day's participation. The workers expected the company to use some of the strike-breaking tactics of the pre-war period. One of the current union leaders recalled watching the pickets massing in 1946 when he was six years old. They carried sticks concealed in their jackets because they didn't know what GE was going to try. He told me:

> The union people were on top of a sound truck in front of the gate, and people who thought the union would round them up said, "We have strike breakers here. We've got to be unified!" That sort of thing. They were getting ready for a battle that didn't take place.

Massachusetts state law prevented women from picketing after 6 p.m. and before 7 a.m., a carryover of protective legislation. This did not hinder their full participation on the day-time picketline. On the tenth day of the strike, over 100 working women and wives of workers with their children marched in the severe cold (*The Berkshire Eagle* January 18, 1946). Police Chief Sullivan, the same person who had been in charge of the 1916 strike, no longer responded to company demands, such as calling in the Boston police, as he had done thirty years before. His commands were limited to forbidding pickets from setting fires in the gutters to keep warm and to restricting the size of signs.

A new management strategy segmenting part of the work force as ineligible for union membership, and therfore entitled to pass the picket line, surfaced in this strike. Management declared that workers such as engineers, commercial workers, cost and accounting workers, production supervisors and personal secretaries should not belong to unions because of the sensitivity of their work. Business agent Jim Callahan approved that a skeleton force in the accounting section continue working, but rejected the need for lab workers, engineers and particularly supervisors of production. When four supervisors gained entry to the plant on February 5, Callahan said, "They will have the stigma of scab attached to them until the day they die; we'll never forget it and I assure you we'll never let you forget it." Management's prerogative in defining the category of union eligibles was supported by a superior court judge who issued a preliminary injunction restricting the union from preventing persons "lawfully entitled to do so from entering the plant." The local newspaper editorialized that "...the decision [to admit ineligibles] must have been made by the company nationally. We do no believe the local company would ever, of its own volition, ask 1,800 residents of Pittsfield, friends and neighbors of strikers, to endanger the cordial and democratic relations between them by asking them to cross their picket lines."

Local community support for the union was strong. On February 2, the City Council voted ten to one for a resolution urging GE management "to enter immediately into negotiations with the union...and alter its present policy in favor of a just and equitable attitude toward the wage needs of Pittsfield's GE employees." Three out of four employees in Pittsfield worked in GE and the eleven-member council included five GE workers. Businessmen as well joined in the support for labor. Leon Mohill, a Cadillac dealer who headed the Citizen's Aid Committee, said that he "unqualifiedly supported the union because their cause was just." He urged the workers:

> ...don't let yourselves be classed as a separate group, Labor, with a capital "L," with a fence separating you from the rest of us... You are the largest consumers, you buy the goods you yourselves and people like you produce. You are the life of the community and there is no doubt about it. Businessmen realize your importance in this community, especially in the last couple of weeks. And if you don't meet a businessman who will pat you on the back to reassure you that he is with you, this does not mean that he is against you. The businessmen know that they earn less when you spend less. Business can only prosper if you prosper.

The manager of the GE works, Emory Paxton, was a respected man. "He was the only manager," a machinist told me, "who would come into the plant alone without a bevy of supervisors surrounding him, come over and talk with you on the job." In a statement to (*The Berkshire Eagle* February 9, 1946) Paxton reflected the sense of mutual dependence that still characterized community-company relations:

> We believe in unions. It is our sincere conviction that the complexities of industrial life today require them. Our company is proud of the fact that it was one of the first of the large companies to enter into a national contract with a union.... After the strike is over, we expect to live with the same employees and with their union. Let us all make sure that we do no single thing today that we may regret tomorrow.

At one point during the strike, he intervened when pickets tried to stop a superivsor form entering and said to him, "I think you've done enough, now." He was clearly not a man whom one confronted directly, and the union newsletter took the tactic of separating him from the corporation he represented:

> ...there is little doubt in our mind that if it were possible for him to personally negotiate the issues at stake, an early settlement might be forthcoming. However, one point in Mr. Paxton's statement stands out above all others — the company still persists in its adamant refusal to arbitrate the wage issue....he must conform with the policy set down in New York. He must continue to support the inadequate offer made by his company regardless of his own personal opinions on the matter.

The business agent warned its own members that they could not bring about a Pittsfield settlement short of a company settlement. For the first time in history, all GE plants were out, along with all competitors in the electrical machinery industry (*The Berkshire Eagle* February 7, 1946).

The strike ended by the middle of March. Workers gained a 10 percent pay increase, slightly higher for those getting less than $1 per hour. Two months later, GE laid off 500 employees (Willison 1957:215).

Structural Changes in Industrial Relation

What do these strikes tell us about the structural changes in industrial relations in Pittsfield? How are these changes related to cultural patterns and beliefs? During the first half century of corporate-community relations, we can see a transformation from a system in which absolute power was exercised by the corporation to one in which two legally incorporated groups, labor and management, engaged in a dialogue that was slowly redefining class relations.

In the day-to-day routines of work and living, the class conflict inherent in the capitalist system of production is obscured in American culture. Charles Walker, who wrote *American City, A Rank and File History* (1937), brought out this contradiction between American culture and structure. "Working class approximate the style of living of the classes above them in America in contrast to the distinct life style of England," he wrote. "Only in strikes do they develop a sense of class solidarity and distinct modes of thinking and acting." In strikes there is a break from the boredom, monotony and subservience of everyday life. The threat of violence provokes some fear, but excitement and even gaiety and festival atmosphere prevail on the picket line, and there is a spontaneous creativity in the tactics, songs and organization. Egalitarianism among strikers breaks down the hierarchy that divides them on the job and links them in a solidified group that is denied in the enterprise. At the same time, it clarifies the break between those who work for a living and those who manage the work of others.

In everyday life one perceives a mosaic of class alliances in which the generational mobility related to the great growth of American enterprises tied an aging production work force to its children. Many of them became technicians, sales representatives and professionals in the expanding service and bureaucratic sectors. A trickle-down of wealth, accumulated in the process of production, enabled blue-collar workers to buy a home, furnish it with refrigerators, washing machines and even air conditions and stereos. By the decade of the 1960s everyone in Pittsfield who worked steadily could afford an automobile and some even had motorboats and campers. Union officials maintained the same lifestyles as other skilled workers which was almost indistinguishable from that of the middle class.

The frustrations of American workers do not evoke the heroic forms of militant action of Bolivia and other Third World countries. The American frustrations are those of having an eighteen foot motor launch and camping gear parked in your garage and not having the time to use them because you have to work overtime six days a week. They include being retired and living in a house with eight rooms and having to keep the thermostat at fifty degrees fahrenheit because the pension you negotiated when you were working can barely cover your food and medical expenses. Or having a right to organize and not trusting the representatives at the negotiating table, or of seeing some of the most militant trade union activists put into supervison and become ineligible as members.

These day-to-day frustrations are forgotten on the picketline. The belly-to-back formation at the gates turned back trucks and cars at the gate. The picketline carries the symbolic freight of this solidarity. This is especially evident when union sympathizers are forced to violate the taboo against entry into the workplace, which in effect is declared polluted by the pickets. In the first half of the twentieth century, workers defined a form of mass action that relied on absolute solidarity, a direct crystallization of the mass production system from which it grew. The main objective was a living wage, and equality based on need rather than recognition of work performed by the individual worker. Homogenization of the work force was a managerial tactic to overcome workers' autonomy (Braverman 1974; Gordon, Edwards and Reich 1982) yet workers were able to turn it to their advantage as the basis for solidarity.

The 1946 strike in Pittsfield set a standard for collective action that was to influence future struggles. It marked the emergency of labor from repressive forms of labor control to one in which labor was incorporated in the power structure through a bureaucracy and a jurisprudence involving state mediation in labor relations.

These cultural features, in which the power of class solidarity becomes manifest, do not necessarily make for structural change. That can only be realized in a change in the balance of power. The trends by which this came about can be traced in the strikes from 1916 to 1946. These can be summarized in terms of (1) changes in class alliance; (2) modification of rules in industrial relations and; (3) national integration of unions along with corporations.

Changes in Class Alliances

At the time of the 1916 strike, city service employees and shopkeepers were separate ethnically and economically from production workers. The police were clearly on the side of the corporation. There was no support for the strikers from the banks and shopkeepers; only the small grocers extended credit to strikers, since these were their only customers. The work force itself was divided; ''foreigners';' reportedly taking over the jobs of the striking workers were Italian and Polish workers often employed in textile factories or in odd jobs for GE outside the factory, as well as the reported black workers. The distinctions based on skill did not separate workers at that time since skilled winders and machinists allied themselves with assembly-line workers in the strike action. GE was able to resist the pressures of the State Federation of Labor as well as attempts by the State Board of Conciliation to bring about negotiations, and there was no higher authority that could prevent their use of strike breakers or special police force.

The alignments were different in the 1946 strike. The City Council was clearly in favor of the strikers; many of them were workers in GE or children of GE workers. But the most remarkable change was in the business community led by the owner of the Cadillac dealership which formed a coalition supporting strikers with money and credit. The American workers had never before been so united. Wearing their uniforms from World War II, the children of immigrants were the patriots and heroes; the managers were the aliens. After the war, American workers shared a common culture, as consumers, with professional and commercial people at the local level. The emic categories, or those stemming from natives in the culture with an insiders view rather than theoretical premises, for class in American culture do not contrast "proletariat" and "bourgeoisie", but rather "little" and "big" people. This distinction was even beginning to surface in the 1916 strike. The workers who were being accosted by the alien Boston police force brought in by GE were standing on their own lawns. Many owned their houses and they were paying the wages of the local police force with their taxes. Although GE could then ignore state machinery in labor disputes, this was no longer possible in the post–World War II period. People sympathetic to labor occupied city and state positions at all levels.

The Codification of Rules in Industrial Relations

Workers' organizations and strikers were legally established with the passage of the National Recovery Act in 1933, the Wagner Act in 1935, and codified by rulings of the National Labor Relations Board. These victories in fact controlled the wage system and labor's position within a structure still dominated by capital, but with the chance for negotiating the economic aspects of that relationship (Brecher 1972:139). In 1916 management would not even enter into a dialogue with the union, but by 1946 the police and courts were acting against managerial abuses of the labor contract as well as those of pickets. Government mediators contributed new rules related to cost of living increases and productivity measures in setting the wage during the freeze. These increased in importance after the war.

National Integration of Unions and of Corporations

The notable structural change in this first period was the development of national industrial unions that confronted the nationally integrated corporations. The impact was more pronounced in 1946 when most of the nationally organized unions went out on strike. This is what startled management into an awareness of a changed structural situation, one that demanded a rethinking of the old repressive mechanism that could no longer be fully exercised.

Production workers were incorporated in the corporate structure as a segmented work force with the organization of work segregated by sex and controlled by management. Paralleling the union and management structures for negotiating labor relations was a government bureaucracy that ensured adherence to ''fair labor standards'' codified in the National Labor Relations Act. The nation was the outer limit for the exercise of these rules. While the labor unions accepted these limits, the corporation began to expand overseas, first in the European markets to get behind tariff barriers and then in Third World countries where low wages provided a better business climate.

In the first half century of corporate growth, from 1880 to 1930, the labor control system moved from outright repression of labor movement to welfare capitalism, in which workers councils were tolerated and minimal pensions established. Yet, as Montgomery (1979) shows, these operated in a context of repression of independent trade unions with communication channeled through company-controlled councils until 1939. As a result, wages remained at the World War I level despite the high market demand throughout the twenties. Although the workers' councils in each plant agreed upon making a wage demand, the company did not heed them (Matles and Higgins 1974). The benefits accorded in the twenties were whittled down at the onset of the depression.

Much as the corporations resisted the terms of the incorporation of workers, they benefited from New Deal programs that redistributed money through government programs to consumers. Their very survival in these potentially revolutionary days depended on the measures they fought.

Chapter 4

Forging Corporate Hegemony

In the post-World War II period nationally integrated unions confronted nationally integrated corporations in a field of battle on which the state held divided loyalties. The basic premises of each of the protagonists had been formed in the preceding decades of struggle. Unions drew their strength from the very conditions of production: uniform, mass production, with few distinctions based on skill produced a solidarity based on similarity of function and wage. Each increase in magnitude of a plant or the corporation as a whole enhanced the power of a unified labor force. In the 1946 strike General Electric became a target for the united work force, which drew strength from the many different branches within the corporation, as well as from competitors within the same industry. Supported by local and state officials, the striking workers seemed to be an invincible force.

The corporation advanced strategies of control over the labor force in three directions. The first was to break up union solidarity through an anti-Communist campaign linked to the Cold War. Second was the decentralization of the firm and expansion of plants in the south where the company found a more favorable business climate in the fifties. Finally, under the leadership of Lemuel C. Boulware, who became Vice President of General Electric in the 1960s, the company promoted a policy of undermining collective bargaining by anticipating labor demands prior to contract negotiations. These policies climaxed in 1969 when unions in General Electric plants throughout the nation achieved a new unity in coordinated bargaining action that fortified the strike called by the IUE and the UE. These moves and counter plays are described in this chapter.

Post-World War II Control Over the Labor Process

While the unions developed a simple defensive structure predicated on organic solidarity, management began to decentralize the structure of the corporation, dispersing production sites within the United States and overseas. Simultaneously it forged a new alliance with the state in the development of the military-industrial complex that President Eisenhower recognized so clearly during his term of office. This was strengthened and fortified by an ideological campaign attacking "communism" in the union and stressing American defense in the Cold War. The attack on labor was administered in an ideological field orchestrated by the corporation as patriotic concern.

Anti-Communism and the Cold War

The cold war became the new focus for mobilizing a defensive structure throughout the world, stimulating war production during periods of peace, and extending a miliary network to back up the advance of capital abroad. Winston Churchill's Fulton, Missouri speech in 1946 declaring the onset of the Cold War gave the cue to industry to proceed in its new attack. Since the legitimization of strikes in the 1930s with the establishment of the National Labor Relations Board, the use of Pinkerton detectives, goon squads and scabs to break workers' resistance (Brecher 1972) had given way to the manipulation of symbols and ideology to win allies in the wider community. The charge of anti-communism broke down the solidarity that unions had demonstrated in the post-war strikes.

The first step in the corporations' drive to curb unions resulted in the passage of the Taft-Hartley Act of 1947. This required a sixty-day cooling-off period, enabling management to plan its counter attack at the same time that it deprived unions of their most effective weapon, that of surprise. The new-found unity of the unions was broken with the requirement that union leaders sign non-communist affidavits. When the CIO endorsed the anti-communist campaign, the UE withdrew from the CIO, and the International Union of Electrical, Radio and Machine Workers (IUE) was formed the following day, led by the former UE president James Carey. In the elections between 1953 and 1956 to determine which union would represent them in the shops organized by the UE, IUE took over half the existing contracts and two-thirds of UE members (Matles and Higgins 1974: 180).

Sam, who had become vice president of the UE Local he helped form (Chapter 4) told me about the split in the local union:

> The worst thing they ever did here was when they split up the union into the UE and the IUE in 1950. They played right into the company's hands. They were fighting amongst each other – Communist, Communist — that was all you heard. But Carey was the one who started it. Carey lost the UE election and Fitzgerald got elected. And right away, the next day, the big headlines, "Fitzgerald Elected by Left-Wingers" and so he [Carey] formed the IUE.

A former chief steward, whom I shall call James Cooley, added to the picture:

> I've always considered the 'I' in IUE to mean imitation. And it's just a poor imitation. They kept the same constitution with one clause added which made it undemocratic. The one clause said if you are part of the Communist party, or in any way support the policy of the Communist party, you cannot hold office. The UE says that anyone regardless of race, creed, political belief — any political belief — is welcome. And they're so far ahead with that. They don't waste any time singling people out for attack

The men and women who built the UE still ask themselves how it happened. Carl, a retired machine tool operator, remembers some of those days

> Our membership meetings were well attended, but we would occasionally have some naive, simple, or lowbrow fanatic stand up and say they didn't like what was going on down at the CIO, being dominated by Communists who were anti-Christ, and His Holiness the Pope said such and such. And everybody would look at him like he was interfering and the guy would sit down. It would happen every so often.
>
> One time around, it became a little more frequent, and then there was a sudden change. Phillip Murray was finally sucked into this anti-Communist deal. Before that time, he used to say that this red-baiting was the most evil thing possible and was being promoted by the reactionaries and so on. He made some very good statements up until that time. But pressure was put on him, especially on the point of respectability, that he was going to be an outcast in society. Here the guy was, making lots of money and playing golf with the big shots and he didn't want to be an outcast. So all of a sudden, he started red-baiting together with a good deal of the national union officers of the CIO. And it seemed to be almost out of nowhere, and I don't recall exactly at the moment how. So Jim Carey came back to life and began making speeches all over with the encouragement of Harry Truman — not openly, but we knew that it was with the encouragement of Harry Truman. And then the IUE was being formed. We said, "Hey, this is a paper thing!"
>
> At about the same time, many business agents were approached here in the local. And our business agent was a weak individual. He suddenly began to yap on the platform, "I am an anti-Communist, I'm a good union leader, and we want good union leaders." Well, he repeated that a thousand times. And all of a sudden we found him an adherent of Jim Carey. And more and

more talk was going on at the membership meetings that communism is permeating the shops. This business agent, he used the maintenance group as his stooges and as his workers. He would win them over by favoring them on lost time, which would otherwise take a lot of explaining to the company. So word would get around that shop that so-and-so was a Communist, that the UE leaders were Communist, that the union organizer that we had with us almost constantly was a Communist. And look what's happening to our boys in Korea, and that sort of thing. So the men openly announced that they were working for the IUE, saying that we must reorganize, vote the UE out and join the IUE. So this went on and on and automatically half of the members went with the business agent, with the church, and so on. Almost all union business was bypassed, just screaming from the platform it was, and we retaliating from the floor, the small number of us, answering their charges, their insane charges.

This business agent bragged about how he met Truman — this must have been in 1948 when Truman was campaigning and he was in Pittsfield and he stopped for a moment and exchanged neckties with President Truman — and he came and told me how Truman was doing a great job. So in a sense it was a giveaway. If Truman did this with a local business agent, he was doing it with others and he was behind all of this, everything to destroy left unions. Because how the hell are you going to wage wars such as Korea if you're going to have the unions oppose you? So then at membership meetings people would come in and sign these anti-Communist affidavits, even though every member wasn't required to sign, just the officers. Now the old man [Jim Matles] who was a national leader, he refused to sign for a long time, on a matter of principle. He said, "If you sign this thing, then it would be something else. The red-baiting would be renewed with increased fury." Which is what did happen because at the last minute, Jim Matles did sign it, and they red-baited frantically from that point on.

His vivid recall of the encounter of union stalwarts like himself with the anti-Communist front reminds us that the outcome was not predetermined as is often suggested in analyses that stress the pervasive power of "capital".

A Phillip Murray award for Americanism still hangs on the wall of the union hall, under the portrait of President Kennedy and next to the American flag. The IUE was certified by the government, and in the local union, the UE was beaten four to one. Most of the early trade union organizers felt that there was a decline in leadership from that point on. "Trade union leaders turned right wing as soon as they heard the word Communist," the former shop steward cited above told me. He concluded,

Democratic Candidates on the Campaign Trail Always Stopped At Local 255 I.U.E. Headquarters. (Photo by William H. Tague.)

The big thing about the UE, and why guys like Truman and the architects of the cold war wanted to get rid of the left wing union was because the left wing unions at their meetings would explain union principles, would explain how various political questions and actions were affecting them, would explain the international situation, would explain how the corporations were consolidating, working against the little people. They'd show movies and slides — nothing like that in the IUE. The education of the membership was what the establishment objected to. The UE used to educate the members. Now all that went down the drain. Yeah, and the union elections, you saw the quality of the leaders go down. The UE used to have an organizer all the time stationed here in Pittsfield who came to every meeting. His job was to keep you advised of the national policies, to see that you didn't do something contradictory. They were very democratic...

The church, according to Carl, was active in mobilizing their membership against what were called Communist unions, joining in the anti-Communist "witch-hunts" from the pulpit and in membership societies.

You know, there were more statements aganst us. They'd have several attacks, especially from Monsignor Marshall, head of St. Mary's Church. He said, "President Fitzgerald of the UE has a fine name for being Irish, but he's as red as the red flag of Russia." People would come fresh from a Holy Name Society meeting. They organized themselves as the "Dirty Twelves" — they themselves called them the "Dirty Twelves" — and they pulled every dirty trick in the book. Even Father Rice, who repented many years later — there was just a small Associated Press news item to that effect in the paper — this Father Rice acquired national acclaim by screaming about national leadership in unions would sell the country downriver to Russia.

A young union leader of the International Federation of Professional and Technical Engineers who was only ten at the time of the division of the UE-IUE recalled the church pressure on the union:

And you've got a priest from the pulpit saying, "This group is subversive." You know, in those days when it came from the pulpit, there's no question about it. It was Father Marshall. He was a pastor at Saint Mary's Church. He wrote a book, *In the City of God* or something. *The Eagle* can give you clippings on Father Marshall going public saying, "We want you to support the IUE. Get away from the UE Communists, blah, blah, blah... They're anti-God, they're anti-Catholic. Look at what's happening in Europe!" There's no question about it. That's why the union went down.

Carl remarked on the direct intervention of these Catholics in the union meetings:

You see, we'd have these people, they'd go to the Holy Name Society meetings which were held at the same time we had our membership meetings, which at that time were Thursday evenings. These people had never attended union meetings before and they were mostly women. You know women, I don't mean to be chauvinistic, but they will tend toward religion a lot more than the men do. Especially conservative women, the Catholics, in those times, and they'd come directly from their Holy Name Society meetings to the membership meetings. Now I'll never forget, I was sitting down alongside a couple of these women whom I knew vaguely. We were just chatting and the business agent was ranting on the platform, and when he got through ranting he made some statements that were way out of line, so I was one of the few who would oppose him. So I stood up, contradicted him, you know. They would recognize this, but of course they had the driver's wheel you know, and the driver's seat, and they'd recognize this. They would let me make my spiel, and these ladies that I was speaking with, together with two-thirds of the people there, booed the moment I stood up. The minute any one of us stood up we were booed, and when I was done talking, I sat down again, and we resumed our chat. They were doing it automatically, as trained, see

In the *General Electric Employee Relations News Letter* there were frequent and reiterated messages reinforcing the "American Way" vs. "Collectivism". Carefully chosen quotations from national figures were inserted throughout the newsletters of 1949 to 1955. "Ideological War will last for years to come and the struggle between collectivism and democracy will go on no matter what temporary peace agreement may be made now in Paris, General Clay, recently returned from Berlin, said at the Columbia University announcement." (*GE Employee Relations News Letter* June 10, 1949). Warnings of what happens under a proletarian dictatorship would in inserted, such as a citation from Polish Vice premier Alexander Zawadzki saying that the three main faults he intended to remedy in the Polish labor movement were the limited production capacity theory with which unions operated, the failure of work committees to prepare workers for self-sacrifice, and the lack of attention to instilling Socialist ideas into women and children (ibid.). The anti-Communist attack on local union leaders resulted in the defeat of the UE in Pittsfield. General Electric management supported the McCarthy committee by firing workers who refused to testify under oath whether or not they were members of the Communist party, a tactic that the local newspaper editor called ''GE's own Fifth Amendment firing policy.''

Decentralization and the New Labor Control System

During the decade of the fifties, General Electric Company was undergoing a new policy called ''decentralization.'' Multi-product plants such as Schenectady, Lynn and Pittsfield were subdivided into divisions with a manager in charge of each major product line. Each division was expected to yield a profit independent of the other product divisions in the same plant. Since the divisional manager's performance was closely scrutinized in the centralized auditing department, he was expected to be more responsible to ''the need for a reduction of plant determination sooner than departmental people.'' In turn, the product manager at the top headquarters expected to see the need for withdrawing a rapidly expanding department from one of the huge plants ''in order to prevent the high employment in the locality from developing into a labor shortage'' (Wickman 1969:24).

In Pittsfield, the new policy was translated into a transfer to the south of production of medium-sized and small transformers. In 1949, General Electric laid off 1,300 workers and put the rest on a short work week. Pittsfield was considered to be a high-wage, militant labor area, and in fact, the average weekly pay of $61.96 was $10. above state averages. The company announced its intention of not expanding the plant size, but holding it stable at 10,000 to 11,000 employees working on transformers and naval contracts (Willison 1957:230). With three out of five employees in the city on the General Electric payroll, the corporation wanted to lower its profile for political as well as economic reasons. Its experience during the 1946 strike had shown the powerful pressures that the workers in predominatly GE towns and cities could exert through their mayors and state representatives.

As a result of this policy, General Electric built a $25,000,000. plant in Rome, Georgia to make medium-sized transformers. Some Pittsfield workers were transferred there to help set up the plant. The IUE-CIO Local 255 business agent attacked the ''Flight of industry to non-union areas'' but the union was unable to stop the move. Even local management was relieved of the decision since it was made at corporate headquarters. In 1955, General Electric built another plant for small transformers in Hickory, North Carolina. Heating apparatus production was moved that same year to Shelyville.

With orders for the Korean War coming in, management at the Pittsfield plant could move workers into Ordnance from the main plant and from the plastics department, where products had been transferred to other plants. Nelly took a three-month layoff when she lost her job in plastics and finally agreed to go back to the East plant in Ordnance in 1951:

So we had to go over there for our fingerprints and to fill out a form. I went into wiring and when it got slow in there, I went into the battery room, underwater batteries. We used to work with pure silver. You had to have clearance to get into that room, and you had a couple of different stripes on your badge. And I was there for a couple of years, and then that phased out. And from there I went to Packing. I loved that. I used to have a restriction on me and I couldn't stand up on the job. I had polio when I was a kid, and sometimes when I put too much weight on it, it was bad. Well this LeMoins who worked there, he took a liking to me, not a liking like you could bribe him. He said, "How come you got a restriction? There's an opening here for a job. I got this opening for a packer. I know you'd like it here," he said, "I'll get your restriction taken off." And I went in and I loved it. It was the best job I ever had. I really loved it. We used to have to pack these things for the submarines. They were like chests. And the girls that got less money, they would wrap all these things in tin cans, vacuum it, take out the air and all, and line them up. It was like a supermarket. Just like you're going in the supermarket, up and down. Then we would have to pack. We would have a navy inspector with us. And you would read your packing list. If there were ten of these, five of these, you would put ten, five, place them in a chest for each one. You'd have to line them up, and when the chest was all packed up, you'd put the screws in and tighten them. Then you'd wheel it down to the fellows, and they'd do the hard part. I really, really loved that job. There were about ten of us and it was really friendly. I always said it was the best job I ever had. And then somehow or other the job got over. That setup was so beautiful, it was just like going in the supermarket, down the aisles of cans all lined up. Mr. LeMoins got the Coffin Award for that. Well, then the war phased out, and they ripped that all down.

Employment in Ordnance production was still contingent on there being a war to stimulate orders and when the Korean War was over, the division went down to a skeleton force. Nelly was kept on:

In 1955 we had a big layoff and I think there were just us three there, just to keep it going. Yeah, because they were expecting work to come in. We used to go in this super clean room, just the three us, and dust, and dust, and how much can you dust? The fellas in there used to do this really intricate work. And we used to go to sleep under the benches. They used to come in with the paychecks, and they knew just where we were, right under the table. And after that, work started to pick up and everyone started to come in. But I can remember when there were just three girls in there. Monotonous? Oh, God, it was monotonous in there. When a little job would come up, you'd run to do it because you wanted to do something. How much can you dust? I don't think the room was any bigger than these two rooms together. And that intricate machinery you had to dust and dust. And we didn't have any work. But they didn't let us go. So we did that for about six months. And it's more work trying to hide.

Al Litano, who was president of the Local 255 IUE at that time, was concerned with the instability of employment at Ordnance. When the Berkshire County Development Corporation called upon the union to send a representative to their meetings, he decided to go:

Because of the broad view that I had of what the employment picture looked like in Pittsfield, as far as General Electric was concerned, I thought, "I'll chair that position myself instead of appointing a member of my board or an officer." And I can recall that when I first went on there, there were all businessmen in town that were members of this commission. And of course, I was treated very cordially by the members of the committee, but I kept pressing the fact the employment at General Electric was going down, and we couldn't depend fully on Ordnance as far as getting contracts from the government to go on.

I personally had the experience in the shop when we were working on the Mark 56, which was gun control that went aboard ship, twice I reported to work in the morning, and was given a layoff. So the government just shut us off, or the contract stopped — "We don't need these units any more. They're outdated. We need to modify them," — and so forth. So from that experience, I knew that we couldn't depend on Ordnance for full-time work, that we needed something else in Pittsfield, either with General Electric, which I pressed on time after time, to put up new buildings, or to repair the old ones, or to expand. And I'm talking about Plastics, I'm talking about Ordnance, also Power Transformer. And I made these people aware of the fact that we needed new industry in Pittsfield. And I urged that we should put up a building some place that would house anywhere from 500 to 750 people, because there was a market opening up for them with the crime in New York and New Jersey. I was reading in the Sunday papers that employers were looking for new fields as far up as this to settle in. But it went on deaf ears. They used to get appropriations of money from the county commissioner to advertize in *The New York Times* and other big newpapers without much success. But I always had a feeling that there was obstacles in Pittsfield. Probably General Electric, Number One; it was the main employer. Number two: whoever was on the City Council and also the mayor. So we never got that off the ground, but I pressed it at every meeting.

The union's inability to force the company to reestablish a diversified industrial base, as Al Litano shows, attests to the growing power of corporate hegemony in local city councils. Specialists in accounting and engineering in General Electric management lent their services and their advice was listened to.

At the beginning of the Korean War, the president of Local 255 was visited by a delegation from Sikorsky Airplanes who had breakfast with him and the business agent to discuss the possibility of buying a large tract of land in Morningside on which they could test their helicopters. Sikorsky had surveyed it and found the wind conditions perfect for an experimental area, but said that they were getting objections from the local mayor and from the General Electric Company. The President of the union tried to attack the mayor for his failure to get in another company to broaden the employment base, but charges in the Local 255 press were never picked up by the local newspaper or by any politicians:

> But anyway, we bailed some hay over that. And of course we played it up in our union news for the next three or four issues that came out. We used to be at 14,200 at the time, and our employment was steadily going down. They were using a lot of the space they owned for storage, but we thought that those areas could be used for either a new product or why should they fight something like Sikorski? Which you know would employ probably 500 people. [I asked if he thought that they were afraid of driving up the wages.] That's exactly the point. GE didn't want to get any competition as far as wages were concerned. Not that kind of competition, especially looking for skilled and semi-skilled people. I think it would have put a dent in GE, especially the short service people because they would figure, "Hey, we're going to do something new here, we're going to be Number One if we put our foot in the door first as far as seniority is concerned." But I think it would have lent an awful lot to the economy as far as Pittsfield is concerned.

Union leaders like the president had an entirely different perspective from the managers of the company. As Litano put it,

> I was born and raised here except for a few years that I spent in
> the service and in North Adams. I'm worried about our grand-
> children. I'm worried about their grandchildren. I'm worried about
> other people's children, you know, because as somebody said down
> at the political rally when Kennedy came, unemployment is a
> problem for the retirees because they don't have their children
> around.

Like most workers, Al's future hopes were related to his children's
mobility. He sent them to the community college, and his son, was
unable to find a job here, and was forced to go to Virginia. His daughter
was a secretary married to an engineer in the GE plant.

General Electric Company's dominant position as employer of
three-fifths of the work-force in the early post-war period had both
political and social consequences for the city. Eight of the eleven
city council members worked in the General Electric Company. Yet
city leaders did not promote awareness of the economic vulnerability
of the city to plans made at corporate headquarters. This problem
became acute in the 1980s as the company was moving production from
civilian consumer goods and electrical machinery to war production.
Because of their commitment to the community, it was leadership in
the unions, not on the city council or in industry, that perceived this
difficulty first. They saw the threat to leave, made by the corporation
from the year of their takeover of the plant in 1903, as tantamount to
a death sentence.

Boulwarism and Labor Strikes in the Sixties

A new personnel spearheaded by Lemuel Boulware, a vice-
president of the General Electric Corporation, epitomized the new
corporate tactics developed in the post-war period. Effectively side-
stepping the collective bargaining process, it maximized the corporations' control over information and minimized the impact of union
negotiation: just before the end of the contract period, the management met separately with local union heads to try to ascertain what
were the minimal, irreducible demands of workers. With that information, the company decided what its offer would be, it did not budge,
but did publicize what it called its "firm, fair, offer" in all of its plants
and in the communities where they were located (Matles and Higgins
1974:251; Boulware 1969; Kuhn 1980).

G.E. Workers at a Meeting of the I.U.E. Local 255 Outside the Pittsfield Plant in June 1959. (Photo by William H. Tague.)

Throughout the fifties General Electric was involved in a policy of decentralization and expansion, both nationally and overseas. By 1960, GE employed 240,000 workers in 166 plants. The IUE had a total membership of 58,000, and there were fewer than that in the UE. It was in this climate of an expanding corporation and a divided work force that James Carey, the man who led the purged ranks of the IUE, called a strike against GE in 1960. As a result of the divided work force, and with many Canadian and domestic plants not affected by the strike, the company had "great flexibility in productive capacity to meet customer's needs" according to Northrup, an industrial relations consultant who was involved in General Electric's expansion and decentralization in the fifties (Northup 1964). Backman (1962:215) quotes Northrup as saying that in the expansion at home and abroad "GE has built second or satellite plants in many cases where operations of the group of plants might be jeopardized by a strike in a sole supplying plant."

Using the Boulware tactic, the company advertized its "firm, fair offer" in the plants where contracts were due to terminate in September of 1960. A full-page ad in *The Berkshire Eagle* (September 1:20) announced that, "Over the past two years, employees have made it clear that their main concern is security. What does that mean?" And the answer management gave was (1) keeping a good job free from worry as to skills becoming obsolete, (2) financial protection in case of layoffs, and (3) opportunities for better pay and medical benefits. "Therefore GE has made a proposal for improvements in present contracts providing greater employment opportunities, income protection in case of layoffs, general wage increases, increased security on retirement, and greater insurance protection."

The IUE leaders tried to whip up enthusiasm for the strike at a Labor Day picnic, focusing their attack on the cost-of-living clause. Before the IUE split from the UE, the contract included a 10 percent wage increase related to cost-of-living increases. This was reduced to 3 percent in the company offer. On Septmber 9, GE ran another full--page advertizement showing, with the aid of graphs and figures, the wage gains that would be made from their proprosal. The 1959 average hourly income of $2.79 would be increased with the new contract to $2.87 and by 1962 to $2.99. In addition, the ad pointed to the "forward-looking security program." The union resisted this salesmanship, and when the company offered to permit workers to vote on the strike proposal at the plant during company time, the leaders called a vote on Sunday in their own hall.

The advertizing campaign by the company increased in intensity throughout the week. On September 23 a full-page ad questioned what the effects of a GE strike would be on job security, which the company had ascertained to be the chief concern of workers. Their answer was cast in terms affecting each of the three divisions of the Pittsfield plant: the Polaris Missile contract being negotiated by the Ordnance Division with the U.S. Navy might go to Hughes, with loss of 300 union jobs; Plastics would lose contracts to competitors causing a loss of 100 jobs; and the Transformer Department might lose up to seventy-eight jobs. The company urged its employees to attend the Sunday meeting to vote. On the following day another ad appeared, with the message, "If you vote for a strike, you will jeopardize your pay, family welfare and job." In addition to advertizing in the local press, the company sent 277 different written communications to all of its employees (Kuhn 1980:231). On Sunday, fifty-one of UE's sixty-six locals voted, and forty-five approved a strike. Pittsfield's Local 255 voted against the strike with a two-to-one margin at a meeting attended by 2,600 of the 4,200 production and maintenance workers. Schenectady's IUE Local 301 also voted against the strike, with a vote of 5,033 to 2,805. In the end, both locals had to go out with the rest of the union.

Carey was wise enough to see the pending disaster and tried to get Ralph J. Cordiner, chairman of the board of General Electric, to present the dispute to a fact-finding board (*The Berkshire Eagle* September 27, 1960). Governors of ten states that would be affected by the strike tried to get both parties to avoid the coming collision, and clergymen from the communities affected sent telegrams urging Carey and Cordiner to settle the dispute. Despite all efforts to avoid the strike, it was called on October 2, and on the following day, each side counted its forces. In Pittsfield there was belly-to-back picketing and the business agent said only 1 percent of the workers showed up on the job (*The Berkshire Eagle* October 3, 1960). The tightest picket line was at the Ordnance Division, where navy defense contracts were filled. By October 4, the union mobilization began to falter. The Burlington, Vermont GE plant was in imminent danger of abandoning its strike when 622 of the 707 employees went back to work, and six other unions accepted GE's original offer. On October 13, Schenectady members of the UE local, which had voted against the strike but followed national orders to go through with it, backed out. In the UE contract, strikes had required approval of two-thirds of the members, whereas the IUE required only a majority of the entire membership. IUE president Jim Carey objected to the withdrawal of Schenectady as unconstitutional, but on October 18 the Schenectady workers were all back on the job.

By October 29 the IUE gave up its fight for a cost-of-living escalator and lowered its wage demands from a two-year contract with a 3.5

percent increase each year to an eighteen month contract with only one increase of 3.5 percent (*The Berkshire Eagle* October 18, 1960).

Despite the unpopularity of the strike, there was a marked change in the city officials' handling of it from their response in 1946 . At a meeting of city officials, including Mayor Haughey, City Solicitor William R. Flynn and Chief Calnam, with GE and IUE officials, Flynn said that as long as there was peaceful picketing with pickets going in concentric circles in front of the gates, on public property, the police had no authority to make them open the picket lines to let the trucks in (*The Berkshire Eagle* October 20). A GE petition for restraint against mass picketing was denied by three superior court justices on the grounds that if the company had taken advantage of the assistance of a panel of mediators of federal service on September 30, the strike could have been averted.

On October 24, the union capitulated and the IUE workers returned to work with no gains made. The only change over the initial offer made by the company in August was the promise by the company to retrain employees whose jobs were being eliminated by technological change. The settlement was, in fact, a loss over the previous contract since there was no longer a cost-of-living increase built into the wage. Management analysts gave a technological explanation for the failure of the strike to mobilize. Northrup (1964) based the lack of unity on the diversification of jobs, related to the great variety of products produced by electrical machinery companies. But union leaders blamed it on the ideological schism between the IUE and the UE. Albert Litano, who in the 1960s became business agent for the IUE, was on the council of the UE after he returned from the marines. When I asked him about the split, he replied:

> I was steward before I left for the marines. After I came back, in 1948, I came in on the council. We started choosing sides, and I was on the side of the IUE... Although I was a "right-winger" at the time, after I got my nose into some book in 1965 I saw it was the biggest mistake to split. I realized that when Jim Carey broke from the UE and formed the IUE, he played right into the hands of the company. Whenever we started choosing up sides, Boulware said, "A plague on both sides!" We should have cleaned up our own house. There was only one card-carrying Communist. In 1960 we all knew we were headed for defeat. Jim Carey played politics from the White House down, with Truman, Victor Riesel, Sylvia Porter....I didn't see that when I got into the IUE. I thought Jim was one of the best when it came to negotiation. But when we saw what we lost, I, along with Jim Matles and Fitzgerald of the national

UE, and John Foley, chief shop steward of the IUE local started meeting. John Foley told me, "You know, Al, unless we get the unions together at negotiations we're not going to get anywhere."

John added that they all went out to dinner, along with Jim Matles. "He could handle anybody," John said, "I don't care who the hell you are, even if he said, 'I'm going to come in here and eat you up!' And he never raised his voice either. He never shouted. And he convinced these guys they were wrong."

The union brought a suit against General Electric for unfair labor practices in the 1960 strike. Although they won the case four years later, there was no chance of regaining the losses. When a strike was called in 1966, President Johnson called for a postponement and Boulware's offer of a 4 percent wage increase in the first year of the new contract with 3 percent increases in the subsequent two years was accepted. The union leaders representing General Electric workers spent their time mending fences. The development of coordinated bargaining was an important advance that helped the locals gear up for the big strike in 1969.

The Challenge to Boulwarism

In the summer of 1969, as the contract deadline neared, the unity in leadership was matched by unity at home. In the 1946 and 1960 strikes, management had appealed directly to the wives of workers to go against the strike. This taught union leaders to extend their lines of communicatoin. Al Litano told me:

> We cautioned the people, "Go home and talk to your wives." In the 1946 and 1960 strike, pressure from the wives was terrific. [I asked why this had changed.] They saw what they had lost in the contracts, especially from 1955 to 1960. They'd see it in take-home pay. Also, the assignment of jobs was by the company, and they would't like the shifts their husbands had to work.

Although a growing awareness of women's effect on a working man's decisions is apparent, the perspective is still that of the male worker, although 40 percent of the work force in the Pittsfield plant was female. In the late sixties, women were becoming more active in the union, and twenty-five of the 265 stewards were women.

October 1, the date for renewal of contracts set by Lemuel Boulware in 1950, gave the company an added advantage because of the cold weather in store for pickets. The climate of opinion, however, was against the company and against the Vietnam War which was becoming increasingly unpopular in 1969. A series of slowdowns, caused by lack of parts, had cut down the pay of contract workers throughout the year. The union demands were for a thirty-month contract with an increase of thirty-five cents an hour the first year, thirty cents the second, and twenty-five cents in the last six months, with fifty cent increases for skilled workers. GE countered with an offer of a three-year contract and increases only in the first year, refusing an escalator clause based on cost-of-living increases (*The Berkshire Eagle* October 27, 1969). Behind these economic demands was the accumulated resentment against Boulwarism, which culminated the year he published his book outlining the strategy (Boulware 1969). By circumventing the ritual engagement in collective bargaining he threatened the institutional arrangements of labor and management. Labor was determined to seize back the initiative.

Both the UE and the IUE were united in supporting the strike and the AFL-CIO backed it as a "struggle against a company ....determined to destroy not only the union but the whole process of collective bargaining," said George Meany (Baer 1975:5-67). On the negative side, there were many more unorganized shops in the electrical machinery industry than a decade before, and northeastern industrial workers were competing with lower-wage workers in the south and overseas. Furthermore, there were many more technicians in proportion to assembly operators, and they often did not join labor unions (Matles and Higgins 1974:273).

On October 27, 140,000 of the 310,000 workers in GE plants across the nation walked out. In Pittsfield, 1,000 pickets were on duty in the morning when the seven o'clock shift came in. The temperature was just above freezing. Most of the incidents that morning, and in the months that followed, occurred at the Ordnance Department where, according to Al Litano, GE tried to break the strike. Community support from local businessmen and professionals as well as other working people was strong. Banks did not foreclose on unpaid mortgages, and local businesses, especially those with a long history in town, gave money and gifts at Christmas, though chain stores gave no help at all.

By November, the area economy was hurting from the strike. The loss of patronage by 5,500 strikers, 20 percent of the county's 20,000 industrial workers, meant the loss of one million dollars for businesses in the first month of the stirke. Luncheonettes closed, barbershops reported few customers, sales of cars were down 20 percent and there was a 5 percent drop in supermarket sales.

General Electric lost orders to Detroit Edison and to foreign companies. Sales dropped almost two billon dollars over the same period in the preceding year, and profits were down 10 million dollars. GE stock hit a five year low, at 79 1/8 per share. GE management responded to the union's elation over its ability to close down production with an advertizement published in the local press: "Lost customers mean lost business and lost business means lost jobs." (*The Berkshire Eagle* November 17, 1969). The company stepped up its attempts to get strikers back to work for Thanksgiving Day; the pickets set up a charcoal grill with a plucked bird suspended over it, bearing a sign: "No more pigeon; let's talk turkey."

Temperatures dropped as the strike wore on into December. GE repeated its original offer on December 5. When the union turned it down, GE filed charges aginst the IUE, accusing them of evasiveness at the bargaining table and violence on the picket line (*The Berkshire Eagle* December 10, 1969). Jim Matles, chief negotiator for the union, charged GE with hiring strikebreakers and giving bonuses to supervisors and non-union workers for recruiting "Cinderellas" — 18- to 21-year-old women who couldn't work on the third shift and were ordinarily the last to be hired. GE claimed that they were not replacements for striking workers. Al Litano spoke of this period: "I had wind of strikebreakers coming in about December. We sent out a call for reinforcements on the picket line. I choked.when I saw some of the pople who came in response, about six-thirty to seven on a freezing morning."

The growing support for the strikers had no effect on the company and the new offer of December 12 was little changed from the first. Pickets adorned a dormant thorn apple tree with Christmas lights, and one of the pickets arrived on the line dressed as Santa Claus, carrying a bag marked "GE's big bag of nothing."

Fifteen congressman attended a meeting in Beverly to bring about a settlement. The father of Silvio Conte, the U.S. congressman from Pittsfield, had worked in GE, and this congressman, along with many representatives, was in support of the union call for government arbitration. Even business journals began to take sides: *Business Week* criticized GE for putting its offer in print and allowing themselves to be frozen into a position, while *Forbes* urged business leaders to follow GE's lead (quoted in Matles and Higgins 1974:285).

With the failure of any new developments at Christmas, political pressure was mounted for a settlement. Senator Jacob Javits, Republican of New York called for a fact-finding board, which was accepted by the union and rejected by GE. Wage losses in Massachusetts were reported to be $3 million a week and an estimated 3,000 employees were on public assistance. Leaders of the AFL-CIO were bringing pressure for a strikers' benefit bill. In response to this, Clement E. Sutton, Jr., GE vice president and general manager of industrial and marine turbines, said, "If the strike benefit bill passes, we'd have no alternative but to set in motion programs for a more serious scaling down of our operations here and further expansion to other states." This kind of threat was clearly in violation of NLRB rulings on fair labor practices.

On January 30, 1970, after ninety-six days of strike the IUE and the UE accepted a new offer by the company, subject to ratification. The UE president, James J. Matles, and the secretary, Albert J. Fitzgerald, called the contract the first negotiated agreement in twenty years. "It took fourteen weeks on the picket lines for the organized GE workers to convince the GE to respect the union at the bargaining table," they announced. There would be immediate twenty-cent increase per hour, fifteen cents in February 1971 and fifteen cents more in April 1972. Cost-of-living protection lost in 1960 would be reinstated — a one cent-an-hour increase for each .3 percent increase in the consumer price index and with an immediate three-cents-an-hour boost. Before the strike, the wages for union-represented workers were $3.25 nationwide and $4.51 in Pittsfield.

Some felt that the final agreement was only slightly better than that offered in December, and both Lynn and Syracuse locals voted to reject the contract. The business agent, Al Litano, justified ending the strike on two grounds: The press had built up the "fantastic offer" that GE was making, but even more to the point, the union treasury was down to a few thousand dollars, no more than a week's strike benefits to the needy. According to Al, this was one of the best-held secrets during the last month of the strike. On the other hand, management was forced to yield because of the refusal by longshoremen to unload ships with components brought from GE plants abroad to fill in for products made in the strike-bound plants.

Some lessons were learned during that strike that are beginning to change the union outlook on the symbolic behavior involved in picket lines. Crossing a picket line had been considered a violation of the most sacred taboo, but union leaders recognized that sometimes that should be reconsidered. John, who was chief shop steward during the strike, commented:

The big show was down here every morning at eight o'clock at the north gate. And we had lines, we had all kinds of pickets. We had more than enough there. And we literally frightenend people by just being there. There wasn't any violence, no threats or anything. It was a pretty well-run line. But there was a woman that you know — Joan — she used to come through the line every morning and she'd stop to talk to you....And some mornings it was just nothing — "The Red Sox got beat," or something else — but she'd tell you, "Joe Smith is out in two months. He's going to be sixty-five in three weeks. Get him back to work." See, you didn't get your full benefits if he was out on strike when his time came up. In fact, I took Bus in through the line. He went in and retired during the strike and he wouldn't go through the picket line. I went down to the picket line and broke it so he could go in without breaking it.

But the most important thing was that they allowed all exempt personnel to go in and discovered that that cost the company money that hurt them more than the union. John drew the lesson:

We learned something about economics that time. It's great to let Theresa go in and sit at her typewriter with nothing to do. However, you've got to pay her. You've got to pay her benefits. There's people who'll say, "Strike! Nobody goes in there!" But when you think about it, it's the right thing to do.

The union was beginning to overcome the almost sacred sanction against crossing the picket line in selectively permitting individuals or even whole segments of the work force, such as the white collar workers, to continue working: I was told that when Bus had to go through to ensure getting his retirement benefits, the whole line disappeared.

The IUE Strike Bulletin summed up the economic losses based on a report by Charles Balas, market analyst at Argus Research Corporation (*Industry Week* 209-70):

lost wages	$ 292.5 million
lost man hours in production	90.0 million
lost sales	2,200.0 million
lost profit	200.0 million
lost taxes	180.0 million
TOTAL	2,962.5 million

General Electric's second contract offer made in December was worth $800 to 900 million in gains to workers' wages, and the final contract was valued at $1 billion.

The consequences of the strike on the work force and the community were far greater than the monetary assessment indicates. The corporation began to reassess its position in cities where it was the major employer. In May of 1970, GE announced plans for a five million dollar expansion of its transformer department in the Hickory, North Carolina plant. Opened in 1956 as a satellite for the GE Pittsfield division, the plant provided the flexibility the corporation liked to have in case of labor disputes. An editorial in the *Local 255 News* (Vol XV, No. 1, February 3, 1971) indicates the sentiment of union leaders regarding these moves:

> In a city the size of Pittfield and with General Electric as its main industry, it is not too hard to see that "As General Electric goes, so goes the city." For this reason we feel that every single business man, professional person, the ABC, all the community agencies, the Mayor and our city fathers, should come forward and offer their services at this time.

The services they called for were to aid in saving the remaining 3000 jobs in the Power Transformer Division. The campaign by the union to save jobs was stepped up as they recognized the increasing movement of General Electrical production overseas. In June 1971, an editorial in the *Local 255 News* pointed out that competition from abroad was the main threat.

> It is very apparent to us that foreign imports are jeopardizing our jobs. Our union has made a profound effort to help combat this and we believe that local management has also made a sincere effort. But:
> GE overseas work force is increasing at more than five times the rate in the US.
> GE owns more than 80 manufacturing plants in 24 countries. (Westinghouse owns more than 40 overseas companies, plus large blocks of stock in foreign competitors.)
> We understand that as a result of these large holdings in foreign countries, both companies have all but abandoned the making of consumer products in the U.S. and orders for heavy electrical equipment, such as generators and turbines are shifting abroad. As we said above we firmly believe that local management is sincere in their desire to keep the work here. They know and we know, that if the trend continues to manufacture heavy electrical equipment abroad, that the Power Transformer Department in Pittsfield will become an assembly line for transformers employing not more than 300 people instead of the present 3000. Component parts will be manufactured and brought in from abroad.

Employment levels have never gone back to pre-strike levels, and expansion of middle-sized transformers continued in the south. Since the settlement, contracts in subsequent three-year periods have been voted and approved without major changes. Contract language is the principle area of conflict. Some members feel that the Boulware position of the "firm, final offer" with little movement in negotiation prevails to this day. The fear of further attrition in the work force is foremost in putting pressure on the unions to accept the company offer.

The Elements of Corporate Hegemony

The basic rules of hegemony can be decoded from the corporate managerial tactics of the thirties and forties. First and paramount is management's assumption of leadership of any initiatives stemming from the rank and file and appearing to have a broad support. Second is the containment of potitical activism in the unions. Finally there is the grounding of these strategies in generally accepted principles that are part of the American way of doing things. All of these rules require a management that reduces opposition to and reinforces the dominance of management over the work force in the workplace and in the community. Gramsci (1973:2177-320) linked "Fordism" with Americanism, and following his lead, I shall relate "General Electricism" to "Americanism."

Cooptation of Union Initiatives

The departure from the corporate strategies that marked the early decades of corporate consolidation at the turn of the twentieth century emerged in the years of Gerard Swope's presidency of General Electric. Unlike other executives of large corporations, Swope did not directly oppose the Wagner Act or New Deal Reforms in the stormy years of the depression when industrial unions were formed. Jim Matles (Matles and Higgins 1974:63) sized up Swope's administrative skill:

> Of all companies, General Electric was most masterful in its control of workers by the practice of paternalism, sourced in the temperment and philosophy of its president, Gerard Swope. After the AFL craft organizations had been shattered by General Electric in the twenties, Swope set up Works Councils which were company unions. But the National Recovery Act of 1933, affirming the right of workers to form their own union, compelled some changes in the General Electric policy of company unionism.

Despite the effectiveness of the Works Councils in fighting trade union activity when it was illegal, the UE made tremendous strides organizing shops following the NLRB decision in 1934. Swope again tried to seize the initiative, publishing labor code GE Q105A, which set forth the corporation's policies on wages, hours, overtime, vacations and employment conditions and anticipated many of the union's demands. Instead of fighting this, the UE incorporated these policies in its first proposed contract with the GE, with the addition of grievance machinery.

When the unions established the machinery for collective bargaining, GE adopted these initiatives as its own. Although Swope fought industrial unions, even tryng to get the AFL to organize the industry when his workers' councils failed, his successor in the fifties, Ralph Cordiner, accepted industrial unions. GE plants across the nation often promoted shop stewards to quasi-managerial labor relations positions.

We interviewed one of these relations men, whom I shall call Herb. He started out as a stock boy just before World War II. His mobility began when he entered that machinist training program when he returned to work after the war. After two years he was made a foreman and then advanced to supervisor of standards and methods. In 1956 he became management's negotiator in union relations and from 1962 to 1968 he served as administrator of union relations. He was clearly a master of the technique of coopting initiatives from labor or government into managerial prerogatives. In discussing affirmative action he said:

> The greatest increase [in intra-firm mobility] has been in the last seven years as a result of a promotional program we negotiated with the unions. The main feature was that jobs were posted, whereas formerly movement came through chance. In the promotional system introduced in 1974, opportunities were made available to everyone.

When I asked whether this promotional system wasn't a result of national legislation, he replied that it was, but that, while it was immediately a response to gender discrimination charges brought to the NLRB against five companies including General Electric and Sears, this "hastened a program that we had been working on earlier. It was well-recognized as a need that we had to have a formal promotional system."

Herb's skill as a mediator between labor and management came from his own origins in a working-class family and knowledge acquired in his years as a production worker, combined with the education and training offered within the corporation. His identification with the firm resulted from his immediate experience in it. He told us:

> GE is the company with the best opportunities and the best pay you can get...Pittsfield has had better relations between management and workers than elsewhere. We don't have that picking up of sides. There is some militance there when it should be, but on the whole, people realize that what's good for business is good for the people in it. They listen, try to understand before making decisions. That's why the relations department developed. We feel that it is to the unions' advantage to understand that business needs mutual agreements benefical to all concerned.

The man and his house, an immaculately-kept Cape Cod cottage set in landscaped grounds, embodied the industrial accord that enveloped all the participants in the industrial setting in a sense of personal progress. According to a past business agent of the union, "That guy gave us a real insight into management." He, like Herb and the other business agents that followed him, are all in agreement that the union should work together with the corporation to get contracts, that the workers need jobs and the company needs workers. This was and continues to be, the basic premise of management's social contract.

Because of people like Herb, whenever the union introduced an issue that proved popular, the company picked it up. One such program was the alcohol rehabilitation treatment promoted by a former business agent of the IUE. The agent found a place in Vermont that offered a six-week program. The GE fought it because they preferred a two-week program in Pittsfield that cost less. The company finally agreed to the longer program but found its own in New Hampshire. The business agent accepted this decision philosophically, commenting that, "GE likes to say it's going to be here not there, 'cause they are paid to be managers and they have to prove themselves."

Prior to 1970, General Electric management coopted issues that were part of labor struggles. Today these issues are increasingly those of general social welfare that management would not be opposed to. A recent example of this occurred in the fall of 1983 when the business agent campaigned on a program to help reduce medical costs, particularly dentistry. The popularity of the issue led to the sponsorship of a Health Fair by the corporation, the union and other business and community groups. The medical director of the corporate headquarters gave the main address, focussing on what he named as the most frequent diseases of the day: cardiovascular and respiratory problems. He claimed that the high frequency in the incidence of these diseases was "more a matter of individual lifestyle." Although an OSHA agent was there in a booth, there was no mention of PCBs, the polychlorinated biphenyls waste that was increasingly being recognized as a hazard for GE workers and the community.

Ideological Containment of Workers

Charles E. Wilson made the new ideological approach quite explicit in an address to the Pittsfield Chamber of Commerce in March 1950. Explaining the newly-felt need for expanding the range of their interests as managers dealing with a complicated market, he said:

> In the beginning [of our business] we confined ourselves to making things, like motors and transformers, and selling them. Today in General Electric, and in almost every other similar corporation, a whole lot of people and a whole lot of dollars and hours are devoted to ideas. If you were one of our employees, you would surely have noticed that during the last several years a good many pieces of printed material, dealing with economic matters, had come your way, as well as some motion pictures, some radio broadcasts, and speeches and discussions. Obviously, we think this is an important activity, and inevitably, we hear it labeled as propaganda....What is it all about?

Dismissing what the "propaganda" was not about — electing a particular political party to office, driving out any particular union or discrediting union organization altogether — he came to what it was about:

> ...we are interested in seeing that organized labor grows up mentally as well as physically. It is a big boy now, with big muscles, and its parents have great hopes for it. It is time that it put away brawling in the streets, lending itself to left-wing politics, socialist or Marxist economics, and alley-cat manners. We want to see strong unions with democratic leadership which has a real sense of responsibility, not only for the individual members of the union, but for the great and successful American industrial democracy of which it is an important part....For its part, General Electric will welcome the day when management and union can sit down together and seek solutions to the real problems of industrial relations with the same friendship and constructive approach that governs a conference of engineers seeking answers to technical problems. (*General Electric Employee Relations News Letter* March 31, 1950)

The translation of political economic issues of struggle into technical problems of organization became central to corporate hegemonic control.

Corporate Leadership in Community Relations

Following Wilson's lead, General Electric corporate managers promoted the involvement of plant managers in their communities. This was spelled out in detail in the *General Electric Employee Relations News Letter* (June 3, 1955) in a list called, "What the community will find General Electric trying to do." In addition to providing good products, good jobs, good purchases — buying goods and services of local suppliers, they detail what it is to be a "good citizen":

> Good Citizenship. We will be found trying at all times in the community to be a good corporate citizen — such, for instance, as being a good taxpayer with no bargains asked; a good supporter of local charities (first, by generous contributions, and second, by our good pension, insurance and other employee benefit programs which insure that we will be chairing on the boards of these local charities); and a good worker in all other worth-while activities aimed at making the community a rewarding place in which to operate, work and live. Incidentally, besides our corporate activity, our individual managers and other employees are encouraged in their own desires to be useful individual citizens of the communities in which they live and work.

> Good Loyalty. At all times we try to be warmly loyal to the good people, good institutions, and good projects in the community. Where it is a matter of our proper concern, we will carry this loyalty to the point of disagreeing publicly, as a matter of duty, with those who seem to be speaking or working contrary to the over-all community interest.

> Good Profit. We try to maintain a profitable operation in the community in order to promote the strength and growth of our activity there and to reward properly the more than 300,000 share owners who risk their savings to supply us with the facilities and backing to make jobs possible there in the first place. All employees there have an opportunity to become share owners under our savings and stock bonus plan, and it has been gratifying to note the increasing number of our community-neighboring who have been choosing to invest their savings with us.

This was followed by a detailed summation of what General Electric needs from the community in order to stay in business. First of all, the costs of staying in business, including local and state taxes, must be kept favorable; second, union abuses in featherbedding, walkouts, improper strikes and labor laws that "either fail to protect the interests of employees, employers and the public" must not be tolerated by the community; and finally "unfair and abusive treatment in politically-inspired investigations, inquiries and hearings or from misguided support when given by the press, educators, clergy, public servants and others of influence to unwarranted attacks on local employers." Citing some of the "old industrial communities" as having particular problems in all these areas, the newsletter stated that the community must perform brilliantly in other areas in order to retain the corporation. They called upon community leaders to help their community get: economic education to ensure that the right thing will be done in their own interests and "in the balanced best interests of all," a moral reawakening to help all concerned that "the right thing is done voluntarily," and finally "political sophistication to guard all concerned against being bribed or fooled by demagogues."

Although the language has changed since the fifties advancement within the firm is still clearly connected with community service. The national Elfun Society makes this explicit to upper level management. Founded in 1928 by Gerard Swope, General Electric's third president, the mission of the Elfun Society was "to promote leadership, enthusiasm, loyalty and team spirit among company management." Its contingent mission was to promote understanding of GE as a corporate citizen, serving "as an important channel for mutual understanding with the community and within the company itself" (GE Pittsfield News Vol. 71, No. 24, June 28, 1985). The continuing mission of the Elfun Society to voluntarily serve the community and improve communication was endorsed by the present chairman of the board and Chief Executive Officer, John F. Welch, Jr.

One of the major activities of the Elfun Society is Project Business, "a program conducted in cooperation with local schools across the nation to help young people develop a better understanding of business and the free enterprise system" (GE Pittsfield News Ibid.). The huge commitment to the program is shown by the 600 members in the local plant who are members of the society.

In addition to the ideological campaign carried out in the context of educational institutions, the corporation makes an award, named after former president Gerald L. Philippe, to employees with outstanding personal service to the community. In 1984 the awards went to an employee who led a sports program for the handicapped; a couple who pioneered a foster care program for the mentally retarded; an engineer who served as scout master and others committed to a variety of different youth training programs. The target population is usually young boys, and the idiom in which their development is couched is sports and scouting.

Closely linked to the service activities of GE employees is the Pittsfield GE Employees Good Neighbor Fund. Called "the primary avenue through which local General Electric employees regularly support local charitable and social programs," (*GE Pittsfield News* Vol. No. 32, Sept. 7, 1984), it promotes, through employee contributions and matching company donations to the United Way and other major charities, a sense of the corporation as a good citizen. Since 1948 the IUE Local 255 has "embraced" the concept of the fund as a means to make one contribution in support of many agencies and organizations. With the theme "Giving that Stays at Home," the Good Neighbor Fund sets up competitive teams in each of its shops to meet the goals that rise each year, even with the decline in employment. Ordnance team members were clearly the winners in the 1984 campaign. The following year, when Ordnance was struggling to improve its image after the conviction on misconduct in contracts and some sense of resistance to defense spending, they were given the leadership positions in the campaign (infra Chapter 8). The half-million-dollar fund includes about $150,000 in a matching grant from the General Electric Foundation. In addition to the GNF drive, the General Electric Foundation has a gift-matching program that enables employees and retirees to double the amount of their tax-deductible contributions to charitable organizations approved by the trustees.

The 1969 strike was the last major confrontation between labor and management in the Pittsfield plant. Since then, the corporation has perfected its latest labor control mechanism, the threat of withdrawing the remaining producton of power transformers if productivity is not increased.[1] As yet labor has not had the political power to instigate legislation that would limit the prerogative of management. In the last contract, negotiated in 1985, the company was committed only to give one week's advance notice of the specific date of an employee's termination. Those whose employment is terminated would be paid 2 percent of monthly straight-time earnings multiplied by the number of full years of continuous services. An employee whose job is directly eliminated by a transfer of work or the introduction of a robot or automated manufacturing or office machine is entitled to pay equal to that which he or she was earning before transfers.

Chapter 5

The Organization of Work

Pittsfield's workers have experienced changes that encompass the major transitions in the development of corporate hegemony. These include: (1) the shift from craft to routinized jobs that Braverman (1974) analyzed in terms of the debasement of labor; (2) the shift from "homogenized" to a segmented labor force that Gordon, Reich and Edwards (1973, 1982) have developed from premises of a dual labor market (Doeringer and Piore 1971); and (3) the shift from assembly and even skilled machinist and toolmaker trades as well as technical and draftsmen's work to automated or computerized work processes (Gorz 1982). Edwards (1979) further elaborated the development of the labor process as one that went from simple repressive controls to technical control through assembly line processes, to bureaucratic control with the development of business unionism.

These processes are not, as Gordon, Reich and Edwards (1982) imply, simultaneous sequential forms found in all industries. The loss of a skill hierarchy that occurred first in the steel and automobile industry took more than two decades to affect the shoe industry (Warner and Srole 1945). Low capital to labor ratios minimizes the pressure on labor control systems in these older industries. Repressive labor control systems that were common in all industries in the nineteenth century and up to World War I have given way to "bureaucratic" forms of labor organization in industries that have become unionized. Coexisting with these industries are small apparel shops and electronic plants where the struggle persists. Louise Lamphere (1979) explores the ongoing struggle in apparel firms in New England to counter managerial techniques of exploitation that manipulate workers in the production process. She contrasts the great array of managerial control tactics in five firms in the Sunbelt where other than monetary incentives to promote productivity are used in addition to piece rates (Lamphere 1986). In General Electric's Power Transformer Division workers effectively gained control of the piecework system in such a way as to make management reassess its strategies and eliminate the piecework system throughout the plant. Segmentation of the labor force takes quite a different form in the plant, as I shall describe below. Uneven development is as characteristic of these older industrial centers such as "Yankee City," "Middletown," or Pittsfield as it is in newly-developing areas. The diversity of firms in terms of capital input, technological advance and rationalization of the labor process coexisting in the same community invalidates an analysis based on unilineal evolution. The textile industry that flourished in the nineteenth century and provided the capital for the electrical machine industry in the risk-development phase weathered the cycles of recession in the first half of the twentieth century by paying extremely low wages in comparison with the major corporation. The only remaining shop, a braid factory, retains its predominantly female work force with paternalistic forms of labor management that defy union organization. Similar practices also characterize the Crane paper company, where the predominantly female work force expresses a loyalty and commitment to work that is rare in U. S. industry. The one garment firm that was in operation in 1982 reverted to earlier repressive labor-relations practices that finally led to its owner being jailed. The newer plastic companies that are spinoffs from General Electric draw upon workers laid off from the corporation. For the most part they are not unionized and pay approximately one-half the General Electric wage. Finally the burgeoning tourist industry, along with the expansion of fast food and retail chains serving the working-class base provide employment without security, advancement or benefits for young workers and women coming back into the labor force.

The sequencing of labor-control systems in Gordon, Edwards and Reich's (1982) analysis is also invalidated by historically-specific accounts. Segmentation of the work force is not just the last of managerial tactics to appear in the annals of labor relations. A segmented work force has existed since the nineteenth century, and, in the textile industry, technological control of the work force has been characteristic since the introduction of the flying jenny. Even in the corporation, where bureaucratic control of the production workers predominates, segmentation of the work force is found in the Plastics and Ordnance divisions and debasement of labor is an ongoing practice as management attempts to limit the control over the job in computerized operations.

This complexity in the system of control over labor is intensified by the fact that industries draw upon a labor force segmented by age, sex and educational background. The great diversity in compensations and benefits is mediated in part by households where members enter into different occupational categories in response to differing demand. The polarization of the work force is currently enhanced by policies promoting employment of highly-educated technical and professional groups in the Ordnance and Plastics branches of General Electric at the same time that there is a severe decline in production in Power Transformer, where many blue-collar unionized workers are employed. In this chapter I shall consider changes in the organization of work and wage compensation in General Electric Power Transformer and Ordnance Divisions, focusing particularly on the blue collar work force. The contrasts in the hiring policy and control over the work force in the corporation and competitive firms will be made in the following chapter.

The Institutionalization of Labor Relations

Critics of the labor movement often cite the bureaucratization of labor relations as indicating the complicity of trade unions with capitalist control systems. From the perspective of those workers who entered the labor force prior to the labor unions, it is precisely the institutionalization of labor relations that was felt to be the greatest gain. Many of the rules guiding labor-management relations were introduced by government mediators during wartime to avoid labor strife in the production of war materials. In the First World War, General Electric resisted the War Labor Board's insistence on shop committee elections of council representatives outside of the shop, stating that "this could bring a parting of the ways of management and employees." (*Berkshire Eagle* September 12, 1918). By the time of World War II, this was standard practice.

John, who started work at General Electric in 1936, was laid off in the recession of 1938 and returned when the war broke out, summed up the difference before and after the union as follows:

> There was a definite change in attitude. You know when I went in there, the boss was king. He could do anything he wanted and he did. [By boss do you mean foreman?] Yes. He was the closest thing to a dictator and the decisions he made were just unchallenged. "No, you go on nights tomorrow," You didn't have any rights. Nothing was fair. It all depended on the foreman's whim. And it went absolutely unchallenged. You talk about someone being infallible, he was it. He might have got hell when he went into the office for doing something, but he sure was king out on the floor. There was more nepotism! To justify anything, "Well, he's my nephew. He's my sister's boy. I've got to take care of him." So therefore, he got preferential treatment. He might even have been a good worker but he wasn't hired for that.

John was very graphic in illustrating the despotic behavior of foremen. One foreman, he said, "who was the best union organizer that I ever met — all you had to do was work for Fred a day, and you wanted to join the union," used to get the workers to do personal jobs for him on their days off. He said that the foremen demanded favors that were never reciprocated. There was resistance, however. One man, a blacksmith in the shop, agreed to prune a hedge around the foreman's yard. He went and cut it down to rock bottom and carted it all away before the foreman came home. Foremen borrowed money and never paid it back. More than one of the older workers asserted that the foremen got their jobs by being Masons. One man added: "It used to be if you wanted to be something in GE you had to be a Mason and you had to have a German background."

The exercise of arbitrary power extended to hours and days of work so that even the regularly employed work force could not count on a week's pay. Sam came to Pittsfield from Portsmouth, New Hampshire after being laid off in the shipyard and got a job in the General Electric making capacitors. He told me about relations in the department prior to unions:

> I'm going to give it to you from when I started. If you came in to work in the morning, if the boss told you to take the day off, you had to go home. You didn't get paid for that day at all. You see, at that time, they used to have a budget to run a department, and I guess they still do, but the foreman run a department, and I guess they still do, but the foreman saved so much toward that budget. So therefore he eliminated you from working. There would be weeks after weeks when I wouldn't get a thing because he used to say, "Well, take the day off tomorrow," the next day, and so forth. And you never got a vacation, you never got a paid holiday. Oh, no. To get a vacation, you had to work there ten years to get it. One week vacation!

The foremen were enjoined to discourage workers from unionizing. Wages were a secret known only to management. Sam said:

> Them days if you got a nickel an hour more, or two cents an hour more, it was a big secret. Do you know that before we organized the millwright's helpers were getting more than the millwright. Foremen's pet. If you were a favourite, you were all set. They found that out after they organized....If the boss didn't like you, that was it. But now the foremens — some of the foremens are still hard to convince, course some of them are very good — but if you have a problem in the department, well, you're supposed to go to the

foremens and then you try to settle it between you and the foremen. But you know some of the foremens are pretty stubborn, you know. You're bound to get someone that's anti-union. Now if you don't settle it right there and then, you go to what they call labor relations. [Sam, like most of the old timers, referred to foremen in the plural as "foremens."]

Whereas foremen used to be promoted from the floor, in the late fifties management began hiring foremen with technical education. Sam commented on this change:

When I was working there then, normally they promoted a man to foreman, they took some guy from on the floor. And now they're not doing that. They bring them in from other departments, different young guys that went to school. They're bringing them in and they don't know the first thing about it. Before when they took a man out, he knew the work. He knew the guys, and some of them guys turned out to be pretty tough.

Those workers who had experienced the change from a non-union to a unionized shop saw the greater dignity workers felt on the job. John sums this up:

I'll tell you one thing about it, everybody worked for the union in those days. There were so many things to accomplish. You know when I went in there in '36 or '37, the company hadn't raised wages in the twenty years prior to that except by five cents an hour. They had been static for twenty years! So the union had a lot of things to do and a lot of places to go. But I think its greatest — outside of contractual — accomplishment was the dignity they gave you in the shop. You had the right for the first time to talk back to the foreman. You didn't have the right to say no before. Young people don't know what we went through to get them what they have now. To argue with the foreman! I had the same foreman for years and we hated him. Still do. Hey, for awhile, for years and years, it was customary to give the boss a Christmas present and we put a stop to that in my department. We said, "What the hell is this?" Well it was not anything great, but just to show your appreciation that he wasn't a bad fellow, a box of cigars, or a pipe. I can remember one guy, we got him a watch for Christmas. You know, that was around thirty-five dollars.

Rules and Regulations

Since the union came in in 1940, workers are represented by the shop stewards in grievance proceedings that are carried out with "labor relations'' men hired by the company. The contract defines the rules guiding relations in production in a general way, but day-to-day upsets require constant reinterpretation. As the business agent of the white-collar union, stated:

> The contract is only one thing, and the interpretation manual is another. What we need is a reinterpretation manual at this point... If you're taking minutes, and you come out with a piece of paper, you say, "That's what he said." Well, maybe I did say something like that, but I didn't mean that. That's why the company has this interpretation manual and why they got eighty to ninety lawyers.

If a settlement is not reached on the floor, there is a three-step grievance procedure. The union representatives ask for a docket number and prepare for a walkout of a crew or section of the plant after twenty-four hour notification. The company is allowed up to a year to respond and since the life of the docket number is only ten days there is often a great deal of frustration working within the regulations.

Despite these frustrations, in operating according to regulations older workers feel that the bureaucratization of labor relations was one of the greatest gains of the trade-union movement. They often criticize younger members of their crews for treating the grievance process as a way of getting out early on Friday and for trivializing the struggle for institution-alized labor relations. In the view of the older workers, the codification of rules is a labor victory, not simply a control system, as Gordon, Reich and Edwards (1982) suggest.

Contract language has become increasingly important with the institutionalization of the labor-management relationship. As I was advised by union representatives, contract language includes everything but the wage. The major points of controversy in interpreting the con-tract have been seniority rights, skill definition and its relation to automation, and provisions for welfare. I shall consider each of these provisions in relation to the segmentation of the labor force.

SENIORITY AND PROMOTIONS. The cornerstone of union tactics has been the use of seniority rights to overcome managerial prerogatives in disposing the work force. As a universal prescription, seniority structures the layoffs and "bumping" — movement to other jobs in the plant — in ways that force both sides into rigid positions. The Pittsfield plant is one of the last pure seniority bargaining units.

There are, however, possibilities of evading the letter of the contract. A former business agent for the draftsmen Local 140 of the International Federation of Professional and Technical Engineers explained how the seniority system worked in promotions:

We have a job-posting procedure that's something of a sham in that it allows the GE to apparently comply with the Equal Employment and Opportunity Commission (EEOC) so that everyone has an opportunity to know there's a job available. But let's assume that everyone was back to rate and there's no one on layoffs. Then what would happen is that they would post a job and the senior person who applied for that would get it. Period. I mean there isn't any ifs, ands, or buts; that's somebody else's because it's based on seniority and minimal qualifications...And that's plantwide, not just in one department, and if you're qualified, you've got the job over somebody in another department with more seniority than you. And that person is not likely to be a minority person. That may change. We're willing to negotiate that with GE if they will give us something else. What's really interesting is that we've offered the company some alternatives to that, and they always depict unions as the most structured, the most narrow-minded, tunnel-visioned type, yet we can't change that because the company structure won't allow it.

The company wants flexibility, but structured in its terms, just as the union does. Each side is responding to a constituency with its own set of priorities. The company would like to be able to move people to different time slots, and to different departments according to its priorities. For this reason, workers with a restriction imposed upon them were not hired when there were many available workers. In the thirties, GE never hired workers under sixteen who had to be allowed time for continuation of school. Later they never wanted girls under twenty-- one, who could not be moved into night shifts. This group — called "Cinderellas" because of the restriction born of ancient Massachusetts blue laws — was hired only in extreme cases such as strike breaking in 1969 or in war time. Currently the company is most concerned with promotion, where seniority curbs their ability to exercise their criteria.

The union, on the other hand, responds to a work force that is more concerned with security in the face of automation and job attrition. In the case of draftsmen, they want to make seniority provisions plantwide. The business agent of the Local 140 summed up the position of unions and what he senses is the management position: draftsmen who worked in Ordnance were better able to find work elsewhere when laid off than those in Power Transformer because of the highly-specialized skills involved in the latter division. In armaments production, draftsmen learn to work according to the military specifications manual that gives them more universally-valid skills. The business agent discussed the differences between union and management regarding bumping priorities:

Since that time [1966] we've always advocated when we have layoffs that people bump back and forth department for department. The company is against that. They'd rather have everyone bump only there, at Ordnance. And that way people that know the products stay with them. And we've always argued, like, hell, get everybody a broad base. But overall that works best for them. They can have a slack period in one department and they can look at the list of people bumped out of there and say, "Harry and Mary and Bill and Joan, they were all there eight years ago; they should come up for that position." But no, they're always trying to get us to incorporate a bumping procedure that says, "If you work at Ordnance you can bump anyone at Ordnance but you can't bump at Power. We'll give you a shot at a job opening at Power, but bumping-wise, you'd stay within your departments. We want that in the contract." That way they can control their work force a lot more. But they've also found out there were times, I can remember and it happened both ways, when one of them would have a layoff, work a deal out to pick and choose the better people from where the layoff was to go to the other department because they didn't have any background. Ironically, six years later when the department that absorbed was on a layoff and the one that was low is high, they had another layoff. The people they didn't want to let go were the ones they didn't want to take earlier, because they turned out to be very good draftsmen.

Sometimes contract negotiations involve prolonged discussion to gain power that is never used. The 1966 negotiations provided for promotion of a merit person, one who had been so designated because of proficiency in a year's period, over one with seniority. This was never used, despite the strong effort the company made to gain that right.

Most American workers accept the fairness of uniform rules regarding seniority applying to all regardless of personality or performance on the job. Immigrants from Latin American countries found it more difficult to relate to such rules. John recalled the reaction of a Brazilian to his attempts to apply rules uniformly when he was a foreman:

This guy from Brazil was an excellent worker. He used to stop me almost daily and say, "How am I doing?" "Great, great," no hesitation there at all. So he was working for me, and I didn't know that there were some layoffs coming. The others were smart enough to know what he was doing. But he had no seniority, so I laid him off. He hit the ceiling. He was belligerent. He told me, "You told me I was a good worker. Not once, not twice. You told me several times.." "You were," I said, "terrific." "But look at that guy, he's lazy, and he's working." He was right again. I couldn't change it if I wanted.

Labor Management Relations

In the day-to-day management of the plant, formal rules are converted into personal encounters where the tolerance of an individual is tested in a gamelike way. For the sixteen years John F. Welch was manager of Plastics in the Pittsfield plant, he evoked considerable admiration as well as fear. Even before he was named one of the ten most ruthless business managers by business journals, Pittsfield workers had identified that quality in him. John said of him:

> You've got to remember that Jack Welch was from here and he was never associated with anything that wasn't high profits. He didn't want just to make a profit. He wanted to make an enormous profit. He's a good guy, by the way. He was good to his help. He was a decent guy to negotiate with. I like him.

John illustrated what he meant by Welch's style of management with a story:

> Woody, who was a foreman in plastics, had a row house up in Washington [a neighboring town]. We had negotiated a contract with Jack Welch some months before that, to put a new washroom out in Plastics. They tore down the old place they had had for 150 years. And what Jack [Welch] did was spend $150,000 for a washroom which ten years ago was enormous. He did the whole room showers, drying rooms, lockers. During the installation, Harvey, a union shop steward for maintenance in Plastics, brought in the plumbing fixtures, sinks, toilets, showers, and the day after the installation, half of them are missing. Jack Welch had a pretty good idea of where they went, so he sent his police department up to Washington, and there are all our items with the plumber installing them. So he said, "Now we got a situation on our hands." So Jack calls me up and says —Jack was never very polite — "Get your ass out here." So he sits there and talks for the first ten minutes, "I'm going to fire that no good rotten Woody." Well I was sitting there and I couldn't care less. I had no responsibility for it; I had no obligation to any foreman. So I just sat there with my arms folded. "Well," he said, "aren't you going to say anything?" I said, "No, Harvey is my responsibility. I'm worried about him. Now," I said, "Harvey just didn't realize that those were the same items. He had nothing to do with transporting them or taking them out. He was doing a job on the side for which he was being paid, and he had a license to work on the side." Jack told me, "You're telling me he didn't know that these were the same items out of the same place?" And I said, "That's right, Jack."

He said, "What kind of a God damn fool do you think I am?" I said, "Jack, if you take this any further, you're going to have a terrible time at arbitration proving that this isn't true." He said, "O.K., Harvey stays, Woody goes. But don't think I don't know the difference."

But that's the way he was. And you could come to an agreement with Jack in less time than anyone I ever knew. He knew what he wanted to do. He knew what he was willing to do for it, and his word was good....He used to say to the labor contract people, "Throw the contract away!" Yeah he said, "Use your head." He used to say that many times. He'd say, "Why did you do that George?" And George would say, "Well, it's on page sixty-three." He'd say, "George, throw the book away." Jack had guts. If he thought something was right, he went out and did it.

The business agent of the Draftsmen's International Federation of Professional and Technical Engineers Local 140 made the analogy of management-union relations to that of a baseball team with the company owning the ball and the bat. "You're up to bat and there's two strikes against you, and that's about where you sit." Like his counterpart in Local 255, he was very conscious of the market both for the product they make — power transformers — and for the labor they sell. The market for power transformers was declining throughout the seventies, and with automated processes that were affecting drafting more than any other segment of the labor force in General Electric, at the beginning of 1980 there were heavy layoffs. These were the two strikes against them, and the third pitch coming up was the threat to close down Power Transformer completely. Eighty-one draftsmen were laid off in 1981 and more were expected to be fired.

Both union and management representatives share a belief in the market as the mediator determining allocation of capital, resource and work force, justifying rewards in the redistribution of wealth. Management persons, at least those in the upper echelons, are fully aware of the manipulation of bids and prices on the supply side. The famous trial of electrical machinery companies in the fifties made it clear that price fixing on distribution equipment bids was not only a common practice but was the way in which bright young engineers move ahead in the hierarchy up to the point that they "had no air cover" (as Engineer Ginn, the "fall guy" at the Pittsfield GE plant said of his own career that ended in jailing [1]). Because the union has few independent sources of information on the firm, they feel required to accept management statements as to market conditions.

The cultural distance between management and workers has narrowed visibly in the last decade. The assistant to the community relations supervisor is 45 years old, the same age as his protagonist in the union, the business agent of Local 255. Both are clean-cut with facial hair groomed in the current styling. Both wear ties at work, though the union agent may have more latitude in working in his cropped shirt sleeves. Education is important in the mobility of both union managerial relations. The union agent may have had an edge in winning the election because of a course he took on labor management relations at North Adams College. Management's community relations man went to Kent State and worked on an Ohio newspaper for seven years.

The careers and life styles of the union and management agents are not terribly different. While the union's business agent is actively involved in the community affairs of Dalton where he lives, GE's relations man is a member of the Red Cross and the Mayor's Committee on Pittsfield Revitalization. Philosophically the two men are not very far apart either. Although the union representative resents being put in the middle when there is pressure for increased productivity under the threat of withdrawing power transformer production, he accedes to it on the score that he does not want to be the one blamed for GE moving out of the community. The management agent puts company policy ahead of his own preferences, conceding the company's right to dictate the terms on which its presence in the community is ensured.

The style of negotiations has changed considerably with the change of incumbents. The ability to make amicable agreements on issues such as the installation of robots in the packing room in 1983, is a stated goal for each side rather than the confrontation approach played up in the press in the 1940s and 1950s. Union sponsored campaigns such as the health fair to increase workers' awareness of medical problems was supported by management and became a coordinated event in 1983. Although problems of cancer related to exposure to chemicals in the plant was beginning to surface, the business agent of the union did not challenge the emphasis that General Electric's manager of clinics and the community relations people put on individual life styles as the main thrust of the campaign. Both the business agent and the community relations man were in agreement that the "compression on wages," i.e. the nearly-uniform rates for all range of work, destroyed the incentive to work and felt that everyone had gained by the 1982 contract giving some improvement to upper level workers. For the first time the percent increases were not translated into hourly rates based on average earnings but rather were applied across the board. The agreement between union leaders and management on this issue signifies the importance of bureaucratic rules in hegemonic control.

Both men offer a contrast to their predecessor, whom I interviewed in 1979. The former business agent had started work as a child in the Depression when he helped his widowed mother support a house full of kids. His first contact with the unions was in the competitive textile mills of North Adams, where he was fired three times (and rehired four) for union activities. At the time he was in office, GE's community relations man was very committed to the community — perhaps too much so for his own career. Some have said the company objected to the way he settled the issue of PCB waste disposal in an amicable way, paying people at fair market price for the houses that had wastes in the cellars. When he and his boss were replaced, those who lived in the area affected were not able to get a hearing with the management. The language, bearing and personal commitments of each was definitely partisan, but both shared a commitment to the community. Their successors seem more committed to their individual careers, and both are said to be desirous of advancing their careers in management.

The very interconnectedness of the divisions in Pittsfield with those in other plants throughout the country makes every decision a weighty one, with widespread ramifications. This in itself builds a certain rigidity in the operation of the firm. As the draftsmen's business agent said:

> The person you're dealing with every day in relations, and his boss is the boss of all relations in Pittsfield, and you start throwing those kinds of things at him, he'll say, "Hey, we ought to check with Fairfield. This will have an impact throughout the country. You know, we've got eight other locals that are similar to you. If all of a sudden we say you can do this kind of work, you're going to tell your brothers and sisters in Schenectady we want to do it too, and it's not just a parochial thing any more." And so it takes them five years to make that decision. We tried to introduce something here like flex time, and they just shudder and say, "Oh, you know what that's going to mean in another location?" And we say, "Let's try it on a trial basis and see what happens."

Many of the best shop stewards have gone on to be foremen, supervisors and labor relations managers. The business agent of the white collar workers explained this movement:

We've got one going this week, got one a month ago, got a lot of good supervisors, cause they know the ropes. And then you get a couple of lousy ones who think they have to impress the company. But these kind of people should be some of the top supervisors in the country because they know right from wrong. Our people are respected. They do know right from wrong, but when they do flub up, they're going to get clobbered by us....The unions train these managers who come in here without any background. There is a rapid turnover in labor managers.

The business agent of the draftsmen's union corroborated the importance of having former union stewards in management when I asked him if he preferred to relate to them rather than to the outside experts:

Yes you can't buffalo them. They're set in their way and they have the faults all of us have as humans, but you can explain your case and it's a good one, they're much more understanding of what's going on. A labor relations man who came up through the ranks who happened to come out of drafting, and they're going to talk to him about a work classification grievance, his advice to the people in management is going to rate higher with management and the union is going to have greater tendency to accept them. You know, I sit across from a guy who's never done anything except draw cartoons in his child's schoolbooks, and he's going to tell me it's not a senior draftsman job, I know all he's doing is mouthing what the manager on the floor told him to say. He couldn't argue with me, so right off the bat, his credibility is in trouble. Now when he comes back later and tells us about the policy regarding sick time, or something else, I'm going to say, "Yeah, this is the same schmuck that tried to tell me that it was only a design job and I know it is a senior design job." It hurts him, and it works the other way around. On your side, when he goes back to management and says, "Hey, look! We said we weren't going to pay this guy what the classification of the work," or, "We were going to upgrade these people and we didn't include enough," or something, they're not going to get smart with him because he represents labor relations. They sit with him and say, "This jerk doesn't know anything. He's only been working here two years. What does he know?" It's the same problem. It takes an exceptional individual to come in from the outside. They have a few advantages; they don't have any pros or cons, but those advantages are outweighed by far by the disadvantages. Labor relations people need their credibility before anything else.

These mediators play an invaluable part in the communication between labor and management ensuring accord in everyday labor relations. The test of their credibility comes in whether management backs them up so that their word is accepted. One of the union leaders with whom I spoke joined management's team a short time after the interview, attesting to his own credibility as an informant. This movement from the ranks of labor to management is evidence of the effectiveness of corporate hegemony.

Compensation For Work

Beyond the negotiations for wages in the contract, there is a constant battle going on in the shop to establish the basis for remuneration. The battle is waged in market terms over the amount produced in relation to compensation. The complexity of the job hierarchy masks some of the inequities that prevail. Each system of compensation is accompanied with an ideology justifying it. The language in which this is phrased has changed over time in ways that reveal the changing relations within corporate hegemony. Labor has shifted from the reference to ''a living wage'' that dominated negotiations through the forties, to a more market orientation, calling for a share in profits and increases in productivity.

The terms in which wage negotiations are phrased have frequently been introduced by government agents during war time. During World War I, the War Labor Board raised the issue of the minimum wage of forty cents. This was turned down by General Electric, but later they gave in. Cost-of-living increases were introduced as the means of avoiding problems during World War II, when labor signed the no-strike pledge and saw inflation eating up their wages. The UE introduced it into contract negotiations following the war, but this was lost when the IUE-UE split broke labor's ranks. Productivity increases, or wage increases based on greater output, was another war time innovation that has been retained in contract negotiations.

The struggle over wages is one of the prime arenas in which corporate hegemony is shaped. I shall focus on the piecework payment and the change to day rate in order to examine the way in which workers can sometimes transform managerial prerogatives in the course of shop floor practice. Piecework evolved in nineteenth century industries as a labor control mechanism. Piecework was introduced in the automobile and steel industries in the early decades of the twentieth century both to stimulate individual productivity and to divide the work force (Gordon, Edwards and Reich 1982:141). General Electric used piecework in most of its production units up until 1972. Carl, a toolmaker in the Power Transformer Division, tried to fill me in on some of the older piecework system in comparison with newer rates to show how workers reversed some aspects of its divisiveness:

At one time they used the Bedeaux[2] system. I think it was in France or England where he promoted his system which was a killer. In other words, it sort of sucked the worker in, in that they were setting piecework rates quite low. And of course, the papers, *The Wall Street Journal*, they played him up something wicked, a genius. The old timers in the shop told me that when he disembarked in this country, there were mobs to greet him. They wanted to kill him. The system was such that they could barely make a go of it on the low prices that they had. But with plenty of experience, if you really made a go of it, you could get above this norm. And for every piece you produced above the norm, the price would be doubled or thereabouts. And I'd say that one worker out of three or four, or say one worker out of two, could reach that norm, and so it was a bonus system in a way. So everybody was working like mad, you know, because they worked like mad to reach the norm, and then when they got above the norm, they'd work like mad to get that gravy.

This was in the twenties, I think. I went to work in the General Electric in thirty-five and they'd already dropped it. It was too much of a killer. The workers wouldn't last. They objected. They'd broken the unions in about 1919 and the people were a bit docile. But it was a hated system. You might say that was the zenith of piecework. From that point on, the left wing, maybe before that, the left wingers always felt that piecework is a terrible thing, and should not have it. They were against it on principle.

When I was working at GE what they'd do is have rate setters, a great many wage setters which increased the office staff, which was expensive and the rate setters would come along and time us for anywhere from fifteen minutes to an hour on the work that we were doing and set a price. Well the price varied quite a lot, especially during the war when there were so many new rate setters who really didn't care. And by the time the war started, I was on machine work and when they came around, we just slowed the machines down.

I asked if the rate setters were engineers.

No, they were often trainees. If you wanted to get ahead in the shop, promotion-wise, first up was to become a rate setter. It was strange, a few men, as soon as they became rate setters. They didn't really care. We had one feller was a minister. He gave us beautiful prices. So the prices varied a lot. A lot depended on the worker's ability, to seem to be working hard while he was being timed, and yet as we say, to screw the bastard. With the machines, we'd always work the machines slower, or shuffle your hands more with hand work, to appear to be working harder. Sometimes the prices were atrociously low, and other prices in the same department, by mistake or something, would be quite high. So we would scream on the low jobs, and fight any attempt by management to cut the price of the high jobs.

Before unionization, the prices were, according to my informants who worked on piece rate, set arbitrarily. As soon as a worker started to make the anticipated earning rate — AER — the company would cut the price. After unionization, there were agreements made with negotiation locally and nationally on how the prices were handled. Workers were always finding out short cuts, or they would run the machine at a higher speed or double up on the tools on a machine doing two cuts at once. They were careful however, not to go too far beyond the ordinary rates so the foremen wouldn't try to retime the job.

Women were even more committed to piecework than were men. They had fewer variations in rank, with most of them being clustered in ranks that were considered only semi-skilled. As a result, the only challenge was in doing the job faster and earning somewhat more. Like the machine-tool makers, women guarded their tricks that enabled them to make out faster and earn more. Nelly explained how this worked:

I got this one woman, she got me under her wing. She was real nice, Boy, she had all the good jobs. Well, she used to make fabulous money. In those days when you made eighty dollars, that was good money. She was tough, though. Lucky she showed me a lot of the ropes. See, each girl had her own job. The new girls got all of the crappy jobs, and the old ones had all the good jobs.

In the old days, we were on piecework. We always had cards punched and you could save up all of these cards for each job and then turn them in all mixed up so that they wouldn't know what the good jobs were. You know what I mean? We used to tape and we used to drill, and we used to file, but you'd mix up seven or eight different jobs. You could make more money than we did, but we used to turn in the jobs that added up to about $80. If you had a tough job, you could take it easy because you had something to cover you to make a good week's pay [laughed]. Oh, yeah, there were so many tricks! So when Leona couldn't handle a lot of her work, she'd say, "I want Nella!" and I'd go over and she'd show me how to mix up all these different jobs. And the boss used to say — I'll never forget — we used to turn around and we'd see him way off watching us. He still couldn't figure out. The minute they figured out which job was the best they'd send a time setter over to you. So he'd always be watching and he could never make it out. So, anyway, he used to say, "You make more money than I do!" And I'd say, "Well I work for it." And he'd say, "Well, I'll catch you yet. I'll find out which is which." But he never did.

When Nelly's job in plastics moved to Taunton, she and the other "girls" used to have to teach the boss and the engineers what they did. In one case, they were supposed to file off the edge of the plastic mold, but instead they put it in a tumbling machine which took it all off quickly. "That's when they caught up with a lot of good jobs," Nelly said.

The lack of mobility for women production workers was partially compensated by piecework. Real skills that were denied in the job description of assemblers were revealed in the speed which an experienced person could attain. When I asked Vicky if there was any chance for advancement in her work, she looked puzzled and then replied, "It was all piecework. If you happened to be a good worker or a fast worker, or a steady worker, whichever — in my case, I was a steady worker more than anything else — and so you made according to what you did." She worked before there were ratings and then when ratings were assigned to women's work, she said it didn't make much difference because you got what you made regardless of your rating.

Constant changes in design and materials meant changes in the prices for each job. When bonded carboloid was introduced into the machine shop, an operation that formerly took an hour could be done in ten or even five minutes but there was more work involved loading the machine. The price of the job went down from eight cents to two cents a piece, but you would have to handle 400 pieces. Other design changes favored the workers, so that fewer pieces were handled. Complications came when there were slowdowns in other departments feeding them materials, or the machines would break down. This was handled with a rate for down-time which became a matter of dispute with variations from one department to another in how it was handled.

The break with this piecework system came in Schenectady where more of the production was related to research and design and many of the men were indispensable. They had more control over the organization of the work and more down-time was claimed. There the management tried a pre-determined motion study, with the rates figured out on paper. This required constant negotiation between union officers and the company. The UE stewards objected on the basis that if they let the company educate union stewards, then the stewards would be absorbed into the company's methods and the workers would have to contend with both the steward and the foreman.

Competition in the bids for the sale of power transformers meant that the company was often bidding below their costs. The company argued that the only way that it could break even was with greater cooperation from the workers. Carl described the response:

> For a long time they were running in the hole. So they split the word somehow and scared hell out of union officers as well as the whole town, that they might have to close out. They would have to eliminate piecework. That was about 1972....The piecework workers were up in arms. They were only about one-third of the workers, with the rest in maintenance and stock delivering....As I used to tell my fellow workers, "The way we produce here, the profits of the stockholders and every damn thing else comes out of what we're doing here." They had already taken about 80 percent of the Ordnance workers off piecework without an ameliorating bonus or anything about ten years before. But their job rates were high. It's high because it's government and because they have to work to accuracy. So they take five times as long to do a piece as we used to....
>
> Now the company had to be democratic about this. So the UE was traditionally opposed to piecework as a matter of principles, but the situation had developed whereby in piecework we made better money and we were not working so very hard. So if the boss came and said, "What are you doing? Always moping. I see ya talking so often, do your work!" Our answer would always be, "I'm making out, aren't I? I'm making my money. I got the skill and the speed and I'm making it regardless. What are you yelling about?" We were quite independent as pieceworkers. We didn't have to have the black whip on our back. When we were on piecework, each of us were individual contractors basically.

The machine-tool makers worked in groups of twelve men who would be rated collectively for raises. Those with higher rates helped the lowest paid. In Carl's group, the men paced themselves so that if they wanted to take a little break, they would work a little harder, and they made more money than the day-rate people. Well, when the union brought the issue to a vote, the piece rates were voted out. The business agent and other officers of the union were concerned with the real threat that the company would remove the Power Transformer Division. Despite the investment in building 100, which the union's business agent felt could be converted to other uses, the gradual attrition of production with the removal of medium and small transformers meant that the threat was realistic. When all of the blue-collar workers, including those who were not on piecework, were allowed to vote concerning piecework, a negative vote seemed sure, but with about three thousand voting, the decision against piecework was won with only seventy-two votes. Some attempts were made to pacify the pieceworkers with a "personal adder," or increment to their weekly pay when they were on day rate for what they lost on piecework but the overall effect was to decrease the incentive to produce. The range of difference in the present pay rate for a worker is not much more than two dollars an hour, with maintenance workers, including sweepers, getting about $10, depending on seniority, and skilled machine workers getting about $12. This comparative factor, along with the loss of pride and accomplishment in making out have dampened the enthusiasm for work. Carl reflected:

> When we took the job, the idea was to learn the job as efficiently as possible so we would get above this base rate. There was a base rate, then an anticipated earning rate and above....Well, the new system was a raise every six months regardless, assuming that a person six months on the job would have improved that much. That is the system they have to this day.

Carl concluded his discussion of piecework with a comparison between General Electric and Japanese enterprises. "It shows that the engineers, the methods of supervision and all, feel that they know everything and we know nothing while in Japan, for instance, all the people are called together and consulted on almost everything. And I always said not only should they do that, but give us true profit sharing and a say in running the place and they would see efficiency."

Ever since the change to day rate, the workers and management have complained about the wage squeeze and the lack of incentive to do the harder jobs which pay only a dollar an hour more. The union was against the piecework system on the basis of the principle of solidarity. In passing the day rate, the company wanted to reinforce the position of supervision on the shop floor since the teams, particularly in the machine shop, had outwitted the system. John, who had served as both chief shop steward for the union and foreman, was one of the members of the union's executive committee who had voted for the day rate. He told me:

> We learned that the union did too good a gob on the piecework system, and the company didn't want to spend money on time studies. They don't make money on time studies, and they lost their shirt. They came out with estimated prices to a great degree, while if you're a union person and they don't have a time study back-up, your job becomes one of going and protesting the lowest prices. And you do this continually. Pretty soon, you've got all the low prices up to pretty good prices and they haven't touched you, they haven't come back at you because of their lack of time-study people. Meanwhile you had the prices in pretty good shape. Then the union took on a program of what we call "extra labor." The prices were set under certain conditions called "normal"...not necessarily normal, but called normal. And then when the working conditions deviated from that, you would go into extra labor. This was not included in my price, therefore I'm entitled to an additional payment. This was generally called "down time." And the union became very proficient at that. The rates went up, the Anticipated Earned Rate (AER), and a guy like me, who was never a good worker benefitted.

His reasons for voting for the day rate were complex. He was afraid that the company would eventually "lower the boom on us" because "we became so good that we defeated ourselves." The vote was held in the union hall although it was not required in the contract. "That made it look like we had voted for it." By including the non-piece rate workers, they were assured of winning. The net result, John felt, was to weaken the union:

> The union lost the way to keep the membership cohesive. You see, everyone was interested in price. Everyone would fight for you to maintain your prices, because if they got away with hitting you, they'd hit him next, and her next and me next. We all understood that. It kept us together. So when we had to fight on prices, we had a lot of support and a lot of backing. Now with this one shift, you go to day work, it doesn't matter. You're measured by the day.... You know, I'm sitting there in the union office and it hit me like somebody throwing a cold bucket of water on me. All at once, all the things I was engaged in for five or six years suddenly stopped. They didn't exist anymore. And all I had was disciplinary

cases. Harassment, and such. Then they started on dope at the time I was there . We always had alcoholics — absenteeism, and there was tardiness, insubordination. And those cases are the most difficult to win. The company goes in there and they give you a credit sheet with a record of absences. Where do you go from there? "Please give him another chance?" So it changed. People sit back and watch this and say, "Now, what the hell am I getting from the union? You know the union's not doing anything any more." You know, it's difficult to operate in a union today.

The management lost a powerful incentive system, and workers claim that production has gone down, but they did succeed in strengthening their hand in the shop-floor proceedings. Herb, the area-relations manager for GE, gave the management position on piece rates:

> This [piece rate] was not a tool that could adequately establish an equitable price. Piecework is good in a highly repetitive system — where it is easily measured, as opposed to building transformers. There a day's work is the unit, and this did not respond to a short-span measure. At the least, the job was measured in one hour or two hour spans. We worked with an outmoded measurement that did not lend itself to incentive. At that time, we hoped to make Power Transformer competitive. In a period when we were hurting from the cost standpoint, we had to do a better job. We went off piecework in 1971.

The settlement was, he said, one that was negotiated, with individual rates adjusted over a period of time with minimum impact on any individual. Some felt it more than others. Those people who had losses were given the adders to make up for the loss. He admitted that it was a system over which management could not maintain control.

The struggle over wages and compensation beyond the base rate brings to the surface the latent class struggle that is masked in the minutely graded hierarchy of the differentiated work force. Management failed to estimate the social relationships involved as piece rates were mediated by unions. In voting for its abolition, union leaders failed to assess workers' motivation to gain individual rewards. Ideological appeals by the union to egalitarianism were effective in the forties when there was a high level of commitment to the union. Yet this breaks down in the day-to-day work routines where the only reward has been translated into the wage. Seniority protects the inefficient as well as the committed worker, and there is, according to most workers, little recognition of merit. In contrast, the piecework system provided not only a merit system of pay but recognition of skill that went beyond the norm. By surpassing the anticipated level of production, the workers felt that they were outwitting the engineers. It gave them a sense of beating the system, of being independent of the foremen, because they were in control of the information on which rates were based. Carl sums this up in his statement "each of us were individual contractors basically." Both the institutions of management and of union were threatened by this. The union's appeal to collective egalitarianism seemed false to workers in the context of a culture that emphasized individualism and rewarded competitive norms.

The only remaining tool to force the workers into greater productivity was the threat of closing the business. This is discussed in a subsequent chapter. We can see that piece rates, once they became self-managed by the workers in the shop, became the antithesis of the competitive practices generally associated with the practice. By building a strong motivation to produce, it obviated the need for discipline, or the "black whip" to which Carl refers. At the same time, workers were careful not to exceed norms so that supervisors would not catch on to their carefully held secrets. Carl, in his retirement, refers nostalgically to the shop, "We made it a good place to work and we promoted the philosophy: leave the workers alone, they'll do their job." The solidarity of the work group threatened both union leaders and management.

Wage Compression

Theoretically all labor union leaders are for principles of solidarity, but in day-to-day negotiations their constituencies balk when uniform rules appear disadvantageous. This is especially true when the issue is wages. The International Federation of Professional and Technical Engineers Local 140 broke away from Local 255 in 1951 at the height of the MacCarthy attack on unions. The break was not over ideology but over wages negotiated by the overall union. The local represents principally draftsmen, who numbered about 500 during the peak years when the Polaris contract was under production at Pittsfield. They were down to 275 when I spoke to the business agent:

> The IUE can ask for a cents-per-hour increase, and most of their hourly-rated people, depending on what that amount is, gets by the majority. And so therefore, they've done their job. Then we just get stuck with whatever that offer is. A cents-per-hour raise for us is just a disaster because we generally make more money than they do. The company says an 8 percent raise; let's say it's

a raise on their $6.15 cents an hour, that ain't no 8 percent raise! Eight percent of six dollars, which is forty-eight cents. That's what it comes out to. We get forty-eight cents and that's a disaster. That's why, we're always considered the crybabies of the Pittsfield works, cause we're always complaining about the rate. And justifiably so. Nobody shows me that cost of living going up in cents per hour. It goes up on a percentage basis. Sure they say we all pay the same for a loaf of bread, and that's nice if we all want to go out and buy day-old bread.... Some of their people, the toolmakers, electricians, winders in the upper ranges of their pay structure, they're getting screwed just as bad as we are.

Management is equally concerned with what they referred to as "wage compression." The vast difference in responsibility between a sweeper and a fork-lift operator is not recognized in the present wage structure. As one shop steward said, "If a sweeper drops a broom, who cares, but if a fork-lift operator drops a big iron casting then there's hell to pay." Even the maintenance crew agrees that there is not much incentive in the wage system. Tony, a sweeper in maintenance said,

Well, over in our place we're not O.K., even though they have some different levels, most people get close to the same. The guys who run the boilers, if something happens, the first thing they [supervisors] do is say, "O.K., it's the fireman's fault," or the water tenders's fault, or the engineer's fault. So they are like a sergeant, with all these men under them; but like me, I'm making $8.54 an hour and these guys are making only $9.60. So their complaint is that all I do is like clean the washrooms and not do the running around that they have to do. And their complaint is, which I can see, is I'm making this much and they're just making a hair over and I can see their point.

The same problem shows up in the white-collar local, where mail delivery clerks get $325 and highly skilled, knowledgeable traffic control clerks get maybe $475 — with benefits for both being 10 percent of the pay. The traffic control clerks had to route transformers across the country, knowing the height of every bridge and road span all along the way. Workers, just as much as the supervisors, object to the protection of incompetence and the failure to reward expertise.

Segmentation of the Work Force

Segmentation of the work force has existed throughout the history of industrialization, but the premises underlying it have changed.

Textile factories, such as that of Pomeroy, kept a core of life-long male employees who might do the same work of spinning and weaving as those hired for peak production periods, but who had the advantage of security. It was not the skill required by the work that made for the segmentation so much as the characteristics of sobriety and industry that defined the status of the workers in the early decades of textile production. Millwrights and machinists were among the growing numbers of skilled employees that were preferentially treated in the latter part of the nineteenth century, as more capital-intensive work processes were introduced into the factories.

The traditional allocation of gender segmentation in the work place, that assigned ''light'' hand-assembly work to women and machine operations to men, persisted in the twentieth century. Other factors such as differential skills, job seniority and supervisory function that were well established in the nineteenth century persisted in the twentieth, but in the twentieth century segmentation was additionally influenced by the level of integration of the firm in the global production system. Large corporations were able to attract a preferred work force, and these advantages were confirmed by industrial union organizations in the decade of the thirties. Competitive industrial firms and services drew upon women and ethnically-discriminated workers. What differentiates the segmentation of labor in the nineteenth century from that in the twentieth is that the negotiations of unions and management in the nineteenth century were not yet bureaucratically regulated. Indeed, a segmentalized labor force is not something that management imposed on labor in an evolutionary sequence, but rather, a coexistent system of labor control that has been endorsed by labor as well as management (see also Littler 1982).

Throughout its history, the General Electric corporation has had a hierarchical and differentially-valued work force. In the 1916 strike, it was the preferred work force of machinists that led the protest for higher wages and shorter hours. It was their union, the International Association of Machinists, that took the lead in organizing the walkout. Machinists and toolmakers have always been the prima donnas of the work place, taking priority over winders and others with very skilled but industry-specific training. The fact that they had a skill that they could take to many other industrial plants gave them the assurance to stand up to management, one very militant toolmaker told me. Many became strong leaders of the industrial unions in the thirties and after World War II. Their history shows that managerial tactics dividing the work force are not directly related to consciousness (Nash 1984). Workers in competitive firms that are less integrated in the world market are paid less and have fewer benefits in the same city. Those comparisons shall be considered in the following chapter.

Etic and Emic Categories in the Work Force

Here I shall compare the differences in the corporation in terms of the "emic" categories — those used by workers and managers themselves to describe their status — and "etic" categories defined by social scientists. However, I will find it necessary to go beyond both of these sets of categories, since they may mask relations in production because they refer to a job and not the labor process. Neither way of conceptualizing the problem captures the workers' consciousness of their condition, qualified as it is by their familial relations with members of the household employed in a variety of different jobs. Nor does it take into consideration the levels of expectation that are activated in the socialization in family and community.

The reference points for managerial classifications of the work force in General Electric are (1) exempt, (2) ineligible for union membership and (3) eligible for union membership. Exempt workers are those whose skill and control of information put them beyond the application of government and union rulings regarding affirmative action or union rules related to seniority of "bumping" rules. Ineligible is a category that includes routine clerical and keypunch operations along with secretarial and other information processing workers who deal with "confidential" material. Until 1960 the ineligible workers could choose not to cross a picket line, but after that was tested in the 1960 strike, management could require supervisors and other ineligibles to cross the lines and work inside the plant. Eligible includes the bulk of production workers except for foremen who, like all supervisors and managers, are ineligible.

EXEMPT EMPLOYEES. Most of the jobs in this category are filled by men. It is a professional status requiring training and education that is subdivided into "individual contributors" and those who manage other people. When women broke into these higher positions after the passage of the Equal Employment Opportunity Act they were channelled into the former category to avoid gender confrontation in the management of men by women. Jane, an "individual contributor" with whom I spoke, said:

> The exempt category are strictly the professional people. When it comes to laying off in General Electric, they very rarely lay off people in the exempt category. The individual contributors may manage a contract or a project, but they don't manage people.

Job security is the principal benefit for this group but, in addition, there is an apparently trivial, but in fact very potent, distinction between exempt and other categories of workers. Exempt workers do not have to punch in on the time clock. This symbolizes the fact that they are given more control in the management of their time in the plant. Competition exists among even these highly specialized workers. Managers will give the task of solving the same problem to two or more engineers and they will often be pitted against each other in coming up with a solution.

When opportunities for women opened up in the exempt category in the early seventies, some of the older personnel managers found it difficult to adjust to the new outlook. The young woman quoted above recounted her experience in being interviewed by the personnel manager accustomed to dealing with male applicants:

> I interviewed for one job at GE where even though you're not supposed to ask people certain questions regarding their intentions of having families or things like that, I was asked... Well, it used to be when I wasn't married, "Do you have a boyfriend? A pretty girl like you, you don't have a boyfriend?" I mean roundabout kind of fashion. The way they do it now is they come out and say, "Are you career oriented or family oriented?" It's the same damn question. I had one man come out and say to me, he mumbled something in the middle of an interview, something about a family, and I said, "I beg your pardon? I didn't quite get what you asked me." And he mumbled again and I said, "I'm sorry, I really don't know what you're trying to ask me." And he finally looked at me and he said, "Well, what about a family?" I said, "Do you mean, do I want to have children and stay home for twenty years and take care of them? Is that what you're trying to ask me?" He said, "I know I'm not supposed to, but that's what I'm asking you." I really was flabbergasted, and I said, "Well, you're right, you're really not supposed to ask me."

When the Equal Employment Opportunity Act first opened up this job category for women and racially-discriminated employees, the company was out fishing for candidates. That wave crested in the late seventies, and management no longer urges women to upgrade themselves as they once did. However, the training courses are open to minorities, including women, and they have greater access to information about openings than they once did.

INELIGIBLE EMPLOYEES. The company controls the designation of jobs as "ineligible" for union membership. All supervisory employees are automatically designated as ineligible, even when they are in charge of only a small group. Because the corporation controls the definition of the job, management can write into the description that it involves the processing of confidential information, and they are the ones who decide what that means.

The head of the white-collar Local 254 was more explicit in his condemnation of the company's interpretation of what constituted confidential work, since this affects his constituency even more than it does the draftsmen:

> Our certification lets this company define what is confidential work, and the NLRB has a very different basis. We are excluded from doing confidential work, so the company says it's confidential work, and they can tell you every job in the GE is confidential work. If they're keypunching the boss's check, they take a whole department away. Or they keypunch a proprietary budget and that's confidential work. Well, everything in the GE is confidential to somebody, and they have brought in that word and we've lost our jobs throughout the years. Our bargaining unit went from 1,296 people eligible twelve years ago to 371 today and the ineligible rank went the opposite. One girl who works in marketing, and we had the job for years, and all of a sudden the company says, "This is confidential." We put a complaint to the NLRB and they come back and they give us the work, but they leave her ineligible. So then the company creates a new job and a year or two later they take away the job. They do it just to pacify us for a year, but they're not giving us information as to what's going on.

The fact that 96 percent of this unit is female gives one a new perspective on the question of why women don't join unions. Their clerical functions, routine as they may be, are easily categorized as managerial, from secretaries all through the information-processing chain. Some women have been reclassified as ineligible while working at the same job, but this is tantamount to grievance provocation. Most of the time, the reclassification comes with the introduction of new processing machinery which integrates them with other information-processing units that are somewhere along the chain classified as confidential. Because so much of the basis for negotiations rest on knowledge of comparable wage scales in other plants, one can understand why management wants to control this information. The computer may become the instrument whereby workers can gain access to that information.

ELIGIBLE EMPLOYEES. The shrinking number of employees eligible for union membership is a clue to managerial strategies in the manipulation of job descriptions to categorize increasing numbers of the work force as ineligibles. The old distinctions between "skilled" and "unskilled" are rarely if ever used. Nor is the contrasting pair, "mental" and "manual," used in the discussions of the job hierarchy by corporation employees. What one hears is the distinction between "production" workers who are "on the floor" and clerical workers in the offices. "Individual contributors" include both production workers and non-supervisory engineers and technical workers. The change in terminology relates to a changing managerial ideology that has moved away from Taylorism and the debasement of the job to "motivational" management techniques.

Eligible jobs are divided into a complex range of differentially-compensated job ratings. In contract negotiations carried out after World War II, job ratings were worked out in production as well as clerical and exempt categories. In the clerical ranks, the lowest is a mail carrier, whose wage in 1982 was $325 a week, followed by general clerks, file clerks, keypunchers, typists, stenotypists and payroll. Until the 1970s, women were never hired in ranks above this. The overt reason was that higher ranks should be able to read blueprints. The union fought for and won training courses in blueprint reading. Women now occupy up to grade 12 ratings where they figure out traffic routes for shipping the large utilities made by the company. The highest pay in this range is $500 a week.

Technological Change

Technological innovation is a powerful means of control over workers since it often means the elimination of work and the introduction of new job descriptions over which the union has little control. The company has complete control over adding duties or taking away some tasks, lowering the rating on jobs or claiming that work doesn't exist. It is resorting more frequently to Kelly Girls, women employed by a private agency which sends in "temporary" workers. These workers are not unionized and work for about half the wage of regularly-employed workers. One whom I met in the course of our random interviews, the spouse of a regularly-employed worker, was actually earning only one-quarter of the top ranking white-collar workers in General Electric. Seeking for outside sources for the production of elements in the Power Transformer Division is expected to increase, according to departmental manager Wise (*The Berkshire Eagle* November 2, 1985).

Machinists and toolmakers have been adversely affected by technological innovation; it has meant not only a loss of jobs, but also the debasement of what had been very skilled jobs that could escape close supervision. Carl comments on some of the impact of technological change in his shop in the late sixties:

> And let me tell you, on the jobs that require skill, it's gone down so badly. In our place they had these chuggers, semi-automatic lathes. A man would set it up and he would have one or two other men with him on these three machines. And there would just be one guy setting it up who would get transferred and the others never did learn. The machine was being run very inefficiently. So the company bought a tape machine which they had hesitated to do before because of the terrible cost — $100,000 for one machine. So now all they have to do is place man there who'll load and unload the machines; everything else is set up for him. No skill, or very little.

The lack of information about future plans for technological change inhibits the unions' ability to plan ahead and advise their workers. As the white-collar union's business agent said:

> I'd like to see a good retraining program we can plan in advance. Say we're getting nineteen computers two years from now, we could say, "How many of you people would like to do this at night, take some courses?" Or "We'll pay your tuition at Berkshire Community College to learn about this."

In the new contract, the union has negotiated a retraining contingency for coping with technological innovation. This is a possible entry into information of the sort envisioned by the business agent.

Draftspeople were hit harder than any other group by computerization when the company introduced computerized drafting. General Electric wanted to classify the new jobs as computer operators rather than drafting jobs because the computer operators were not unionized. The alternative route which the company offered was expanding the job of the draftsmen to include programming of the computer and thus to classify the job as exempt, that is, technical-professional work that is free of all union restrictions. Either course would be detrimental to the union. Union attempts to gain greater flexibility in the job description and upgrading of their personnel was met with stiff resistance by the company. The business agent of the draftsmen's union parodied the company's reaction:

> The classic argument between the union and the company is, "It's much easier for a draftsman to become a programmer on a drawing than to teach a programmer to be a draftsman." And off the

record the company will say, "Yeah, we agree with you, but you damned drafting people, you'll claim that work is yours. You'll be organizing all of them. You'll be saying all of those twenty guys over there belong to you. We can't tolerate that." And we've tried to assure them that we won't do that.

It is a power question that the contestants relate to in technical terms without raising the basic issue of jurisdiction.

Gender Segmentation

With the attrition of the work force, the hierarchy of skill levels collapses and the apprentices, oftentimes youths or affirmative action people, are the first fired. In drafting there were no apprentices, and no one with less than ten years' service, since these positions had all been eliminated in the early part of the layoffs in the mid-seventies. The few women who worked in the department did, for the most part, routine tasks such as compiling data on a varitype machine — a typewriter that types notes on a drawing. One such woman was reduced to a clerical position even after thirty-one years of service. A few women, some of whom had come in during the Korean War, were offered opportunities to advance when the EEOC was putting pressure on the company.

Production workers have up to twenty-five ratings ranging from 8 to 28. These are supposedly based on skill, difficulty or hazard in the job, and special training required. Until the seventies women never rose above an R14 rating, which was chiefly in testing. Following the passage of the EEOA in the early seventies, jobs were posted; several women applied and gained jobs as truckdrivers, cleaners and in big assembly work. The only woman to sign up for the heavy assembly job was Joan, who had lost $45 in weekly pay when she and all the other workers were taken off piecework. She commented:

> To upgrade yourself after we lost piecework you had to take on a man's job. Foremen tried to discourage you there. It was tough to take on a man's job. "This is heavy, that is heavy; you've got to climb way up there." It was tough to take on harder jobs just to make up the money that you had lost. If you're working for yourself and your ramily, this is what you had to do.

Joan worked inside a tank loaded with PCB-impregnated oil. She was the only woman on the night shift, which she took to get 10 percent extra in pay; there were hundreds of men. She moved to an R19 rating, and with the "adder" which was compensation for the lost piecerate, she was making more than her husband, who did the same job. Her marriage went on the rocks after fifteen years and five kids, but she denied that it had any connection with her new earning status. On the job she wore dungarees and shirts, covered with oil but after work she changed to street clothes, the trim polyester pant suits with California-style blouses that she wears in her duties as shop steward. When she left this job she went to a woodwork shop, which had also been a male domain and where she worked with a swing saw. When she started work there, Joan said,

> The boss didn't want the other gal who came in with me because she was too small. As though size made a difference! Because there were little men in there. But we always had to prove ourselves, whereas a man just got hired. There can be twenty guys in a shop and one woman on the job and the supervisor asks, "Is she doing it right? Why is she standing still? Giver her a broom to sweep." But you stand out.

Nelly belonged to the generation older than Joan that went to work just before World War II. Unlike Joan, she resisted being put on "men's" work during the war:

> I remember one time they came up with this job. It was something to do with a small bomber. It used to come off the presses in half, and then they'd put them together. And you used to have to buff it, you know, with these wheels. And two or three girls had tried it and they couldn't do it, so he asked me to do it. You know, if those wheels went so fast, they could snap that right out of your hand. And I was short and I didn't reach that big wheel. You couldn't even hold it. A woman couldn't hold it. I told him I couldn't even hold the dishes they're so big. "It's dangerous. I'm not going to do it." So he says, "Well, you go home." So I said, "Well, I'm going home." He says, "You go home and come back when I call you." That was before the union.

In the early 1970s when she was close to retirement, Nelly was offered another opportunity to take on a "man's job," but this proved equally futile.

> After I had inner ear trouble, this women's lib came in. The boss said, "I have just the job for you." "Yeah?" I said, "What?" "In the other room there's wiring. You have to climb a ladder to do work up there." "You mean I have to work with the men?" You had to work with them up there. "Yeah, you have to work with

men," he said, "but they're good." And the men at the beginning
weren't for the women's lib. He said, "You can get about twenty-
five dollars more in your pay." "I don't care. I don't want it." Well
he pestered me a good three or four weeks. The union kept bothering me. Labor relations kept bothering. They couldn't understand
why I would turn them down. Now I was getting annoyed by this
time. I said to the union, "You're just as bad as they are." Imagine,
I was out six months, then I worked a little, and I had to stay out
another two months. That is the first reason I didn't want it, because
I got sick again. I said, "What good is it? If I put my head up too
long, I would go black because of the equilibrium. And in the
second place," I said, "would you want to have to come in in
overalls?" He said, "No," and I said, "Well, neither would my
husband. Well," I said, "don't bother me no more." And I says
to the union, "And that goes for you too," cause they came in the
room that time.

Then I was offered quite a few higher paying jobs. I turned them
all down. I said, "At this late stage, I'm not going to bother." And
so the girls took all these heavy jobs. They all stuck together so
they would do all the heavy lifting and all and help each other.
You know, that heavy work there, a woman should not take on.
I know I have enough pride in myself so I wouldn't. One of those
girls, she would do anything they would tell her. You know, some
girls they don't care as long as they make that extra dollar.

Now there was this one girl, very friendly with me, we'd eat
lunch together and everything, and she had her breast removed.
She really went through heck and after that, she said she was
going to work four years. That would be when she was sixty-five.
So anyway when I left, if they asked her to work seven days at
night, she worked seven days until 7:30. And I said, "Josie, what
do you want to work all those hours for?" — She had a husband
too, and he was working in a store on North Street. And everybody
used to talk about her, especially with her breast out.... Well, after
she took another upgrading, and all the girls said, "You wouldn't
believe what she's doing. They have these cable jobs, big cables
with all the wiring inside and they're all covered and you've got
to get on your hands and knees and tie these." And this is what
she was doing! I said, "Josie, I don't believe what you are doing!"
A lot of the men — it's a man's job you see, she's on her hands
and knees doing this heavy dirty work and the fellas, when she
was doing it without a fight, they would be out on a coffee break
and she would be on the floor meanwhile. And I would say, "I
don't know why you're doing that." Like I say, I like the girl, I
don't know what she wanted the money for. She never spent
anything on herself. When I quit work, I gave her two suitcases

of clothes. I could dress up pretty nice. It wasn't a dirty job. I don't know what kind of a husband she has. I said, "I don't believe any man would make his wife work that hard." Course he don't see her working, but what he must realize the more money you get, the harder you work. It isn't always that way. Sometimes the more money you get the easier it is. But she got the particular jobs that are heavy and hard.

Nelly shows a sure sense of what was culturally appropriate for a woman of her generation to do. For her, a sense of pride meant avoiding the heavy, hard work that women's lib advocates were challenging as being for men only. Husbands and fathers should intervene, she felt, to establish the limits on these activities. Otherwise a woman lost the respect of her co-workers as well as her self-respect. Men of Nelly's generation were also critical of such changes, and many complained about women asking them to help with the heavy loads. Supervisors were told not to help the women, and some men said they could not tolerate seeing a woman struggle with a heavy load and defied the prohibition. Nelly observed that the women stuck together to help each other out. The real threat was that women would do the dirty, heavy work without resisting demands, in part to prove themselves, even working through coffee breaks to keep up. The cultural commitments to ways of relating to the opposite sex, to styles of dressing and to the limitations of women's work to primarily sedentary activities were ways of overcoming the opprobrium attached to factory work during Nelly's youth. These cultural commitments will remain a difficult obstacle, even if the legal battle for ERA is won.

In the case of eligible workers, equal opportunity regulations opened up higher paid but heavier and dirtier jobs for the most part. Only a very few women entered into the really skilled production jobs such as toolmakers or grinders. Men complained that these women often did not have the strength for the job, and they rarely saw the change from the perspective that Nelly raised, nor did they observe the women sticking together to get the job done.

The real skills that were involved in what was categorized as semi-skilled work when done by women were rarely appreciated. Nelly worked on wiring panels for aeronautics communication equipment. The navy would fly planes up to Pittsfield in order to have her check out panels that were not operating correctly and yet she never rose above an R14 rating. In order to get any higher she would have had to do the dirty, heavy — but far less skilled job — that had been categorized as a man's job. Her description of the work she and her co-workers in Ordnance did reveals its complexity:

One of those girls did beautiful wiring. She could read those blueprints like nothing. When I first tried to read blueprints, I had a hard time. And her and the other girl, they taught me. But their blueprints are a little different from the regular ones; they are a little harder. Good thing they had a lot of patience! Cause I really wanted to quit, but they said, "Oh, you stay there." I said, "I want to go up to the main plant and look for a job with better work." If it wasn't for her, I would have quit. But my brother told me to keep away from any of those tough people [in the main plant].These two girls really taught me to read the blueprints, and they would help me with some of the jobs. She had so much patience, and she was the type that worked slow and easy, and her work was beautiful. You had to lace the wires, and hers were so perfect. Well she did a job one time that was better than the picture. They sent it to our building and the other building, they wanted everyone to see it. Now she must be about sixty.... She had the patience of a saint, and her hands were like magic. She loved the wiring.

Nelly, who had a great deal of pride in her work, was frustrated by supervisors who did not appreciate what was involved in the task and simply urged her to hurry up and push the work through. When she retired, she was replaced by three women. The job, inspecting wiring panels for complex radar devices, was increasingly done by machines run by men who got higher rates of pay than she. She complained to me about their work:

And when the work got so bad, you would have to tell the fellas on the machines that it was wrong. You would be getting a lot of stripped wires and the connections, sometimes they'd jump and you'd get two wires on the spool. And then I'd have to come in and fix the machines, and tell them — who were getting big money — what was wrong with the machine. They didn't like that! I knew what was going wrong with the machines. They probably knew, but they used to race to see who would get the most wires on. And so many wires would be their count. I never saw a boss from morning to night because they didn't know themselves what the job required.

Segmentation and Union Jurisdiction

The definition of boundaries is increasingly a prerogative of management since they control the information regarding job descriptions. This was particularly frustrating to the white-collar union and to the professional and technical engineers who would find that their attempts to recruit members were blocked by claims that their work was "confidential" or that it was "exempt" because of certain eligibility requirements. As a result the jurisdiction of the union is defined by work qualifications that are determined by management. The draftsmen's business agent illustrates how this works:

> Well, when you go after your certification with the NLRB after an election and say, "We want to represent these people" and the company will take one of two approaches. If they want to totally defeat the issue, and they think they have a good chance, they say, "Well, you can't just go after these 200 draftsmen; you said you wanted technical people. We want you to include technicians, lab technicians." You get a big mix of people who say, "Well, I don't mind being part of an organized group, but I don't see why we should be part of them," and so therefore the company stands a good chance of having an election and having the union badly defeated. Or they go the other way, if they're positive that one particular group is going to belong to it — that was our case —one particular group is going to vote to unionize. They'll say, "Well, OK, that's it, strictly people who are draftsmen."

Most of the grievances center around work done by people who are ineligible for the union but who do the work that is covered by union regulations. The company will then argue that the union represents a defined category of people that has nothing to do with the work. When the Professional and Technical Engineers Local 140 tried to go beyond the draftsmen to organize other people who might feel that they are being treated unfairly by the company, the company settled the problem quickly. The business agent for the draftsmen recalled:

> We had people there that are called architectural designers, illustrators, or whatever. They came to us once and they attempted to organize because of some short-changing they got regarding wages, and before we could even get cards out, the company somehow came through with about sixty-nine of these people getting cost-of-living increases. They said, "Thanks for the help, but we're not interested in organizing now."

I asked him about the claim by the business agent of the white-collar union that so many positions were declared ineligible because they deal with company secrets such as payroll, and he said:

> The company will always claim that. To the best of my knowledge, unless the individual is dealing with classified relations, that is,

information on the union individual in terms of a discipline case, or planning for manpower.... these technical and clerical people would be eligible.

New technology has accelerated the process of redefining jobs as ineligible in addition to cutting down the number employed. Fred explained how this worked:

About six years ago they come in with the CRT machine and they put them in all the formerly eligible jobs down in a certain building where the same work had been done by keypunchers. We used to do all the keypunching throughout the plant. They were eligible workers up here in the main plant. That machine, it would look at the work, keypunch it and it would go directly to the computer. It would eliminate the cards, the tape and the direct access. We had about seven keypunch machines back then, about seven years ago, in the building. We still have the seven, but throughout the plant they have 200 which ineligibles, exempts and supervision now run. They claim it's like a pencil — you don't own it. But before we did own the keypunchers. They claim they had a right to run a business and according to the contract they do, but we strictly fight for the work and not the particular individual doing it. And we've been successful with the NLRB. They come in here and make this company furnish information. They tell us in advance about new machines and we have a right to ask them for an update. We're not against these new things. We want to be a party of it, we want to take care of our people, to get them trained, to get these jobs rather than lose them.

Fred told us that the company did away with the training program, instituted by the union in 1973, which taught clerks blueprint reading. As a result of that program, women — 86 percent of their membership is female — had been able to upgrade themselves and take on new jobs involved in changing technology. Some of the work has now been contracted to non-union shops in North Adams or in Springfield to avoid the union. The GE News is printed in North Adams, resulting in a layoff of two of Pittsfield's union people. Fred looked forward to having an integrated training program, with information from the company advising union members with sufficient advance time so that they could train their people at the local colleges or even in the union office.

Control Over The Work Process and Union Apathy

All of the union leaders report apathy among members, despite the many problems that confront them in declining jobs and loss of income in the face of inflation. With national averages in attendance at union meetings running about 6 or 8 percent of the membership, the unions have a hard time getting a quorum to run their affairs. Older trade union leaders who built the union attribute the apathy to the systematic uprooting of political concerns that had been part of the industrial trade union organization. Carl says:

> The UE used to educate the members and this is one reason the government, like Truman and the others, jumped on the UE, wanted to smash them. They were educating the members, that's what the problem was. In business sure — be greedy, that's what it's all about, grab! And people should realize that's what business is all about. But in government, which is supposedly for the welfare of the people, or the union working for the welfare of the whole, you need dedication. Simply playing politics will ruin a union very quickly or ruin a government.

Apathy among leaders is as rampant as that among rank and file members. Carl elaborated on this point:

> The feeling has been growing, what's in it for me? Get the job of steward, you have simple seniority. Or get elected to negotiations and you get a vacation with pay, a few days off with pay, even have money left over. If you're on the grievance board, you get done and you can stay out the rest of the day. These things attract leaders today.

John emphasized the difference in the UE approach to negotiations from that of the IUE. The UE, he said, "did their homework" before coming to a meeting. They used to take the GE profit and divide it by the number of workers and then they'd come back into the shop and say, "Last year, GE made $8,951.36 on you. For each employee, they made $8,500." The gains made by the union were immediately perceived, he said. One important symbolic battle was winning the right to smoke in an area designated within the shop. In those days, "Lighting up a Lucky," or whatever brand, was so closely tied to being able to relax that it was considered a significant gain.

To explain the same apathy, younger trade union leaders put more emphasis on the many more distractions for workers now than in the past. The draftsmen's business agent said:

> There are so many things today that people are involved in. I think of some of the old movies where the working man had his family and his job, and probably his church. And those things kept him

going for 99 percent of his week. He might have a chance to
stop by and have a beer, and he might have one night out to
be active in something. Today the worker has so many things
to do, from his kid's Little League team to activities they've
got.... And this plastic money, if you don't have the money,
take it now and pay for it later. It's an attitude, "Hey, I'm not
hurting," and the companies today will say, "Well, at least you've
got a job. Be thankful you've got a job." So when people take a
good look, they say, "I'm not really that badly off. I'm better
off than my parents. I've got two cars, color TV and my kids
belong to the local club that's got a pool." You can tell that guy
that there's danger out there if conservatives are elected and he
will say, "What are you talking about?" He never has the time to
look into it.

Based on his own experience as a candidate for political office,
this union leader said that if you want to get support on a labor
platform, you go to the older workers, the young ones do not vote.
When he first became president of Local 140 in the sixties, membership meetings were so large that they had to rent a hall for the 200
or so members that showed up. Today they can't get a quorum. This
withdrawal of political issues from the union agenda was a direct and
effective result of corporate hegemonic attack on political interest in
unions.

Bureaucratization and segmentation of the work force are coexisit-
ing forms of labor control that operate concurrently in the setting of
the corporation. Most of the production that one could "debase" was
women's assembly work in electrical appliances and plastic casings.
This work has been transferred to other sites in the U.S. and overseas.
Segmentation of the work force based on education and gender
persists, despite federal legislation on fair employment practices.
Women are most subject to layoffs and the loss of their jobs to other
sites. Bureaucratization of the work organization is lessening as the
numbers of union workers, now down to about 3,000, or less than one-
half of the work force, shrink still further. But because bureaucratization
displaced the cultural roots of worker resistance, which had been based
on ethnic identification or commonality of interests in craft
specialization, worker resistance has been weakened.

In their fight to control the workplace, management has consistently denied the creativity and motivation of workers. In the
compendium of managerial practices issued in the fifties (General
Electric 1956, Vol. II: 74). The company rationalizes the minute fragmen-
tation of tasks in Durkheiminian terms:

Like all other concessions to living in a civilized society, recognizing and using such specific language, or classification, represents a voluntary concession from complete individual freedom to the end that common purposes rather than anarchy may prevail in the resulting organization.

The deviations that could have been absorbed in earlier days, the writers go on to say (General Electric 1953-9, Vol.II:75) "will necessitate correspondingly closer integrating or teamwork efforts by managers, and by professional, technical and other individual contributors." Throughout the four volumes of this massive compilation of managerial strategies, the authors never used the term "manual workers" or blue collar workers, preferring the de-classed category of "individual contributor."

The net effect of the reorganization of work in ever more specialized tasks was to alienate the intelligence and motivation of workers. As Gouldner (1954:66) states in his analysis of a wildcat strike among gypsum workers, "The drive for efficiency had the unanticipated consequence of impairing one important source of efficiency, the motivation to work." There is, in most factories, a continuous, conscientious withdrawal of efficiency. For the assembly-line workers, resistance to managerial control is a daily struggle marked by occasional sabotage of products and even of foremen who are not liked. One foreman who told workers to stop bringing their radios into the shop (not the Pittsfield plant) had his tires slashed and his dog was shot on the doorstep of his house. "Manufacturing consent," that Burawoy (1979) found in the small machine shop where he worked, is more typical of plants in the competitive sector, especially where piecework is involved. Piecework makes even a dull job interesting as you count up your gains capturing the same capitalist ethic that motivates managers and salesmen. Even in the General Electric, piecework continued to engage the interest and energies in the machine toolmakers unit until it was banned, as Carl has described. Although often epitomized as capitalist control system, when it operates in a small tight shop with long job cycles the workers can gain control over it.

One of the experiments through which management has recently tried to overcome alienation and to stimulate productivity is that of quality circles. In its introduction into the Pittsfield plant there was a considerable modification from the Japanese model. The white-collar union's business agent described it as a threat to unions:

Yeah, it's just starting up here. It's called a quality circle. And this can be a threat to unions. Our international has given the blessing to it with the proviso that the union is involved, because they can do this without us, O.K.? They get all the non-union members they want. The boss says, "Come out here in the office." They don't have to have a union steward unless someone requests it, and people aren't going to request it. And they come in and there's ten or twelve on a team. "How's things going?" "Pretty good. We need a better light over here." Now these are the things that the union used to do. All you got to do is moan to the union, and we'll make sure you get a better light. "We'll get it for you, no problem." They're the miracle makers. "You and the group, you didn't make out enough. James Jones didn't make enough." Now the people are pitted against the people, and this is the way they get one to fight another. We would rather be part of it than have them do it on their own. Because we can see where it could be very, very detrimental to the union, where the young people years from now say, "What the hell you want a union for? We got all these circles here." If we get involved with it we can more or less control what our items of responsibility are. But if we say we're against it, they won't even invite us in. They can call people who will work against the union. "How would you like a ten-minute, twenty-minute break in the morning? You got it." We can't get that no matter what we do.

In the current period with the organization of work controlled more and more by management, with a work force faced by layoffs, and with apathy toward unions intervening in the work process, management is increasingly resorting to threats of leaving the town in order to gain increased productivity. The Lynn Local IUE responded to the pressures by voting to work more hours and accepting new work rules, in return for assurance that GE would build a 51.7 million dollar plant in the city. Among the new rulings was flexibility in shifts, such that twelve-hour shifts would be accepted when imposed by management. The facility that they are building is largely automated and will employ few of the blue-collar workers that are accepting the demands imposed.

Blue-collar workers in the Pittsfield plant banded together for the first major unified strike in June 1986, called because of a company crackdown on absenteeism. The union argued that disciplinary measures were unfair since they were applied only against production workers and with inconsistent criteria in the point system on which the discipline is based. Union leaders claimed that 2,800 workers stayed out, demonstrating the unanimity regarding this issue. The sense of workers as a class "in themselves" resulted from managerial actions which disproved the public relations' claims that everyone at GE is an individual contributor.

The Social Construction of the Labor Force

The labor market is socially constructed in a local, national and increasingly international setting. Corporate managers and labor union officers enter into and define the sectors of the population that are channelled into jobs differentiated in pay, stability or continual employment in jobs that offer opportunities for advancement. This "segmented" labor market is not, as Gordon, Edwards and Reich (1982) maintain, strictly a managerial tactic to reduce labor unity and control the channelling of workers. Cultural assumptions shared by labor and management about gender and ethnicity in the population inform and validate the way that this is done. Responding to these assumptions appropriately is a key element in the construction and reinforcement of corporate hegemony. For example, by playing into assumptions about appropriate gender roles, during the depression the corporation managed a layoff system firing women and holding on to men with dependent children in such a way as to minimize workers resistance. During the present layoffs, in Power Transformer, as the company prepares to close the division, by allowing the union to manage the bumping rules management has kept union members busy managing the crisis in such a way as to avoid resistance to the decision. The daily preoccupation with grievance cases minimizes attention to the wider issues in which the union is caught as production jobs are eliminated and the scope of their operations within the corporation minimized.

General Electric developed a labor relations interface team hiring some of the best shop stewards as representatives of management in the daily negotiations on the shop floor. They provided a medium of communication minimizing confrontations in production. This fortified corporate hegemonic control in the plant by providing mobility and opportunities for the outstanding workers, in the wider community.

How control over the work process operates in competitive capitalist firms in the community, and how the coexistence of firms differently integrated in the world market affects interaction will be discussed in the following chapter.

Chapter 6

Competitive Firms

Small corporations and companies that operate in competitive markets coexist with General Electric in a symbiotic relationship. That relationship is forged in the labor market but realized at home, where families pool and redistribute the earnings from their work in the different sectors of the economy and put together their version of the culture. The existence of a large plant establishes a broad base for recruiting workers for industries in the area. In turn, the cyclical nature of production in General Electric requires alternative occupations that keep workers in the same area to be called back when the need rises. In those households where there are two wage earners in different companies, the continuing paycheck brings relief in slack periods. The smaller companies, particularly those in the same production lines, such as the plastics firms that have sprung up in the area, can call upon the expertise of General Electric's technical and professional staff on a consultantship basis. Indeed, some of these firms have been started by former employees of the General Electric when the production they were involved in went elsewhere.

There are also tensions resulting from the uneven development of these competitive capitalist enterprises. Wages and benefits won by organized labor at General Electric are often twice those at other plants in the city, even those that are represented by a union. The starting wage in General Electric according to the 1982 contract was $8.40 while that of the next largest firm, Sheaffer Eaton of Textron Corporation, is $6.00 and that of most of the small plastics companies is $5.00 per hour. This results in a lesser commitment on the part of workers to the smaller companies. When General Electric calls, they respond, oftentimes to their own regret when layoff's occur. These firms are currently being destabilized by their incorporation in conglomerates that are not committed to the area in the way that owner-managed firms were.

General Electric and other large corporations were created in the first wave of mergers in the period 1897-1903, motivated by the desire to stabilize the markets for which they were producing. If the ultimate motive was profits, the net effect was to vitalize the productive capacity of the country. In the 1960s another wave of mergers brought about the conglomerates. Conglomerates are corporations combining unrelated activities, not simply different products for the same industry but often products for totally distinct markets (Steiner 1975:15). Since they showed no attempt to control any one market, the conglomerates did not encounter the anti-trust legal opposition raised against horizontal and vertical mergers. Yet conglomerates have had possibly an even greater negative impact on communities than the earlier mergers. I shall try to show with the current conglomerate purchases of nineteenth century firms in Pittsfield that the speculative motive introduced by conglomerates balancing different markets introduces an even greater arbitrariness in production schedules than the mergers motivated by the anti-competitive drive to stabilize — and produce — for a given industry. In two major cases, a plastics and a paper company organized by local entrepreneurs were bought up, milked for profits and sold within a decade of their purchase. In the speculative financial markets in which they operate, firms taken over by conglomerates must not only produce a profit but a huge margin that sets them ahead of all competitive ventures. Even the major corporation, General Electric, is taking on some of the characteristics of conglomerates as it moves away from power transformers, electrical machinery and other related products to credit corporations, communications, and other enterprises acquired only for their anticipated earning rate.

The presence of the small competitive firms is essential for the survival of the community. Even though they experience the same recessions and respond to them with layoffs, their decisions are not always coordinated to the same schedules. Unlike General Electric, they cannot gain tax abatements or other concessions on the threat of leaving. The greater the balance that can be retained in the mutual dependency of communitiy and industry, as Arensberg (1942) remarked, the greater likelihood that the democratic process will be retained. Because of the presence of small competitive firms, the impact on the community is not as great when there are layoffs at General Electric since these smaller companies may offer interim employment that delays the relocation of workers, and wages of these workers sustain commerical enterprises and municipal servics. Since they rely on a secondary work force, principally women tied into households with other earners, layoffs in small firms are tolerated to a greater degree. Although there has been a net decrease of 8.9 percent in factory jobs in the county in the 1970s, there was an increase in the work force of manufacturers of small and intermediate size. The expanding businesses are paper manufacturing, printing and publishing, plastic molding and metal fabricating. (*Berkshire County Development Corporation Directory of Manufacturers* 1982; Massachusetts Division of Employment Security 1982).

Paper and plastics lead the smaller industrial enterprises in the Berkshires and in Pittsfield. Paper production dates back to the nineteenth century when the major plants, Crane and Eaton, were established on the basis of available raw material supplies and water power. Plastics is an outgrowth of the General Electric Company's elimination of production in consumer goods such as radio bases, control buttons for electrical products and other items that were produced in the twenties and thirties.

A few other industries survive using plants and even equipment that date from the nineteenth century. Turner and Cook leather company is often considered to be the Berkshire's oldest industry. In September of 1977, when the firm was sold to Strattners of Sandisfield, the *Berkshire Eagle* (September 14, 1977) announced that "The new owners will discontinue the manufacture of leather whips, introduced in the early 1800s, by S. A. Turner, and of leather belt pins, introduced in 1888 to keep the business in step with the Industrial Revolution, but will continue making leather mallets." The A. H. Rice Silk braid manufacturing company celebrated its centennial in 1978, shortly after the firm was sold to Gerli and Company, a small multinational textile company, but the name was retained and a descendent of the original owner continued in a consulting capacity. The owners have kept up with the industrial revolution by turning to synthetic yarns, first with nylon parachutes in World War II and now with thread for Converse sneakers. The firm was experimenting with a return to silk in 1984.

In order to understand the employment potential of these smaller firms and how the organization of work related to General Electric, we reviewed the history of these firms and interviewed the managers of the most representative companies. During the research period from 1982 to 1985, with occasional return trips to update the manuscript, five of these plants went out of business. The loss of these buffers to economic cycles in the major firm suggests the greater vulnerability of the economy.

Paper Companies

Paper and allied products make up one of the oldest industries in Massachusetts, particularly in the western part of the state. The natural advantages in abundant water supplies for energy and pulp are still of some importance in the production of paper in the area. The retention of the industry is due more to the historical circumstances of its having been founded where a market grew around it and where, in the case of Crane, government contracts permitted its survival when more competitive areas in the west lured other industries. Searlemen (1979) sums up the reason for the resistance of the industry to the flight southward in terms of the Factor Price Equalization Theorem: when the costs of production inputs will tend to equalize in all affected locations, the firm will stay put. As supporting evidence, Searlman shows that wages and benefits of workers in Sun Belt firms have risen to approximate those in the Northeast.

In 1977, employment in the paper industry in Pittsfield totaled 669, or 2.1 percent of the total employment in the city. Employment rose in the period 1977 to 1982, when there were more than that in the firm of Sheaffer Eaton alone. The number of paper workers in the county declined from 3,880 to 3,470 in 1982, but Crane company, with plants in the neighboring town of Dalton as well as Pittsfield, held on to a steady employment of 975.7

The importance of the industry to the economy of Pittsfield is even greater than these figures indicate. As a basic productive industry, it sustains a share of the service industries in the area. The paper industry led to the development in the nineteenth century of the E. D. Jones Company which made much of the machinery for the early factories. The E. D. Jones Company remained in business when it became a branch of the Beloit conglomerate that produced equipment for the paper industries. In the recession of 1981 and 1982 it weathered the sharp decline in demand for paper by securing orders from Taiwan and India. However, in 1985 the owners were looking for a buyer.

Sheaffer Eaton

The rise and decline of the Sheaffer Eaton Company is a classic case of the merger mania of the 1960s. Eaton is an outgrowth of the Hurlbut Stationery Company that became the largest producer of fine stationery in the world, incorporated in Pittsfield in 1893. It operated with a succession of partners, including Hurlbut, Crane, Eaton and Pike, and later became known as the Eaton Paper Company. The company was sold to Gorham Corporation of Providence, Rhode Island, a corporation that had bought out the Sheaffer Pen Company. In 1959 Gorham became a division of Textron, a conglomerate producing aerospace and electronics products as well as other industrial products. Its subsidiaries, including Eaton Paper Company were merged with Textron in 1967. The paper division was combined with Sheaffer Pen Company in 1976, and Pittsfield was chosen as the corporate headquarters for three domestic firms that manufacture their products in plants started by small scale entrepreneurs. The company still retained its identity as Sheaffer Eaton within the "family" of Textron-owned companies. With other plants in France, Australia, Canada and the Netherlands, the corporation employs a total of 3,000, with a little over a third of these in Pittsfield. Textron is included along with ITT, LTV, Gulf and Western and other major corporations as classic conglomerates in that there is "no natural ambit within which they operate" (Steiner 1975:18). Management still occupied one of the fine old brick buildings that the Eaton company built when we interviewd a middle manager in 1982. The advantages in retaining the Pittsfield site, according to our informant, is the skilled labor supply as well as the paper suppliers in the vicinity. They purchase all their paper stock and just elaborate it in items such as specialty correspondence stationery and At-a-Glance calendars. The corporation spokesperson in 1982 asserted the confidence his managers felt in the Pittsfield plant, based on their million-dollar investment in capital improvements. Yet in 1987 the corporation withdrew production from the Pittsfield plant and put it up for sale.

Employment in the period 1977 to 1982, when General Electric experienced its greatest number of layoffs to that date from the Power Transformer, was fairly stable (Table 6–1) in Sheaffer Eaton. Most of the people hired in the last half of the seventies were young, with the majority being women under 25 years old (Table 6–1). This group has experienced the greatest number of layoffs at General Electric, and the marked complementarity in sex and age composition to that of General Electric can be inferred from the fact that the average age at General Electric is around fifty-three. In the Sheaffer Eaton Company the average age for males was going down when the age of General Electric workers was rising: it was forty-two in 1977 compared with forty-one in 1979 and for females it has gone from forty-eight in 1977 to forty-seven in 1979. But when we compare the age groups in Sheaffer Eaton in 1977 and 1982 the complementarity was even greater, since the vast majority at Sheaffer Eaton were under twenty-five and over fifty-five with General Electric[1] absorbing the preferred, experienced labor force between ages twenty-five and fifty-five. The cut-off in hiring at General Electric and the lay-offs of those with under ten years of service has made available the group that Gordon, Reich and Edwards (1982) would put in the "dependent primary work force."

Table 6–1

Hourly Workers, Employment by Age and Sex in Sheaffer Eaton, 1977–1982

Age	1977			1982		
	Male	Female	Total	Male	Female	Total
20–40	20	12	32	2	39	41
25–29	32	36	68	54	37	91
30–34	15	19	34	42	41	83
35–39	21	30	51	38	42	80
40–44	14	27	41	34	38	72
45–49	22	27	49	13	31	44
50–54	21	75	96	24	46	70
55–59	24	91	115	20	62	82
60–64	13	38	51	16	56	72
65–over	6	8	14	16	10	26
Total	188	363	551	259	402	661

Source: Personnel Manager Sheaffer Eaton Co.

In comparison with General Electric, where the sex ratio is about 80 percent male and the average age is about fifty-three the work force at Sheaffer Eaton was younger and weighted toward females. In 1982 the base rate at Sheaffer Eaton of six dollars per hour was about 75 percent of the GE rate but since the firm still had a piecerate system, experienced workers could earn up to ten dollars an hour, the top rate made by one of the assembly workers who set letter tabs on the At-a-Glance calendars.

The kind of assembly work done at Sheaffer Eaton was similar to many of those operations that had been done at General Electric when consumer goods such as irons, radio bases, electric bulbs, etc. were produced. This work is considered semi-skilled and speed is the essence of whatever skill is involved in these short cycle operations. The women wore radio headphones tuned in to their favorite programs — this represented a change over the old assembly lines with piped-in music where everyone marched to the same drummer. Other elements of their work were more individualized than one would have found in an old assembly line operation. The personnel manager described the work scene:

> Their work table and stations are personalized and nobody else dares sit there, even the second-shift person. They have to sit at

their own table. Everything is laid out so that it's most efficient for them. The table heights, the chair heights, the foot rest, the lighting, is individually controlled.

Management had not yet devised a machine to do the hand set operations as cheaply and efficiently as these women. The hourly people were organized by United Papermakers and Paperworkers Local 882 and Local 1090. The manager felt that it was the superior work force that made Pittsfield a preferred site for their operation. He said:

> There's a value in as far as the work force is concerned. If we were to pick up and transplant this thing into the Sun Belt we would have a very definite training problem where we would expect lower production, quality problems. You save a little bit in labor probably; you save a fair amount in energy; there may be some tax advantages at least for the first number of years. There may very well be capital expenditures in the beginning. It would turn the decision to stay in an old facility such as this, that is pretty well depreciated. It doesn't cost a lot as far as the plant and equipment are concerned, and as long as we can remain competitive operating on a multi-floor, relatively close-column speaking kind of manufacturing environment, raw material handling doesn't get to be too much of a problem as long as we don't outgrow the acreage that we have.

Shaeffer Eaton maintained a fairly stable year-round production schedule since they had three product lines operating on different demand cycles during the year. One peaked in the summer, the other at Christmas time, so there was a lot of internal movement. The explicit concern of the company with holding on to its superior labor force gave Sheaffer Eaton a competitive edge with General Electric, despite the higher pay in each classification in the latter company. The manager gave us his perspective on that:

> General Electric is out in front; they're the community leader, classification by classification, it's almost always a substantial advantage in GE. GE on the other hand has the reputation in the community of being a very cyclical employer, here today, gone tomorrow. We have a fair number of employees that came here when they had the opportunity to go to GE for that reason. They wanted a smaller, more family-oriented environment. There are others that are hired out of school, high school, college, Berkshire Community College or whatever, worked here for a couple months, a year or two, got some training under their belts and went to General Electric for the buck, not too concerned about other things.

And then there's a third category of people that did that and then said, "I'm tire of that; I want some roots," and came back.

Shaeffer Eaton impressed us as being unusual among conglomerates in not threatening to leave the community at the sign of any problem with labor, and in promising stability in employment. The president of Sheaffer Eaton, Louis S. Bishop, told the *Berkshire Eagle* reporter (July 29, 1981) who reported on a year of prosperity achieved at a time that General Electric's Power Transformer Division was laying off hundreds of workers, that "a pivotal factor in the health of his company in Pittsfield will be cooperation between management and employees on their mutual interest of achieveing job security." A year later, when Sheaffer Eaton was "forced" to lay off 150 of their 900 people, they instituted a four-day week to hold on to as many of the remaining people as they could. This was only done in firms where there seemed to be a collective identity among the personnel such that all were willing to sacrifice a part for the whole.

The apparent success of this conglomerate came to an end on February 26, 1987 when the Textron's corporate headquarters announced the proposed sale of the local plant in order to reduce the debt it incurred when it bought Ex-Cell-O Corp., a maker of Aerospace and auto parts for one billion dollars. The collective commitment of the work force did surface at the time in a movement among workers to buy some of the product divisions of the firm to keep them in operation.

Crane Paper Company

Crane Paper Company is identified primarily with the neighboring town of Dalton, but the plant producing government bills was on the Pittsfield side of the border until 1975 when that operation was moved to the Dalton plants and the Pittsfield plant now produces stationery. Despite the fact that the company has sold to an international market and produces the paper for all U. S. currency as well as American Express checks, the character of the firm has remained that of a cohesive, family-oriented enterprise. This is changing as the last of the Crane family, who served on the board until June 1985, was replaced. One of their employees who quit before mandatory retirement age said she could not tolerate the "GE rejects," superintendents hired from GE who had a different managerial style than the old foremen.

The Crane family has played a significant role in Dalton charitable activities, and the community as a whole reflects the characteristic stability and concern for long-term employeees that has been a hallmark of the company. The total corporate payroll of 980 includes 730 in the Dalton and Pittsfield operations and the remainder in the Excelsior Process and Engraving Company and the Excelsior Printing Company in North Adams and Standard Process and Engraving in San Leandro, California.

The combination of a family-owned company identified with the community and region, along with government contracts in currency that stressed the loyalty and quality of workmanship that required a committed work force, insulated the company from some of the managerial techniques that were beginning to characterize other businesses, including General Electric.

Plastics Companies

Approaching Pittsfield from the south a sign announces: Pittsfield, Plastics Technology Center of America. This image has been created and reinforced by the development of twenty-two small to medium plants that make plastic molds and products for industrial and consumer usage. Plastic has become the centerpiece of industrial revitalization efforts in the city.

The old porcelain plant where Vicky worked when Plastics Avenue was still called Ceramics Avenue, expanded rapidly after 1937 when over one hundred moldmakers were employed. But as production was moved elsewhere in the forties, about a hundred men were laid off. More than a dozen plastics companies were organized by former employees who did not want to leave town. Another exodus from General Electric in 1968 resulted in the formation of two more plastics companies.

For many of the entrepreneurs in plastics, their roots in Pittsfield extend back to growing up in the Lakewood neighborhood and many of them worked together in the plastics department at General Electric. Their identity as a group is still recognized and reinforced in the "Plastics Alumni" bowling team which brings them together every Friday. Kinship ties unite them with others in the group. Most of the firms experienced some expansion in the late 1970s and in 1979 a new company, Richwell Mold and Tool Company, was started with the help of the Pittsfield Development Committee. The biggest of the plastics companies, Marland Mold, was bought by the conglomerate Ethyl Corporation along with Imco and Greylock. Within the plastics industry alone, one can see the full range of American capitalist ventures from owner-managed operations to a division within a multinational

Small Plastics Firms Have Been Organized by Former G.E.
Technicians Such as Richwell Mold and Tool Company.

corporation. The diversity in ownership arrangements is matched by
the range in management-employee relations; there are union shops
with workers earning $6 to $12 an hour as well as non-union shops
where women earn the minimum wage of $3.25.

Just as in the case of Sheaffer-Eaton, Marland Mold tells us a great
deal about the impact of conglomerates on indigenous industries.
Marland Mold was one of the first of the ventures into plastics by
natives of Pittsfield. It was started in 1946 by Paul Ferland and Valentino
Marchetto, whose names were combined to give the firm its name.
After ten years' service with General Electric, Mr. Ferland left the firm
and worked in a Connecticut mold company for a few months, returning to Pittsfield in 1946 to open his own shop. In the early years, he
sold molds to General Electric, including the radio casings that Vicky
worked on at General Electric before they were phased out. He,
Marchetto and other collaborators were graduates of the General
Electric apprentice toolmaker training program. They opened a shop
in the Tillotson mill on Fourth Street, moved to Newell Street in the
Lakewood neighborhood, and finally bought the Elmvale mill on Peck's

Road when Elmvale went out of business in the fifties. This had previously been the site of Peck's Woolen Mill, with a fine brick main building built in 1863 and meant to last a lifetime. There they opened two shops, Imco and Greylock.

Ferland credits General Electric Company's training program as having given him and his collaborators a start (*The Berkshire Eagle* April 1, 1960). He sent his employees to apprentice classes at Pittsfield High School, where they were taught at night by General Electric engineers. In 1969 the company was bought by Valve Corporation of America with corporate headquarters in Greenwich, Connecticut. This was dissolved when Ethyl Corporation bought it in 1974.

The Greylock shop did injection molding of finished products and Imco blow molding for making a variety of products, including tools using Marland molds. The injection molding requires a less skilled work force. Greylock had thirty employees in 1962, with both men and women working on machine operations. Except for the third shift, there were more women than men. In 1982 when we interviewed the administrative supervisor for the combined firm, there were ninety-five employees, 80 percent of them women doing both machine operations and assembly work with men primarily involved in technical operations and tool repair. Women are employed as material handlers, janitors, technicians and in three supervisory positions.

The company still makes radio cabinets, knobs, pens, speakers, pill dispensers and medical cups. Suppliers of finished products such as Greylock were having more trouble getting material in 1974 and welcomed the bid by Ethyl to buy the company. Ethyl closed a plant in Puerto Rico that same year because of labor protests and "troubles," along with poor financial performance. The advantage in being a subsidiary of Ethyl during the acute material shortages of the mid-seventies seemed obvious. Ethyl doubled the capitalization of the firm.

The IUE organized the shop in 1976. The supervisor felt that it improved management-labor relations because it provided objective principles and procedures for layoffs and raises. The company could not play favorites with a union, nor could it be forced into doing so by the workers themselves. The union succeeded in raising the salaries slightly, from a little over the minimum that was the pre-union rate to $4.33 to start. Continuous operations of the machines, run on three eight-hour shifts, was important to maintain the heat generated in the molding operation. Absenteeism was a constant problem, and the management tried several techniques, short of wage incentives, to keep people with low absentee rates. One of their techniques was a "bingo" game, with a number drawn every time an employee worked every day of the week.

The company was more independent of General Electric during its affiliation with Ethyl than it had been in the early days. Since the parent company produced its own feedstock, it was no longer necessary to buy it from General Electric nor did they require technological help since this came from Ethyl Corporation. Training of their technicians was done by their own staff, with help from other Ethyl plants. While there was little advantage to the corporation in the Pittsfield location, there were no disadvantages except for higher taxes. The company received help from the Massachusetts Investment Credit Corporation in the form of low interest loans, and the state offered a tax abatement if the company bought equipment which would be operated by women. Such incentives, the supervisor guessed, were of greater importance to the small companies than to a big corporation. She felt that the company had "the best of all possible worlds": a small company that retained its distinctiveness, absorbed by a larger company with expertise and feedstock.

Six months after our interview, Ethyl closed Greylock injection mold, keeping Marland Mold going. The supervisor to whom we had spoken learned about the sale only when she read it in the newspaper. She felt lucky to have been transferred to Marland Mold only a short time before. I spoke to one of the IUE organizers, whom I shall call Pat, who had worked at Greylock. She told me that there was no clause in the contract about advance notice, and given that, the owners were "pretty decent" about giving the more senior people a pension plan and severance pay. Before the company was sold to Ethyl, the owners would work weekends along with the workers to get out a rush order. After the corporation started running the business, there was not as great a commitment. "They're big enough, they're powerful enough, and they have enough money so they don't have to depend on one small shop," the organizer said. Some of the workers were able to get jobs in Marland and in Polymetrix, where there is no union but many of the women in the fifties were not able to get employment.

Greylock workers organized when the company took away Blue Cross and Blue Shield coverage. The organizer had been working in the plant when that happened:

> When they took away our Blue Cross and Blue Shield, they did something terrible. Well, I mean, my wages were alright, and all of a sudden they pulled the carpet out and people did what they did…. They did the same thing at Imco. We tried to organize them

three times and they would not sign up. I was in there on the campaign and the company bought them shoes and shirts, and I sat there and said, ''Wow, I don't believe this! ...a new pair of shoes!'' And then there's the threats at the other end. ''You're going to lose your job! We're going to close down.'' You know, everything illegal, but who's going to tell? If I'm a person in the plant, and someone's threatening me, I'm not going to go and tell. You know, that's my rear end on the line. And then in this economy! You know, you're so afraid in the first place. Yeah, they tell you your job is out the door if you sign a union card.

Pat's experience with organizing extended to other states where such threats were common practice. She saw the reductions in union membership, because of plant closings, plant moving and layoffs. The decision to close Greylock, the labor-intensive phase of plastics production where companies rely on low paid labor, was surely related to the entry of the union. Mold making, which requires a skilled work force that is better paid, still held an advantage in an area where well-trained workers were available.

I assumed that there would be some stability because of this factor, but one year later Ethyl sold Imco to Brockway, a manufacturer of glass, plastic and metal containers which employs a total of 12,500 people in eleven plants, the parent company of which is in Brockway, Pennsylvania. The plant was down to forty hourly and ten to twelve salaried employees when it was sold to Brockway. The new company was not unionized, yet hourly workers had been earning $5 to $12 an hour. This was higher than Brockway paid in its Nashua facility. Within a year and a half, Brockway closed the shop and moved to Nashua, New Hampshire. Since blow molding is a specialty that no other plastics shops do in the area, the workers were expected to have difficulty finding other employment. (*The Berkshire Eagle* December 5, 1985). In January 1986 advertizements for a moldmaker and foreperson to be responsible for an eight-man tool shop and willing to relocate to southwestern New Hampshire appeared in *The Berkshire Eagle*. The flight of these competitive industries, even within such a close range as neighboring states, is an important dynamic in the manipulation of a labor market.

The instability of these firms once they are taken over by conglomerates is a growing concern for leaders in community development. The seed money given to small owner-operators like those who started Marland is a public resource that later provides the infrastructure for conglomerates who buy them out, milk them for a short time and throw them away when competitive opportunities beckon their foot-loose owners elsewhere.

There is greater stability in some of the other plastics companies where management is made up of family members and friends, who frequently move on to form separate companies. This is the case with Moldmasters. The first such company was started in 1946 by Kushi and four other GE "alumni" in a shop next to the grocery store on Newell Street in Lakewood, and is now a family business run by Kushi's sons after his partners left to start their own businesses. Their sister, who used to do the company's bookkeeping, married a managerial employee who left to start his own business in 1964. Most of Moldmaster's sales have been to Sprague Electric Company in North Adams or to General Electric. They also get business from former employees of General Electric who have gone on to other companies or formed their own companies elsewhere. They have enjoyed a good relationship with General Electric in getting supplies, particularly in 1974 during the oil crisis when feedstock was scarce. "We've been good neighbors," one of the brothers told us. Now that gynal has been phased out by General Electric they will no longer be able to "pick up what we need on weekends and then tell them on Monday morning" as they used to, but other exchanges of information and training continue.

The brothers have a great deal of family pride in their business. In the small reception area of the modern brick structure is a large portrait of their father, banked with potted plants. "He got us down to the shop to sweep the floor, work there, from the time we were in school," one of the brothers told us.

This business feels it is performing a community service in giving jobs to a local work force, particularly youths from Lakewood. In order to maintain a priority on quality, they chose to remain small to "keep our company manageable." The company now employs fourteen to sixteen women on two shifts, and about a dozen men in the tool shop. "With our work force," one of the Kushis told us, "we can put anyone anywhere. They are flexible and well-trained by us. We have a company clambake and we also get together in the shop with the workers and discuss problems." The brothers are proud of their own commitment to working in the shop and rarely take a vacation. "We've got people working here who have more vacation time off than we have." They contrast their hiring policies, favoring local youths, to those of competitors who hire minorities at lower rates. Kushi told us:

> We are competing with shops that hire minorities. We do our training and want workers we train, since we work with expensive materials. We don't make junk. Some of the materials cost $4 to

$5 a pound, and our customers know what's good. They are mostly industrial concerns with quality consciousness. They check us out very carefully.

In fact, there is a gender segmentation of workers with female workers exclusively involved in finishing and some others mixed in with the male work force. It is the male workers who get the more extensive training and who go on to form their own companies.

One of the trainees who took an apprenticeship program at ''Marland Mold College'' and then went on to form his own company is Richard Rilla. He got further experience in two other plastics companies and then bought out American Mold and Tools, a small local operation, for $30,000 including all the equipment and a customer. He now operates with seven full-time employees and three part-time employees in the office. His wife keeps the books, a preferred pattern with these family businesses. In 1980 he split with his partner and moved his business from Hancock to Pittsfield, with the help of the Community Economic Development fund and a federal grant for solar energy.

Rilla estimates 80 to 90 percent of their production is for companies outside of Pittsfield, with Sprague Electric in North Adams one of their regular customers. Although the local General Electrics plastics operation does have a need for mold makers to test the work for the materials they are developing, he says that they usually go outside of the area. He estimates that they could keep four to five shops busy in the area, but for reasons he did not know, they sent the work outside. Rilla maintains a higher pay scale in his small shop and emphasizes expertise in turning out parts with extremely close tolerance in their injection mold and compression and transfer mold work. This requires a thorough apprenticeship, teaching people to work with the machinery.

Rilla's reasons for staying in busines in Pittsfield are personal rather than rational, since the tax rates are higher and transportation, both for his employees and for sending out materials in a rush, is deficient. He stays simply because he likes the place. He has been a member of the ''Plastics Alumni'' bowling team since the sixties and is now president and secretary-treasurer. ''We're a fun group. We get together on Friday night, just to break away from our everyday humdrum duties and what not. And ironically it's the same people I do business with and am in competition with.... One way or another, we all still enjoy life.''

With these commitments, Rilla has a different outlook from corporation executives at Ethyl and Brockway. It is unlikely that his company

company will be a target for a takeover if he remains small enough, since they usually turn to larger companies. Then too, it seems that the conglomerates are turning to lower-wage areas, such as Nashua, for further investment.

Several other small plastics companies are located in the old mills, the choice made by Greylock and Marland Mold in Pecks Mill. Precision Mold and Pittsfield Plastics Engineering are located in the Pontoosuc mills built in 1826. The venerable buildings lend distinction to the new companies, according to the manager of Precision Mold. In Precision Mold, which is a branch of McKenzie Company on Peck Street, there are six mold makers and apprentices who do work for Boston firms primarily, but feel that the presence of GE Plastics Research center provides available expertise and a stimulus to the business. The other company is run by a brother-in-law of the Kushis. His business, which he started in 1967, was somewhat larger, with twelve machine operators and four skilled mold makers. He gets orders through General Electric and their branches in other areas, and attributes all of the mold-making business to General Electric having got out of plastics. He has moved away from custom molds to standard molds for spools of a wide range of sizes.

The small entrepreneurs remark on the difference in production in their shops and at General Electric where, one of the owners said, the average guy is holding up production.

> A small shop cannot afford that. Every guy has got to produce. We'd go out of business if they felt that way. ...But over in General Electric the union runs that place. They can walk out any time they want to..... They don't want to work. I wouldn't stay in business if I had a union in here. Here we depend on big business. We can do it cheaper, and it works out good. They have the market and connections and can place their work with us.

This probably sums up the relationship between the corporation and the small plastics businesses as well as anyone could. Since these small, non-unionized shops can exert more pressure on the work force, General Electric uses them as sources for many parts that require labor intensive operations.

Other plastics businesses have been served more directly by the mayor's development committee. Polymatrix is one of the firms in the Downing Industrial Park just off East Street that started in 1965. Like its neighbors, Polymatrix is a large, pre-fabricated aluminum building situated just across the street from the Lakewood Molds and up the street from Berkshire Beef, the first company to locate in the industrial complex. Although the owner, Bill Rufo, grew up in Pittsfield and graduated from the Pittsfield High School, he did not come from the Lakewood section where many of the plastics "alumni" originated. His father, who worked as a fabricator in General Electric, inspired him to start his own business. He worked at General Electric for thirteen years and then went to work for his brother in Lakewood Mold. His brother got his experience in the Marland Mold company. He opened up Polymatrix in 1975 with three partners, two of whom supplied the capital, with additional funds from a local bank. A later expansion was funded by the Massachusetts Industrial Financing Agency which, unlike the banks, puts no restrictions on the use of loan money.

Polymatrix has a work force of eighty-five people, seven men and the remainder women. They pay people the minimum wage, which was $3.25 an hour when we interviewed Bill in 1982. Foremen make around $350 a week, plus overtime. Needless to say, there is no union at Polymatrix. Bill told us that Ethyl, which was the only plastic molding firm with a union, "has the wherewithall to contend with unions." He has a high, but for plastics "normal," turnover which he attributes to the fact that the work is boring and repetitive with a lot of noise.

Rufo has a much higher capital investment in modern machinery and automatic feeders of the supply than the other companies we visited. He has $600,000 in buildings; $1.5 million in molds, with ten molding machines costing $90,000; another $500,000 in auxiliary equipment; and an automation system costing $150,000 which had not been hooked up yet since they have been too busy. He has been able to take advantage of the small business supports provided by the city and state, and the partners put everything back into the business, not taking anything out for their own use. The production arena was impressively clean, a remarkable fact since he has no separate maintenance crew. Every worker, apparently, cleans up after himself.

This firm is completely independent of General Electric both in terms of supplies — it uses a lower grade of plastic — and of market — it makes cassette cases that are sold throughout the United States, "from Massachusetts to California." Unlike the other plastics manufacturing firms, they were not as severely affected by the 1981–82 recession as those plastics companies producing industrial tools and products. Despite its autonomy from General Electric, the fact that General Electric has located the plastics center in Pittsfield makes it a more attractive location for all the small industries like his own, Rufo said. There is a large pool of skilled workers and the area can attract and hold well-trained supervisory staff. Despite the disadvantages of taxes on the high side and poor transportation, the advantages out-weight the drawbacks.

Cavalero Plastics moved from the old Pontoosuc mill to one of the many old schoolhouses that were offered for sale to businesses in the seventies when the school population was drooping. The golden oak floors had just been refinished when they moved in 1982. The slate windowsills and arched brick-framed windows are touches that one could not find in modern buildings. The owner told me: "Ours is a family closed corporation." His son is production manager of a work force of fourteen divided equally between males and females. This level was down from the usual twenty to twenty-two workers, a reduction made necessary by the 1982 recession, but by 1984 it was up to forty. The firm has hired some CETA workers in the past. There is no union.

Cavalero has taken advantage of the Massachusetts Industrial Finance Agency with a loan of $260,000. All of their profits go back into the firm. Like many others, the advantage for them in being in Pittsfield is the good work force and the nice location for plastics business; the major problem is the poor transportation to major market centers and the high taxes.

The newest firm to enter the group is the Stuart Allyn Company, which has occupied a site in the Taconic Business Park since 1985. In addition to the production of precision molds, they offer design and consulting services. Like the others, Stuart Allyn Co. is a family business — the firm name is made up of the given names of the father and son. The owner, Allyn Scace, Serves as president, with the son the vice president in charge of manufacturing and the wife as treasurer and office manager. Only four other employees work in the shop. A graduate of the Taconic High School apprentice program, Allyn Scace worked in Marland Mold and later Richwell Mold and Tool.

These are among the twenty-two small plastics firms that represent the future prospects for industrialization in Pittsfield. The set of expectations created by the companies themselves and the development committee working with them continually generates new firms within the field. It is significant that all of the entrepreneurs are linked through common experiences at the General Electric or in the firms started by the GE alumni. Expansion is, like that of segmentary lineages of Africa, a replication of the same structure in a different locale, as each trainee extends the pattern in a new small owner-managed firm organized around a core of family members. All except one of the owners interviewed insisted that they were not competing against each other. Since their production operations are small, they serve different markets, each doing a very specialized operation.

The reproduction of this form of capitalistic enterprise is assisted not only by the direct credit and subsidies given by the state and local government but also by the state-subsidized University of Massachusetts research center in polymers. General Electric Company makes direct contributions to the center and its graduates in turn serve the industry and the smaller firms with it. It reaffirms the centrality of plastics to the public and to the industry in this area. The limitation comes when the firm gets swallowed up by a larger conglomerate that then begins to judge profits in terms of what could be made in other places. Both Ethyl and Brockway closed shop when the wage rate exceeded levels at their other sites. Another limitation exists in the structure of labor-management relations. The mere threat of unionization confirms decisions to close operations. Since they are competing with government programs in Aid to Families with Dependent Children and unemployment in gaining a work force, they also firmly set against what one of these owners contemptuously called these "give-away" programs such as unemployment compensation and mother's aid and the like."

To the degree that they are successful, these companies have an advantage in establishing close personal relations with their work force and turn out high-precision work with high productivity ratios. When I asked one of the owners whether they used quality circles, the new buzz word at General Electric, he asked "What's that?" Yet they are closer to fulfilling the norms that are said to make quality circles work in Japan than are General Electric supervisors. The continual interaction of managers and production workers and the proven possibility of moving into their own business overcomes the alienation that is endemic for production workers in General Electric.

The mutual dependency of community and industry is best realized in such small industrial firms. This is expressed most eloquently by Richard Rilla:

> The local business community, primarily the banking interests, don't recognize the fact that we're in business to try to grow. We supply the local economy with wages, taxes and so forth, and I think the mold-making industry is probably supplying the city of Pittsfield to the tune of some six or seven thousand people through their families, employees, and as consumers through a broad range of services. We are dedicated to the Pittsfield area primarily because of our New England ideology, the way we were taught to live, taught to experience. What we're doing, where we are and who we are, the work ethic is instilled in us, work hard, push ahead, just keep on working.

The "New England tradition," as Rilla so aptly phrases it, embodies the reinterpretation of that nineteenth-century outlook that resulted in the first wave of industrialization in the second and third generation of immigrants. The cohesiveness of the Italian community of Lakewood provided both the shared experience and knowledge and support that made possible the risky venture into small business in the fifties and sixties when the corporation saw diminishing profits in the field. The recent entry of multinationals buying out the larger and more successful of these ventures does not lead to sustained growth. The greater sensitivity of these large corporations to wage differentials in distinct geographical areas, and their lack of commitment to the area that inspires most of the owner entrepreneurs to weather the recessions means that they deny the real growth of industry that comes from a wider distribution of the gains of production in terms of real wages.

Mary stayed at Elmvale Worsted Mill even after she got called by G.E. during World War II, but the mill closed in 1959.

The Textile Industry

Four textile companies that were organized in the nineteenth century remained in business up until World War II: the A. H. Rice Company, T. D. Peck Company, the Russell Mill and the Pontoosuc Woolen Company. These were taken over by three new companies in the early decades of the twentieth century. The Berkshire Woolen company purchased the Upper Mill of T. D. Peck Manufacturing Company in 1915. The Elmvale Worsted Mill and the Wyandotte Mill started in the thirties, taking up quarters in old textile factories, the former in the Russell Mill and the latter in the Pontoosuc Woolen Mill, which had gone out of business after the stock market crash. Elmvale stayed in business until 1959. Wyandotte made U.S. Army blankets in World War II and kept in business until 1963. Women worked in carding, men on the mules, bobbins, looms and heddles which women fed. When the company introduced the spinning frames, women took over men's jobs in the roving machines. In the thirties, the industry employed 1,500 workers. The Berkshire Woolen Mill and the Wyandotte were organized by the textile workers in 1939.

The lability of textiles in the twentieth century illustrates the strategic importance of wage costs in determining location and staying in business. Mitzie, the daughter of a silk weaver who kept moving the family as he went from Canada to the New England mills as they closed successively, shows in her family history this process. "You know how the mills are," she told me "They closed and moved South. We kept moving. Rocky Hill was one, Willamantic was one, then Norwich. I was quite young and the mills didn't stay around all that long. Finally he [her father] came to work on the Adams wool mill." Her older brothers were weavers working in wool, silk and cotton. Her sisters started out as weavers in the mills, but they got married quite young. As the youngest, she was able to get a high school education and later work in the General Electric company until her marriage.

Those who stayed in the mills found the work hard, poorly paid and with few benefits. Women were constantly subjected to sexual harassment by foremen, but felt they couldn't complain for fear of losing their jobs. Some stayed on even when they were offered a job in the General Electric during World War II, thinking that they would have a better chance of holding on to the job after the war. This proved mythical, since all but one of the mills closed.

A. H. Rice is the only one of the many textile companies that originated in Pittsfield that is still in business. Founded in 1878, the family retained control over the operation of the plant until it was sold in 1982, though the grandson of the original owner is still kept on as a consultant. The machinery for braid, which is the specialty with which they started manufacturing, was purchased from a liquidating company. It is eighty-five years old and requires constant vigilence by the two men who have been working on it the past fifty-five years. They came to work when they were fourteen years old, just two decades before the machines went out of manufacture about the beginning of the Second World War. Other machinery is from thirty to fifty years old. The company's willingness to do small orders with special needs for color and spinning of the threads means that they fill a niche with few competitors. The labor force in 1984 included 120, 70 percent of whom were women who worked in the shop while men filled the maintenance jobs and the dye shop. The maintenance crew earned the highest wage, $6 to $10 an hour, with $3.90 the average for production workers.

I spoke with John H. Rice, one of the grandchildren of the founder. He is a frequent contributor to the local paper's financial pages and an important figure in the social and charitable affairs of the company. His response to my question as to why he thought the company was able to stay in business when so many others failed was succinct:

> One reason we were successful was that we selected particular markets that we thought we had a product to offer and we concentrated on that. We didn't attempt to become giants. There were markets that we thought we knew something of so we stuck to those. And as new ones came up — we got into the jogging business at the very beginning and sold thread to Elders and Converse and several other companies that began making jogging shoes at the beginning. I think the fact of family ownership and family management is important, and I like to think we were a little smarter than some of the others. The companies that didn't make it around tried to go into areas they didn't know anything about, and they got knocked off by other people.

In addition to making braid and stitching for shoes, they make shoe bags used by companies for advertizing, and a "wing walker," or shoe bag for airline maintenance crews.

This company's biggest employment period was in the early seventies, when they employed 280 people and were a major supplier for the automobile industry. A. H. Rice is known as a firm that could never be unionized. Early in my field work one of the men who had helped organize the UE at General Electric said, "One place they tried to organize but they never could was Rice's Silk Mill. The moment they heard someone's trying to organize over there, my God, they have somebody standing right outside. Oh, if a stranger comes around, "Oh, you're not welcome here!" I was curious how it gained that reputation, and in my interview with the then retired former owner and manager of the company, I asked whether the family philosophy affected labor management relations:

> We never had any labor troubles here and we don't now. There were several attempts in the late forties and early fifties to unionize, but nobody felt confident enough to call an election. So we never had an election and never had a strike. We had some informational picketing by the textile union. There was a company around here that unionized and within a couple of years they went broke. So I think the people realize that might happen here. We had people whose families had been with us quite a few years and there was some transferable loyalties..... I think one of the reasons we haven't had a union is that we did everything we could, we tried to accommodate people, if not to the point that we let people have three hours off in the afternoon to stay home and take care of the children. They weren't quite that flexible. But very often we would put material into inventory just so we wouldn't have to shut down. We repaid loyalty by being as considerate as we could. With a small company you can do that.

I asked what level that was true and he replied:

> At the shop level. A lot of our people in production are women, whose husbands work at General Electric, and so the women were happy to have a supplementary income. They were not dissatisfied when there were layoffs when business was somewhat slack and they were happy to go home and take care of their houses.

I asked if he had a more flexible working schedule to accommodate the double day that married women had:

> Yes, so the chances for dissatisfaction were somewhat less there than they were at other companies. We never got into flex time, but we did have periods of short time that family women could avail themselves of. There was no set pattern.

The "short time" refers to the four-day, ten-hour shifts that most people prefer in this shop. They started that schedule, with fewer than ten daily hours, when they were short on orders, and kept it on when people showed a preference for it. They also noticed an increase in efficiency on that schedule. The plant supervisor indicated that they do, in fact, have a non-institutionalized flex time for people who ask for such considerations. They found that this too worked to their benefit. The supervisor remarked as he was showing us around the plant:

> In the summertime, and again maybe because we're not a union shop, because people like to get home early in the afternoon, we start earlier in the morning and leave early. We also have people who come in on odd shifts if their children need to go to school first, and they go home later. Particularly if a person has an expertise that we have to train again. If someone comes to us and says, "I have a problem, can I do this...." We have a young lady working in our finishing department, she comes in at two because her husband works odd hours, and then comes home and takes care of the kid. And she requested several months leave to do that. Actually it works better in our operation. We can make some things in the morning and she can finish them at night and we can get them out of here a day earlier than we could. So we do work with the people. In fact, it's to our advantage.

The basic consideration for the needs of the work force, including giving each worker his or her birthday off, is the factor to which they attribute the stability of the firm. Beyond that there is the structure of the work force, which is predominently married women, many married to men who work in General Electric. In addition to having a major medical plan and a non-contributory pension plan in the shop, they receive medical insurance and access to pensions won by the primary labor force. There is little incentive to move toward unionization given the threat of the factory closing down. Their 1983 earnings of $4.80 an hour could be upped by piece rates. When the new management took over in 1982, the president encouraged workers to relate directly to him. According to former management, "it raised hell with the management structure."

Affirmative action has not been a conscious goal of the firm except on the government contracts they get. Even so there are women who are superintendents and foreladies, and this was common even before the Equal Employment Opportunity Act. There is even an executive vice president who is a woman. But Mr. Rice assured me, "we aren't a matriarchy yet."

Since its purchase by the Gerli Company, the A. H. Rice firm seems to be carrying out the same procedures, maintaining a small size in a select market. The other mill owned by Gerli is the American Silk

Company which is in related manufactures, weaving silk and velvet fabrics for apparel and decorative fabrics. Unlike the conglomerates that buy up firms only to wrest the last remaining profit margins from them, they appear committed to an industry and to a place.

Garment Industry

The only garment factory in town, The Workshop for Designers, operated on a shoestring budget in a rented building downtown. The few firms that compete in this field in the region are most concerned with maintaining low labor costs in order to remain in operation. The Workshop for Designers became the site of a five-month strike, the longest in Pittsfield's history.

The case is worthy of attention because of the implications for labor relations in such firms. It is an extreme example of the failure of U. S. industrial policy to protect American workers from competitive production in the low-wage countries. In Pittsfield, the working underclass employed in this garment firm was primarily female, and many of the women are the principle breadwinners in their families. The company also hired people with criminal records, and they ran a subsidiary company called Berkshire Ltd., where they employed retarded workers to finish garments.

The strike was called in March 1982. The owner, having received a big order from the army to make parkas, called in a time-rate man, and on the basis of the scales set, the wages were to be much higher than usual. According to striking workers, the boss then arbitrarily cut the rates in half. Most of the women walked out when the owner fired a woman who had made contact with the International Ladies Garment Workers Union. While they walked the picket line, and suffered aggravated assault by the owner of the firm, who at one time drove his Cadillac into the line injuring a picket who had to be hospitalized, scabs had taken over their jobs. After 157 days of strike, the women went back to work, pending a NLRB settlement. The NLRB filed thirty-seven violations and eleven subviolations charging the owner with failing to bargain in good faith in December 1982. The settlement in July 1983 required the owner to reinstate, with back pay, employees fired for organizing and the workers gained a contract, with the ILGWU as bargaining agent. Shortly afterward, the firm reduced employment, then dissolved as a company.

Arbitrary management policies precipitated this strike. That it involved many women who were heads of household contributed to the greater militance of the strikers, who were more aware of the inadequacy of their wages for supporting a family.

The case has significance for understanding structural changes in the economy. Small plants operating on reduced profit margins rely on a work force that cannot find more permanent positions in industry because of their own family commitments or past problems affecting their employment records. Aside from some of the more bizarre aspects of their behavior during the strike and after, the owners saw themselves in a crusade to preserve small competitive firms and viewed the government, in the guise of the NLRB, as pitted against their survival. In the expansion prompted by the first large contract the company ever had, a company that had employed twenty employees handling $400,000 in production in a year grew to a four million dollar operation employing eighty workers. The rapid expansion caused a breakdown in the personalized relations that had formerly characterized relations between the owner and the workers, most of whom had called him by his first name. Once the personal relations were broken, the family-managed concern could not adapt to bureaucratic procedures demanded of the employer as relations became formalized. Comments by workers in other plants in the city, as well as members of the Chamber of Commerce, indicate that the owner had no support in the community and that his behavior was considered a throwback to the twenties and thirties. He was last reported in the western highlands of Guatemala where he commented on the favorable conditions for business.

General Electric and the Competitive Firms

In the growing integration of production throughout the world, large, oligopolistic firms tend to expand into less developed areas of the United States and overseas. Small, competitive industries were more likely to be contained within their existing areas, hiring a "secondary" work force at lower wage levels than those offered in the large corporation. The stability of this sector has been broken down as conglomerates have bought and sold those that were yielding a greater profit in recent years.

A community study of this sort allows one to see the great range of variations in the degree to which industries are organized, and how this affects the wage levels as well as the structure of economic opportunities at a local level. Thus the basic factor of wage costs in the decision to move is not so much affected by the average wage in each region, but the wage given to the particular sector of the work force that is involved. In the restructuring of the large corporation, changes in the division of labor have resulted in a smaller proportion of the work force being involved in eligible union jobs. The proportion of union eligible workers in the General Electric plant in Pittsfield has declined from over one-half of the employed labor force to less than one-third. The conglomerates exhibited a similar intolerance for unions. Sheaffer Eaton and Ethyl laid off more than half their work force when they were organized and the union contract went into force. Shortly thereafter both companies shut down production entirely.

Another factor affecting management is the degree of capital-intensive production. Where there is a significant degree of automation resulting in high per capita employee productivity, the significance of wage costs is diminished. General Electric has eliminated many of the products that involved a large number of production workers at an earlier state in its development in Pittsfield. With the decline in Power Transformer Division, there was a steady erosion of the remaining production jobs until it too was closed. In the early seventies, General Electric made the significant moves to minimize this part of the labor force by expanding the Rome, Georgia and the Hickory, North Carolina plants for small and middle-sized transformers. The present curtailment of production in the eighties is according to management statements, a response to the diminished demand for power distribution machinery along with a loss of some of the existing market to overseas competition. Yet the company has not fought to regain its preeminence in the field of large transformers not because there was no profit but because of the low returns compared to Ordnance production and other lines of activity such as the credit corporation with phenomenally high returns. Given the prevalent view that Pittsfield has a militant labor force, particularly after the 1969 strike, General Electric decided to minimize its role in such production involving a large blue-collar work force. Priority was given then to the Ordnance Division in the Pittsfield plant.

From my first interview with the sub-director of community relations, it was made clear that GE's decision to move the small and medium-sized transformers to the south was made for reasons other than that of lower labor costs. Indeed, within a few years after their departure, IUE organized the plants in the south with the help of some of the Pittsfield union leaders. The important factor was to minimize the presence of the firm in the community so that it was not the target for community opposition whenever decisions were made regarding the work force. This threat was clear during the strike, when mayors of the communities that had a large General Electric presence got together with state and national representatives to bring the company to arbitration. The potential pressure of such public interest groups exerted on the corporation reinforced the desire to "take on a lower profile." Consequently the plant experienced attrition throughout the seventies as the oil embargo put pressure on costs and reduced production in many industries within the United States. The only growth in the corporation occurred overseas.

Thus General Electric's decisions are not simply controlled by cost factors. Larger numbers of organized workers in their plants throughout the country mean that their labor costs are more equalized. Their size makes their decisions a political factor related to external group pressures. In contrast, competitive firms, even when they are a part of a large conglomerate such as Sheaffer Eaton in the Textron group, are not as capital intensive and their production schedules do not affect the entire economic climate in the way of the dominant firm. The decisions of these smaller firms to stay or leave are strongly influenced by the threat of unionization.

Another case in point is that of the A. H. Rice Company. The wages for the non-unionized workers in this firm are about those of national averages, only slightly above minimum wages. Since this is a major cost factor, the other considerations of transportation energy costs have not yet made for a sufficient differential to justify movement in terms of the theorem. The non-economic factor of management preferences for living and working in an area with many cultural and recreational facilities has thus far prevented movement.

Municipal Industrial Development Efforts

The mayor's Office of Community and Economic Development stepped up activities to win new industry as the economy declined in the early eighties. In its publication, *The Pittsfield Economic Revitalization Plan: An Industrial Development Agenda for the Eighties,* the committee, headed by Janet Goldberg, pointed to the advantages of a highly-skilled work force, attractive physical area with low population density, high quality education and a good raw material base with lumber, sand, gravel and other materials. The committee called for zoning for a new industrial park on the site of the old Taconic mill and preparation of a parcel for industrial development near the airport along with a by-pass highway connecting the city with major interstate highways. The economic forecast was bleak, with over 8 percent unemployment, the loss of 9 percent of the population from 1970 levels and a dependence on General Electric that accounted for 66 percent of all manufacturing jobs and 43 percent of all jobs in the city.

During Janet Goldberg's term in office, the mayor's office succeeded in getting eight closed school properties into use and providing a stimulus for new industrial parks as well as the existing Downing Industrial Park. The committee assisted industries in getting the Industrial Relief bonds; even larger companies such as Beloit Jones were helped by these loans, which required no needs qualification. With the incentive of a 121a tax break, General Electric made the decision to locate its international plastics research and development center in Pittsfield.

By 1985 two of the projected industrial parks were nearing completion, with some leases arranged. Janet Goldberg's successor, William J. Angelo had been a contract manager for the city and before that had run a demolition program. A much more optimistic outlook had developed in the intervening years, and the first two objectives of the committee had been realized with a zoning law and the infrastructure for the airport industrial park well under way. Angelo spoke enthusiastically about the projects underway.

> There are three major acres where development is going to take place. One is the 200 acreas adjacent to Tamarack Road; second is the airport area itself; and third is the Barker Road area of 30 acres.... We have started the development of the last area. We're putting a road down there; that's up to bid right now. We've run a sewer down to it. We built a new connector road from the airport to Route 20 and 7. We've hired a consultant and are using bi-weekly meetings we have for a public forum about what we want to do with the airport. In the interim, we've negotiated with the state for funding for this road.... The whole thing is pretty near locked in. I think it's ready to go.

The last obstacle that the leaders in the revitalization movement see ahead is failure on the part of much of the populace to envision this developed future. "We have to think of things much more positively," Angelo stated bluntly, "[and] not badmouth ourselves. I think we have to sell ourselves to people in the Berkshire before we can go outside the area."

An unstated concern is the question of unions, particularly those related to the large corporations. One of the development leaders put it this way, "How do you get someone like Wang or Digital, which is not unionized, coming into the area and having to deal with the issue?'' The vision of the development agencies for the future does not include unions or even government programs for promoting the skills and education of those who stand outside the frame of high-tech development. A decade ago when leaders in the IUE sat in on the development committees, they tried to get the city leaders interested in wooing big business. Union Carbide was looking for headquarters in the seventies, and there was a rumor that Sikorsky Airlines wanted a testing site. When Al Litano brought it up at a meeting of the committee, they didn't follow through:

> So I said, ''We've got empty buildings in Pittsfield that we probably could renovate, get some money in, and these people could use them.'' I said, ''We've got the airlines here, they want to be close to New York City, and they want to get out of the huddle and muddle of the big city. This would be the appropriate place for them.'' Well we never got a report back that they did follow through on this, never. So I got a call from this friend of mine, and he says to me, ''What the hell is going on?'' He says, ''There are people looking around the Connecticut area because they haven't been contacted by Pittsfield at all, through my inside information. Is there anything going on? Any contacts?'' I said, ''No one reported contacts to me, but I'll lay the question on my next meeting,'' So I make the question at the next meeting, and all I got was evasive answers, and nothing direct that they were contacting them. So the next thing I know, after a period of about three or four months go by, I get informed that they knew that in Danbury, Connecticut. I was so upset, and they knew that with the GE employment down, got a lot of skill plus four states they could draw from.... And I raised holy hell about it at the next meeting that I went to. I checked it myself with a friend of mine that had lived down in the Hartford area, like the wage scale, which was higher in Danbury than in Pittsfield, cost of living was higher in Danbury than in Pittsfield. We had so much going for us.
>
> Some of the board members told me later, in the recession of 1982, ''You know, Al, I always believed in the things that you said, but unfortunately my eyes weren't opened wide enough to project the future, but everything you said was true.... But you must remember what one of our problems is. GE is number one, and a lot of us do business with General Electric, and if we had pursued your thoughts, a lot of us would have been knocked off the list.'' That's a big fear of theirs, that they had over their heads.

The staff of the Office of Community and Economic Development face increasing contradictions as the attempts to plan and direct change come into opposition with conflicting established interests. Planners who opted for industrial development were criticized by tourist interests. Attempts to improve roadways or construct bypasses to channel traffic to the new malls were attacked by the old downtown shop owners or homeowners who protested change affecting their neighborhoods. "Not in My Back Yard," (NIMBY) was becoming a local as well as national slogan (cf. *New York Times* June 18, 1988) as change threatened old patterns. Deeper ideological debates emerged as leaders within and outside city government questioned the use of public funds of tax-free agencies to "help MacDonald's stands" or to provide infrastructure for profit making corporations. William J. Angelo's successor in the Office of Community and Economic Development, David A. Maynard, left the office under a cloud, announcing that he felt "caught in a system where the roles had become so blurred and confused it was difficult to work effectively" (*Berkshire Eagle*, June 20, 1988, p. B1).

In the changing industrial development in Pittsfield we can see transformation of a corporate hegemonic alliance between industrial concerns that provided jobs and expanded opportunities for workers to expansion sales outlets, tourism and service industries with low wage jobs. This trend that began in the 1970s and bore its fruits in the 1980s will be described in the following chapters.

Chapter 7

Buying and Selling in Pittsfield

Pittsfield's transformation from an industrial base with one large corporation dominating a field of small diversified industries to a limited employment, high technology center has brought with it a proliferation of sales and service enterprises. The loss of over 10,000 industrial jobs in Berkshire County since 1970 has been more than matched by increases in retail and wholesale trade as well as service jobs, but these are low paid and insecure employment of a largely unorganized sector. This has had a marked effect on neighborhoods and families polarized by growing wealth differences. Two income families strive to retain the standards of living to which workers in a thriving industrial economy had become accustomed, but increasing numbers of single wage earners, often female-headed families are falling below poverty levels.

Pittsfield's Economic Revitalization Corporation pricked the illusory bubble of prosperity experienced in the high spending years of the 1970s and 1980s by taking a hard look at the economic vulnerability of a region that had turned from basic production to buying and selling as a way of life. Compiling figures from the U.S. Census, the U.S. Department of Commerce, and the Center for Economic Development, the report issued by the Corporation called "An Economic Base Study of Pittsfield and Berkshire County" shows a decline in manufacturing employment throughout the county from 24,140 jobs in 1967 to 17,216 in 1985, a percentage decline from 41.3 percent to 28 percent. In the following three years, 1985, 1986, and 1987 in manufacturing 1000 jobs were lost each year bringing the total decline to 10,000 jobs in two decades. The increase of 3,500 jobs in retail trades and 5,500 jobs in services from 1974 to 1984 (County Business Patterns) are, for the most part, low-paid jobs employing predominantly women. In Pittsfield alone there was an increase of 2,865 jobs in these two sectors from 1970 to 1980. Fast food chains were trying to lure young workers with extraordinary measures such as "Bonanza's" raffle of an automobile to each applicant.

In Pittsfield, men predominated in the 7,100 manufacturing jobs in 1980 when there were 5,109 men and 1,991 women, while in retail trade women have a slight edge with 2,067 of the 3,970 jobs and in services they have 4,295 of 6,589 jobs (U.S. Census). The average wage for manufacturing jobs in 1985 was $25,518, for retail jobs $9,984 and for service jobs, $12,562. As a result of these changes, there is a greater decline in the young male population that is projected to increase to 10 percent by 1990.

The commercial life of the city of Pittsfield has always been dominated by the level of production and employment at the General Electric Company. Housing and real estate, stores, malls and the old "downtown" shops all keep a careful watch on hiring and layoffs at the plant as they calculate their inventory and plan their sales. Pittsfield was chosen as a key center for studying blue-collar purchasing habits, and the sales rung up in the registers of the major supermarkets provide market analysts with an index to predict the popularity of goods throughout the U.S. Just as the rhythm of life is set by the daily occupations that absorb at least forty hours a week of the 12,000 people who are in the labor force, its counterpoint is the commercial traffic that occurs after work hours. The flow of traffic on the main arteries of East Street, Tyler and Dalton Streets swells at the shift changes at 7 a.m., 3 p.m. and 11 p.m. as thousands of workers hurry to the parking lots to rush off to the supermarkets or to their homes. Oftentimes couples with children have tightly calibrated schedules so when one arrives home to take over child care and household responsibilities, the other is rushing off to work. Supermarkets and chain outlets in the malls are geared to the working routines of production workers. Some of the food chains stay open around the clock and recent changes in the state codes for mercantile activity permit them to stay open on Sunday.

The changes that are occurring in the commercial sector tell a lot about the changing work force as the new young professionals take their places in Ordnance and Plastics Research and Development in the General Electric plant. Commercialization of all the basic and extended needs of life reflects the growing polarization of wealth in housing developments, clothing shops, supermarkets, restaurants and car lots. Ethnic identification is woven into the commercial life of the city as it is celebrated in fairs with the sale of foods and arts identified with national origins of immigrant populations. Religious holidays and patriotic days stimulate a market for costumes, floats, bugle bands and banners. Maintaining the commercial vitality of the city has become a central concern of the city officials as well as state and national political representatives as they try to promote the economic base to sustain these activities. In their efforts, salesmanship of the city to attract new enterprises has become a driving force in planning policies.

Neighborhoods and Commercial Development

Each section of Pittsfield has a special character formed by its past history combined with the reworking of those traditions by the current generation. Attachments to the landmarks that gave meaning and substance to one's formative years have become a recognized part of planning commissions that, in the sixties, would start with bulldozers and only think about what should come after when it was too late. These traditions are being reworked in the new commercialization of housing developments. Construction companies keep pace with the decreasing ability of those in low income brackets to buy new homes and the rising demand for high-income housing by rehabilitating old houses on the north and east side while building in colonial or Georgian styles in the more prestigious neighborhoods on the south side of town.

The outlines of old neighborhoods defined by the textile and paper mills are nearly obliterated as the growing commercial interests proliferate in shopping malls and housing tracts. One of the few surviving boarding houses of the Berkshire Woolen Mill was converted into a gourmet restaurant filled with the memorabilia of the Italian-American family that manages it. A Venetian panorama painted on the rear wall incorporates the likenesses of the proud owners. The row houses for workers in the nineteenth century mills were nearly all replaced in the early decades of this century by the duplexes and tenements built near the General Electric plant which attracted first generation immigrant families. The rent received from one half of the house paid off the owner's mortgage. Frequently relatives teamed up and bought these houses jointly. These houses have survived the generations of tenants who often lived under the guardianship of the owners. Theresa lives with her husband on the top floor of one of these houses and looks after her elderly tenants on the first floor to make sure that they are getting along allright. Al divided his duplex in half laterally, his brother living in the east wing and he and his wife in the west wing. Duplex arrangements such as these cultivate a more organic relationship among kin and even non-relatives than the statistics on independent households would suggest.

The tract housing built in the fifties in Morningside has gradually taken on the individuality of the homeowners as trees, ornamental bushes, porches, dormers and fences have modified each plot of land

and house. Pat lives with her husband and new baby in a Cape Cod cottage on a tree-lined street in one of these post–World War II developments. Lakewood, within a stone's throw of the General Electric plant, retains the strong neighborhood feeling that characterized it when Italians first settled and built their houses here. Nellie lives there with her mother and husband on Newell Street just across from the Kushis' mold-making business.

Somewhat to the west, on sites formerly occupied by mill housing, multiple-unit public housing built for veterans after World War II has been joined by trailer camps. The Polish population settled in the grid of streets radiating from North Street where they built their church and clubhouse. A bakery that sells Polish specialties serves a neighborhood where houses carefully maintained by workers abut rental units that the city redevelopment authority keeps threatening to demolish if their owners don't come back from Florida and fix them up. Despite the dim view that the city fathers hold of this part of town, some new construction of modest multiple-unit housing for rentals has been started. For the homeowners in an area where the only talk from city development people is of putting the by-pass through their neighborhood, the sound of the construction crews working late in the evening to meet the scheduled completion date for their bank loans is welcome. Alex, who lives here with his wife and three daughters in the house that he "owns with the bank," (while paying off his mortgage) commented, "That's music to my ears!"

Most of the new construction is on the south side of the city bordering Lee and Lenox. This is the preferred residential locations for managers, although only a few decades ago some workers like Vicky and John acquired old farmhouses on which they have lavished their skills and knowledge — in the gardens and the upkeep of their homes. The new houses built in courts off Holmes Road sell for $225,000 to $250,000. A development called Yankee Orchard Park off East Street, near where it joins South Street in Dalton, has thirty houses under construction that the developer expects to sell for $120,000 to $160,000 to highly-paid technicians and white-collar workers. In the forties Bus bought his fine old farmhouse nearby for a few thousand, but it was a big move for him then. The spurt in housing construction that began in 1984 and 1985 is related to the lower interest rate as well as the backlog of demand for houses. New housing reflects the increasing wealth differences of the population.

For over a decade the southwest side of town contained a vast crater along West Street, an old Italian neighborhood where kids living in crowded tenements above the bars and shoeshine parlor and corner groceries burst out in the street to watch the cops break up fights or carry off the drunks. Nelly's mother had a grocery store here where she helped many of the Italian families coming in to translate their documents. A few blacks were beginning to displace Italian families that were moving to the outskirts of town when it was demolished in the urban rehabilitation wave of the sixties. There has been little replacement for the two and three story buildings though the city with the help of the state built some brick mulitple-dwelling units for the elderly and those with low income on some of the land vacated. Sam lived here with his wife in an efficient one-bedroom apartment, with many shared recreational and communal rooms in the building. The supermarket built nearby in anticipation of new business and residential occupation closed down when the butchers struck for higher pay. Its new owners have seen business pick up as the newly constructed corporate headquarters have been filled with employees.

In this congeries of neighborhoods with a wide range of life styles it is hard to find that "whole way of life" that one could call a culture. Yet there is a coherence to the pattern that is, for the young, linked to the public schools within each neighborhood and associational life that draws together the adult population after their day's work or their life's work is over. Nelly's mother proudly asserted that you could play bingo seven days a week in Pittsfield. Whether it is bingo, board meetings of charitable institutions, body-building in the YMCA, aerobics in Morningside School, meetings in the union hall or the Atheneum, canoeing on the Housatonic, ice fishing on Lake Pontoosuc or duckhunting in the hills, these activities give purpose and meaning that people miss when they move elsewhere in search of a warmer climate or higher wages.

Buying and Selling

The reproduction of this cultural core requires a vast array of commercial enterprises, interspersed in the industrial landscape, that draw upon national and international sources to secure the many thousands of parts that go into building, maintaining, remodeling and restoring the houses, automobiles, garages, pools, sports arenas, public buildings, theatres and stores. Most men are engaged in do-it-yourself construction and remodeling projects that, though money-saving, depend upon the ability of individuals and families to acquire the cash for materials. The income related to the sale of one's labor power, professional skills or training is the primary basis that makes it possible

You Can Play Bingo Seven Days a Week in Pittsfield.

to meet the culturally-induced standards. Inability to perform in the labor market because of age, disability or childrearing responsibilities are partially mitigated by public and private development commissions and welfare agencies.

Driving north on scenic Route 7 after you cross the border from Connecticut into Massachusetts, you pass through the town of Great Barrington where Stanley put to use his first alternating current generator lighting its streets, leave behind the quaint villages of Stockbridge, Lenox and Lee, and feel a quickening in the tempo of commercial life. Motels, restaurants and shopping malls have larger signs drawing in visitors. A computer retail outlet has taken residence in one of these motels. Spacious tarmac parking lots invite the passing motorists to stop and fuel up, eat, spend money on a Mercedes Benz, a basket of fruit, shoes or clothes for the family. Factory outlets elbow fruit stands and automobile displays. A sign announces that you have arrived in Pittsfield, Plastics Technology Center of the World.

The extraordinary mix of elegant shopping and bargain basement spending, of thrift stores next to high fidelity recording and musical instruments stores, of fast food chains and pizza huts next to gourmet restaurants, of book stores and sports shops, is based on a vibrant commercial sector that mediates the cultural elements defining the different class, ethnic and generational groups. Industry coexists with commerce that responds to the consumption interests of managerial elite and production workers, as well as professionals, school teachers, tradespeople and artists who prefer the more vigorous mix of American Social groups that one finds in the more precious art centers in south county. This "hodgepodge," according to New York consultants who were hired by the city to encourage use of the commercial outlets, is not enough "upscale" to impress even local consumers let alone the visiting tourist.

The grid that defines Pittsfield's commercial activity is constituted by the compass point streets of North and South, that intersect with East and West streets at Park Square. There is little remaining of a once-thriving commercial sector on West Street, after the abortive move to rehabilitate it in the sixties. The Pyramid Corporation, a construction development group, proposed to build a multi-million dollar shopping plaza at the intersection of these major arteries that was defeated by a coalition of community activists and business intersets concerned with preserving the unique features of the community. The Bank of Boston building, the pride of Pittsfield in the centenary year of its founding, was the focal point for the fight against the mammoth mall project.

It has been restored to much of its original appearance except for the lost mansard roof. Occasionally the local press prints photographs of the old West Street, and many long for a return of the three- and four-story buildings that contained many small shops and the offices of professional people who moved out of the center of town as zoning laws changed and individual car ownership permitted a wider dispersion of shopping. People particularly lament the loss of the railroad station, a stone building of unusual design that took full advantage of the skills of Italian construction workers who had recently arrived in 1907 when it was built. A small shelter for the one passenger train with a brief stopover in the city replaces what was once a terminal for north, south, east and west traffic.

The tract called Parcel 3 became the focus of a great deal of conflict and nostalgia for the old shops — Curtin's Package Store, Gaetani's Barbershop, M and J Shoeshine Parlor, Pickwick Hotel, Jack Mulcare Motor Supply, Dearstyne Brothers Tobacco, Berkshire Fish, Smith Brothers Coal and Oil, Angelina's Submarine Shop tucked in with the Haddad Motor Sales and Smith's Supersonic Carwash — that were demolished in the 1960s. If preserved, they might have been restored to the contemporary version of a quaint New England village as in Stockbridge or Lee to the south of the city. The developers of the eighties are aware of the great loss. William J. Angelo, who worked on the mayor's downtown development committee when we interviewed him in 1984, is most cognizant of this:

> Twenty-five years ago, North and West street were complementary to each other, like two limbs of a body. Take this (showed a picture of cars parked along a busy West Street) they were like two lungs of a body. And now it's hard for one to work without the other. In addition to having a number of stores and shops down on West Street, there were three major restaurants and a train station in a half mile. It was a very, very beautiful, quintessential New England type of town. That was destroyed in the old 1967 urban type of philosophy. And they took down a lot of houses around there. They destroyed them. That was basically the economic base for downtown Pittsfield. They did their business downtown. They wiped them out of there, and they wiped out a lot of the stores and you're operating on one lung. Now it's come back to a philosophy we think is appropriate to downtown Pittsfield. There are plenty of shopping plazas to go around, but Pittsfield is different.

The outlook of those who shape the architectural outlines of a city

today differs considerably from that of the sixties, when removal and
new construction, not renewal, was the guiding theme. The revitalization plan announced by the mayor in June 1985 was a modest contribution by the city of $20,000 and a call for $60,000 from businesses
along North Street. It was the climax of three years of small changes
affecting the facades of several buildings and a major reconstruction
of the bridge that spans the railroad crossing. The two cinemas that
could no longer attract a capacity audience were scheduled for conversion, one to a theatre for the blossoming Berkshire Public Playhouse.
Morgenstern's Clothing, The Candy Place, Soda Chef and Ruffer
Realtors occupy a one-story block where the individuality of each
business can emerge in the signs and displays. A three-story building
was imaginatively renovated to include a beauty parlor and a shoestore
in the basement, bookstore and clothing store on the ground floor and
restaurant on top. North Street was, one owner of a haberdashery
proclaimed, a success story when the Male Ego was burned out and
returned to another site on North Street.

The transformation of old and new styles of consumption related
to the changing composition of the work force is continually reflected
in the changing retail stores along North Street. Kay's Coats and
Richman's Cards reopened on North Street, and several businesses
including The Candy People, Either/Or Books, Taylor's Sound and
Pittsfield Sporting Goods have expanded. Mod, Mod World, Boutique
134, Luv Bug and New Concepts Fabrics coexist with older businesses
like James Jewelers and Englands. These names denote the changing
trend in retailing that promotes an escapist world of image making
rather than relying on established family names. A new park sports
iron work and old fashioned lamps that cultivate the reappearance of
New England charm. When North Street was finally able to reopen
all lanes of traffic in 1984 the mayor cut the ribbon to the sound of the
Royal Garden Jazz Band as cider and apples were handed out in the
crisp October evening. The re-emergence of the mall wars in 1986,
when Pyramid made a successful bid to take its project to the neighboring town of Lanesboro, again threatened the revitalized mainstreet.
The main anchor to the downtown shopping center was lost when
England's, the main department store for a century, decided to go out
of business.

Tyler Street is probably as commercially active as North Street, but
it is even more diverse in its business establishments and less planned
in its development than North Street, where the government-aided
programs are concentrated. This is a street that expresses the American

Small Businesses Flourished on Tyler Street. (Picture by William H. Tague.)

dream of owning your own business, from the bars and pizza houses to the bookstore, pet shop, boat sales, carpet store, bathroom fixtures, hardware store, antique and used furniture stores, gas stations and a Chinese laundry. One of those who succeeded is Anthony Crea, who started Frank's Berkshire Marine on Tyler Street with a $10,000 investment twenty-five years ago and built it into a $1.5 million dollar business by 1982 and who was featured in an article in *The Berkshire Eagle* (August 29, 1983) about this neglected street. Some businesses that got their start on Tyler Street went to the more prestigious North Street when they became established. While some call the street "tacky," its low rents encourage the kind of diversified entrepreneurship that is the mark of a vigorous commercial life.

East Street merchants benefit from the trade of General Electric workers on their way out of the main building. Lunch rooms and gas stations cater to the needs of workers on the job, and hardware, gardening supply stores and construction supplies provide them with the materials for the many projects with which they are constantly involved after work. Automobile sales stores, power equipment of all kinds, chain saws, plumbing installations are all available here to fashion and refashion the well-maintained houses and gardens that impress the visitor to this city. A Goodwill store recycles the goods that one party discards and others find useful.

Beyond these arteries lie the shopping malls in what was once the meadowlands of Allendale Farm and the Coltsville paper factory. In the swampy area where only billboards stood before World War II and where Carl and his friends sought shelter to plan the organization of the union, the great sprawl of chains grew up in response to a rising consumer market after the war. Only a stone marker on a miniscule triangular park bearing the names of Coltsville boys in the service is a reminder of the past neighborhood that surrounded the old factory. Most of these shopping plazas attract the big chains such as Bradley's and Zayre's that have sprung up in the same arenas as the old catalogue outlets like Sears Roebuck. At Christmas time some of the chains stayed open twenty-four hours, where, newspapers announce, you can shop until you drop in the frenzied atmosphere of the season. Brooks Drugs, Price Chopper and Stop and Shop provide incredible displays of the world's goods that flow in an unending stream into the city. In Berkshire County as a whole in 1985, people spent 169 million dollars on food, nine million on drugs, eight million on health and beauty products, seven million on household appliances, four million on TV, seven million on audio equipment, six million on furniture, twenty-six

Huge supermarkets have taken over the malls in what was Coltsville.

and a half million on men's and boys clothing, thirty-five and a half million on women's and girls' clothing and ten million on footwear. Another fifty-two million went to restaurants, sixty million to gas stations, seventy-four million on automotive equipment and thirty-five million on building and hardware material. The expenditure of one-third of all retail sales on food reveals the strong weighting of a blue-collar, family-oriented consumption pattern in the budget expenditures.

The commercial life of a city is a visible index to changing life styles. In the lands once occupied by farms, factories and warehouses of nineteenth century industry, the spread of malls in the 1950s and 1960s were a sign of the greater affluence and wider spread of incomes. Today the competitive "mall wars" of the 1970s and 1980s result from commercial activity promoted by construction developers removed from the real needs of the communities they serve. In Pittsfield the Pyramid construction corporation is developing a site only a few miles from the Allendale shopping mall constructed in the Coltsville area shortly after World War II. When their bid was accepted by the neighboring town of Lanesboro, Pittsfield accepted the offer of a competitor, Simon Associates, to build an alternative site just south of the proposed Pyramid project of the late 1970s. Pyramid won this round and was able to prevail over environmentalists, who opposed building sites on wetlands, and those concerned with the downtown area. The victory of the malls is a defeat of the old multi-functional areas close to residential areas where owner-operated shops provided the cultural materials for a local interpretation of nationally celebrated holidays and family celebrations of birthdays, anniversaries, weddings and graduations. Interspersed with lunch counters in J. J. Newberry's and restaurants, North Street provided havens for the retired or youthful unemployed where they could sit and get warm in a place where they met others in their own condition or where the tellers and clerks from banks and shops could relax away from the job without a boss's supervision. The behavior of people in malls is highly coded, directed toward specific purchases. Dominated by chain stores leased by corporate owners, they drive out of business the small shop owners who provided space for the scout's cookie sales or church raffles, and who extended credit to striking workers. The annual fund drives for various charitable organizations and leafletting by quasi-political organizations have been warned off of the malls in what may be a curtailment of the first amendment, as yet not recognized by society.

Fairs, Celebrations, and the Associational Life of the City

Pittsfield's celebration of religious festivals and national holidays is intimately linked to the commercial interests of the city. Parades follow the major shopping route of the old downtown center on North Street. Whole shops and departments of larger stores are devoted to the masks, costumes, cards and reminders of sacred and secular events. Industries and shops underwrite the expenses of bands and floats, and public figures often participate in the parades.

Here I shall consider only Halloween and the city-organized art fair and ethnic week to show how the dialectic of commercial reproduction of the culture responds to individual needs and societal selection of significant events. Because of their particular relationship to the military-industrial complex, Memorial Day and the Fourth of July will be described in Chapter 8.

Halloween

Halloween had already devolved into a children's celebration with tricks and pranks the order of the day when the first parade was inaugurated in Pittsfield in 1923 "to keep the young from tearing the town apart,'' (Willison 1957:134). For this first celebration, General Electric workers made a huge, self-propelled dragon accompanied by monsters lit up with thousands of the electric light bulbs that they still made in the factory. The tradition was maintained as the parade grew to accommodate school children, veteran's groups, local businesses, and was sponsored by the recreation department and *The Berkshire Eagle*. The transformation of the city from an industry dominated town to a commercially oriented economy can be seen in the changes in Halloween.

The construction of the floats and the preparation of the costumes for those who join the parade on foot or on one of the many trucks requires weeks of planning and collective effort. Two magic and costume stores that operate year round have a wide variety of masks and clothing to replicate Mae West, Cleopatra, flappers, gangsters, werewolves, devils and witches, Batman, Spiderman and a complete line of animals from elephants to butterflies. The General Electric display was always the one most anticipated until it was discontinued in 1957. As I got in line to view the start of the 1982 parade, one of the men who had worked on the dragon in 1957 said it was a block long and carried a dozen witches. Macy's even wanted to buy it and put it in their Thanksgiving Day parade, but General Electric didn't agree to that.

Hundreds of people lined the street, mostly kids and their parents, the smaller ones sitting patiently on the curb clutching balloons. Some of the spectators wore costumes. The Pittsfield High School band entered from the Girls' Club on East Street promptly at 7 o'clock followed by the fire truck loaded with trick-or-treaters in a variety of costumes. A float with witch- and pumpkin-headed children followed and then a walking hoard of trick-or-treaters holding strings so they wouldn't get lost, followed on foot. The leader of the next group was a kid with legs upside down on his head. Cheerleaders for the Lee High band in orange and black preceeded the Sacred Heart float. ET, the movie character from outer space, was popular in several floats, and there were girls in middle-Eastern attire and an extraterrestial group with ape beaks and sunglasses. A whole troop of kids wearing shiny plastic smocks made of garbage bags and sprouting bug-like antennae from their heads walked while a witchmobile with ghosts in sheets, witches and a ''Spooky bus'' drove by filled with ghosts shining flashlights. The crowd gave a good applause to the Wahconah Regional High School jazz band and to an ambitious ''Kid Konstructed'' pirate ship with many pirates and clowns on deck.

A huge Mack truck carrying a massive foam figure titled "A Hallowe'en Troll" was driven by as shrieks issued from the interior. The themes, worked out in commercial enterprises and in the schools with parents assisting the teachers, who supervise the children after school hours in making the costumes, are wide-ranging interpretations of what is in in popular culture. It is an exciting event, particularly for children, and engages their imagination more than any other public event. The projection of another identity, the essence of putting on a costume, is the attractive element for the young children especially. But the enthusiasm for the General Electric float that used to be the central part of the parade shows another element in the work scene that overcame the alienation of the workers. For many workers who told me about these past creations, it seemed that 1957 was not only the last year that they made the float, but it was also the last year when Power Transformer was in its glory as the principle unit of the local plant and the largest producer of power transformers in the world.

Artabout and the Ethnic Fair

Two themes that have been pushed to lure some of the tourists up from south county and get people off the beaches and into the stores are the Artabout and the Ethnic Fair. Each event differs in content and representation, but the format is similar. In 1982 North Street was roped off from auto traffic and a staging was set up. Performances ranged from Bach to rock and actors from the surrounding summer theatres joined featured artists in the Artabout celebration. The cultural attractions of the Berkshires were given an opportunity to draw a new audience from that tuned in through high-culture outlets and the upper-class tourist hotels.

The Ethnic Fair celebrated the varieties of cultures that had come to make up the work force for the factories. It took me two performances in sequential years to see the underlying dynamic. The main show was the ethnic dances. These were performed by folk dance groups hired by ethnic associations such as the ITAM lodge. In contrast to Third World ethnic arts, where people transform certain of their native themes to something that will find a market with tourists, ethnic groups in America become a market for an all ready commoditized version of their culture. There were few spontaneous entries in these highly-scheduled performances. A polka orchestra stirred some passers-by to dance and the Vietnamese bride of a veteran stirred more of the audience to applaud, but the most active involvement in the production of their culture were the Afro-Americans who sold southern American and African food in a booth with musicians drawing crowds with African music.

The celebration of ethnicity is a recognition of the effectiveness of corporate hegemony in drawing the immigrant populations into the mainstream of American life. Although many of the cultural traits of their ethnic identity were suppressed at an earlier time, these are now valued emblems of the roots they are rediscovering. But in that discovery, the ethnically uprooted people who came to work in the construction gangs and factories have become consumers of ethnic arts now, for the most part, produced by others.

Selling Pittsfield

The logic of competitive salesmanship to bolster the economy has entered into and defined the way public and private agencies are responding to the crisis caused by deindustrialization. The Pittsfield Chamber of Commerce has joined with city officials and political representatives at state and national levels to promote a campaign for "selling Pittsfield" to attract new industrial and commercial enterprises. Even the community relations agents for the General Electric Company that formerly discouraged competition for labor in the area are now actively cooperating in the campaign. This logic, visible in the construction corporations' promotion of ever-greater shopping malls discussed above, is central to the emerging hegemonic action that dominates policy making in the city. I shall trace this development in the Chamber of Commerce promotion of the city for new business, the city officials planning for development, political party programs for stimulating enterprises, and the General Electric Company's agenda in the changing economy of the city.

The Chamber of Commerce

The voice of the commercial sector is the Chamber of Commerce, which includes 700 businesses, 500 of them small — under five million capitalization. The director, James W. Wallace saw his part in the revitalization of the economy as one of accumulating statistics to show growth potential, and of promoting legislation in the local, state and federal government to enhance the business climate. When we first spoke to him in 1982 the unemployment rates had gone from 7 percent in February 1981 to 8.5 percent in February 1982 and jumped another point in April. He saw this as the major problem, remarking that it had stimulated some communication between unions and businessmen.

As a result there had been government-backed proposals with concrete aid. "The Chamber of Commerce does not do anything by itself," he said. "We are, if you pardon the expression, a pimp, bringing together people pivotal in change — businessmen with politicians." I asked if this included unions and he agreed. I learned later in the conversation that by unions he related primarily to the construction industry, where contractors operate like individual enterprises.

When we spoke to him again in 1984 he was more optimistic. The decision by General Electric to base its world headquarters for plastics research and development in the city was expected to attract other small plastics industries. Ordnance was "going crazy" and bringing in high-tech jobs.

Jim's philosophy diverged from the usual homilies about a Chamber of Commerce outlook. Assessing the outlook of the area, he said:

> The pluralistic system is the basis of the strength of our country. The minority around here are vocal enough to prevent any new development and to maintain a pluralistic base. The corporation people who stay on here are not willing to change. There is a pride and slight hint of damn Yankee — a mountain outlook. "We like it — you can go home." They slam the door to those outside. A couple might come in with income and education, but they are not always welcomed.

Trying to overcome this isolationism is one of the tasks he has set for his team. He criticized the people who objected to developments like the Lakecrest condominium project, a $20 million dollar residence facility that he saw as broadening the tax base and providing a second home for people who would pay $125,000 dollars for a unit. "The Ridge Avenue crowd got into this and opposed it because they do not want traffic."

> A small minority gets active and fights things, and there isn't a vocal opposition to them that could get it going. With the by-pass [a projected connector road to the Massachusetts Turnpike] over the last thirty years there have been neighborhood groups all over the city who try to prevent development in their back yard.... Many of the environmentalist groups are defending their own backyard; green is a smokescreen for privilege. Anything will get opposition. And those who might benefit by this with new jobs, they are a relaxed, not a vociferous reaction.

Jim's office is the main thrust behind the campaign to sell Pittsfield to potential enterprises. His office arranges for the wining and dining that Mayor Smith gladly leaves to him. He reflects the optimism the other town leaders expressed and is a strong booster of the Berkshires, pointing to the "fascinating blend of rural and urban" characteristics, the fine arts programs and schools of the arts and "a quality of life that is mindboggling." Its potential, he said, can be seen in the fact that it is a metropolitan area 262nd in size but 62nd in median income. He expressed the heightened awareness of the need to attract the kind of industry that will preserve the mix of rural and urban element that makes the area attractive both to tourists and the new professionals they are trying to lure in. The town itself was becoming increasingly segmented, with the earlier Downing Park near the Power Transformer Division on the east side of town considered a lower-level operation and the newly-zoned area near the airport on the west of town for more glamorous high-tech industries. Jim painted a picture of this future development in glowing terms:

> Picture yourself on the 128 strip [Route 128 outside of Boston with the heavy concentration of high-tech businesses] or down in New York, and, "Hey, Mr. Corporate Executive, here you should locate in the City of Pittsfield of the Central Berkshire Area." His first question is going to be, "Well, O.K. where?" "Well, gee, that's really a very good question. Where are you going go put it?" What I've been saying is that we've been taking some very positive steps, and we have positive answers. Here's where you're going to go, and here are the financing programs available to you, and here are the tax programs that are available to you, here are the training programs that are available to you, and hey, the public sector, the private sector in the community are working together. We're going to work in your behalf, and we're going to make it happen. So it's a totally different animal that's starting to appear from my perspective and I want to see it continue. I think that there is a much more positive attitude between the business community and the mayor. I think the mayor's been working very hard with us, and we've been working hard to work with him, and it's going to happen. There's no question in my mind. It's exciting to watch the barriers fall. Slowly. This is the Berkshires.

The last obstacle that the leaders in the revitalization movement see ahead is failure on the part of much of the populace to envision this developed future. "We have to think of things much more positively," Jim stated bluntly, "[and] not badmouth ourselves. I think we have to sell ourselves to people in the Berkshires before we can go outside the area."

City Planning for Development

Despite the signs of revitalization in the eighties, a declining population that dipped from 51,974 in the 1980 census to 50,395 in 1984 and went below 50,000 in 1985 cued city officials to problems that the mayor tried to address. A drop below the 50,000 level in the next federal census would mean a loss in the block grants that the city was using to attract employers. City clerks made a special effort to record every resident, emphasizing the importance in permanent resident status to receive Social Security, nursing home care and other benefits. A campaign to encourage newly-hired employees of local enterprises to live in Pittsfield was one part of a redevelopment planning program to promote residence through more jobs.

At the same time, real estate property values were climbing, from $696,335,990 in 1980 to $839,826,898 in 1983, somewhat more than inflation levels. The new, higher-paid positions at General Electric, Beloit Jones and Sheaffer Eaton were bringing in buyers "who did not flinch at 13 percent or 14 percent mortgage interest rates" when they come in from higher-priced real estate market areas (*The Berkshire Eagle* November 5, 1984). Commercial real estate was increasing in value after a long slump. One realtor almost tripled his price for a two-story building on North Street between 1983 and 1985. While realtors looked at each other in amazement, they were quoted as saying, "What happened here?" "It's crazy!" "Twenty percent jump in 18 months!" others were concerned with a bursting of the balloon (ibid.).

While inflation was skyrocketing in the private sector, the total city budget of $40.8 million in 1984 had changed only slightly over the 1974 $39.1 million for the major departments of education, parks and recreation, the Housing Authority, licensing board, law, public health, buildings, planning board, public works, water department, veterans' services, police and fire departments. This was a period of rapidly rising costs, and the reductions represent a loss of services that go to the less-privileged citizens. In the public health department, the clerical staff was reduced by one-third; schools were reduced by 207 employees in the 1982–83 period; public works were cut from a $5½ million budget in 1983 to 2 million in 1984; and in the same period firefighters were reduced by fifteen from the staff of 122 employees. The police department benefitted from a reduction in crimes from 7,582 in 1982 to 6,951 with the greatest reduction in the crimes against persons. Skeptics attributed it to the loss of youthful males in the population; they have the highest propensity to commit crimes.

Mayor Smith put the greatest part of his attention on the development and planning office headed in 1984 by Bill Angelo. The sentiment that he was anti-business during his first term of office because of his opposition to the huge shopping mall on North Street turned around in 1983 when General Electric approved the construction of the Plastics Research Center. The development office succeeded in converting two of the schools that were closed because of a declining enrollment into small businesses, and in opening up two industrial parks, one near the airport and the other on land donated by a hardware company (Chapter 6). The city put in the sewer and water lines as well as street lighting and access roads to the industrial park, and contributed to the credit needs of the new businesses with state and local financing. The lots in one park sold for $10,000 each, all bought within six months.

The mayor's committee is coordinated with the Chamber of Commerce, but they have independent responsibilities. "We're delivering the sites, and the Chamber is going to market outside the county. It's a kind of hand-in-glove operation," Bill Angelo told us. The mayor set up a program for matching city funds with private dollars for "those wining and dining functions, bringing those chief executives and their families in and introducing them and letting them stay here a while at a suite in the hotel, and letting them enjoy our facilities, and our cultural activities, and all of our recreation, and let them know about our quality of life here." That role, the mayor said, is for the Chamber of Commerce. For a mayor to play that role would be counteractive to his image as a public servant concerned with all the people. He wanted to avoid the "bigwigs" and let the private sector take care of the sales pitch while he concentrated on the administrative work. He summed up some of his achievements while in office:

> One of the things that you've probably noticed about Pittsfield is that we're rather innovative and we're not afraid to take a chance on something that's innovative and something that will save some dollars. For example, we built our Vicon facility where we burn all of our rubbish and sell the steam to Crane and Co. And it happens to be the best and most efficient facility in the world... And it works very well. No more land fill, now, no more dumps in the city of Pittsfield. We're also in the process of bidding for a water improvement facility for twenty million dollars, a water filtration system, and also a plant that will improve all of our water, which hasn't been improved for years. We're using a brand new process called Krofta Process, invented by Dr. Krofta, a local engineering firm in Lenox. We were originally going to build a water infiltration plant which was going to cost us forty million dollars. With Dr. Krofta's system, it's only going to cost us eight million dollars. This will equalize the pressure throughout the city. So these are the kinds of things

that industry and business look at, and they see that kind of progress, and they see all of the things that we're doing to benefit that.

The mayor considers himself to be very non-partisan and willing to work with all. In his efforts to gain development of the commercial and industrial basis, he made every effort to avoid being "tagged as big-business oriented" and to relate to the working-class people so that "everything that you're doing when you're helping business and industry and the large corporations is to ensure them that they have jobs and that their children have jobs and that everything is directed for the working mass."

In line with this philosophy, the mayor made sure that representatives of labor are on all the boards and commissions related to development planning. "They feel more comfortable feeling that their people are represented in what happens and have some say in it," he said. When Proposition 2½ came in limiting the increases in municipal spending, the mayor called in a management study team that, he said, is working very well. They have "eliminated all the fat and cut all the deadwood," making each department more efficient in the reorganization. He said he was able to maintain 90 percent of the city services including the schools while cutting 45 percent of the budget over a three year period. Human services, he claimed, were not cut at all. It was his own personal goal to see that anyone in need was taken care of:

> I just feel that any leader in any community has a responsibility to the citizens who are in need, to see that they are taken care of. You can't have people out there who are hurting and having needs and suffering because they can't make it. I think that's important. You have to see that the people are comfortable and pleased. I have a tremendous relationshiop with the elderly and I try to provide not only the elderly but also the poor and the handicapped. I try to provide them with as many services as I possibly can in order that they are comfortable.

In the face of economic decline in the blue-collar industries, the mayor, the development committee, the Chamber of Commerce and other agencies are rethinking the town. The new conception involves a changed facade for the commercial sector and a hegemonic control that relates to different people. The way Bill Angelo sees it is that the town is moving from "a tank town to a white-collar, very professional yuppie type with Ordnance and with plastics." As a result of General Electric bringing in a lot of high-priced talent, the whole outlook of the city is changing, he feels. There is an increased demand for artistic and cultural resources and a developing interest in art, theatre and the ballet. He expects to attract a "very high-class business." Both he and the mayor would like to bring in a "Wang or a Digital" plant, but felt that "they have to exercise care not to compete with existing vested interests." Neither Wang nor Digital is unionized.

Mayor Smith also saw the same problem that Jim Wallace pointed to — the need to cultivate local pride in "selling" the city:

> Well, we're doing all the things we can to promote our city and to sell our city. I think one of the toughest things was to sell it to our own people. You know you have a tendency to take things for granted when you live here all your own life. You take it for granted that it's beautiful here. We have four seasons and beautiful recreation areas to take advantage of all of them.... Oh, we've done all kinds of things. We've worked very closely since I've been in office with the arts to promote the arts in this city. We were very instrumental in getting Berkshire Public Theatre underway. And that brings industry in too, because people in industry like to feel that everything is there for them.

The mayor's challenger in the 1985 elections criticized his handling of Proposition 2½, saying that he caused the collapse of city government in the process. The voter turnout for Smith, who got twice the votes of his opponent, reaffirmed the support of Pittsfield's citizens in the wavering economic setting.

The impact of the combined effort of public and private agencies courting new enterprises may be "robbing Peter to pay Paul," as Margaret Pantridge of *The Berkshire Eagle* (November 20, 1985) staff commented on the case she calls "The Courting of Kay-Bee." Kay-Bee, a chain of children's toy stores, that had previously employed 200 people in the neighboring town of Lee was seeking new corporate headquarters for its outlets. In the desire to develop Parcel 3 behind the Boston Bank building on West Street, the Pittsfield Central City Development Corp. urged the mayor to provide tax incentives under Chapter 121A of the state laws as well as free land and site preparations on the underveloped remaining part of the lot to lure Kay-Bee to Pittsfield.

While negotiations were proceeding, there were rumbles of discontent in the "Letters to the Editor" column. Julian N. Lichtman of Richmond (*The Berkshire Eagle*) objected to public money going to a corporation in a free enterprise system that "meant companies and individuals use their own money to erect buildings, buy equipment and pay taxes." He called this welfare to business an example of a zero-sum game "where nothing is created, merely moved from one place to another with taxpayers footing the bill."

The courtship proved successful and on the vacant lot in the shadow of the bank building where the homeless used to congregate a luxurious building rose up to shelter the new corporate "welfare" recipient.

Political Party Promotion of the Business Climate

Politics at the local level requires an adroit management of particular issues relevant to one's constituency combined with the ability to reflect party programs going on at national and international levels. Improving the business climate is accepted by both labor interests and business and corporate leaders as the most important target in the mid-eighties. This is the crux of corporate hegemony in maintaining a dominant position in political and economic life.

State representatives were careful to back some of the local initiatives mentioned by Mayor Smith. The Republican Senator Peter C. Webber took some of the credit for getting state funds to back the industrial parks and other projects involved with downtown development. He supports financial assistance to businesses, an issue that has not been challenged by the unions, even though many of the entrepreneurs helped by these projects reject labor organizations. His goal, like that of the mayor, is to sell the area to potential businessmen:

> We need to market the area. There are industries in the state that have labor shortages and are looking to expand.... It's a good place to live. I've tried to get some of our colleges around here to actually quantify it so we can use that to actually go out to sell.... We need a basic outreach where we can identify, with the help of state leaders, those companies which are looking to expand, go out and invite them here, and show them what we've got. Visiting sites, financing, tax benefits and also transportation, those kinds of things. All the pieces are there, site inventory, that is all done and we should be reaching out and bringing them in. Clearly we've got to hold on to the jobs we have here the best we can. We have to help the companies struggling, and things that are beyond the forces of anyone's control.

Republicans and Democrats fundamentally agree on what the solutions should be, although they differ in their emphasis on the kinds of industries needed. Senator Webber tended to support industries such as tourism and publishing that would "fit in the Berkshires" more than the large production facilities that unions prefer to increase blue-collar employment. State Representative Robert F. Jakubowicz, a

Democrat, supported the industrial park along with the senator and the mayor, but he mentioned in addition to tourism and publishing the continued need to get new product lines into the General Electric plant. He was more concerned than the senator that many of the enterprises brought in to the industrial parks were non-union, and that there were generally a low level of pay.

> This is my personal view, and maybe it's completely wrong, but it seems to be that instead of — sure, everyone would like to see that factory with the 1,500 jobs — I think that we should forget about that, and think about what practically can we do here. What you're really going to have to try to do is sell people on coming here as a nice place to live, not necessarily the blue-collar people, but to get something here that's going to attract other industries on a small scale. We did have a publishing firm that went out of business. I don't know how you do it, but it seems to me on at least the drawing board, to target the kind of business or industry you want, and then that's where state government can pass special legislation and make the effort to reel them in.

These differences in emphasis mask a basic adherence to the logic of capitalist reproduction. Both are, in the words of Jakubowicz, "trying to preserve what we have, because we're losing what we have, and then of course trying to get something new." That "something new" included the industrial parks, the improvement of the downtown shopping area and a by-pass artery for the inter-city traffic. When we asked him whether he felt that most of the development effort was bipartisan, he explained concretely what the procedure was:

> Well, what happened was that Bill Angelo, who is our — well, I don't know what they call his office, Economic Development? they keep on changing the names — contacted both myself and the state senator early last year, and he came to a meeting with the city administration and showed the idea at least for the proposal. Bill was informed at that time to get the thing set up, in other words, get the proper zoning, assurances from the people that they're not going to object to this because there were objections to the traffic, running in the water lines, that kind of thing. Bill went back and put all these things together, and he came back, and we again sat down and talked. This took us to the point where the city council said they were going to consider this thing very seriously. Every time the governor came out here we lobbied him and took him around to different people, and the governor partly committed himself to say, "Yes, I'll come up with the money." Then it was just whether he would find the money from federal dollars or from

state monies, and they just made a decision about a month ago that it would be state dollars. They would want an environmental impact study and it would delay the time tables. So I don't know what you want to call that, partisanship or whatever. It was essentially Bill Angelo, the state senator, and myself who initiated it. Well, we with the initiative of Bill, took it to the governor and walked it along.

Hegemonic relations require this carefully orchestrated, bipartisan action to ensure reproduction of the infrastructure for private capitalist expansion. There is no basic disagreement on what should be done, although the rhetoric about who should do it and whom it should serve changes. Everyone agrees that the city should be ''sold'' to private entrepreneurs who would bring in industry. Senator Webber and Representative Robert Jakubowicz were rated as the two top business supporters in the county selected by a foundation composed of chief executive officers from all kinds of businesses. Their rating was based on an analysis of voting records on pro-business bills, with Senator Webber having a 1984 voting record of 73.44 percent pro-business and Representative Jakubowicz 59.91.

The most successful candidate in relating to local constituency is Silvio O. Conte, who won his fourteenth race for Congress in 1984. The son of an Italian-American who worked many years as a General Electric foreman, Conte married the daughter of a French-Canadian from Springfield, thus, as one of my interviewees told me, sewing up both the major geographic and ethnic populations in his constitutency, which stretches from Springfield and the east to Pittsfield on the west.

Given his background, it is anomolous that he is a Republican in what had been a solid Democratic district. His responsiveness to his constituency and the powerful position he occupies as a senior congressman in the House of Representatives enables him to retain his position in the Republican camp while keeping a labor vote. He balances his votes — backing the first Reagan budget but voting against aid to the Contras in Nicaragua — in a way that minimizes the opposition and cultivates his stronghold with a mix of blue-collar voters and professional liberals. He makes every effort to direct federal spending to industries in western Massachusetts, introducing an amendment in a 1986 energy bill designed to give U. S. manufacturers an edge in price competition against foreign competition. (*The Berkshire Eagle* June 18, 1986). Each defense contract that is awarded to the local General Electric plant is announced through Conte's office. Yet he has also been a strong advocate of a freeze on defense spending to cut the budget deficit. As a representative in a state where education is a major

industry, he is a strong supporter of colleges and educational institutions, fighting for increased appropriations and the guaranteed student
loans that benefit the lower and middle classes. In recognition of this,
he has received sixteen honorary awards from educational institutions.
In a congressional district with a large elderly population, he sponsored
the low-income fuel-assistance program and the Social Security disability legislation as well as the cost-of-living increases for Social
Security recipients. In an economic setting where women make up a
large proportion of the work force, he supported ERA and sent personal
response letters to all those who urged him to vote for the bill. He listed
as his supporters in his last campaign the major unions in the area,
educational organizations, Veterans of Foreign Wars and environmentalists. His success can be measured in the 2.7 to 1 lead over his
opponent in the 1984 election.

In spite of his support for what are called ''special interest constituencies,'' the business community thinks of him as their strongest
champion. One leading representative of that community told us:

> I'm not sure I totally like all of Sil Conti's programs, or all of his
> spending. In his behalf, he's caught in the same trap as everyone
> else is. The one thing I will say is business in Massachusetts, and
> our district in particular, has a real friend there. I know people don't
> recognize the power that he wields. He put together a panel for
> businesses to visit in Washington, he does this every two years,
> but I went for the first time this year, and I will sell the heck out
> of it for my membership the next time around. When you see the
> director of the Federal Reserve, Secretary Regan, as head of the
> treasury, and when you see the director of the EPA, who's a tall
> dangling guy and with a tremendous sense of humor, and when
> you see George Shultz, and Secretary Doyle, all on the same
> program and that's only four, there were five, all rounded up in
> one day, that says to me that we should re-elect this man as long
> as possible, because of the unbelievable amount of power at his
> disposal, which he has focused for his constituency in western
> Massachusetts.

The function this businessman refers to, called the Business-
Government Leadership Symposium, attracts ''some of the most
influential political leaders on both sides of the congressional aisles,''
according to Margaret Pantridge in the local press (*The Berkshire Eagle*
May 24, 1986). Schultz asked the audience what he, as secretary of
state, was doing at a business symposium, but the purpose was made
clear when Conte said the secretary of state told him of the need to
up appropriations for foreign aid and embassy security as he escorted

him to the Congress. For Conte it provides "a very clear message to his constituents that he has an incredible amount of power and influence," a former state representative told the reporter. Democrats relate more to working-class constituents than their Republican counterparts and this support was organized through the unions. When Senator Ted Kennedy comes to Pittsfield on the campaign trail, he always touches base with the IUE. Al Litano introduced him to the meeting of retired and active workers in the IUE hall in April 1981 as a person who always showed cooperation in his assistance with labor problems. John F. Kennedy's portrait still hangs over the podium in the main auditorium, and Litano told the audience that "some people called this place the Kennedy altar."

Senator Kennedy addressed the concern that "the working men and women see that their purchasing power over recent years has been diminished despite efforts to get cost-of-living increases in their contracts." He berated the presidential incumbent, without naming him, for his attack on Social Security and the safety net for the aged, his withdrawal of student aid "to go to some of the fine schools and colleges in our state of Massachusetts," and for the reduction in home-care funding. He related the turn from human resource programs to the insensitivity to the concerns of labor. The reduction in unemployment compensation, he said, forces people who are heads of households to take on minimum-wage jobs when their unemployment compensation runs out after only thirteen weeks. The cutbacks in these programs assisting workers occurred at a time when the oil companies, the tobacco industry and other special interests were getting even higher subsidies. Contrasting the tax reduction of $140 for the family making $10,000 a year with $25,000 reduction to "those of you who are making $200,000 a year" [laughter] he concluded his speech by saying that he intended to fight to make sure that the benefits of a tax reduction for individuals would be spread to the middle-income people of Massachusetts and the nation, and that the senior citizens would gain the recognition due them from someone who recognized their needs because his own mother was ninety-three.

Political speeches, like the political action that is related to them, are geared to special interest groups. This reinforces the sense one has in Pittsfield of the segmentation of age, sex and to a lesser extent, class groups that prefer to have their special interests addressed. It is considered appropriate for candidates to personalize their predilection for serving a particular group because of their own personal commitments. This contradicts some of the assumptions about increasingly universalistic criteria of action with industrialization, and it certainly contradicts a rising class consciousness. Most Pittsfield citizens have found their own niche and direct their political activities toward preserving it. The successful politicians in the region seem to have picked up on this theme, whether they are Republicans or Democrats, and are able to act within these boundaries to reconstruct in their own behavior the corporate hegemonic relations that their own and their constituents' lives.

General Electric's Community Relations Agenda

Just as General Electric has institutionalized the role of labor relations, so has it institutionalized the role of community relations. As public relations became more demanding in the 1980s the job of the relations staff in ''selling'' a good image of the corporation became ever more important.

My requests for information were turned over to this public relations department. In the six-year period of my study, I perceived a change in the character and approach of the three community relations managers I interviewed. In 1978, the manager of community relations to whom I spoke was an affable, well-informed man who had come to the area in 1962 and decided to make it his home rather than moving upward and outward. He occupied a two-room suite overlooking the transformer department and the slogan on the overpass, GE FIRST IN SAFETY. His secretary offered me a cup of coffee and we spent two hours talking about the industry's prospects. He spoke quite frankly of the uncertainty about Power Transformer, given the lack of an energy program in the Carter administration and the continuing recession caused by the oil embargo. The city had already lost 7,000 people from the population of 60,000 when he first came to the plant. He rejected my use of the term ''flight'' to the south of middle transformers, preferring to call it a ''spinoff,'' responding to the ''better business climate'' in Shreveport, Louisiana and Rome, Georgia. This was not, he asserted, a result of lower wages — that tended to even up over time. Rather, it was a combination of factors including lower electric rates, fewer state regulations and a more ''hospitable'' state administration. He waxed eloquent about the beauties of the Berkshires, the nature reservation near his home and the Halloween parade in which he served as a grand marshall.

During the summer of 1981 when the Power Transformer Division was being written off as an unprofitable venture, headhunters were invited into the General Electric plant during the July break. The director of community relations had gone to the highest corporate bidder, Westinghouse, along with his boss. The next time I visited the relations office, his successor was installed in a small side office. The new manager had had only one month to get acquainted with his job when I visited him and he had to refer most questions to his secretary, who had twenty-five years service in the company.

Like his predecessor, the new interim manager justified the layoffs in Power Transformer as a decision "to limit their entry" into the transformer market since the three major producers, General Electric, Westinghouse and McGraw Edison split a market which had declined from an annual growth rate of 7 or 8 percent to 1.9 percent. The strategy to "scale down the business to take the fat out" was made so that a situation of "three big guns fighting for the market" would not result. Unfortunately, he added, that meant reducing the number of employees. The plant then employed 7,700 overall, with 3,000 in the Power Transformer Division. Layoffs in the hundreds were expected in the next six month period, with some people being bumped to other departments. While salaried exempt people would be found employment, he said that there was not much "we" could do about union eligibles, adding that "if we were to try to move them and settle them in other plants, it would be exorbitant, but we have been successful in placing a few in the transformer department of McGraw Edison." Ordnance was expected to pick up some of the workers laid off, but that would take at least three years, he said, until Reagan's emphasis on defense would show up in the industry. The aging work force was a sure sign of the attrition. In 1979 the people of age fifty-five and over were 29 percent of the work force, whereas in 1981 they were 35.8 percent.

In the course of our conversation, it was clear that the crisis for the community did not threaten his position, nor did it enter into the concerns of upper management. When I questioned whether there had been a great deal of anxiety stirred up by the talk of shrinking the division of Power Transformer, he replied:

Formerly buyers used to favor the one big supplier for all their equipment, but now they tend to cut up their purchases and GE no longer benefitted from the monopsonistic position they once held.

This reasoning left out of the equation one of the factors that I had learned from union leaders. Power Transformer was making some profit, but not nearly the level of other division, particularly Ordnance and other high tech products favored by the Chairman of the Board. Bottom line profits compared throughout the corporation determined the decision to downgrade the division. I asked what plans GE had to ease the transition, and he replied:

> I don't think the business is going — just cutting down to a break-even point.... You will hear Mayor Smith say that GE owes the city. We think the city owes GE. We have a payroll of $190 million.... It was felt that it was more humane to place as many people as it could and to try to trim the business to make it. Everyone describes the love-hate relationship with the community. Sometimes GE is described as a villain, but with the Good Neighbor Fund, GE gave $470,000, 47 percent of the one million dollar drive.

A year later I returned to visit his successor, who replaced him when he was sent to an overseas plant. Power Transformer was down to 2,200 employees. The laid-off workers we had interviewed were mostly young men and a few women with short service. The new relations manager raised the issue we had heard discussed at the union about threats of withdrawal if productivity did not increase. He was very emphatic in denying this.

> To my way of thinking, that would be unfair labor practices to say that, if we can't get what we want, we will not operate the plant. It is not, however, illegal to state business realities. It is a fact that transformers are not doing well and that we have been losing money on them. But we are not Chrysler. They went to the other step, but GE would not be in that position.

The new director was adept in co-opting the adversaries' position, asserting that the clause requiring at least six months' advance notice of plant closing won in the last contract was a "positive gain made in open communication about the corporation's plans." In fact, the corporation fought that clause, according to the business agent of the local union. The relations director elaborated his point:

> GE is not unwilling to communicate. Corporations are not human entities, but they are entities none the less and do have moral responsibilities. GE has a high moral caliber; we would not simply close down over the weekend [this referred to a remark I had made about a small electronic shop in the neighboring town that had left a sign on their door for the employees coming to work on a Monday morning reading, "Gone to Jamaica"] GE can't go to Jamaica and hide.

He summed up his view of community relations as follows:

Well, I'm looking at this through a one-year window, but I see the relations with the community are superb, especially with the political leadership and the human social sector leadership.... I have heard stories of the fifties when the GE lobbied against the other industries coming in to the community. I can tell you that now we spend money trying to get other industry in. We can no longer afford to be Daddy Warbucks. There is a need for other industry — tourism will not do it. The technology center will bring with it small plastics molders to the Berkshires.... The Berkshires stand a chance of being the Silicon Valley of plastics.

This summed up the "moral commitment" of the corporation to the community in terms that they were able to communicate to workers and politicians in the recession of 1981–1983 before their expansion in Ordnance picked up some of the slack. The business agent accepts the "realities of the market" along with the developers and the local government. As yet there has been no backup to Representative Frank Jakubowicz's request to General Electric that they bring in more product lines, a request that was met with a negative response from John F. Welch, chairman of the board of General Electric.

Nicholas Boraski, supervisor of Ordnance Systems, lent his name to the brochure selling the unique virtues of locating your business in Pittsfield, commenting "If you are looking for quality of life, try Pittsfield for your industry," a clear appeal to the new face of high tech enterprises.

In the face of economic decline in the blue-collar industries, the mayor, the developement committee, the Chamber of Commerce and other agencies are rethinking the town. The new conception involves a changed facade and different people enabling them to overcome some of the barriers to expansion that held them back in the past. The vision of a high level enterprise engaging high-tech engineers and professionals includes such firms as research and development, electrical component manufacturing, investment banking, computer software, light metal fabrication and data processing. Yet the development comittee is very aware that the very attractiveness of the Berkshires for such firms — the relative serenity, slower pace, and scenic views — could be destroyed if they were too successful.

The interdependence of the corporate philosophy of competition and bottom-line profitability with the individual ethic stressing free choice is given fullest expression in the commercial and associational life of the community. The availability of a large variety of consumption goods satisfies, at least minimally, the desire for self-expression denied in the workplace. This plays an important role in the labor compromise with corporate capitalism. The attempts to maintain that flow of goods and the wages that make it possible to purchase them has become a part of the job of mayor, his or her development commission, the Chamber of Commerce and the groups that promote the associational life of the community. The town has embarked on a vast campaign to sell Pittsfield to business enterprises that will come to the beautiful hills and generate the jobs that will keep it all going. The advice of a management consultant firm to "sell" the town's assets since "It's just a question of marketing it properly," (*The Berkshire Eagle* June 11, 1988:C1) is taken seriously as city leaders reduce a complex set of economic and political decisions to salesmanship.

The central myth in corporate hegemony of the market as a natural regulator of the economy is played out in the commercial life of the city where the ability to balance supply and demand exemplifies adaptive success in a rapidly changing economy. Responsibility is accorded to the individual entrepreneur in such a way as to mask the political manouvering that regulates supply and demand factors at every level of commercial exchange. The strategy of salesmanship pits one community against another as cities attempt to lure enterprises with tax rebates, free or low-priced land, and relaxation of regulations. Pittsfield's winning Kay Bee's corporate headquarters was a loss for the neighboring town of Lee.

City planning officials have only lately begun to question the promotion of commercial enterprises and to ask whether a service and sales economy will generate sustained prosperity. The questions now being raised by the Pittsfield Revitalization Corporation take on an additional urgency in an economy threatened by cutbacks in defense spending that has lent an ephemeral prosperity in the 1980s. This is discussed in the following chapter.

Chapter 8

At Home with the Military-Industrial Complex

> *The world we live in is a battleground upon which the adver-*
> *saries are democracy and totalitarianism. The conflict is one*
> *of social systems...of methods through which society makes*
> *its decisions in social, political and economic affairs. The*
> *weapons which are in use are military, political, and economic*
> *intellectual and religious. The test of these systems will lie*
> *in their effectiveness in attaining the satisfactions — material,*
> *human and spiritual — which are the goals of any society.*
> *This war of methods and ideas gives rise to new problems*
> *and it underscores old ones with which we are already*
> *familiar; it is the source of the greatest uncertainties of our*
> *own world.*
> > *Marvin Bower, quoted by R. L. Cordiner,*
> > *president of General Electric (1957:87).*

> *While the law of competition may be sometimes hard for the*
> *individual, it is for the best because it ensures the survival*
> *of the fittest.*
> > *Andrew Carnegie, quoted in* GE Pittsfield
> > News *Vol. 71, 36, October 11, 1985*

The philosophy of the corporation embracing the central values
in corporate hegemony draws on the social-Darwinian struggle for
survival. War is a challenge that brings out the best competitive
qualities, and through this engagement, the success of the firm, and,
it follows, the community and family, is ensured. War is linked with
the good things in life — jobs, security and strength — through the
defense contracts that have made Ordnance the largest divison in the
local plant. The linkage is expressed in the Family Day that initiates
employees' families into the work they do, and through Hollywood
films like Star Wars and Rambo I and II shown at special orientation
events by the local GE plant. It is also manifested in the display of the
Bradley Fighting Vehicle with its gear shift made in the Pittsfield plant
in the Memorial Day parade. The language of the board rooms — at
least that which gets published in the *GE Pittsfield News* — and of
employee briefings is replete with Spencerian phrases.

The culture of war is a delicately-managed enterprise that absorbed the energy, inventiveness and ingenuity of over 62 percent of the personnel in the local plant in 1985. It is not without its critics, found even in the very institutions that are major supporters of the defense program. These include the local union, the veteran's organizations and the political system extending from local to national levels.

The military-industrial complex that President Eisenhower warned the nation about in his farewell speech in 1961 became the dominant force in the U.S. economy in the eighties, affecting costs, productivity and planning in all other sectors of the economy. The fluctuations in the dollar at home and abroad, influenced in part by military expenditures, and the resulting debt, limits the market for all other goods produced in the country. These trends affect all communities because of the high interest rates putting a brake on alternative investments or government spending or other pursuits. They particularly affect those communities like Pittsfield that have become a home for major producers of armaments. The restructuring of Pittsfield's economy in the 1980s devolved around Ordnance as investments and personnel were shifted out of Power Transformer into defense production.

The Business of War

National Impact of Military Production

Armaments production promotes capital-intensive, automated processes that result in unemployment of large sectors of the work force and reduced tax revenues. Comparing the impact of government expenditures, Robert W. Degrasse of the Council on Economic Priorities (1984) estimated that while 24,000 jobs are created for every billion dollars spent on military hardware, an equivalent investment in public transport would create 32,000 jobs or in education 71,000 jobs. The inflationary impact of military expenditures is, according to Seymore Melman (1979), a consequence of the decline in U. S. productivity because of a consistent and long-term trend toward maximizing costs because of Pentagon subsidies. Since the capability of a machine tool, not the cost, became the issue in armaments production, high bids and cost overruns became the norm (Melman 1983). U. S. machine tool prices rose an average of 85 percent from 1971 to 1978, while in Japan they rose only 51 percent. Melman (1979) cites a former congressman who, when questioned why these former enemies should not share costs of military production, said that we could not compete even in arms manufacture and would lose that industry. As a result, machine tool orders in 1984 were only one-half their 1979 levels and employment was 30 percent below 1979 levels (*New York Times*, July 8, 1984, Section 3:1).

Industries producing for civilian markets could not replace equipment and many have been forced out of operation. This, in turn, raises the cost of unemployment for the community and puts additional pressure on price increases for these goods. Melman (1983) puts the brunt of the blame on management concern with short-term profits, wasting the abilities of skilled machinists and turning to overseas investments to maximize profits. This opinion is shared by Harley Shaiken (*New York Times*, July 8, 1984, Section 3:1).

Whatever corrective tendencies operate in a market economy are mitigated by a disproportionate investment in military production. Military contractors' profits dipped only slightly during the 1980–1983 recession when durable goods manufacturers experienced dramatic losses (UPI, published in *The Berkshire Eagle*, September 7, 1985). Accounts of fraud, waste and abuse by military contractors further distort the economy.

General Electric Corporation epitomizes many of these problems in the policies promoted by John F. Welch, Jr., who became chair of the corporation in 1981. The major emphasis is on the expansion of computer-aided design and manufacturing systems. The purchase of Calma Company and 23 percent of the stock of Intersil of United Telecommunication, a producer of automated production systems, was the first step in GE's entry into high tech, an industry that is, according to *Business Week* analysts (May 14, 1979) geared to inflation since they have declining unit costs which can be translated to rising profit margins.

Entry into continually higher Research and Development operations that are tax write-offs is another growing commitment in the eighties. GE's proportion of expenditures in this area increased each year from 1975, when they represented 38.0 percent of investment, to 1981 when they were 48.1, with a dip to 45 percent in 1982 (Securities and Exchange Commission 10K Report 1983).

A great deal of research and development is invested in aerospace and aircraft engine operations, another of General Electric's priorities. Reporting on the entry of GE into competitive bids for a 40 billion dollar aircraft contract, *Newsweek* (August 29, 1983:54) called it "Neutron Jack vs. the Shark" — a reference to John F. Welch of General Electric and Harry Gray of United Tech. The Pentagon promoted the competition so that they would not become overly dependent on a single supplier after some exchange with Pratt-Whitney over the F100 fighter. Their wager that the two companies would split the contract in an election year was realized, and *Newsweek* concluded that both companies would win and "the only loser would be the taxpayer" (August 28, 1983:54). The scientific management involved in the collective effort to assembly the various parts of complex military equipment is transforming U. S. industry.

General Electric's acquisition of RCA, which includes the television network NBC, for $6,278 billion unites two major Pentagon bidders, thus reducing the competition in that field as well as consumer electronics in which both companies produce (Ralph Nader in *The Berkshire Eagle* Dec. 28, 1985). In a rather contradictory statement, John F. Welch, Jr., Thornton F. Bradshaw, chairman of RCA and Robert R. Frederick, RCA president stated that the merger is "an excellent strategic opportunity for both companies that will help America's competitiveness in world markets. We are creating a company that will successfully compete with anyone, anywhere in every market we serve." (*The Berkshire Eagle* December 12, 1985).

Welch has been directly responsible for the shift to financial operations since he headed the General Electric Credit Corporation. Started during Swope's presidency to help promote the sale of durable goods, it has become a leasing agency for commercial airlines and provides a cheap source of credit for internal use. It has continually shown high earnings in an inflationary setting with rising interest rates, and is responsible for a large share of the gains in the Services and Materials category of GE revenue reports. The SEC 10K Report of 1982 showed a strong lead, with two billion dollar assets, confirmed the following year in Welch's report (*GE Pittsfield News*, Vol. 69, 38), that earnings in the Credit Corporation were 32 percent ahead of the previous year in the third quarter. *Fortune* (May 4, 1981) credits it as a "tax refund cow" that can be milked for rebates from the U. S. government.

Linked to these strategies is a shift in production from blue-collar assembly work to steel-collar robots. The employment trends can be seen in the SEC K10 Report. In 1982, the company employed 367,000 people, over two-thirds of whom were in the U. S. Only 93,000 were in bargaining units: the blue-collar, production workers and lower-scale white-collar workers. This is down 20,000 from the previous year, when there was a work force of 404,000 with 289,000 employed in the U. S. and with 110,000 employees in bargaining units. *Monthly Labor Review* of September 1982 points out that in the 1982 contract settlement production workers were being shifted to lower-rated jobs because of transfers of work and automation. The corporation has more flexibility in carrying out automation than their overseas competitors because, according to *Business Week* (August 9, 1982) "they have worker compliance." Summing up Welch's career in 1983, the SEC notes that he sold forty-five operations for $500 million, including small appliances to Black and Decker and Utah International, and bought fifty high-tech and service firms.

General Electric's present strategy grows out of trends that go back to World War II and continued, with some interruption after the end of the Korean War, to build up throughout the sixties. Priorities in production were clarified in the decentralization moves of the 1950s. The objectives stated in *General Electric Professional Management* Vol. I (1953:43) were "to place the authority and responsibility at the level of each one of these divisions or product line segregations so that we will have the flexibility, equal to that of our most agile competitor and yet use the storehouse of information and cooperation which is available from the other operating areas, and particularly from the staff officers and members of their organization." Since this meant that each division was to be judged in terms of its own record of profit and investment, it gave a great deal of power to headquarters to deploy investments, with the accounting department the whip in the operation.

Since 1950, when that report was formulated, the corporation has grown from 117 plants in ninety-eight cities of the U. S., dispersed in twenty-four states and Canada, to 230 plants in thirty-four states and Puerto Rico with 135 in twenty-five other countries (SEC 10D Report 1982). In his role as chair of the board, John F. Welch probably has the greatest power in the history of the firm to sell operations that do not match up to the dominant players. This clearly involved a reduction in Power Transformer. The industry nationally has gone from 180,000 million volt amphers in 1974 to 62,000 in 1980 and most analysts (quoted in *The Berkshire Eagle*, April 2, 1984) were convinced even before the decision was finally made in 1986 that Welch would "leave it to Westinghouse and RTE to fight it out" in the power transformer market.

The Local Impact of Military Production

The buildup in the defense industry is correlated with the decline in the production of consumer goods and peace-time capital goods throughout the nation. It is more striking at the Pittsfield General Electric plant than nationally. A variety of consumer products have been transferred to other plants in the U. S. and overseas or have been phased out of production. The most dramatic shift has been the decline from divisional status to that of departmental status of power transformers, the pioneer product on which all others depended. When production of medium and small transformers was transferred to southern plants, a move first made in 1957 and followed by massive withdrawal of production after the 1969 strike, there were no backup orders to keep continuous production in the large transformer department. This became particularly acute in 1982 when the demand for large power transformers declined precipitously. While the growth in the Ordnance Division, where naval balistics systems including Polaris and Trident and the Bradley Fighting Tank are produced, took up some of the laid-off employees from the Power Transformer department from 1982 to 1987. The need for specially trained and educated personnel in Ordnance meant that many others have not found employment. It also meant a shift from union-eligible to exempt employees. In 1988, Ordnance was beginning to experience a similar attrition when cuts affecting 900 defense jobs were announced (*The Berkshire Eagle* May 18, 1988).

A productivity drive "to make Pittsfield production [of power transformers] competitive with that of Westinghouse and McGraw Edison" resulted in layoffs locally of 600 workers but failed to give security to remaining workers. The layoffs brought the unemployment rate in the Pittsfield labor market area up to 7.3 percent in September 1982, (*The Berkshire Eagle* November 30, 1982) and the rate increased up to 7.6 percent in the following year (*The Berkshire Eagle* December 3, 1983). As a result, the Pittsfield labor market area was declared a labor-surplus locality. This designation, which the congressional representative for the region claimed credit for, enhanced the firm's bidding on federal contracts, giving it an almost 6 percent advantage over other firms. (*The Berkshire Eagle* July 30, 1983). This incentive to lure defense contracts, combined with the negative attitude toward blue-collar production in a city that had the reputation of being anti-business and strong union, confirmed managerial decision making that the Pittsfield plant should be primarily oriented to Ordnance. Nicholas Boraski announced the decision to the press (*The Berkshire Eagle* January 21, 1984):

> Ordnance, with its defense business, is well-positioned to take advantage of the commitment in this area. The strength of Ordnance and Plastics' stability will offset a further shrinkage in the transformer operations with 1984 remaining relatively stable. Employment will be at or near the 7,100 figure at year end.

The laid-off workers were for the most part not the bulk of the newly-hired employees. As a result, there was a massive migration of people in the young-worker age group as almost 9,000 people left the city in the period 1970 to 1985, bringing the population down to 48,000 in October 1985. Furloughs of four weeks at the end of each year in Power Trnasformer helped defer additional layoffs.

The new Plastics Division, linked to worldwide expansion projects in Osaka, Japan and in Bergen Op Zoom in the Netherlands, promised to maintain rather than increase employment. Since it is exclusively a research and design operation, the personnel are highly-trained exempt employees. Production might be done in one of the dozen plastics injection and mold businesses that have grown in the city.

Employment in the three divisions reflects the shift in emphasis. The Power Transformer Division that once employed 5,000 workers was down to 900 employees in 1988, while Ordnance had grown from a few hundred following the Korean War to 5,000, almost completely reversing the proportion of those in civilian and war production at the end of the sixties. Throughout the growth period of Ordnance, the company advertized for new hires in national engineering journals rather than in the help wanted columns of daily newspapers. In these ads the manager of professional personnel relations stressed the civilian usage of Ordnance contracts. "stretching and redefining engineering missions" to attract a new kind of personnel.

Production in Ordnance

> Be not too proud, great bird, I can whisper intelligence into the brain of other great birds in their nest beneath the sea, thrust them forth into the air, and help guide their unerring flight through wind and rain, across the face of the globe. Yes, your eye is sharp, but not as sharp as mine. I can spot an enemy speck in the sky, seen or unseen, move tons of metal and track it with precision, and call into play guns and missiles if I must to protect my home — the ship upon the sea and what are you on land, great bird? Can you, as I, turn, stop, reverse and swim giant vehicles across the swamp and mountains, keeping their fighting eyes steady in a world of dust, heat, spray and motion? Yet all this I can do, great bird, because I am ORDNANCE SYSTEMS.
>
> GE *Pittsfield News*, September 15, 1979,
> Family Day 75th Anniversary Souvenir Issue.

By 1985, the Ordnance Division of Pittsfield reached a "Fortune 500" size business (*GE Pittsfield News* October 11, 1985), according to Tom Lavery, general manager of the Engineering and Manufacturing

Department in Ordnance, at a meeting of some 800 managers and "individual contributors" (read workers). Announcing that the division had just received an eighteen million dollar contract for work on the fleet ballistic missile, Lavery predicted that the division would receive more than a half-billion dollar return for production related to the Trident II fire control systems and guidance systems in the coming years. His remarks printed in the *GE Pittsfield News* (October 11, 1985) exemplify the outlook cultivated in the industry:

> OSD sales have grown by more than 70 percent in the past two years.... It is now clear that defense businesses are operating in a very competitive environment, quite similiar to commercial businesses. OSD is aggressively pursuing new business, such as SMAINS and Liquid Propellant, in a new, tough, competitive environment. As our environment changes, we too must change if we are going to continue the history of success that OSD has demonstrated in the past. We are successful.... we are winners. Feel good about that and continue to demonstrate that winning attitude every day. We can feel good, but we cannot relax. Our job is to make this good business better!

GE has consistently emphasized the commercial extensions of defense-oriented Research and Development, in part to overcome employee skepticism about career commitment to defense production. Summing up the areas in which Ordnance Systems technology contributed to other divisions, *GE Pittsfield News* (Vol. 69, no. 32, September 2, 1983) reports that GE Net, the bus interface system developed at Ordnance, is a key element in the new factory automation and in the CT scanner used in medical technology.

On March 28, 1985, the Pentagon imposed a ban on bidding on new defense contracts by the Space Systems Division of General Electric Company, following an indictment charging that the firm's Space Systems Division defrauded the government of $800,000. Nicholas Boraski, general manager of Pittsfield's General Electric plant, sent an open letter to the Pittsfield Ordnance Systems Division charging employee misconduct in the allocation of time on time cards. In an interview with *Berkshire Eagle* reporter Margaret Pantridge (*The Berkshire Eagle* June 5, 1985) John F. Welch claimed that GE was singled out because of its visibility. He reiterated the charge that it was "low-level engineering folks" and that the corporation was unable to find the guilty person. The corporate ombudsman urged employees to report any suspected violation. The company paid a fine of $1,040,000, hardly more than the alleged $800,000 false charges. The ban against bidding on new defense contracts was lifted in April, and that on Space Systems Division at the end of July.

In order to assure a flow of defense contracts, General Electric finances a Washington, D.C. headquarters with a staff of 120 at a cost of $1.3 million a year for rent, according to Thomas B. Edsall *The Washington Post* (reprinted in *The Berkshire Eagle* June 8, 1985). These "corporate beachheads" that GE constructs in almost every branch of the government are, according to Edsall, "designed to mesh a private sector conglomerate with the public sector conglomerate - the U. S. Government," with the goal of "manipulating the Washington market, lobbying on aircraft engines, aerospace radar, electronics flight simulators and weapons systems as well as nuclear power plants. In addition, these GE lobbyists try to influence legislators on a host of tax, labor, environmental and other issues that concern their business. An exhibit of an Avenger model with an all-electronic turret stabilization system used to fire the Stinger air defense missile was declared a "hit" at an Army show in Washington in October 1984.

Community Response to Military Production

Union Initiatives

Through the end of the seventies, the business agent of the IUE Local 255 called for management to bring in more product lines to make up for the declining demand for large power transformers. As the layoffs rose in the eighties, F. Bruce Ferin, the business agent who entered in 1979, accused the company of deliberately moving out product lines. He predicted that the Pittsfield plant would eventually become a "repair and assembly unit" employing fewer than one thousand workers" (*Local 255 News*, February 17, 1984). According to the business agent, each demand made by management during that period was phrased in such terms that if the workers did not accept, management would close the Power Transformer Division. Workers accepted the elimination of piece rates with the promise that more work would be brought into Pittsfield. Far from making this a reality, the company eliminated work by transferring the production of medium transformers and bushings to the south. Shop steward Choc Gonzalez called foremen in the Power Transformer Department "hatchetmen" who cut jobs and piled work on others in a frantic attempt to improve productivity and gain compliance with the managers (*IUE News* April 3, 1979).

The decline of Power Transformer Division made the union vulnerable to management initiatives in the eighties. Despite the reluctance of many of the workers to engage in defense work, it appeared to be the only alternative to closing out production. Those who did resist transfers to Ordnance felt that they lost opportunities to advance, since there was little or no mobility in the Power Transformer Division. The union put its major effort into gaining transfers to the Ordnance Division of workers laid off from Power Transformer. The gains they made in that direction minimized the initiatives of the previous decade in fighting for new consumer product lines.

Peace conversion was on the agenda of the union for a brief period. The national IUE headquarters in Washington hosted a delegation of trade union leaders from Europe who were touring the U.S. in July 1983 to discuss the effects of international peace on trade unions. In the union headquarters they visited they raised the question of how to preserve jobs in a conversion from military-oriented production to production of alternative socially useful products.

> 'If the Peace movement ignores the needs and interests of working people,' said Klaus Mehrens of German's I. G. Metall Co., and if peace is won at the expense of jobs, then millions of workers will oppose peace plans. Ron Todd of British Transport and General Workers Union stated that there is a vital role to be played by trade unions in developing those policies for conversion. (*National IUE News* July 1983)

The visiting union leaders claimed that it is a myth that military expenditures create jobs and urged unions with contracts in defense industries to negotiate with employers for alternative-use committees. German trade unionists recalled that their movement opposed rearmament prior to World War I and World War II and that they would again oppose military buildup.

Alternatives to defense production were supported by the Amalgamated Clothing and Textile Workers, United Food and Commercial Workers, the American Federation of State, County and Municipal Workers and others that were not as intrinsically involved in defense as the electrical workers. But since the electrical production workers had failed to recover from the 1982 recession except in those plants with defense-related production, the incentive to search for peace alternatives was weakened. *The Monthly Labor Review* (Bulletin September 1982, 105:44–5) report on the downgrading of 100,000 electrical workers nationwide indicated a growing trend. Plant closings, rather than the search for new products, was the major concern of the unions.

As a result of their perception of the vulnerable position of electrical workers in the labor market, the IUE did not advance the movement to peace conversion. The Committee on Political Education of the Pittsfield plants's Local 255 refused to endorse the Democratic candidate for senator in the 1984 elections, John F. Kerry, because of his position on the defense budget. When Senator Edward M. Kennedy came to Pittsfield to campaign for Kerry in October 1984, Local 255's business agent tried to get him to ''send a message'' to John F. Kerry counseling him to withdraw his opposition to the Bradley Fighting Vehicle, the Trident 1 and 2 and the Aegis, all of which contain components made at Ordnance. Kennedy tried to convince them that Kerry was only opposed to the MX missile and Strategic Defense Initiative weapons, and that by fighting the high military budgets and trade deficits Kerry's policies would stimulate manufacturing jobs in the U. S. He failed to convince the local's Committee on Political Education (COPE) to change its stand of no endorsement for either Kerry or his opponent, Shamie. ''We're not for Shamie,'' a union spokesman told labor reporter A. A. Michelson who writes the ''Beacon Hill Weekly Commentary'' (*The Berkshire Eagle* November 3, 1984) ''because he's too Reganistic. On the other hand we don't like some of the Department of Defense changes that Kerry is calling for.''

Although Kerry did win the senatorial race in Massachusetts, there is a large and growing block of voters who are supporting, or at least not actively opposing, conservative candidates because they fear the loss of their jobs. Despite evidence that government money spent on transportation, solar energy, housing and other consumer-oriented production creates more jobs, the issues that dominate workers' thinking are bread and butter concerns about union members' own jobs in their own locality.

Although the union did not officially support a conversion-to-peace movement, some members of the rank and file initiated activities in collaboration with peace activists in the county (infra page 319). Individual workers sometimes chose not to work in Ordnance Systems because they did not want to work on armaments. I asked one worker whom I shall call John why he had left Ordnance and why he chose to return to Power Transformer. He replied:

> I did not really leave there. I was laid off one transformer and they sent me over there to work. I didn't want the job. I told them I

didn't want the job, that they were forcing me into it. They couldn't understand why I didn't want the job. I told them it wasn't that I didn't want the job itself, per se, because a job is a job. I told them I would do the job to the best of my ability but I would be wearing my five or six buttons [bearing political slogans]. They were working on a number of things. Part of it was still Trident at that point, and in 1981, by their own admission, GE had 231 weapons on contract. My job was a split and pokey job; it was really two jobs, one being an inspector of wiring, and the other was working in the metallurgy lab calibrating the tools that they use out on the floor. I was calibrating within two millionths of an inch. I would have liked that aspect of the job. It was interesting and a challenge. And a lot of use of math. ...So I would have liked that. They said that in two or three months they were going to administer the color-blind test for all new people coming in the inspection program in Ordnance. That would have been my ticket out of there. I was color blind when I went into the air force. Anyway the next day the instructor said, "Look, you don't want to be here, right?" And I said, "No." He said, "Well, what if we move up that color-blind test." And I didn't pass. I say now, I should have passed that test; I should have gone to work there, because what's really needed is people in there talking. I should have kept my mouth shut at that point in time. I didn't have the heart to work there. But if I had gone, I'd have done my job. I'm sure I would have done that. I stand on my work. I'm a worker. I know my job. Every aspect about my job, I want to learn it.

John's ambivalence about the work in Ordnance — liking the work itself but objecting to the end product — was shared by a number of employees, including draftspeople who chose to continue at Power Transformer despite the greater opportunities and challenge of jobs in Ordnance Systems. They were not, like John with his buttons, openly advocating peace-time conversion, but their latent advocacy of peace-time production exists as an option that might be rallied as a movement gets started.

Ordnance Systems pervades every aspect of the city. Managers of Ordnance Systems are integrated as residents, with their children often enrolled in local public schools. All of the top managers have served as voluntary chairs and members of boards of directors of the local service agencies, and as leaders of fund drives to fund these agencies. Their multiple roles reinforce their position in the corporation at the same time that these integrate the division they head into the community. The Gerard L. Philippe Award, named after former chairman of the board of General Electric, is given to those employees who perform outstanding services for the community. Among those awarded it in 1985 were Bob Saydlowski, a man involved in disaster work for the Red Cross who served on the board of Hillcrest Hospital; Skip Thompson who was the director of the Pittsfield Boy's Club Alumni Association and co-founder of Pittsfield Parks Department's Junior City Basketball League; Tom Lareau, a decorated Vietnam combat veteran who devoted about twenty hours a week counseling veterans and who opened a center for these veterans; and a group of Ordnance and Plastics employees who organized HOPE to help the starving people of Africa.

The recently-retired manager of Ordnance Systems, Gene Peterson, exemplified the multiple-role commitments during his twenty-three years of service in Ordnance Systems. His two years of service in World War II on a U. S. destroyer were probably as important as his degrees from Bowdoin College and the Massachusetts Institute of Technology in gaining his appointment as manager of Ordnance Systems in 1960. He served as chair of the board of the Pittsfield Boys' Club, the United Way and other organizations. The new manager is, like Peterson, a native of the area and fits easily into the life of the community. He has served on the boards of many Pittsfield and Dalton associations.

The Good Neighbor Fund is the primary entry into redistribution of some of the earnings to the local society. Each year the entire General Electric Plant is mobilized to raise money from employees and managers. In 1984 the drive organization chose the showing of the film "Star Wars" as a promotion setting off the competition among five teams from different divisions of the plant. To make the entertainment even more attractive to GE employees and families, free popcorn and soft drinks were provided to all who attended. The teams were color coded and named according to product specialities: Weapon Control Programs and Shipboard Equipment Programs, Ordnance; Bushing and Arrester Products, Transformer; and Finance, Plastics, etc. In this program the elements of American cultural life are integrated with the military reference system that increasingly gives shape and form to life in the community.

Probably the most outstanding event symbolizing this trend was the first General Electric Family Day organized by Ordnance Systems. In the past, Power Transformer had organized this event which annually familiarizes the families of General Electric workers with what is going on inside the plant. I attended the 1985 Family Day on an Indian summer day in September when the brightly colored tents were set up around the main building occupied by Ordnance Systems.

Clowns offered balloons to the kids, and a jazz band from the University of Massachusetts played Dixieland melodies in the refreshment tent. The logo for the day was a button showing two adult figures, male and female as proven by pants and skirt, and two smaller figures of each sex embracing each other. In an arch above the united figures was the inscription: "Ordnance Systems Division," and below their feet, "Family Day 1985." The theme for the day was a take-off on an old nursery rhyme — "Good, Better, Best, portrait of a growing division." The manager of Firing Ballistics Missile Support Project explained the purpose of the event: "In addition to providing an opportunity for family members to see where dad or mom works, we would like to show our families all the work and energy that is going into making this historically excellent business a new force in the General Electric Co. and a growing entity in the rapidly changing defense market today."

On the day of the event over 14,000 GE employees and their families lined up to take the two-and-a-half mile tour of the buildings occupied by Ordnance Systems. Children were allowed to "draw a house" on the drafting computers that, as one of the tour guides told me in an aside, were costing many drafting jobs throughout Ordnance. Toy-like replicas of the Trident, Polaris I and II painted in pastel colors were on display along with a miniature vehicle like the Bradley Fighting Tank. Youngsters could don full battle dress and ride in it. Another great hit with the children was a tiny robot produced by Ordnance engineers with the help of students in the area. Children were allowed to draw a house on the computerized drafting screens. Toy-like replicas of the Trident, Polaris I and II painted in pastel colors were on display along with a miniature vehicle like the Bradley Fighting tank. The youngsters could don the full battle dress for a driver and rider. Another surprise feature was a tiny robot produced by Ordnance engineers with the help of students in the area. A videotape showed the operation MK and Trident guidance system intercepting an enemy missile.

It was an impressive exhibition of the techniques the corporation utilized to overcome fear and potential hostility to military production encapsulating it within familiar, positive social institutions. In a souvenir edition of the *Pittsfield Ordnance Systems Division News* (Vol. NY, No. 31, Sept. 11, 1985:4) group pictures of the "family" members who have been with the programs for a long time "prove what people working together" can bring about. The fact that the end product is a potentially destructive system of armaments is justified in terms of the "challenge" posed by the enemy. Sometimes the enemy is named, but more often it remains a mythic force, available for promoting a sense of the need for the defense network. As people exited from the grounds, just as they picked up their souvenir gift of a first-aid kit, their last image was that of a full-sized Bradley Fighting Vehicle. The presence of Ordnance Systems in the community is also felt on other occasions. One of the Fourth of July parade attractions was the Bradley Fighting Vehicle mounted on a float that moved down North Street with some GE employees on board. Occasional ceremonies bring the Department of Defense to the city when awards are given and the linkage between the plant and the Pentagon is re-inforced. One such occasion was the Department of Defense award in September 1983, for GE support of employees who serve in the National Guard or Reserve. The Ordnance systems manager is often shown in newspaper articles giving the General Electric Foundation grants to schools and colleges. It is significant that the manager of Ordnance, not Power Transformer or Plastics, is chosen for the ceremonial act that reinforces the linkage between Ordnance Systems and educational institutions that ensure a future generation of trained personnel. A picture published in the *GE Pittsfield News* (Sept. 30, 1983) showing the dean of the School of Engineering at the University of Massachusetts at Amherst, shaking hands with the general manager of Ordnance Systems, with heads of the minority engineering program, university deans, and Ordnance managers of employee professional relations smiling at the camera, epitomizes the hegemonic relations of corporate military production and the universities.

The influence of Ordnance System pervades decisions regarding many community activities. When the Berkshire League of Women Voters was denied the use of a regional school for a talk on the pro-liferation of nuclear weapons, people guessed that the decision may have been influenced by the fact that four of the five school commit-tee members who voted against it were employed at GE's Ordnance Systems.

Cultural Elements of Militarism

Memorial Day is the annual event that brings together all those who have served with the military along with schoolchildren, scouts and others recruited to give public recognition of the sacrifice wounded and killed veterans made to their country. Initiated as a day to remember the soldiers who died in the Civil War, the ceremony has become generalized to recognize all who died in any war. Richard Nunely, a columnist for the local press, remembered back to his youth when the last Civil War veteran rode in the parade in the back of an open GAR roadster, and the Civil War was still the featured memory:

> Other wars had occurred, to be sure, but World War I was remembered, on Armistice Day, the Spanish-American War was ignored and the various Latin American forays apparently unknown. Decorator Day was the Civil War, and the memory of it still hushed people, made them feel sickish with awe (Nunley, BE May 30, 1984).

For most Pittsfield residents the Civil War is nearly forgotten as members of the American Legion, the Veterans of Foreign Wars and the Vietnam Veterans recall the dead of World War II, the Korean War and the Vietnam War, placing a poppy in the memorial urn in Pittsfield cemetary. The last World War I veteran died in 1983.

The main speaker in the 1982 Memorial Day observations made a point of the special problems faced by the Vietnam veterans who not only are ''still suffering the ravages of their wounds'' but also ''the lack of the full respect and honor of their countrymen.'' His speech may have given an opening for the most forgotten group of veterans to make their entry in the 1983 parade.

On May 30, 1983 Pittsfield's Vietnam veterans marched in the annual Memorial Day parade for the first time. While the other veterans, of World War II and the Korean War, wore dress uniforms, they wore camouflage battle dress with green berets as they marched down North Street to the cemetary. It was a significant change, for them and for the community, for these veterans, to appear in public at such an event. The stigma they had borned for fighting in an unpopular war, the first one that the U. S. had lost in the 200 years of independence, was not over, but the burden had shifted. They were now becoming incorporated in the mainstream culture.

When I attended the Memorial Day celebration the following year the Veterans of Vietnam stood in their camouflage suits directly opposite the canopied speakers' platform, with the Veterans of Foreign War in the rear and the American Legion in front of it. The speaker, a lawyer who was a veteran of the Vietnam War and who had been named outstanding young man in American, spoke of the sacrifices made by the dead soldiers but went on to question the military solution to problems. He said:

> We live in a country with more freedom, more wealth and opportunities than any other. But could anyone have imagined a century ago how American soldiers would be asked to go throughout the

globe to African deserts, Vietnam rice paddies, and to be blown up in Beirut?

and concluded with a quotation from "a great modern warrior, Dwight Eisenhower:

> Fire, famine and pestilence are the weapons of today's wars. I have come to hate war. War settles nothing.

Veterans' organizations and those linked to them through the Ladies' Auxiliary are age graded. The legionaires include most of the older veterans from World War II. In their parade slacks with gold braid and their white shirts and ties worn under jackets often emblazoned with medals, they look more like comfortable businessmen than military figures. Veterans of Foreign Wars wear the dress uniforms they may have worn when in the service. But the younger veterans of the Vietnam War were clearly distinguished not only by their battle gear, but many wore their hair long and sported beards instead of the clean-shaven trim haircuts of the older men. The high school bands and drum majorettes wore the parade uniforms of a Gilbert and Sullivan opera version of militarism, the epaulettes, braid and brass buttons a gaudy burlesque of the military theme. Even the beds of red tulips seemed to be standing at attention as the ceremonies were quickly carried out in the light spring showers.

These were not the Memorial Day celebrations that William Lloyd Warner characterized as "An American Sacred Ceremony" (1953:3). He emphasized the continuity in the celebration. Warner failed to examine his own assumptions as a native of the culture when he commented that it was a "ritual integration of many small comunities from which people derived deep satisfaction." Ethnic exclusion characterized the life of the New England communities he studied in the thirties and forties and must have found its expression in the absence of many veterans from the celebrations. I recall as a child growing up near Yankee City in those decades that it was the professional and business men who marched and gave speeches, not workers. The Vietnam veterans of this decade who led the new organization were from working-class families — an index of the recruitment process that enabled the prosperous families to keep their children in colleges or exempt professions. The divisions were not so easily glossed over in the speeches as in those earlier decades, as speakers in the Pittsfield Memorial Day parade expressed shame for the war that caused so much sacrifice, and a growing awareness that sevicemen who most suffered from it were asked to bear the burden of guilt alone.

The major veterans' organizations maintain a military presence during peace time with good works directed at hospitalized veterans and the youth. The oldest organization is the American Legion Post, which owns an impressive four-story building with a dining hall, auditorium and sports field. Organized in May 1919, it is called after Charles A. Persip, a black man whose service to the post and the community merited the honor. "He was more or less self-employed," I was told, "doing odd jobs for people in the southern part of the city" (the wealthier district) so that he could reserve his main efforts for community work, raising money for the Jimmy Fund, the March of Dimes, the visits to the Pittsfield Hospital. It was clear that community service was a priority to a post that recognized such a man as their most honored member. The post raises money for the Boys' Club, the Boy Scouts and scholarship funds allocated to three high school boys. Although the major emphasis is on the development of boys, the Ladies' Auxiliary does some fundraising for girls' activities. The 14 percent of the Legionaires nationwide who are women, have worked to gain facilities in the Veteran's Administration's medical center, and there are now several women commanders in local posts as well as a state commander.

The local American Legion Post commander, John Henderek, works in the Veteran's Affairs Office in City Hall. He said that veterans in need are taken care of through this office so that they can avoid the humiliating experience of applying for welfare. The local office handles $4,300,000 for pensions and compensation for veterans and dependents in need. The legion brings gifts and cookies to hospitalized veterans at Christmas and other holidays. (They have recently given up bringing cigarettes, formerly standard offerings.) They decorate the graves of veterans on Memorial Day. The major problem the post now faces is the number of World War II elderly with chronic illness.

The relationship between the American Legion Post and the other veterans' organizations is, according to the post commander, one of unity. "They want to be separate and apart, but definitely they want that unity, togetherness," he assured me. The VFW commander personifies this since he is a member of the American Legion as well. Their mission, like that of the American Legion, is to support veterans and the community. "My Ladies' Auxiliary," he told me, "works very hard. They have a bingo party once a week and raise money for the community." Recent donations include the Girls' Club, Boys' Club, and Friends of Wild Acres totalling about $4,200 a month. When the Red Cross ran out of money, the ladies raised over $4,000 dollars.

The VFW post commander expressed the same philosophical ambivalence about war that I had heard frequently. When I asked him what he thought about the arms buildup, he replied,

> I don't like it. I think it is necessary, but I don't like it. I don't like troops in the Middle East or in Central America, looking for trouble, poking their nosie in too many pies. I don't ever want any more members of foreign wars eligible for entry into the VFW. That's my goal in life!

But when I asked him what he thought would happen to Pittsfield if we didn't have an arms buildup, he responded, as did most General Electric workers, with a concern for employment:

> I don't like to think. But small as Pittsfield seems, we're one of the prime targets in another war. Last I heard we were eighth on line because of the Ordnance plant. I worked there thirty years. Without that, where would we be? But I hope some day we can produce something else besides armaments.

The sense of impotence that most people in our random sample of General Electric workers expressed (Chapter 11) was echoed in his response to my question as to whether there was anything the people can do:

> I wish people could talk with the guys who are pushing the buttons. Ask them why people are killing, for what ends. Why are they fighting for a piece of desert land. [The interview took place at the time of the Lybian offensive in 1982.] I don't understand. I did my duty because my country told me to. I'm proud of it, and I like the guys that did it. But we've got to defend ourselves. There are always fights. Cowboys fight Indians, Indians fought for their land. Norwegians fought for the ocean. I think it's just natural. Brothers and sisters fight; families fight. [I intervened to say that they don't fight to kill and he replied,] Some do. In GE they tell me, "How come you are so cooperative?" I say, if you want to you can have cooperation. Countries should do the same. We need the Middle Eastern oil, they need our food.

The sense of dissonance between his pro-peace sentiments and the role that the VFW commander played was overcome by cultural reference points that supported his thesis that war must be natural since everyone does it, including family members. Yet his vision of cooperative mutual service to others was a guiding value in his work and volunteer services.

The Vietnam veterans suffered in a far more poignant way from the dissonance that others tried to resolve through such cultural reference points. Until 1978 their sense of a loss of identity in coming back to a country which they had served only to find themselves ignored or even condemned resulted in private, internalized psychic shame. The organization of the Vietnam Veterans of America in 1978 was, according to Larry, the head of the local chapter, a response to the homecoming of the American hostages from Iran. He told me:

> The coming home of the American hostages, the amount of publicity, the hero-type welcome that they got — this started the action and it's just taken off. A lot of the Vietnam veterans wondered why they got a hero's welcome, not that they were not heroes, but we actually were fighting a war.... So we took a cold, hard look backward and said, 'Gee, these guys [the Vietnam Veterans] did not get their just reward.'

The organization is far less formal in its organization than that of other veterans' groups, with about 130 members attending its issue-oriented meetings. There is a great deal of fluctuation in the membership because, I was told, "they just don't believe in the thing." Much of their discouragement comes form the experiences they had upon their return from the war. In the anti-war climate, the victims of that war felt that they became the scapegoats.

One of the major problems for the veterans returning after the Vietnam War was unemployment, particularly in North Adams but also in Pittsfield, where people were being laid off from Power Transformer because of the shift to the south. Although employers were formally committed to giving veterans the jobs they had when they left, they would claim that the job no longer existed. This happened to Larry when he returned to Sprague Electric Company. He, like some of the other veterans, decided to take the GI benefits and go to college. This gave him an entry into government jobs in housing and redevelopment.

As a result of their own problems with unemployment, the Vietnam Veterans have made employment one of their prime efforts. They set up a special booth in the State Employment Service office and advertised for Vietnam veterans to come and talk with counselors. They became familiar with the training and leadership programs available, and members of the organization would go around to area businesses that deal with the federal government and would "make sure that they fulfill the rules for veterans."

Agent orange is another concern. Local veterans did not feel that a settlement made with the chemical companies in 1984 was just, in terms of money or assessment of the possible damage. Larry summed up the feelings of the veterans:

> I think a lot of the Vietnam veterans wanted the chemical companies to admit they did wrong, but they didn't. It was a compassionate settlement to the Vietnam veterans, not a settlement of guilt. It didn't really help us. I kind of look at it personally like Richard Nixon. He never admitted he was guilty, but he resigned from office. And I think the chemical companies did the same thing.... The cash settlement, I think, shows that they feel they were guilty. A lot of Vietnam veterans wanted to see them go into court because of the press that it would get... The issue was getting these people and these issues dragged out and to show what happened and what they did over there... The other thing I think is very important is that most Vietnam veterans I talk to say the settlement has nothing to do with the government, but they also blame a certain amount on the federal government being the one who quote unquote knew the danger of agent orange, knew the problems of agent orange. The chemical companies only manufacture it. The government was the one who actually used it.

Meanwhile the Vietnam Veterans are trying to get information on what military units were in what areas and which ones were spraying in order to press legal claims in the future. This information is being collected by the 131 chapters, but because the government has classified a great deal of the information on where agent orange was used for twenty to twenty-five years, the veterans are having difficulty collecting information. As Larry commented, "You look at it and say, 'My God, he's going to die before it becomes unclassified.'"

The other major health problem Vietnam veterans face is psychological trauma. Larry drew a vivid portrait of what it was like to be in Vietnam:

> I think that what has happened with the Vietnam veterans is that we were under a lot of pressure in a very jungle-like environment. We had people who were not distinguished as enemies. We've seen kids with grenades on their bodies — little kids that you would like to go up to and say 'hi' to. The main thing about unconventional warfare, you think of wading through jungles with rice paddies and shells going off and trip wires, and you become very paranoid. Now one day you're in the jungle, and the next day you're in the streets of Pittsfield.

For Larry, and possibly many other Vietnam veterans, their goal was not to avoid just any war, but to avoid "any war action without 100 percent backing of our government, and 100 percent backing of the American people." This would require "a clear sense of being threatened."

> The most important thing is why are we committing these troops to this place? Why are they on foreign soil... I've always said that today Vietnam is now an adjective. It's used for everything.... They say, "We don't ever want this to be another Vietnam war." I watched the news summary on television last night and they said that, in essence, all of the people of the United States are victims of Vietnam. It was a part of our history, and everyone had a feeling for it. I hope we learned our lessons from it.

I commented that when the Vietnam veterans find their voice, they can get their message across to higher places, and Larry responded,

> That's what all the members of the veterans' organization are saying, get to the men who are pressing the buttons.

But there was a clear sense of the limitations of their power in influencing such decisions. Larry felt that while the Vietnam veterans could influence little conflicts like Salvador and Central America and places like that, but that when it came to the issue of nuclear war, there was nothing they could do. As for employment in defense production, many Veterans work in war plants because the plants by law have to give preference hiring Vietnam veterans.

> I don't like to get into the thing that if you're building them you're doing it to use them. I don't know if that's really true.... What scares me the most is that I hate to play games like when you're a little kid, "I'm not going to fight Joey because he's bigger than I am." Well, someone along the line is going to say they are going to fight Joe, and they'll go into World War III. And we're sitting here and bluffing all these countries. If you hit us, we're going to hit back harder. It scares me. I think it scares a lot of us.

Berkshire County has the largest number of Vietnam veterans in the state, perhaps because it contains more blue-collar workers and fewer children went to college. It also had fewer peace marches than other counties. But when the veterans returned and found that they were not welcomed as heroes, as their fathers had been, they felt bewildered. The war memorial they plan for Park Square is an attempt to recognize that sacrifice without glorifying it. Larry referred to the national memorial with the 58,000 names of soldiers who died and said,

> How can anyone ever look at this war memorial and ever want war again? When you see these names and how small they are and they were human beings, and they were like you and I — You see this stone, just a mass of names, how anyone can see this and commit another conflict like that? I don't see how they could possibly do it. The marines' memorial with the Iwo Jima flag, it's a different story. That doesn't show the price, that doesn't show the cost of war. You look there and say, "Wow, this is great!" But this memorial of Vietnam has an impact that to me is great. I'd like to show my family. And when you think of it, how many politicans went to Vietnam?

The failure to give public recognition to the special problems of Vietnam veterans was highlighted by the case of two veterans who burned down a Buddhist shrine in the nearby town of Cheshire. A psychiatrist called as a defense witness explained the burning of the temple as "an outgrowth of post-traumatic stress syndrome" One of the veterans was "plagued by feelings of guilt and anger from his service on a B-57 bomber in Vietnam... when there would be indiscriminate bombing of villages... and the other was forced, out of mercy, to kill his buddy who was sprayed with napalm. The psychiatrist asserted that the problem for the Vietnam veterans is where to put the anger, and when they see Vietnamese driving around and doing very well, they take their anger out on Orientals. (*New York Times* January 5, 1984).

Political response to the Vietnam veterans initiatives grew in the 1980s. In July 1984 U.S. Congressman Silvio Conte joined the relatives of servicemen still missing in action in Vietnam and announced a campaign to gain a full accounting of those missing in action. In the following year the Vietnam veterans received some of the belated respect many felt was due them as servicemen. In March 1985 the twenty-six from Berkshire County who had been killed were honored by former veterans and by the Vietnam Veterans of America. This day of memorialization was quite different from the celebration on Armistice Day at the end of World War I. It was a solemn occasion when the members of the small audience were called upon to assuage their guilt rather than the jubilant memories evoked about the victorious wars preceding Vietnam.

A Vietnam Veterans Center was opened in August 1985, and a state grant of $62,400 was given for staffing it with an outreach specialist and secretary. The center planned to give out information about agent orange and testing for exposure and to provide referrals for jobs and educational opportunities. The staff members of the center intended to follow through with each case, giving assistance in filing claims, gaining emergency assistance and even standing in line to support applicants who looked for aid in the conventional veterans' centers. The center also welcomed members of families in which the veteran "may not be ready to admit he has a problem but the families are aware of it," said president of the chapter Thomas G. Lareau. In May a model of the planned Pittsfield Vietnam memorial was unveiled, a four foot by six foot grey marble with the outline of the map of Vietnam which would join the statue of a Civil War soldier holding the flag of the Grand Army of the Republic on the Park Square lawn.

The incorporation of Vietnam veterans into mainstream society may deaden the negative response to military solutions. Yet the social injustice suffered as personal guilt by the young men whose lives were destroyed by the war required intervention by the local power structure, which had at first ignored them, As yet the national government has failed to recognize even the minimal claims for medical compensation to those exposed to agent orange. As local chapters, like that of Pittsfield, gain ground, and as state and national congressmen support their issues, the pressure for national recognition will come if the democratic process persists.

Peace Activists

Anti-Soviet sentiment is almost a reflex of the socialization process in the U. S. John, a GE worker involved in the peace-conversion movement, said that when there were demonstrations going on about Vietnam in the sixties when he was in high school, he marched around Park Square saying, "America, love it or leave it!" He began to question the Vietnam War when he was serving in the air force in Texas. It was not until he was discharged and went to the Berkshire Community College on his GI benefits that he began to become aware of his unstated assumptions. In questioning them, he became a peace activist.

While I was in college I became active in GIRO, Global Issues Research Organization. Some of the members took a trip to the Soviet Union, and they came back with slides of the Soviet Union. I thought, Jesus, these are people too! They could have houses over there, and there's cars and busses and trucks. People wear clothes there (laughed). And all of a sudden I asked, What did I have in my mind on those people before? And I realized that I had nothing in my mind. Nothing good, just bad things.

The following year, John went to the Soviet Union and found that there were many ways that exchanges could help each country. John was a realist about his planning for peace. He told me his philosophy:

Most people who talk about conversion planning today say that it means coming up with different products that, say, Ordnance GE can make and turning it around and converting the factory so that it can make it so that Pittsfield is not in the arms race. Well, I don't think it's that easy, because under that philosophy, where does anyone address the ideological differences between the United States and the Soviet Union? Where does anyone lessen the charge of unilateral disarmament? Besides, I think every defense contract ought to have required by law conversion plans of what they could make if it wouldn't be military, and keep making the military thing. Both sides should continue making the plans and sending them along to our arms control negotiators and have them look them over. They could look them over and ask for changes here and there and come up with real good plans. I think the plans should be multifaceted. We could help our own economy, the Soviet economy, the NATO economy, the Warsaw Pact economy and the economies of Third World development. So then we exhcnage the plans with each of them, go to the Soviets and say, "Look, these are our military strengths," and they know pretty much within 5 percent what they are and we know what their military strengths are. It will have to be small confidence building measures because we have no reason to trust the Soviets, and they have less reason to trust us. But then you've got a bargaining chip. Space satellites warfare, that isn't a bargaining chip.

The current way of planning, John maintains, nullifies the potential for production of peace time goods. He gave me an instance of that kind of planning:

A couple of weeks ago there was an announcement that GE got a 30 million dollar contract for Midgetman. Now that Midgetman was scheduled for deployment in the 1990s. They have all these different conceptions for the year 1990 into the year 2000. Where are the plans for peace? We're talking about ten or twenty years from now, and all they're talking about is war. To get back to that contract, it was split three ways. It was a 187 million dollar contract. We got thirty million, someone got sixty million and someone got eighty million. Most of that contract is going to that guy with the eighty million dollars. Cause each place is coming up with its own version of Midgetman. And then the air force is going to choose between the three to say which one is best. Most likely the one who spends the most is going to be chosen and will get the contract.... That's just spreading the money out, keeping the constituents happy. It's so absurd.

In the years of growth in Ordnance, people have grown not only to accept it, but to think of it as offering more job security than the peace time production that preceded it. John often encountered this argument to the conversion idea:

People say there are risks involved in conversion planning. What if we go into conversion planning, and what if the Soviets then end up having their missiles stashed up and then take over twenty or thirty years down the road? Well, there's risks in this arms buildup. And the risks there are a lot more dangerous than the chance that they may keep a few missiles stashed away and exploded 'em on us. The risks here are greater. Throughout history, hasn't it been shown to us that in order to reap benefits you gotta take risks?

What was really unusual about John was his willingness to enter consciously into affecting history. He had gone to a conference on peace conversion the previous year and had been accused of being a CIA agent when he was taking pictures.

Well, I was really taken aback by that. And afterward I began to think to myself and I said, Well, wait a minute. What have you got to hide anyway? I'm proud to be working for peace and trying to bring peace about, and trying to be level headed about it. I like to look at things historically speaking.

It is one thing to come to an awareness of peace issues, and quite another to convince others in Pittsfield. When John invited co-workers to meetings, he said the phone would ring off the wall for a week with people calling and saying "What are you doing letting that Communist son-of-a-bitch speak?" I asked him where his critics were coming from.

Where are they coming from? They're coming from having served their time in the military. Being, having the mentality of America, love it or leave it. America's right; might makes right. They're not just the older people from the McCarthy time. They're mixed. I've had young people and older people. What I tell people is that my

mother and father, well, they worked at GE Ordnance. I'm a
product of GE (laughed). What we ought to do is make more
products like me! My father went in the Army Air Corps in 1942.
He caught pneumonia and was discharged early. He came back here
and he went into Ordnance and he met my mother there.
Throughout the years, my father worked in Ordnance off and on.
My grandfather worked there. He was in security, in the boiler
room. Well GE is my family, right? My brothers and my sisters,
right?

I remarked that I didn't think the people on top appreciate that.

> I don't think that they do either. You know, Nick Boraski last year
> talked about the Pittsfield mentality. He talked about it in a
> detrimental way. I wanted to go to him and say, "You know, mister,
> you've got it mixed up. It's the Pittsfield mentality that made GE
> what it is. It's Power Transformer that carried GE for many years
> and enabled them to get into these businesses.... Pittsfield mentality
> is really good mentality. There's good people over there in GE. A
> lot of my friends, my brother works in Ordnance Systems. A lot
> of good people work in Ordnance. I'm not trying to close down
> Ordnance or close down the jobs. I'm trying to bring peace about,
> you know. How do you do that? How's it done?

John is convinced that, as long as we have freedom of speech, we
should be outspoken. When he first started his peace activities in 1982,
collecting signatures for the freeze, no one knew what it was, but
nowadays he says you can't talk to anybody who doesn't know about
it. He feels that the same may be true for the conversion idea. He was
not discouraged by the low turnout of twenty-five at a meeting in June
1983, sponsored by the Nuclear Weapons Education Center of
Williamstown and held at the IUE Local 255, nor has he given up trying
to involve the union in a more active commitment to conversion ideas.

Donald Lathrap, professor at the Berkshire Community College
who started GIRO with his wife Marion, became active in the civil rights
movement in 1964. Although their attendance in Quaker meetings is
an important factor in their commitment to political activities, they
consider their motivation to be based on humanist rather than religious
principles. Donald was a veteran of the Korean War:

> When I got out of engineering school I had a six-month tour of active
> duty. At that time you took tests and you could stay in college;
> otherwise you went to Korea. There again it was selective cannon
> fodder. I ended up six months in and I had to teach there. I thought

the service was abominable, but teaching was exciting. I enjoyed teaching even in the military.

When Don and Marion went on the civil rights march to the south, they were aware of the danger to the marchers and made out their wills. On the twentieth anniversary of that event, they saw the difference between the first occasion when Martin Luther King gave his speech and everyone was well-dressed in suits and ties, and the reuniting of the group when everyone was in tank tops and shorts. These days, even in the peace movement, things "are not really dangerous." They have found that the police are trained to behave differently.

In the sixties, Don was teaching and working in the summers as an engineer at GE, where the increment in salary enabled him to support a growing family. Don became involved in the peace movement when he went to a conference on the arms race in 1977. Marion said she resisted it for quite a while:

> I couldn't deal with global things. Give me personal problems. I didn't think I could really handle the attack on peace activists as being odd balls. This was 1977, 1978, 1979 and even up to 1980 and 1981. I think this past year [I interviewed the Lathraps in 1984] it's just blossomed with "The Day After." Even though I don't think it was a terribly great movie, it wakened a lot more people. With Reagan's budgets and all, people are realizing what that is doing. We went to the Soviet Union in 1980, and there were still a lot of people that would say, "Why would you want to go there?"

Don joined in about their trip:

> We were over there only three weeks, but we met with peace committees in five big cities. [I asked whether the peace movement were condemned over there and he replied:] Oh, it's co-opted in a sense.
> Marion added, "It's the ones that are not condoned by the government that end up in jail."

Don was interviewed on Russian television by a woman "like Donahue or something" and since she didn't speak English, the interview was conducted through translators.

> Well, it took a half an hour to get her to understand what the peace movement was. We were treated as though we represented THE PEACE MOVEMENT, as though it were a monolithic organization,

a single entity. When all we've got is an office in this old house on the second story and the executive director lives there and he has a secretary and his wife helps. What they do primarily is circulate reading materials around the county and arrange tours and do a couple of special little things. But it's a miniscule little group. A Yale professor left an endowment and they're able to carry on. So we tried to explain that we were not some AFSC or some big group. Just twenty or thirty small groups that I could think of just like that. And she didn't understand it at all! But the wonderful thing was, she said, "Well, what does the government do to help peace in your country?" And we realized that "peace group in the U. S." is defined as oppostion to the government. It's defined as support of the best that government has to offer over there. And our mouths just hung open. And you know they're being misled, I think, to a certain extent. Nevertheless they don't think of peace as in opposition to their government, whereas here, it sort of defines the peace movement in one way or another.

GIRO, the group that the Lathraps helped organize, plans conferences and brings speakers on global issues of the environment and peace to the campus and community. It provides a broader context for the consciousness-raising than most of the single-issue advocacy groups.

The peace movement is a loose coalition of the "Stop the Bomb" and the "Nuclear Freeze" student-teacher organization, "People for Peace," mostly in South County and the few involved in "Conversion to Peace." A new coalescence of peace activities is emerging in the opposition to intervention in Central America. Each group sponsors meetings in school or church facilities. A state-wide delegation converged on the Statehouse in Boston to urge a referendum on a nuclear freeze, a move supported by all of the Berkshire representatives. The Berkshire delegation announced its mission with a mockup of the Cruise Missile and signs calling for a freeze.

The anniversary of the bombing of Hiroshima on August 6, 1945 has become an annual observation with public demonstrations or vigils in Park Square by representatives of the various peace groups.

In 1983 a few people from People for Peace appeared at the Ordnance gate singing and showing placards calling for disarmament. When I asked one of them whether they had any members who were GE workers and how they felt about Conversion to Peace, he said:

They were against our being here today because we've been trying to approach people to talk to them about converting production to peace time uses. And the feeling of the activist was that we would alienate them [the workers] and they wouldn't want to talk with us. My feeling was that unless we make the point, people are not going to be thinking about it in the first place. As long as we respect each others' positions.

Despite the frustration of not being able to reach workers who feel that their jobs are on the line, the People for Peace have seen growing support for their nuclear freeze activities and support for the resolution to have a referendum in South County. Looking back to the sixties, they remember growth in the war resistance from a time when resistance was considered far out to the point where it was part of the mainstream.

The Pittsfield Stop the Bomb group held its demonstration in Park Square in 1982. When I asked about their goals, one of the high school students said:

Well, it's the whole range. Stop Nuclear War is specifically against nuclear war, and I think nationally it's for the freeze. It's an organization of high school students. Personally, I guess I'm a pacifist. I got involved in this four years ago. In this area, I think there's about three times as much support for the freeze as there is opposition.

The young man I spoke with was also involved in the opposition to the peace-time draft registration, but he was careful to keep each issue compartmentalized. One of the students commented that his father was a doctor, so he did not get pressure from home about being in the Stop movement, but the father of one of his best friends is an engineer and does try to discourage them. When I said that I had talked with the group over at Ordnance they were eager to know how many there were and added, "We didn't want to antagonize the people so we didn't go there." They then debated whether to go over and join with them, but decided against it and thought that maybe just one representative from the group might pass by. A young woman with a baby in a stroller joined the group for awhile, and when I asked her if she was in the Women's Strike for Peace she said she was afraid of getting into too many things.

In 1984 the Nuclear Freeze demonstrators drew a crowd numbering 100, according to the local newspaper, with a rock band and speeches on the dangers of a nuclear holocaust. Park Square is a realatively neutral zone, compared to vigils or leafletting at Ordnance Systems where some peace activists, usually from out of town, prefer to go. One of the locally active People for Peace explained their reluctance to go there:

Some of the people want to go over there [to Ordnance] and put
the pressure on them, have vigils there, and leaflet and cause some
disturbance and even try to get into GE. Because that happens in
other cities like Philadelphia and Boston and New York City and
other places. You have these manufacturers all over the place and
they demonstrate and make a big scene and get arrested. But the
feeling is that in New York, or Philadelphia, people who work at
these plants are rather anonymous people. You don't know them
and they don't know you and they aren't going to have any other
contact with you. And in Pittsfield you're neighbors, and you're
relatives, and you are alienating two groups, which is what confrontation would do. You're not going to change anything. You're
just going to make two camps.

Probably the most general interest in peace is supported by the
church groups. The primary concern of the established religious
congregations is consciousness, although national ecumenical groups
sometimes take more vigorous action. In 1982 the interfaith Center on
Corporate Responsibility of New York proposed to the shareholders
of GE that they call upon management to halt the nuclear arms race.
GE recommended that its stockholders vote against the resolution.

The educational director of the Catholic churches in Pittsfield told
me in an interview that bishops have given strong support to education
for peace in their parishes. In the revamped education program, the
diocese, centered in Springfield with four counties of western
Massachusetts, will have a segment on peace and justice issues. This
movement, which, he said, "comes from the top down" faces the
"most ticklish issue" on deterrence; most will condemn the nuclear
weapons because of the massive killing of civilians, but when it comes
to arms for deterrence, many support it. There is "qualified support"
of weapons "in the context of negotiations" but the church condemns
the stance of nuclear superiority taken by the Reagan administration.

As a result of the strong commitment to peace of the "church
hierarchy," the educational director is concerned with "how the
message can best be translated to the laity." They have dispersed "tons
of literature" from National Catholic Education and weave programs
on peace into all education. Personnel at Ordnance have appreciated
the church's effort and, he said, "see the church as a moderating
influence overcoming the search for profits." A number of parish
councils have endorsed the nuclear freeze.

An Interfaith Task Force supports ecumenical services, with
speakers such as the Reverend Sloan Coffin, a prominent opponent
of the Vietnam War; Judy Scheckel, a former nun and now staff

member of the Traprock Peace Center specializing in disarmament; Reverend Daniel Berrigan, who engaged in many acts of civil disobedience during the Vietnam War; and the Reverend Robert F. Drinan who is professor of arms control and disarmament at Georgetown University Law Center and U. S. congressman from 1971 to 1981, when he withdrew from elective office upon orders from Pope John Paul II. These nationally recognized speakers provide a focus for local activists to crystalize their own ideology and extend their networks.

Throughout 1984 and 1985 the peace groups were sponsoring conferences and lectures concerned with the buildup of the ''Contras'' in Nicaragua. Activists in the Witness for Peace group involved ecumenical alliances of Baptists, Catholics, Methodists and people of any other religious conviction concerned with the spread of hostilities. The Berkshire Committee on Central America organized a trip to Nicaragua in 1984 and the following year members of this group decided on an action of civil disobedience at the marine recruiting station. Sixteen protestors entered the station asking to show slides of their past years' trip. The marine sergeant called the police after the group refused to respond to his request to leave. While the group included several Williams College students, the age range of the seven women and nine men was from nineteen to seventy-three and they came from five different towns in the area. The action was given wide coverage in the local daily press and the weekly *Berkshire Sampler*. Pointing out that these were people who went jogging, tended their gardens and were parents, the *Sampler* questioned what motivated them to carry out this act of civil disobedience. The answer seemed to be moral outrage and frustration that all the other actions they and others had taken had failed to change the government policy of intervention. In response to clear messages opposed to military solutions from his constituents, U. S. Congressman Silvio Conte has consistently voted against aid to the ''Contras'' although he is a Republican.

In the summer of 1985 a group of Witnesses for Peace traveled to Nicaragua. One of these witnesses wrote to the local newspaper of her experience listening to the prayers of Nicaraguans fasting for peace in a church on the Honduras border, and commented:

> Are we as a nation so polluted by power and arrogance that we cannot respect the self-determination of a small country of three million people? What values are we promoting when we use terror to show the Nicaraguans who is boss? The contras do not deserve our support. The United States must stop funding murder. (Karen E. Rott in *The Berkshire Eagle* September 5, 1985.)

Peace action in the community stresses a moral concern rather than a more overtly political or economic struggle. Corporate hegemony is reinforced by the growing dependency of workers on the defense buildup. Labor unions try to make small gains in getting the corporation to hire laid-off workers in the constantly growing Ordnance Systems rather than demanding new production lines in consumer-oriented production. Qualified attacks by the major religious institutions on the arms buildup curb, but do not oppose, the need for defense industries and limited wars of containment. The peace activists operate outside of the established institutions to voice their alarm at the military expenditure and their outrage with the Central American intervention. As yet they are few in number, and neither the unions nor the municipal administration have confronted the corporation in its defense buildup. But the more experienced peace activists point to the history of the civil rights movement and the Vietnam War protests to show the potential for such actions growing into mass movements.

Pittsfield is eighth on the target list for a nuclear attack as a result of the presence of Ordnance Systems. In a pamphlet detailing strategies to follow in case of a nuclear war, the Civil Defense Committee reported that "if you were at General Electric Ordnance, this would disappear into a crater 20 stories deep" and "the rim of radioactive soil would extend to Dalton Avenue, East Street and the Boston and Albany Railline." Everything within a two-mile radius would be demolished, and "if one were boating on Onota Lake, most would be killed by the burnout." There is little comfort in having the General Electric facility in their presence, and yet there is an equally prevalent fear of its leaving.

Chapter 9

Family and Community in Pittsfield

In the process of industrialization, families constituted the most important institutional nexus ensuring survival of working class (Hareven 1975, 1982, 1987; Humphries 1977). Families make up for the insecurity in the labor market by pooling resources. They organize the division of labor within the household in such a way as to make otherwise incompatible schedules of wage work and housework plausible. They extend the remuneration of wage earners to the non-wage earners doing housework, attending school, or in retirement. They provide the basic motivation for a steady commitment to employment to wage work even when the conditions of work and the remuneration are deplorable. Family life compensates for the lack of attention to, or concern for, basic welfare interests of the society within capitalist structures. Through their own sacrifices to provide mobility for their children through education and training, the parental generation proves the success of corporate hegemony in providing expanding opportunities.

The positive attitudes and rewards of family life are coopted in the commercial and industrial life of the community. Stores, restaurants and businesses use it in their titles: there is a Family Affair Restaurant, a Family Appliance Repair, a Family Health Center, a Palace Theatre Family Entertainment, a Family Tag Shop, a Family Thrift Shop, a Family Therapy Associates and a Family Practice Associates. The General Electric Company calls its yearly tours of the facilities a "Family Day," to help relate the job to spouses and children.

Despite this positive outlook statistics for family breakdown in Pittsfield follow national trends. The number of separated and divorced women doubled from 1970 to 1980, going from 1,291 to 2,155. Since most of the men left the area after divorce or separation, their numbers actually decreased. Women have in these cases assumed the responsibilities for playing both parental roles while entering the work force.

The burdens borne by the family are becoming recognized by public and private agencies that provide supportive and compensatory assistance. Most of the associational life in sports, the YMCA, the Girls' Club and the Boys' Club promote family programs that bring the members together in recreational activities. The greatest fear in economic recession is the loss of family contacts as members leave the community to seek jobs elsewhere. Family counseling is offered in the training programs for displaced workers. With the heavy burden the family carries, breakdown is expected and in this chapter I will focus on the intergenerational dynamics of family life, reserving governmental and quasi-public mediation for the following chapter.

Generational Changes In The Family

Generation, ethnic origins, wealth and class influence but do not determine the functions and preferences of family life. While it is generally assumed that members of the same family of origin share the same socioeconomic position, this is quite often not the case, and members of the same family may exhibit the whole gamut of alternative structures and styles within the same generation. This replication of the societal structure within the nucleus of the family promotes and strengthens corporate hegemony by affirming the mobility, independence and freedom of choice that are central to the value system. The fact that siblings, children, and/or extended family members occupy different positions in a socioeconomic hierarchy is proof that one can make it in the society if one has the ability and drive. This makes failure more difficult to bear at the same time that it provides resources to assist one who is in trouble.

The other characteristic of family life in Pittsfield that reinforces hegemony is the redistribution that goes on within the family, supplementing and atoning for the inequities in the market system of distribution. The complementarity of male/primary, female/secondary employee comes about when households pool resources of men and women. Without a male breadwinner in the family, women are more sharply aware of the inadequacy of their pay to meet the needs of the family and are, therefore, less likely to accept the system as it is.

These two processes — the replication of the social structure in the family and the redistribution of pooled incomes in the household — will now be considered in terms of generational change, alternative family forms and compensatory social service agencies. The dynamics of these processes vary considerably over time and between family units that are differently constructed. Social service agencies of the state and local government, particularly those organized in the period of President Johnson's Great Society movement, are directed towards overcoming some of the major distortions in the operation of the system.

Max Gluckman (1968) said that:

The structural duration of an institution is that period of time required to work out the implications of its rules and customs within the biological, ecological, and social environment. This period of time, the duration, is contained in the structure of the institution, and it is only in terms of expositing the institution through that duration that we can work out the interdependence, the systematic structure, between the elements that comprise the institution.

For families, this structure relates to the four generations required to see the biological processes of mating, reproduction, maturity and death worked out in a complete cycle.

Within four generations, one can also see the social processes of enculturation and incorporation in the community. By enculturation I mean taking on the forms and meanings expressed in behavior and belief in a community. Since the family is the primary institution in which this takes place, it acquires a double importance for people who have come to a place from another culture. When the migration occurs within the four generations of significant social formation, the "duration" that Gluckman refers to, it is the family that takes on a great deal of the task of gaining a position in the new society. "Family time," as Hareven (1975) points out, is distinct in its institutional cycle from "industrial time." Families that retain a high degree of cohesiveness are those that benefit from combined resources to gain greater mobility (Hareven 1987; Sennet 1970[1]).

I shall try to show how the life experiences of members of several families illustrate the processes of replication and redistribution within this four generational cycle. These families were selected from among the 100 respondents to a survey questionnaire administered to employees of General Electric on the IUE's active and laid-off list, as well as people whom I contacted while attending community affairs.

Replication of Social Hierarchy in Families

The great successes of many immigrant families can be traced back to the support offered in extended families. I have selected some of the families that illustrate both the success of individual members and the range of variation within a single generation to show how families mirror the social class differentiation. Age order and sex are extremely important factors conditioning the ability of individuals to take advantage of family resources. Older children go to work earlier, and their contribution to the household goes toward helping younger children. As family fortunes improve, younger members can stay in school longer, enhancing their mobility. Females tend to give a greater share of their pay to the family and this, combined with a tendency to negate their entry into advanced educational or professional institutions, reduced their mobility. How this works can be seen in the following families, whose names are fictitious but suggest their ethnic origin.

The Bartolinis

Vicky Bartolini immigrated to the U. S. in 1921 when she was thirteen years old. She came with her parents and brother from what was, until 1918, known as part of the Tyrol. Her family had been evacuated from their village, which was part of Austria until after the war, when it was taken over by Italy. She was able to get four hours a week of schooling in the town where they lived during the war in what was to become Czechoslovakia. Her father came first to America in 1913 to earn the money to bring them over. He sent money over twice; the first time it was stolen by the travel agent. It took another year to get the money together again. As soon as they arrived in Adams in 1921, Vicky went to work in the Hoosac Cotton Textile mills and there she was able to go to school half of each day. Her father worked in the Arnold Printworks and her mother stayed home. Mr. Bartolini had been an itinerant shoemaker in Italy but he couldn't use his trade in the U. S. since shoes were factory made. Vicky got her first job in the General Electric in 1924 when she was sixteen. She was helped on her first job by the fact that her foremen, the father of the Republican congressman for western Massachusetts, spoke Italian and taught her the job.

Vicky was laid off when she got married but went back to work in the textile mills after the birth of her child because her husband's carpentry jobs were irregular during the Depression. She moved in to a two-family house on East Street with her mother, who helped her take care of her daughter. She was rehired as a machine operator during World War II. After the war, she bought a little house with a large tract of land where her husband planted and worked a garden and set in fruit trees. Vicky's daughter went to work in Washington and, following her husband's death in an automobile accident, went on to become a director of Peace Corps recruitment in California. Her granddaughter visited her summers and met an engineer who works in the General Electric. They now live in a new house they built on Vicky's land. Vicky spends a good deal of time with her great-grandchildren who are still small. She hopes to live long enough to see them grown up. The contrast in the two houses and the life styles that they contain encapsulates four generations of change in working-class culture. Vicky's cottage still retains the simple spare lines of its eighteenth-century origin, with small rooms and a sunlit porch full of plants. The only modernization is in the kitchen, which is filled with the electric appliances that most workers acquired after World War II. Her granddaughter's house is a spacious ranch-style split level with a patio and barbecue pit. Her great-grandchildren have rooms stuffed with toys.

Vicky has made several return trips to the village of her childhood, which is now a part of Italy. During World War II, Vicky's mother used to send clothing and money to her relatives in Italy who were desperately poor. Now, Vicky says, some of them are better off than she is. But she quickly adds, "I'm lucky I live in America and not over there, even though they're all much better off than they used to be.... America is a land of liberty. Yes, you can do things here. Here, no matter who you are, you're just as good as the next one, whereas over there they argue how much money you got." At another point in our conversation she reflected that, "in reality, you work harder here than over there."

The Leonardis

Within four generations the Leonardi family moved from Italy, established a home and raised a family in Pittsfield, saw their grand-children born and raised to college age and the mother has lived to see five great-grandchildren born. In four generations their family members moved from the father's status of a contract laborer on a railroad gang to professionals working in General Electric and in the community. John, a retired General Electric worker who was born in 1913, recalled what he learned of his father's progress in the United States:

> It started out with my father coming to this country when he was a boy. He went to Colorado first, and he worked on what you call a gang in a railroad. They had shandy work — everybody worked in a shandy and one man was appointed to do the cooking and everybody bought their food and the railroad paid them back. As a boy he made a few dollars there, which was the accepted thing then, come over to America the streets were lined with gold. Go back to Italy and get married and come back to America with a family. Which he did. And he came back here, and came directly to Pittfield because there were friends here at the time that he wrote to, telling him how wonderful it was getting over here to get a job. Because conditions in Italy at that time were bad. Because if you worked at all, it was in agriculture, and if you didn't have a little

plot of ground to live off of you didn't eat very well. You had to have your own sheep and livestock; sheep was the main thing, and if someone was rich and really lucky, they had a cow. Only the cities were really industrialized, and that was in the northern part of Italy.

John's father went back to Italy to get married, because, he said:

If an Italian married an Irish girl at that time, he was ostracized by both sides. He was just a non-conformist. He was what you call today a rebel.... Ethnic groups are very clannish. And you can't blame them. They're both [the Italians and the Irish] the same, they both did the same thing to the other. The younger generation moved in, they started going with each other. And still to this day there's an undercurrent of, "Well, Jesus, he's Irish. What the devil is she going to marry him for?" Now it'll take one or two generations more before they're really all American. And I doubt then that it will become erased anyway.

John's parents had two children who died in infancy in Italy, but when his father, who had returned to the U. S. alone, had earned enough money to bring his wife over, they settled in the center of Pittsfield and produced four children, three boys and a girl. John was the eldest child.

John started work in 1929 when he was sixteen years old because his father had been injured working in the GE and there was no insurance. With four children and no wage coming in, his mother took in boarders and he got a job as an office boy at General Electric for $5.50 a week. He got married when he was twenty years old and took on the five jobs he described in Chapter 3. In 1936 he went back to work at General Electric when his first child was two years old. The work force was still ethnically divided, but some Italians were employed inside the plant. John pointed out:

Up until 1929 they were first generation Polish, German, you name it, because they came over during the First World War, but during World War II and this generation coming up were more Americanized, were more modern, were more knowledgeable and were educated, much better educated because you had to go to school in this country. In the old country if you had money you went, and if you didn't, you didn't. And then education played a tremendous part. If you got a real smart Italian boy like Faccioli, he was one of the electrical engineers who had a lot to do with what they said over there [in the General Electric]. He was also connected with Steinmetz. He was a genius. He helped many Italians.

John married Dora in 1933. Her mother had come to Pittsfield when she was seventeen years old. Her mother's father had a barbershop on West Street. Her parents had their wedding breakfast in the railroad station's restaurant just after its construction. Her mother later ran a grocery store and knew everyone on the west side of town. Her father was a welder in the General Electric all his life. Dora was the eldest of six children, all of whom have stayed in Pittsfield. One of her brothers, who went to college, is a fire captain. Dora wanted to go to college to study nursing, but her father objected:

> My father felt that a girl shouldn't take care of men, and you know how the older Italians were. He was broad-minded in a lot of things, but that was one thing where he was very set in his ways. I was so disappointed. But ah, it's one of those things. At that time, if the parents said no, that was it. It isn't like today. You listened to them then. He didn't like the idea of his daughter being a nurse. I often wonder how he would feel if he knew that we have a daughter that's a nurse.

Dora worked in the General Electric, along with her father and her brother, as a packer in radio bases. She said:

> My first pay from the General Electric was about $18.75, I can remember. Seventy-five cents was the spending money I got at the end of the week. You know how your mother doled it out to you.

John also turned all of his pay over to his father and mother until her got married. Dora lost her job after a year and a half when production was transferred elsewhere. She went to business college and got a job in a newspaper magazine distributing company. Her sister, Nelly, was "one of the top girls" who worked on the GE wire assembly-line, working on Poseidon.

By the time World War II came, John and Dora had two children. Right after Pearl Harbor, he signed up for the service, but his boss urged him to stay to break in a new man on the job. Because he was in essential industry, those deferments extended throughout the war.

The first home that they bought was in the city, but by 1953 they had an opportunity to buy an old farmhouse on New Lenox Road. "The bank and I went into business together," John said. There he had the land to grow a big garden and his wife canned food. The youngest child was then seven years old.

Their children went to the community college and became professionals. Two are working in General Electric, a daughter who is a nurse in the clinic and the youngest is a computer analyst in payroll. He wanted to enlist in the army during the Vietnam War, but his father insisted that he get his college education first. A grandson is working as a mechanical engineer at Lynn General Electric. His sister worked in the General Electric laboratories while she was still in college and is now graduating. Another daughter works for the Hartford housing Authority as a secretary for a judge.

The Leonardi's are one of many immigrant families that achieved the American dream within four generations. John attributes some of their success to the corporation:

> As far as I'm concerned, working for the General Electric Company has been a very beneficial thing. You've got to have someone smart up there. There again, you've got to point out to the younger folks, especially when you're walking a picket line, "Oh, that GE is a lousy company, this and that," and "The GE don't know what it's doing." Well, I tell them, "The General Electric didn't get to be as great a company as it is today by having stupid people at the top. You've got to have someone smart up there."

The Ronzinis

The Ronzinis show the full range of class relations within the second generation of eleven children, five of whom were born in Italy and six in the United States. Their father had gone to America to earn money to bring his wife and children to the United States. He worked very hard to get the money together because of the looming threat of World War I and the fear that Nick, the eldest, would be drafted. They arrived in the U. S. in 1913 with the eldest, Nick, who was already twenty-three years old; Alex, who was eight; Mary who was five; Jeanette and May, the baby. The children enjoyed the ride in steerage, running around free because their mother was sick most of the time. They and the other children lined up for warm milk which was poured into tin cups, and they soon learned that the steward dispensing the precious fluid did not remember how they looked, so they would come up for seconds and thirds. They could smell the steaks cooking in first-class passenger quarters.

When they arrived in America, they went to live with their father in Buffalo, where he worked on the railroad with their Uncle Jim. Not long after that they came to Pittsfield and lived with another family, the seven of them crowded into one room. Soon, they moved into a rented apartment on Fenn Street in a third-story walkup. Fenn Street was all Italian then, and there were several Italian stores where the father bought beans in large sacks to feed the family, going from one shop to another to compare prices. Then they moved to Fourth Street, where for the most part Irish and Yankees lived. That helped them learn English faster, but the boys had to fend off the bullies. It didn't help that their mother told them not to fight or they would be put in jail because they were Italians — that meant that the boys ganged up on them even more. The house grew with them and six more children were born there. As the boys grew, Jimmy, the son who had an aptitude for carpentry, built additional rooms making four four-room apartments out of the double house.

The family was, like other Italian families, very patriarchal. Alex used to wish that his father would not walk in front of his mother when they walked down the streets. Their father did all the accounts because his mother "couldn't tell one bill from another" and was totally illiterate all of her life. Alex commented:

> Well, he knew how to handle it. He was quite a provider. I don't care what suffering you went through, you did it for the whole family. And Pa seen that you'd get food for the family.

The father was intending to leave the house and all the belongings to the boys because they were supposed to be the providers. But his wife intervened and said in America the girls also had to inherit something. Boys were allowed greater freedom as they were growing up, and while they could come in at any hour, the girls had to be home early. Theresa remembers vividly when she came home from a date, "There would be a big conga line with bread to be kneeded on Friday nights." They also made wine and everybody got in to their special rubber boots to stamp out the juice from the grapes.

Alex, who was born in Italy, remembers the humiliation of going to school and being put in grades with five year olds when he was eight. "When we used to sit on the floor in a circle," he told me, "I must have looked like a janitor with the rest of the kids." He left school as soon as he was fourteen, the legal age for quitting, and went to work in the Rice's mill. His brother Jim, who was the first one born in their Fourth Street house, "got along with the teachers, strangely." Jim explained his success with them:

> If somebody got noisy in the room, it was my job to shut 'em up because I was tougher than the rest of 'em. I got along fine, but, uh, I used to pride myself when I was in the third grade that I could lick everybody through the fifth grade. I think it made a difference when they had me in their class because the teacher used to cultivate

me a little bit, you know. They used to treat me awfully good. If
they wanted somebody to go down to the store, she'd send me
down.

Jim worked for a painting contractor with Alex and later organized
his own painting contract business. Jeanette worked in a laundry and
Mary clerked in the family store. May married at an early age. Joe
bought an old-age nursing house. Theresa was the first child to
complete high school. She got a job at the General Electric in 1936.
The youngest brother went to Williams College, where he was the
captain of the football team, and graduated to become a reporter and
later the editor of the Williams College Alumni Magazine. Each of the
children turned over all of their money to their father. Alex did so until
six months before his marriage when he started saving for his wedding.
Theresa asked her father, ''Pa, can I do it like the Americans?'' That
meant to pay just room and board. She continued to give over $10 but
was allowed to keep $1. But when she was laid off in 1937, the family
did not expect to be paid room and board. This is the crucial difference
between a household economy and a market economy.

The children took very different paths although they stayed most
of their lives in Pittsfield. Mary went to Connecticut with her husband,
who deserted her there, then she returned with the help of welfare
to Pittsfield, where she worked in the Elmvale mill until it closed in
1949. Jeanette bought the dry cleaning service where she worked and
prospered there. Alex and Jim prospered in their paint business,
especially with some good contracts from General Electric. Jim owns
over a million dollars worth of land and houses in Coltsville. Alex was
happy to be able to help his brother Ralph invest in a book store that
he ran for many years in Williamstown. When Theresa married an
Irishman, she was excluded from the Italian congregation of the
Catholic church. She kept the job she first got in the General Electric
even after she married and had three children because her husband,
who was in construction, was an alcoholic and she had to support the
family. Her sister Jeanette helped her out, getting clothing and shoes
for her boys when they were growing up.

Patriarchy is a complex set of relations that provides benefits to
the dependents which have assured its survival. The centralization of
earnings controlled by the father enhances his position in the family
as he redistributes income to family members according to his own
criteria of what is appropriate.[2] When the Ronzinis celebrated their
fiftieth wedding anniversary, Mr. Ronzini gave Mary $100 to get her
mother a dress. Mary and Theresa went to England's the downtown

department store, and found a fuschia dress with rhinestones for $15! When they told their father they got a dress for $15 he said, "What kind of a dress did you get? A rag?" Theresa added, "So Ma put the dress on and he liked it. She said she was going to be buried in it. And she was too." The parents went to stay in Joe's old age home and there, to his dying day, their father took care of and worried about their mother. "Pa stayed alive as long as she lived because he had to take care of her," Theresa told me.

The Lantenaris

Life was hard for these immigrant families, but when one of the parents died before the children were grown, it was even more difficult. Al Lantenari was born in 1917 and his father died when he was nine years old. He and his five brothers grew up on West Street when it was a daily fight for survival for a boy. He recalls these years:

> Of course, we were on welfare, and my mother, outside of a few words of profanity, spoke very little English. We continued going to school. She had six boys to bring up. We had girls, but unfortunately they passed away at a very young age. She was tough with us. She made sure bringing up six boys that we were going to toe the mark. We did get into a little trouble here and there, you know. Boy trouble, nothing serious. That's one thing that I am often thankful for — because of the strict rules that she laid down for us that none of us ever got into any serious trouble. None of us. She set curfews for us if we went to the Boys' club, and she'd say, "I want you home at 8:30." As we got older in our teens, she'd say, "I want you home at ten." You better be home at ten. She had a favorite stick there, maybe two inches in diameter and maybe about four feet long, and she used to role macaroni. I can remember when I was thirty-five years old, she lived next door when she was alive, and we went over there one day. I think that it was the Christmas holiday. She was sitting down and I'd done something to her. I'd either pinched her or something playfully, and she raised her arm and I flinched. She scared me from when I was a kid, and my brothers were all the same way. We just feared her because of the discipline that she used in the house. People used to tell her that the boys do this and the boys do that, and she'd say, "Don't you worry, I'll take care of them."

Discipline within the family, such as Al's mother exercised, was important in the tough neighborhood he was growing up in, where people made booze during the prohibition and others came to drink it. Al saw a man they called "the banana man" (because he let the kids grab the bananas that fell off the stalks as he worked in the fruit department of a grocery store on West Street) fall off the West Street bridge into the river. Another time while he was licking an ice cream cone he saw a man kill his son-in-law over a fight about the proper length of the skirts that his daughter should wear. Al's mother was able to keep him going to school until he reached sixteen. Then the welfare department insisted that he go to work, although he had only one more year to get his diploma. He went back to school after he was married and learned a trade, reading blueprints, and machine shop theory, when he was laid off and on unemployment.

Al joined the service in 1941, although by that time he had one son and one daughter and could have gained a deferment. His children have gone to college and two remain in Pittsfield. One daughter is a secretary in General Electric and his son is supervisor in the Massachusetts turnpike service.

Impact of Familial Social Hierarchy on Consciousness

Within four generations — what Max Gluckman (1968) called the "structural duration of an institution" or "time required to work out the implications of its rules and customs within the biological, ecological and social environment" — these families were incorporated in the community. As the primary unit of enculturation, the family was particularly important with immigrants since it took on the task of gaining a position in the new society. Each generation surpassed the past in education and class position, although there was variation in the level of success achieved by individuals. The Ronzinis exhibit the most extensive range of variation, but all of the members I spoke to attributed their success to the American system. The successes experienced by the Leonardis are attributed to General Electric as well as to the country. The Lantenaris experienced the sting of welfare when the mother was widowed, and this may well have influenced Al's commitment to union organization before it became socially acceptable. Yet he was among the first to respond to his country's call when war against the Axis was declared.

The advances each generation made are visible proof of the opportunities available in the United States. Patriotism and commitment to the institutions that reproduce the society are reciprocal concomitants that rise not out of false consciousness, although they impede the development of class consciousness, but out of an awareness of betterment within their family cycle. The replication of social hierarchy in families proves to most people's satisfaction that opportunities are available for all and it is up to the individual to take advantage of them.

Redistribution in the Family

These families reveal the strength and resiliency of the institution that made not only for survival but also for rapid mobility in the span of two or three generations. This was achieved by the redistribution of wages within each family in such a way as to enhance the opportunities for the young and more often, male members. Even when the death of one parent threatened the family unit, the strength of a person like Al's mother made it possible to go on with welfare assistance. Although the nuclear family was a distinct unit with its claims over the individual having priority over the extended unit, the wider family encompassing three generations was an important support structure.

The variety of experiences within the same generation is directly related to the sequence in the birth of the children and to the mobility of the family. As each of the older children in turn helped those younger by contributing their pay to the family, the successively younger children could stay in school longer and longer. This help contributed to a greater cohesiveness in later life. The experienced reality of mobility engendered a sense of commitment to the family and through it to the social system as a whole. Women accepted the authority of men, their fathers and husbands. The reciprocal of this dependency was a devoted attention on the part of the men that lasted throughout their lifetimes. In the Ronzini family, the mother enjoyed this up to her last days in her son's old age home, where her husband stayed alive as long as she did in order to attend to her. This was not the fate of their children, however. Theresa and her sisters became full-time wage earners and assumed the head of the household position that was not recognized by General Electric or the wider society. Their children, however, appreciate the fact that it was their mothers who ensured their survival. Vicky also lacked the economic support of her husband, although she more than upheld her share of the household burden as chief breadwinner and housekeeper. In her family, ideological commitment survived a generation beyond the reality of the behavioral support system.

The Leonardis sustain the patriarchal authority of the father even when the women are full-time workers. They accepted his decisions even when it limited their self-development. The fact that Dora's father discouraged her from taking up nursing denied her access to a career that interested her, and, at the same time, confirmed her dependency on her husband. The women in the Ronzini family subsidized the large family that their father engendered at the expense of their own careers and social mobility. Yet they accorded him the respect of a patriarch until his death.

Generational and Ethnic Variation in the Divison of Labor

Family resources include the wages and income of its members and the labor they control. The expropriation and allocation of these resources follow a pattern based on an ideology about gender hierarchy and control within the family. But there is a wide latitude in what that ideology consists of, so that each generation gives it a different specification. It is influenced by the employment context in which members of the family are engaged. I have already described above the effectiveness of pooled family resources in gaining mobility for some members in the wider society. Here I shall show some variations, as changing family forms and functions affect the redistribution of resources.

The major change is from that of pooling all the income of the children, which is put under the control of the father, to individual autonomy of each wage earner, who simply makes a contribution of board and room. When the father was in charge of pooled resources, he was expected to save a portion of the wage which would then be returned to the children when each wished to get married and set up their own homes. This redistribution reinforced the authority of the father and put the mother and children effectively under his control at the same time that his care and concern in shepherding these resources validated his position as "head of the family." All the families I have talked with had shifted to what Theresa saw as the "American system" where working children, although still living with their parents, hand over only a specific portion of their wage to their parents for board and room. The generation that graduated during or after World War II could call upon familial resources at least for another two years of community college training beyond high school. If they worked, they might help pay those expenses, but beyond some nominal contribution for food, they had control of their wages.

Not only have the intergenerational patterns changed, but also the set of expectations between spouses. Until very recently, the preferred pattern of nuclear family roles was that of a single breadwinner. This was never realized by the entire community, nor even by an overwhelming majority of it, but when women like Vicky and Theresa worked full-time they found it necessary to explain why they did so. Before the union, the corporation always treated them as expendables and even after they gained some job security, their pattern of interrupted work because of family responsibilities cut down the seniority that was the essence of security. During and after World War II, when more women took on part-time work, their pay was expected to cover "extras" — meals in restaurants, entertainment, new furniture purchases and other exceptional expenditures. But when the woman's job is a full-time commitment, as it now has become, women's contributions are allocated to education for the children, clothing for themselves and the children and a major share in the purchase of food.

In our interviews of 100 active and laid-off production workers selected from the IUE lists of "eligible" workers (see Chapter 5) we found that women's commitment to work varies with the number and ages of their chldren as well as the stability of the husband's work and the kind of work they themselves perform. Our interviews, about one-half of which were carried out in the homes of the subject with both husband and wife present, revealed that the spouses of forty-eight or 63 percent of those who were married and for whom information on the spouses' work was acquired, did work, and for all but three of them it was a full-time job. Three women went into full-time work when their husbands were laid off. Nine worked in General Electric along with their spouses. Sixteen were engaged in service jobs such as hairdressers, nurses, sales persons, waitresses, etc., a category that comprised 43 percent of the working spouses of sampled workers. Thirteen percent, or five, were schoolteachers. Of the five women workers in the survey, only two were married and both the husbands who worked in the firm. Since most of the production work that employed women in assembly of electrical products had been relocated to the south and elsewhere, there were few women in our random sample and three of the five were on lay-off. Most of the women who remained in the plant were in the clerical staff or numbered among the recent employees to fulfill equal opportunity rulings on defense contracts.

Allocation of Roles in the Household

Visiting the homes of workers we were able to see the great deal of flexibility in the household division of labor among those couples where both worked. All the working women continued to shop, a preference on their part. The outside/inside work division that characterized families with non-wage-working wives persists, with some modifications. The major contrasts are between members of different generations. Vicky, whose working career began in 1921 when she was fourteen years old, continued to do all the housework even though she was the main support for her family, which included one child. She describes her weekend routine after she was forced by a lay-off at the General Electric plant to seek employment in New York State, where she stayed during the week:

I liked my job down there very much, but I had the upkeep on the house. My husband was here and all the expenses were the same or even more. I used to work six days and come home for three days, then go back to work six more days, then have three more days off. I came home on my three days and cooked up a storm so he'd have food here. That was in 1953.

Although she never expressed resentment about this uneven division of labor in the several interviews that I had with her, I noticed she laughed somewhat scornfully when I asked her if her husband minded her working, and when we were raking leaves that fall, she swore that she would cut down a pear tree her husband had planted. It seemed almost a symbol of the extra work he heaped on her even after his death.

Theresa was able to continue working as a clerk in General Electric's traffic control office after her marriage in 1952 because the union had eliminated the company's right to fire married women. Although she worked full time, she was forced to take on full responsibility of the house and getting the children to day-care and schools. Added to this was the burden of caring for the man himself after he became an alcoholic and worrying about his whereabouts when he was not home. She turned to her own family for help, and was proud that she never had to go on welfare.

Men and women of the younger generations who entered the work force in the sixties have a much more flexible division of labor. One young couple in their mid-thirties acquired an in-ground pool, a gift of the wife's father. Their division of labor used to be inside/outside, but the pool changed things:

> I take care of maintenance outside work and she does the inside. She will sometimes do the mowing, but mostly I do it. Oh yes, the wife takes care of the pool. We have an in-ground pool the wife's father helped with getting. There was a patio pool, but she wanted an inground pool and my father-in-law decided that it should be a good pool. I don't know what he does, he seems to have a lot of money to throw around. So she wanted it and she got it. It's her pool. I used to come home from work and vacuum the other pool. And suddenly one day I thought, "What's going on? I come home from work, and while they are sitting around the pool, I'm vacuuming it." So I told my wife that she could vacuum the pool while she was sitting next to it anyway, and she agreed, and I accepted to bow out quickly. So now she takes care of the pool. I'm not a pool person. My wife does all the cooking, cleaning, shopping, taxiing.

For most of the men, outside work is extensive and so there is a more balanced division of labor than one might find in cities with greater proportion of rental units. One man wired his house, built a family room, put on a porch and maintained his own and his mother's house in the two-year period when we were collecting budgets. He also helped his brother-in-law build his house in a neighboring town. A man over fifty was helping his son build his house when we interviewed him; he was a carpenter at GE. Many families collected wood on weekends for their heating. Some, like Bonnie's husband and the father of another family in our interview, made their own wood stoves and even sold them when they were laid off. In these projects they expend the strength, skill and ingenuity that is often denied an outlet on the job.

When women work outside of the house, the spouses arrange their shifts so that one will be at home when the children return from school. Tight schedules involve complex routines in the delivering of working spouses and children with one car and two jobs. A change in shift for one spouse involves readjustments for the other. Women like working at the Berkshire Medical Center with its full twenty-four hour work schedule that offers a range of part- and full-time shifts that they can work in with that of their husbands. They also like teaching because it allows them to be home when their school-age children come home. Because of their double responsibilities, women find forced changes in the hours of work even more stressful than men, particularly when there are young children. When women work, particularly when they are mothers, as Lamphere (1986) shows, there is a greater impact on the organization of work in the household.

Men are becoming involved in more than superficial ways inside the house. Three men who were laid off have undertaken full responsiblity for getting the kids ready for school and preparing their lunches. We have observed men during interviews who managed the children very successfully and apparently without resentment, responding to the little crises of cuts and fights in an experienced manner. Working women all preferred to continue doing the shopping themselves, an indication of greater managerial responsibility in food preparation, but men take charge of meals that they prepare for themselves and the children while their wives are working and both share cleaning and laundry chores.

When men are forced to live away from home during the week because of employment at a distance, the double burden falls on women. When Bonnie's husband was laid off in Pittsfield, he went to Connecticut where he stays all week. She was working at General Electric until she was laid off. Now she has the full care of the three children and stays home. She talked to me about the Monday morning blues:

> Today is bad. All Mondays are bad. The baby gets up, you hear him about the first and I give him breakfast. My husband leaves Monday at 3 a.m. and comes back Friday at 7:30. Weekends we get wood. We have a wood furnace he made. When he was out of work, that's what he did. He makes beautiful stoves. I do the housework when the kids are at school. If my girlfriend has the day off, we go horseback riding. That is for me. I also have projects in Artex [a brand of craft production kits] and I paint and do ceramics. My brother is unemployed and my sister in unemployed. He's painting the house now. He was working in Connecticut, traveling a lot. Two other brothers and one sister are laid off from Sheaffer Eaton. I don't know what's going to happen in Pittsfield. My husband heard of a power plant in Arizona. Maybe we will go out there. How do you hold a marriage together? Then at 12, or 1, we have lunch. The children eat at school two times a week and I give them money every day. In the afternoons I go for a walk with Wesley, or if he is crabby, he naps. I hate Mondays. Today was bad. Fridays are the best. The kids come home about 3, and they do their homework. May helps a lot. She takes Wesley out, and Jason's got the garbage. May does the dishes and at 5 or 6 we eat supper. Jason goes out on his bike and gets in at 7 or 7:30, and May at 8:30. In the evening I do arrangements [flowers] and watch TV and I'm in bed by 11.

Bonnie feels that she used to get more done when she was working:

> I love the weekends after I have been working. I used to do so much more canning and freezing then I do now being unemployed. So far this summer I have just canned twenty-seven quarts of tomatoes. I had a beautiful garden when we lived in Cheshire in the nine-year span when Jason was growing up and before Wesley was born.

She was cleaning at that time in a nursing home but was able to come home and clean her own house and care for her garden. In the brief stint when she was taken on at General Electric, she did not have even weekends and evenings because of overtime:

> When I worked at the GE, that's all I did was work. The normal schedule is forty hours, but then it was twelve hours a day. The

only day I took off was Memorial Day. At the beginning, I kept the machine cleaner than my house. I was like living in GE. I worked Saturday and Sunday. I was making good money, but we didn't save it, not a dime.

The redistribution of the daily chores such as child care and house tending rarely involves extended family ties, but takes place within the nuclear family where it is not ordinarily observed. Even when Bonnie was working fulltime with overtime, her mother did not come in to care for the children, although she lives in town. She had raised fifteen children, and that part of her life was over. Because there was a wide age range, the older girl took over many of the tasks. This was the pattern her mother followed, as Bonnie explains:

My mother worked at the Boston Auto Gauge and at Rice's. She worked while we were growing up. There were fifteen children. She had three with her first husband, with two more that died, and ten with the second, nine of them living. I used to baby-sit with the younger ones. She went to work at 3 p.m. That taught me a lot. My husband had everything he wanted when he was growing up, and he has a different way of looking at things. He got a welder when he was ten. He kicks a TV if it doesn't work. He thinks that I work the kids too hard. His sister got a hi fi and mini mike for Christmas, and if I got just a game, I was happy. His father was a sheet metal worker.

The set of expectations one grows up with conditions the expectations in a marital relationship. Regardless of wealth levels, however, the principle of internal responsibility for maintenance of the family, both financially and in services rendered, holds for working-class people. All of our respondents in the 100 random sample interviewed, except for four unmarried youths, lived in their own homes, and only in one case did a family in which the wife ordinarily worked have the assistance of the wife's mother living with her to help care for the children. Another woman's mother tried to take care of her daughter's children, but they both agreed it didn't work out well and a baby sitter was hired. Despite this privatized daily management of the household, there is a great deal of assistance among extended members of the family in long-range tasks of house building and maintenance.

Table 9–1
Work Activity of General Electric Respondents' Spouses

Age	Male Respondent Number of Children							Female Respondent Number of Children					Total
	0	1	2	3	4	over	?	0	1	3	4	over	
20–25													
No spouse	5												5
No work													
Works part time													
Works full time	1												1
26–30													
No spouse	2							1					3
No work		2											2
Works part time													
Works full time	1	1								1			3
31–35													
No spouse	1							1	1				3
No work		1	1			3							5
Works part time													
Works full time	2	2	1										5
36–40													
No spouse													
No work													
Works part time			1								1		2
Works full time		1	1	3							1		6
41–45													
No spouse	1												1
No work		2											2
Works part time		1											1
Works full time		2											2
46–50													
No spouse									1				1
No work		1	1					2					4
Works part time		1											1
Works full time		2											2
51–55													
No spouse													
No work			2	2									4
Works part time			1										1
Works full time		2											2
56–60													
No spouse													
No work								2					2
Works part time		1	1										2
Works full time		3	3										6
?		2											2
61 and over													
No spouse													
No work			1										1
Works part time													
Works full time		1	2	1	2								6
TOTAL	13	9	15	13	9	2	3	2	4	3	2		75

There is no discernable pattern in women's decisions to work full time, although fewer women with growing children work than those who are without a spouse or whose children are grown up. Women who do work have highly organized schedules meshed with those of working husbands. Marriage is a preferred pattern, and most people are married by their thirties. Women who work at General Electric are less likely to have a living spouse than are men. Women's commitment to work full time and acquire the seniority that has protected their job in times of layoff is a corollary of their need for the paycheck and the benefits.

The data on division of labor within the household seem to conflict with Heidi Hartman's (1981) summary of the studies done in the sixties and seventies on housework responsibilities when both spouses work. She concluded that only minimal and insignificant changes had come and that the major difference was that fewer hours were spent doing housework because of more efficient organization of time and better technology. I found considerable differences among generations who began work in the thirties, sixties and eighties, with continually more progressive attitudes as well as activities related to sharing responsibilities on the part of both spouses. These findings seem to be corroborated by a study done by Elizabeth Maret and Barbara Finlay (1984) in two periods, 1974 and 1976, showing consistent trends towards greater sharing of domestic tasks in that short period. More recent data indicate a discernible shift in expectations of husbands' participation[3]. Blau and Ferber (1986:128) report that the proportion of time spent by husbands and wives on housework and wage work moved more actively together in the 1975/6 to 1981/2 period than during the preceeding decades.

The balanced reciprocity that occurs between spouses in the household may break down under stressful conditions. One man's first marriage could not survive the 101-day strike of 1969 when his wife went to work full time (outside of General Electric) and berated him for failing to support the family. Women who went out on strike in the garment shop also describe the intolerance of husbands when they were involved in organizing meetings. These women also seemed less willing to tolerate demands on their time and energy by their husbands when they became politicized by the union drive. Three women I interviewed separated from their husbands in the course of a four-month strike. Joan, who took a ''man's'' job when affirmative action opened up some of the segregated job opportunities in the plant, made more money than her husband, who was working in the same shop she entered, since she received an ''adder'' (amount added to regular

wages when piecework was abolished). Although she denies that her
marital breakup resulted from this threat to her husband's position,
their fifteen-year marriage, during which five children were born, did
end shortly after.

What seems to happen is that personal transformations, brought
about by the structural changes occurring in the wider society, raise
questions about a given set of accommodations and precipitate new
decisions. It is not simply an accumulation of grievances experienced
over many years around the same set of expectations, but rather, a
break in the expectations that precipitates a crisis of consciousness. The
division between family and the industrial market place is a fragile egg-
shell, subject to shattering internal obligations no longer conforming
to external demands.

The sense of exploitation women may have at home or on the job
is tempered by an awareness of the greater danger and hardship men
experienced in those jobs classified as male jobs. Older women resisted
the breakdown in gender segregation in the plant because of this
factor. With the implementation of the Equal Employment Opportunity
Act,[4] when a woman was bumped from her job she was presented
with both "male" and "female" jobs to be bumped to. Older women
often did not want the strenuous, dirty and dangerous jobs, yet they
could not turn down more than two such jobs without being permanently laid off. Equal-opportunity openings, in this sense, play into
managerial control of the work force to an even greater degree than
the sex-segregated jobs that gave women the option to refuse a whole
category of those jobs. Younger women, particularly those who are
single heads of families, need the bigger paycheck and are willing to
sacrifice themselves more for it.

Class Variation in the Gender Division of Labor

Class is a concomitant of generational mobility as educational
opportunities and the changing structure of occupations transformed
patterns of work in the family. In the following case histories of children
who have surpassed their parents' class positions, I have drawn from
interviews chosen from among contacts I made with people in the
random sample of blue-collar production workers. Some, in fact, are
children of the workers whose case histories appear above.

That is the case with Donna, the daughter of Al Lantenari. She
is thirty-three years old and has two boys aged three and six. When
I interviewed her in 1982, she worked as a secretary to a manager at
General Electric. Her husband is an engineer at GE who, like many
of the young men who want to move upward in the corporation, works

evenings on further schooling. She reflected on the difference between her own and her mother's life:

> My mother never went out to work until I was in high school. I think she was very frustrated with it because there's an awful lot of stuff that she wanted to do that she never did do because — it wasn't for us, it was because of my father. For her, her whole life revolves around her family, and she never took time out for Marie, [her mother's name]. Never ever did she, I've never known her to do it. And I refuse, I've never gotten quite deep into psychology. I've wanted to get my degree in social services, and that's what I'm going for.

Donna's day starts at five when she gets up and gets ready for work which begins at 7 a.m. and ends at 3:30 p.m. She used to waken the baby when she got up so she would have some time with him before going to work, but now she lets him sleep until she has to bring the two children over to her sister-in-law, who lives next door. She added:

> It's just too hard for them to get into my routine so early, and they would drive me crazy. In the morning — I'm not a morning person — and I'm glad that I work 7 to 3:30, because, then I come home from work and I'm full of energy. And I'm so excited to see them. Whereas Bruce [her husband] is more of a morning person, and I'm very pokey, I get up for work, and oh! But he gets up at 7 and if he has the time, or if they're hungry, he'll feed them. But I get home at about 4, and when I get home, they help me. I do the shopping, and most everything. Bruce was very helpful before he got an upgrade, and it's more involved and he works a lot of overtime at General Electric. He just started two years ago and there's a lot of pressure on his job.

Bruce is an engineer and is trying to get his master's degree taking courses at night:

> So his role when he's home is very small; this is my opinion, he might disagree. The kids are number one when he walks in the door and he gives them the time, whatever has to be done. But other than that, I do all the washing, the cooking, the cleaning. Anthony — Christopher is too small yet — he has his duties taking care of his clothing, putting them in the hamper if they're dirty. They have to clean up the toys, that's standard, whatever they use. Anthony sets the table, he helps me with the supper. He might peel the carrots, he might peel the potatoes, and I talk to him. It's the only time I can get what's fresh on his mind from school, have

a conversation with him because if I don't, I'm too tired. And then we eat. Bruce doesn't come home until later.

After supper, I save all the housework to do then, when they're around because I think they enjoy that. Especially Anthony because he's at a very impressionable age, and it makes him feel important that he can contribute something to help make it easier for me. Sometimes when I get home, he says, "You have to come upstairs and see what I did before school." He folds the clothes, and he folds the towels for me, really cute, he puts everything away, and it really makes me feel good.

Donna's sister-in-law prefers staying home, and so their households are very complementary. Donna's husband worked in an investment firm when the baby was born. Since his insurance didn't cover everything, it was very important for her to continue working, and she preferred to do so. Her children sometimes ask her why she has to work and why she doesn't want to stay home with them. She never tries to say that it is to get them material things:

I say, "There's things that mommy likes to do, and I like to work," and he says, "Don't you like to stay home with me?" I say, "I love to stay home with you, but this is something, it's like a toy for mommy, it's something that makes mommy feel good," I said. "I hope that you can understand, and if you don't I hope that I can explain it to the best of my ability." I don't want to get into the materialistic things, you know, "You want this, well, you want that, mommy's got to work." I couldn't do that to him. I didn't want him to grow up on the value of the dollar because that's what society stresses is the value of the dollar. They'll learn that, they will, "I want this and I want that, and let's go here." I don't even have to tell him that. "I want this bike," you know.

On weekends, Donna goes shopping, often taking the children unless they want to stay home and watch television. Their father reads to them, and they work together on homework. I wanted to know what her parents thought of her working:

When I went back to work, they'd joke about leaving them, "How can you leave a little child!" Oh God, every time I'd come home, I'd tell them I wanted to. But I would cry, I used to get so upset, "Am I doing the right thing?" It was so hard. I was really emo-tionally traumatized. I really had a hard time coping with that, 'cause I really didn't know if I was doing the right thing. My mother didn't want me going to work. She didn't. She said, "You know, you bring these kids into the world for what? To go off and leave them with someone else?'' I feel that it's not the quantity of time, it's the quality. I think that I've given more to my kids than a lot of mothers who sit around watching television, watching their soaps from 1 to 4 o'clock in the afternoon, glued in front of the TV set. Whereas I don't have time in my life for TV.

Barbara is a young woman who works with her husband as an exempt employee in Ordnance. She does analysis of manufacturing schedules and costs. She took courses in the financial management program at General Electric and advanced to her current position. She lives in a new spacious split level on the southeast side of town. She has no children and when I asked her if she was planning to have one, she said, "I have a dog." "That's a start," I commented. She rejoined,

> I don't know, I think at some point we would like to have a family, whether we adopt children or have them biologically is one decision that we'll have to make. We thought of doing both, maybe in a couple of years, have one child biologically and if we wanted to increase our family, adopt a child. There's just some things that I would like to do at work before I take some time off. I graduated from college in 1975, and I turned twenty-nine this year.

I asked about the division of labor in the household:

> Michael is pretty good. Recently he has taken a job that he is pretty involved in so that I've been carrying probably, — I know the greater burden than he is in keeping up the house and all. We, I don't know, I guess it's pretty traditional. We take turns cooking, one cooks, the other cleans up. He does most of the mechanical type things; he makes most of the repairs on the car 'cause I have no interest in learning how to do that. We both do some things, like cut the lawn. It's basically a function of who has the most time.

Michael has been working sixty-five hours a week, which is rather common for engineers. They both get up at 5:30 in the morning. Barbara said,

> I recently changed to the 7:00 to 3:30 shift. I never used to be a morning type of person. If I had my druthers, I'd probably stay up until the middle of the night and sleep all morning. But I just find that being on the 7:00 to 3:30 shift, it allows me to get out of work and do the duty type of things, like go to the dry cleaners and go grocery shopping and run different errands or I spend my whole weekend doing that. So it really is a bargain. So we have

breakfast in the morning, at least I do. He doesn't always.
I eat breakfast just because I can't function if I don't. By 10:00
I'm just wasted. I'll eat some cereal or a piece of toast or something. But that's something we each have to take care of ourselves.

Barbara has an exercise class twice a week as well as her classes in
accounting at General Electric. They generally eat late because of the
activities they have. She may watch TV or read. She does needlepoint
and keeps plants. She has a flower and vegetable garden in the
summer. They see friends from work on occasional weekends, dining
at each other's houses, but because Barbara and Michael see each other
so rarely during the week they like to be together.

I had expected that there would be a significant difference between
production workers and engineers in the amount of shared household
responsibility. Although I have too few cases of the latter from which
to generalize, I found that the job pressures on engineers to upgrade
their knowledge by taking courses in the nearby colleges and in-job
training meant that they were away from home much longer than the
normal eight-hour working day. This left their wives even more in
charge of the home, whether they worked or not. Although there is
only a slight difference in age between Donna and Barbara, there is
a marked difference in attitude about domestic life and career. Donna
has a lingering sense of guilt, played upon by her own mother, for
working outside of the home. For Barbara, there is no question of the
importance of her career. Children are an option, whether biological
or adopted, and what she calls a "traditional" division of labor, in
which her husband shares cooking and other household tasks, is in
fact a recent innovation.

The household as an arena of redistribution is indeed an important
stage that conditions the wider social struggles. The quiet revolution
that is taking place as men are becoming familiar with domestic chores
may become a paradigm for change in other arenas. It is only in doing
these devalued domestic tasks that men will learn to recognize the value
and difficulty of the many tasks involved and, more importantly, the
complex managerial involvement. Pronounced differences in the degree
of responsibility men undertake in the home is correlated with age,
and the trend is toward increasing participation in household tasks
measured in time and commitment. These changes were not legislated,
as in Cuba where the law makes it possible for a woman to bring her
husband to court for failure to perform household chores, but an
ideology that used to dictate full-time responsibility regardless of a
woman's work outside of the home is now changing. The changes are

in the realm of custom, where new rules and expectations are bringing about transformations in personal relations and roles related to gender. Vicky would not have considered it possible to neglect her husband's meals even when she worked away from home and commuted, while Joan would not tolerate her husband's demands after she moved into a man's job at General Electric. Some younger women even expect to see a hot meal already prepared when they come home from work.

Single Heads of Family

The increase in single heads of families in Pittsfield parallels that in the U. S. (11.7% in 1980). Most young women have worked at some time during their lives, so separation or the death of a spouse is not as difficult a transition as it is for older women. Generational contrasts are the single most important variable in defining the paths women take in the transition form marital to solitary status. I shall illustrate this with the discussions of Sue and Mary at the Women's Service Center talk which I attended.

Sue worked continuously in her adult years:

I'd like to tell you a little bit about my working career, the struggle I'm now involved in. I'm separated so I'm a single head of household. I have two children ages four and six. I've been fortunate; I've been able to work before my marriage, throughout my marriage, and now as a single person; I've worked steadily for eleven years. I work for Workroom for Designers. It's a small factory, most of you know, on Pearl Street. I'm employed as a sewing machine operator. It's run by husband and wife, and most recently their son has joined forces. One clear advantage to working in this place (and you'll wonder after I've talked for a while why I've stayed there) when I got married, of course I wanted to take a little bit of time off. My boss said, "No problem; you'll get your job back," and that was great. And of course when my first child was to be born, I of course needed another leave of absence, and he said, "Fine, your job will be here when you get back." Of course, this was an unpaid leave. So through a couple of surgeries and a couple of children, I've had occasions to take a couple of months off here and there, but I've always been able to get my job back with relatively the same amount of pay that I enjoyed before I left. And now as a mother of children — and I don't care if its a single head of household, or a two parent household, most men don't share in the problems and responsiblities of chidlren — I might need a babysitter, and my babysitter can't come until 7:15 in the morning. The rest of the shop was in to work at 8:00. I was able to go in to work at 7:30 in order to wait for my babysitter. You don't often find this. And also I can say to my boss, "My son or daughter is sick. I have to stay at home." Or, "This one had an appointment, I have to have a half an hour here or there." He's always been very agreeable, which is something you don't often find.

These considerations made an otherwise ill-paid and trying job situation tolerable. According to Sue, the shop was filthy and there were few amenities for workers. The employer was said to have a very bad temper and was likely to scream and yell at the workers. When the boss made some arbitrary cutbacks on their piece rate, the women started to organize. They were fired, and then went out on strike for over five months. During that time, Sue and the other women had time to reflect on their condition. Sue sums up the sentiment of the sixty workers who walked out:

> When he started taking away from my paycheck, that was the last straw for me. I don't ever want my son or daughter to work in a place like that. I have a commitment to my fellow workers, the sixty people on that line for twenty-seven weeks now and nobody has tried to go in. I would be the last person, strike me dead, to ever walk through that line. Those people, we've become very close. We're all working towards a mutual goal. We're very, very strong about it, also for future employees.

The owner of the firm was alleged to have driven his Cadillac into the line, injuring a picket on duty, who had to go to the hospital. The women asserted that he and other members of his family used foul language each day as they cut through the picket line. She and the other strikers were relying on donations from the IUE and other unions in town. Their commitment to change in the workplace was a threat to their responsibilities to their families. Sue's answer to a question raised by one of the audience, "Why do you picket and expose your children to this violence?" brought this out clearly.

> Because I feel very strongly about it as a worker, as a woman and as a mother. I feel that I should be able to make a decent week's pay for my children to live. I feel very guilty the entire summer that I am not able to do a single thing with my children except to bring them to the picket line with me. As I said before, I cannot afford to send the children to a babysitter. My family is not sympathetic to this. My family has not made an offer in any way

to me, whether it is to watch the children for a day or buy me groceries or anything like that. My mother, incidently, she works at GE, but she will not belong to the union. She doesn't believe in unions. While I know that I don't like my children exposed to the language that he [boss] is using, they're going to grow up with this kind of thing. I don't use this kind of language in front of my children. They know that this kind of language is used. They've heard it, but yet they don't repeat it. They understand what it is, where it's coming from. I just want them to know the kind of struggle that's involved.

Another large and growing group of single heads of families are widows. Often these women have had no work experience outside the home, and their homemaking skills are not given consideration by employers. The Women's Center has addressed the needs of this group in a program called "Displaced Homemakers." The director of the program defined the term:

She is primarily a homemaker for a substantial number of years, she has been a dependent on the income of another, and that income is no longer available to her because her spouse has died, separated, divorced, was disabled, and she has to seek work. She's going to have a hard time getting back into the labor force. Other aspects of this definition are, a woman who has been a single parent and is receiving aid to have the dependent children, when those children reach eighteen, she is not going to be eligible for that income any more. Or women whose husbands have died and they are receiving Social Security in order to raise their children, when their children are eighteen years old, that Social Security will cease in that household and that woman will become a displaced homemaker. So these forces are acting very strongly to propel women who have committed themselves to the homemaker role into the job market.

The program director introduced a woman as the widow of a farmer who had worked until his death on a small farm in Peru, Massachusetts. She was in charge of the house, the garden and canning and the children. She was also involved in community work, the daughters' campfire group, the church and served as town clerk, working for a nominal fee. This all changed when her husband died suddenly:

I went to sleep on Saturday night as a loved, cherished individual (and protected), and I woke up the next morning to find my son and the next-door neighbor giving my husband CPR on the floor while they waited for the ambulance. In that instant I became a

> non-person. The person I was disappeared; since then, I've been
> searching for myself.

The search involved seeking a livelihood, since her husband left little
insurance. After a briefing at the Women's Center, she went out on
some interviews:

> And what strange questions they asked me. "How much do you
> want to get paid? How much did you figure you're worth?" I didn't
> know, I had no idea. So back to Tina (the director) to find out. Then
> the next question was. "What could you do?" That I knew a little
> bit better. But I had to convince other people that what I had done
> through the years was worth money. I'm still not sure of my ability
> compared to other people, and I'm not sure you should compare
> yourself with others. What I was thinking, as I was sitting through
> that interview was, "Can I work eight hours a day straight? Can
> I work fast enough? What if I can't learn it and I mess it all up?
> And, What happens when I make mistakes? Are they going to shoot
> me out the door?"

One of the consultants at the center suggested a cleaning service,
and she found a job with one and then opened her own business. She
now has several women working in the business. Counseling is
important in overcoming the sense Mary and others who have not
worked in the labor market have of not possessing valuable or
marketable skills. Their own resistance to the commoditization of
services that were identified with family status and ties stands in the
way of transition from (in Mary's words) a "loved, cherished and protected" individual to a full-fledged member of the wage labor force
or a small business.

Government Mediation in Family Welfare

Sue and Mary were both successful in the search for a personal
identity. Sue became a labor organizer and Mary has been featured
in the *Berkshire Sampler* and small business ads. Other women who
dropped out of the middle-class or secure working-class category
because of death, divorce or separation from a spouse have fallen into
poverty. For them the answer is welfare or a constant struggle to maintain themselves and their families in marginal jobs at the minimum
wage. Welfare intervention is considered to be a temporary expedient,
resorted to only in extreme emergencies.

Welfare has changed along with the times, but not in a uniform progression. In the thirties, when welfare picked up where private charities left off, the rigid rules related to welfare often imposed precipitous changes that interfered with life careers. Al was forced to end his schooling one year short of his high school graduation because in the twenties when he was growing up children of sixteen years of age were supposed to be out working. When he came home from the service and could not get back in the General Electric because of his union activities, welfare forced his wife out of a five-room apartment where she had spent the war and put her in a three-room apartment because her husband was now about to leave the service and was expected to contribute to the household. At the same time, when their son was having a heart operation in Boston, they could only communicate with the doctors by phone and welfare took the phone out. The anguish that Al felt turned to anger:

> Anyway, this day when I went down and they said they were going to remove the telephone, I jumped over the counter. I give him a couple of shots [fistcuffs]. So the girl that was the secretary called the cops. They were right next door. So they brought me in and arrested me for assault and battery. He [welfare director] was bleeding a little in the mouth, you know, and he came in to make a statement, and the chief was in there and he says, "Who the hell do you think you are anyways? You get home from the God damn service, you think you run the town? All you guys are the same." I says, "Am I under arrest?" He says, "You're under arrest." I says, "Beautiful! That's exactly what I wanted. Now I'm home on leave. I'm not discharged. Thirty-day leave. Wait until I get into court tomorrow morning and there's a newspaper reporter there and I'm going to tell them how this man here moved my wife out of five rooms, and wait until I tell them that he cut down on her food stamps or whatever it was then." Then he threatened me to take the telephone out of my house and my son's going to be operated on. "I'd be more than happy to go to court." I said, "I don't care if I get any time, but you better move out of town, I'm coming back after you." So he says, "You got a big mouth!" He closed the door on me in the room and made me wait there about an hour, and then he comes back in and says, "All right, get the hell out of here. Don't let me see your face around here again." So they let me go.

When Al did get to work, with some pressure from the Veteran's Administration to get him rehired at General Electric, he bought a duplex with his brother and lives there to this day.

Mary always worked, even after her marriage and three children. She had the night shift at Tillotson's and her husband stayed home, then sometimes he went to work in the day when she came home, but often he "would work nothing." They moved to Connecticut and he picked up with another woman and went to Illinois. The State of Connecticut moved her and the children back to Pittsfield during the war:

> And so we settled here, and then my son got a job in the Rosa restaurant part time. We were better off without him [husband]. The State of Connecticut rented a five-room apartment on Oak Street. Moved all our furniture, every stitch we had. We had a supervisor and a nurse, traveled with the kids and I. And then when we got here, well, we settled here.

Mary went back to the Elmvale mills. With one son working she was able to support the other two. She worked there until the mill closed down.

Welfare intervention has changed with the times, and though the rules are still there, there is greater latitude in administering them. Telephones and cars are considered a necessity to operate in the labor force, and welfare does not deprive clients of these when they are needed. Bonnie recently had to resort to welfare when both she and her husband were temporarily laid off in 1981:

> When he [husband] was unemployed, they [children] got a state lunch. He was getting $156 a week when it ran out and there was no insurance, so we went on welfare. When I went for the baby in the hospital, we had to get welfare — $400 a month. I hated to do it, but what can you do? Then he went to Vermont on a job, and I went right down to welfare and told them to take us off right away. I don't like to be on. One thing, people complain a lot about welfare cheats, but I'm telling you, it's there when you need it. I hate going up to unemployment, welfare office. I just want to work.

This resistance to accepting financial help from the government is the bottom line in being a part of the system of independent, self-sustaining workers. This even extends to subsidized housing projects, and neighbors fight any plans to set up public housing. Nick Speranzo, a man who grew up during the Depression and works in the Pittsfield Housing Authority, regrets this attitude:

> If they would think of their brothers and sisters — but they are terrible. I know a guy whose wife died and the family moved out

of town. Then he had a triple bypass. Now how the hell is he going to live without help? He's a human being; he's a fellow man. But most people don't think it's going to happen to them.

In those neighborhoods that retain the strong sense of community that was part of the immigrant experience, there is some retention of mutual aid. Nick was brought up in Lakewood, where the tradition of sharing in adversity was strong. Nick says of Lakewood:

> I was born in Ward 3, of Lakewood. Really nice there. Everybody knew each other. We weren't deprived of anything. Other wards had more money, but Ward 3 was really working people. They really survived by selling bootleg liquor. They never let a family starve. We ate good.

Lakewood has survived, but the entry of single-occupancy housing broke up West Street. To solve the problem, all of the buildings were torn down, but the problems of the people living in poverty and leading lives that are disorganized by alcoholism did not disappear. They are dispersed in pockets of poverty found in various wards. Morningside is now a target, and Eveningside, on the northwest side of town, is slated for the road by-pass by the development committee.

With luxury condominiums and weekend vacation homes crowding the field, it is hard for the poor and their welfare mediators to find housing. In the fall of 1984 welfare mothers were unceremoniously evicted from a motel to make room for deerhunters in what became a scandalous highly publicized statement of values. The Women's Service Center found the mothers a place in the YMCA. The center has since tried to buy four abandoned schools to set up more permanent shelters for women with children. Their ultimate hope is to provide centers with day-care for the children, work rooms where women can produce articles for sale and learn a trade and housing in the same unit. As yet the financing has not been available for these combined services. Welfare is limited to providing the finances for buying shelter, food and other necessities on the regular market. Recipients of AFDC report a reluctance on the part of landlords to rent to them on the assumption that ''you're going to destroy the property,'' as Liz Holzman, a divorced woman on AFDC, told reporter Stephen Leon of the *Berkshire Sampler* (November 3, 1985). The kind of penalizing that the Omnibus Budget Reconciliation Act has instituted for anyone earning income while receiving aid has upset the transition to independence through employment. Since most jobs available for women are poorly paid and temporary, they prefer not to risk losing the welfare payments, as difficult as those are. Holzman slipped into the poverty category when she divorced her husband. Like many of her friends, this meant an abrupt change from a comfortable home with a modern kitchen and bathroom to a dreary walk-up apartment. (Table 9–1)

The greatest unmet need is for day-care, both for employed women and women who would like to get off welfare and become employed. The Girls' Club instituted a service with ninety-nine positions in 1982. A public agency, the Berkshire Center for Families and Children, operates a day-care center which was an important resource until it came under the cloud of an attendant accused of molesting several of the children. This kind of experience, which is found increasingly in day-care centers throughout the U. S., is raising further obstacles to the development of this service. The Berkshire Life Insurance Company is the only private enterprise in Pittsfield that provides day-care for its employees; a service it started in 1984. By 1988 General Electric was beginning to move in that direction as the new cohort of professional women put pressure on the company. The low pay for service workers and the high turnover exacerbates the problem of getting qualified and dedicated workers. Lack of child care is the single most important factor in women's engagement in full time work (Boulding, 1976; Cowan 1987)

Pittsfield's families are increasingly burdened with the problems of social welfare as they are shirked by the Federal government. The privatization of these cares poses a special burden on women, and especially single female heads of households. They are the most militant in labor circles, and their issues must become the vanguard of union organizations if they are to survive in the future. Poverty rates in Pittsfield reflect national statistics showing an increase in youth, female and black impoverishment. The failure to address their needs within the present structures of corporate hegemonic relations poses the central agenda for political mobilization in the nineties.

Chapter 10

Government Mediation and the
Survival of Community

Government mediation is only a partial entry in arbitrating and reconciling the claims of various groups.[1] Limited as it is, the necessity for action by the government is denied in corporate hegemonic ideology. Even when disinvestment policies pursued by the corporation increase the needs for such intervention. Since government funds are derived from sectors of the population that may or may not benefit from them directly, the political interpretation of redistribution does not follow from class relations in production. In Pittsfield unionized production workers have a hierarchy of values related to government programs that categorize the programs funded by input as "victories of the labor movement" and those with a means test as "bureaucratic government spending." They try to avoid falling into this second category, often at great personal cost. Women, like those who went on strike in the garment factory (Chapter 9), worked full time even with small children at home and at minimum wage rates lower than what they would receive from AFDC, and I have been told about old people eating cat food rather than applying for food stamps. Retired workers would prefer to negotiate their claims for higher pensions with the company than with the state. "We built General Electric," retired workers who have organized the Local 255 Retirees Club say, "and they owe us a pension that permits us to live in dignity." Dignity means without the help of children or welfare payments. Each year the retirees picket the plant, asking for donations from workers and making known their claims on the corporation. Their commitment to some of the corporate hegemonic ideology directs their preference to make claims on the corporation rather than the government.

The evolution of legislation concerning the human resources and welfare needs of the nation responded to structural changes in the population as well as to economic cycles. Each major demographic shift prompted reevaluations of what the reciprocal rights and obligations of workers, cititzens and family members were. Only some of these emanated from production, where they were defined in terms of contribution to production. Others originated in the family and community and were related to problems of people who were not a part of the work force. Recognition came slowly that there were not only the "deserving poor," but that the very nature of capitalist production required intervention to sustain those who suffered layoffs during industrial cycles. Comprehensive federal legislation to provide for those who suffered from industrial accidents or disease, the aged who could no longer work and youth entering the work force did not come until the thirties. The special concerns of women who were the sole support of children first came in the form of aid to widows in 1919 and, only after professional welfare services replaced religious charities, to the divorced or never-married mothers. The aged are a growing constituency who unite the problems of retired workers with those who were never in the work force.

Each increment of welfare meant a concomitant admission of the inadequacy of the economic and social institutions that were part of corporate hegemonic relations. At the same time, it required a self-definiton on the part of the recipient that made explicit their needs. The slow progress reflected the resistance both on the part of the conventional institutions of work, of family and of community to admit their inadequacy, and on the part of the clients to admit their needs. The ideology of the free market pervades both donor and recipient classes in the United States, possibly the reason the country lags behind most other industrialized countries in social welfare (Wilensky 1981). It is one of the clearest indices of the viability of corporate hegemony.

The process of penetrating these obstacles to redistribution of the social product requires the combined effort of public and private agencies working with the population that is to be served. First, it is necessary to identify and enumerate the consitituency that is in need in order to convince legislators. Then it requires mobilization of the target population in its own defense. This often necessitates a cognitive reorientation overcoming socialization practices within corporate hegemony that stress independence, individual solutions and suffering in silence. I shall discuss three groups whose needs are addressed by public and private agencies: the youthful unemployed, women who are heads of families, or "displaced homemakers", and the retired in relation to their place in the changing composition of the populations.

The evolution of custom and law promoting the redistribution of social production shows the interplay of ideology and behavioral norms responding to sectoral disparities in income and level of living. This was not an axiomatic response. Public recognition of a need was often a belated response to the increasing numbers of the cohort in the population. When the retired workers began to live longer in the decade of the sixties, they became a political force to reckon with. As the youthful unemployed increased in numbers, they found an advocacy group. And as divorced and unmarried female heads of households increased, programs related to their needs sprang up. What is needed with each group is a critical mass that will attract the attention of congressmen and senators. The following table shows trends in Pittsfield compared with national trends in the decade 1970–1980.

Table 10–1

Population Trends by Age Group in the U. S. and Pittsfield, 1970–1980

Age Group	United States		Pittsfield	
	1970	1980	1970	1980
	%	%	%	%
Under 5	8.4	7.4	8.0	6.0
5–14	20.0	15.0	20.3	14.9
15–24	17.5	18.4	15.3	17.2
25–34	12.3	17.0	10.3	14.6
35–44	11.4	11.6	11.1	10.1
45–54	11.5	9.6	12.7	10.9
55–64	9.1	9.6	10.2	12.2
65 +	9.8	11.4	12.0	14.0
Total	100.0	100.1	99.9	99.9

Source: U. S. Census

Change in Pittsfield is in the same diretion as national averages, toward an older population, but at a greater rate. The percentage over 65 is 14, up two points from 1970 while national averages are up 1.6 percent. Whereas there is a lower percentage in the youthful dependent category 0-24 (38.1 compared with 43.6 percent) national averages dropped less precipitously: from 45.9 to 40.8 percent. The city has the same percentage in the earning years from 25 to 65 years: 47.8 in Pittsfield compared to 47.8 nationally.

The changes at the lower and upper ends of the population pyramid will have cumulative effects on the distribution of the social product. Predictably there will be more recipients of pensions and fewer donors to funds such as Social Security. Youth unemployment will further limit the contributions to the wage fund that is the major source of redistribution, particularly since corporate taxes have been increasingly cut. Nationally in the period 1970-1982, female-headed families doubled, comprising 28 percent of families in central cities and 17 percent in suburbs. Among black families, those that are female headed are in fact the norm, with 52 percent falling in this cateogry. These structural changes in household composition are correlated with increases in the number of women in the labor force and with increases in recipients of Aid to Families with Dependent Children (AFDC). The percentage of female-headed households below the poverty line in Pittsfield has doubled from 345 in 1970 to 719 or 11.7% of households in 1980 (Table 9-1) but it is rising. Women are fast becoming a critical political force by virtue of these changes shifting them from the status of dependent wife to independent wage earner or dependent welfare recipient. The political change has been noted in the "gender gap" in voting behavior. The most marked change is in the proportions of the elderly: the life expectancy of forty-two in 1850 in the U. S. rose to seventy-three in 1979.

Youths, blacks and women who head households are, in Pittsfield as in the rest of the country, the categories with overlapping constituencies who were most hurt in the recession. Women had reached a critical mass in numbers as well as proportions of the population to become advocates for reform related to employment. Blacks and Hispanics, comprising 2 percent of the population in Pittsfield, do not have the force that minorities have in the industrial city of Springfield to gain relief for their youth and adult unemployment. The black poverty rate has more than doubled in the 1970 to 1980 decade. Action for government intervention is analyzed in relation to each of these age and gender groups below.

Youth Programs

Youth programs have moved from private, religious charities to public and private secularized agencies. At the turn of the century the goals of the programs were cast in moral improvement terms, while today they are cast in the idiom of sportsmanship and competition. The YMCA, the Boys' Club, the Girls' Club, the Catholic Youth and the Jewish Youth address the interests and problems of the young. The YMCA in Pittsfield was organized in 1888, the Boys' Club around the turn of the century and the Girls' Club not until 1924. This reveals the greater concern for boys running wild if they did not have parental supervision. The YMCA's 3,500 members include many family groups drawn from middle-income groups. The 5,100 members of the Boys'

The Boys' Club opens its doors to all the boys in the City. (Photo by William H. Tague.)

Club include many children with single parents, and they are generally considered to be from lower-middle-class income groups. All of the clubs are concerned with the development of "a complete person, morally, physically, and mentally." They serve different populations and their approaches differ. "The Boys' Club shoots with a shotgun at their clientel," the director of the YMCA told us. "We have a more rifle approach. We're after a concern, a task, and we aim for that group and we deal with it." Others see the difference as the Boys' Club responding to the needs of lower-income families where both parents work or where there is a single parent, and the YMCA as cultivating family group activities for a more middle-class group. The most devoted alumni come from the Boys' Club, and many profess that whatever success they have had in life came from the guidance of the Catholic lay people that staff that organization. The Girls' Club, which does not have as much funding as the other organizations, has introduced bingo games that enable them to carry through on innovative programs, including day-care.

Movement from childhood into adulthood assumes movement from play to work roles. During the sixties, recognition that prosperity did not automatically integrate all Americans in the rising economy led to some innovative programs designed to circumvent the welfare system while attending to the problems of the disadvantaged. Vista, the Job Corps and community action programs recognized the disparities in education, job opportunity and socialization processes. Initially the Job Corps was conceived for boys since, Sundquist (1969:43) says, "it was typically young men rather than young women who were dropping out of school and the labor market." Later the CETA programs involved the whole population, including youth and mature workers of both sexes and all ages. Job creation was included along with job training in private industries. This meant that the service sector in other agencies was expanded by the employment of the trainees in park work, hospitals, museums and school lunch programs.

When CETA was transformed into the Job Training Participation Act (JTPA) in 1983, the immediate impact was a cut in the budget. In Pittsfield, the budget went from $7,500,000 in 1978 to $1,000,000 in 1985, and none of those separately funded efforts was secured for more than a few months. Job creation was removed, causing hardships in other agencies that had relied on the help provided by the trainees. The failure of any given participant in a program meant that the agency was given reduced allocations. In effect, this meant that all the financial risks of working with lower-class populations was shifted from public sources to these human service agencies themselves. The emphasis on numbers of participants recruited and moved through the program as the chief criterion in judging the programs further discouraged any creative activities.

Despite these setbacks, a dedicated staff of thirty to thirty-five, some of whom were recruited during the sixties, and seventies when expectations were high about overcoming inequality, try to respond to the many unmet needs that a staff of 100 used to address. They assess what is needed in the existing labor market and adjust their training to that. They now have a sales and marketing program with North Adams College and a word processing course at the Berkshire Community College as well as on-the-job training in about 200 different businesses. These include machinists, secretaries, dental assistants and plastics mold makers, medical technicians and nurses aides. The programs tend to be aimed at an existing set of low-level entry occupations. This, combined with their dependent, step-by-step funding discourages any attempt to develop more creative careers. Employers benefit from the free employment services provided by the state as well as the wage subsidy during the training period and for a short time following full-scale employment. The further provision of tax credits to those employers who take on such trainees provides, in effect, welfare to the entrepreneurial sector.

Head Start, part of the Great Society Program that has operated in the city for thirty years, began with classes for sixty-five students in 1965 and has increased to 242 classes in nine centers in Berkshire County. The program continues to take the holistic approach to health, nutrition and social services, in addition to the educational facet that marked its origins. The program enjoys strong support in the community and its twentieth anniversary was marked with awards presented by the federal congressman. The program has served 3,900 children and their progresss was duly noted on the occasion of the anniversary.

Women Heads of Families

Women are bearing the brunt of changing family norms, both in increasing poverty levels and as victims of abuse by husbands and estranged mates. When women lose access to the resources controlled by men, they become the underclass of marginal workers, earning minimal wages or dependent on government welfare. Nine-tenths of single-headed families are female headed, and the numbers of female-headed families have doubled for blacks and increased by 75 percent for whites (Weiss 1984; HUD 1984). The percentage of children growing up in poverty nationwide in 1983 ranged from 11.7 percent of white married couples to 23 percent of black married. But with female-head families, 47.6 percent of white and 68.5 percent of black families were classified as impoverished. President Reagan prided his administration for cuts of $2. billion in AFDC and $2.3 million in food stamps, but these cuts have removed the incentive for people to work and thrust more families below the poverty line. According to HUD (1984:283) the "harsh rule that prohibits an AFDC recipient from disregarding any earnings after four months" makes AFDC recipients "reluctant to plunk into uncertain jobs" with the resulting problems of child care and complicated travel arrangements.

Women heads of households are an increasing part of the work force. They were the population most affected by the recession of 1982 (Table 10–2).

Table 10–2

Unemployment by Age Group in Pittsfield, 1981–1982

Age Group	1981	1982
Both Sexes 16–19	19.6	23.2
White	6.7	8.6
Black	14.2	17.3
Married men	6.0	7.4
Women who head households	10.4	11.7
Men 20+	6.3	8.8
Women 20+	6.8	8.3
Total civilian population	7.6	9.7

Source: Unemployment Survey, Current Business 63.7 1983

Unemployment dropped to 5 percent by 1987 as jobs for youths opened up in the service industry and the unemployed left for other areas.

The Pittsfield Office of Welfare serving Berkshire County in 1985 had a staff of fifty-five, including thirty social workers, three administrators and fourteen clerical workers. I spoke with one of the social workers, a man who grew up in a neighboring town and who was well aware of the changes that have taken place in the twenty-three years he has worked in the office. Deinstitutionalization of the mentally disturbed and low-intelligence patients from state institutions has put an additional burden on the office at a time of severe budget cuts. The case load has dropped from an average of 1,789 clients in 1982 per month to 1,383 in 1985. This is not due to a reduction in need, but an inability to do the outreach needed for those who are in need but cannot seek help, I was told. The case load, my contact assured me, does not reflect layoffs and unemployment in the community, but, rather, the political climate. The major factor affecting the numbers they serve is how eligibility is figured, and with the present strictures since the Omnibus Budget Reconciliation Act, these have gone down despite rising needs. When people use up their unemployment compensation, most either take on lower-paying jobs or relocate. The spokesperson said, "Our program is related to politics, not need. How eligiblity is figured does not have any relationship to General Electric or the job market. We have not seen any increase despite layoffs at the plant." As a result, the increase in needs as a result of unemployment and deinstitutionalization is not taken care of in the present budgets.

Table 10–3

Poverty in the City of Pittsfield by Household Type and Race in 1970 and 1980

	1970	1980	% Change
Number Below Poverty Level	4,219	5,295	+25
Percent of the Population	7.4	10.3	+40
Under 18	1,458	2,177	+32
Over 65	1,160	567	−51
Families	718	1,223	+50
Families with Female Head	345	719	+108
Blacks	118	323	+273
Unrelated individuals	1,346	1,259	−7
Black Poverty Rate	10.8	24.2	+140

Source: Bureau of Census, reprinted in *An Economic Base Study of Pittsfield and Berkshire County*

Cultural definitions of the minimal standards of living have changed considerably since the Depression, my interviewee,who was born late in the thirties, told me. Contrasting contemporary standards with earlier ones, he said:

> During the Depression, it was a question of not eating, not a question of having a telephone or heat for the house. We did not need cars then. Families would have them for Sunday driving, but it was not considered necessary.

In the new needs assessment, cars and telephones are necessary parts of contemporary society. Evaluations made for the nation are, however, always faulty, the welfare spokesperson told me. With two neighboring towns in the same county, just moving across an invisible line from North Adams to Williamstown is like moving from Appalachia to affluence.

Some of these differences relate to the personnel policies of the dominant industries in the towns. Contrasting the policies of the major firms in neighboring towns, the welfare spokesperson said, "I once took an application from a sixty-five year-old worker who had worked at Sprague for forty years, and he was getting only $40 a month pension." Sprague is, he added "a naughty, punitive parent" whereas Crane, a nearly two hundred-year-old paper company in the neighboring town of Dalton, "is a parent that gave to its children and the community.... it is a loving, caring family." In contrast, he called General Electric "a very petulent grandmother that threatens to withold her wealth, leave town and reduce the work force" whenever she doesn't get what she wants.

The greatest need is an increase in services to those "who cannot move through the bureaucratic maze," the welfare adminsitrator said. These people include the deinstitutionalized mental patients, alcoholics and older people who reject welfare. Some of the cases that fall through the net are cared for by the Salvation Army and Christian center which provide emergency rations and shelters. When welfare and food stamps are used up, or during the three weeks after application when a family waits for welfare, there are seven emergency food pantries that serve about 375 families in the course of a month. The Northern Berkshire Community Action gives surplus government foods and a $25 supermarket voucher to the needy. Supplemental programs such as the payments for energy costs and for weatherizing the homes to reduce fuel consumption enable those on fixed incomes to remain independent.

Welfare is, for some, addictive, my contact added. The subsidized rental, heating supplements, food stamps and basic income, from $315 for a family of two to $445 for a family of four, are extremely attractive in a fluctuating economy with layoffs continually threatening a wage earner and with rising prices cutting into income. It is, according to the welfare spokesperson, "Very traumatic to leave Mother Welfare. It is a very warm and secure, though sometimes demanding demeaning, institution." The Reagan cuts minimized the opportunity to combine income earning opportunities with welfare subsidies and this has cut off exits from full dependency on welfare.

The increase in the numbers on Pittsfield's welfare roles and of charity clients reflects the rising numbers of people below the poverty lines. In 1982 there were 34.4 million nationally, with estimates of two million more in need who were not receiving help. Reagan's answer was the truckloads of surplus cheese distributed through the church groups and state offices.

Several groups began to develop private initiatives in response to the rising needs of women and children. The Women's Center began as a volunteer group in 1975 and grew to a $175,000 operation in 1982. Their first activities were intervention in times of crisis, usually precipitated by wife abuse. The center provided legal advocacy for divorce proceedings, a hiring hall and job counseling. When a ''hot line'' for receiving calls was established, the numbers of calls increased from 295 in 1980 to 412 in 1981. The ''Displaced Homemakers'' program, begun in 1983, was financed by the Bay State Skills with funds equaling that of the entire Women's Center operation in the previous year. The program is directed at those women whose lives were predicated on their roles as wives and mothers and who suddenly lost whatever claims to wage redistribution or Social Security benefits because of death or divorce of the spouse. The social worker who worked with these women compared them to veterans, who, she said, ''are also committed to carrying out society's goals of protection of the nation and our home and our values,'' but whereas veterans will receive educational benefits and be given preferred status in training for jobs, widows find that their skills and experience are considered negligible.

The dilemma women face in politicizing their claims is that of losing their rights defined in relation to dependent roles in the household while seeking autonomy as wage workers or as claimants for public assistance (Peattie and Rein 1983). The failure of the Equal Rights Amendment to pass state legislatures and become national law indicates the fear some women have of losing their claims as dependents in a society that has thus far given them a share of the social product by virtue of their status as wives and mothers. In this period of transition, any move to equalize their position in the labor market may be construed as a threat to that status. The legislation that came out of the New Deal, according to Erie, Rein, and Wiget (1982:2), ''confirmed the dependency relationships of women and the deserving poor.'' In contrast to this legislation, supported by the working majority, the Great Society programs may have threatened that same group (Piven and Cloward 1982). Their sacrifices to advance their own mobility and that of their children seemed to be negated by those programs that seemed to assure the security and advancement of everyone regardless of their commitment to work and save.

Despite the many contradictions that exist in their political position, Pittsfield women have become an increasingly vocal sector of the population in their attempts to redress the losses they experience as they move from the dependent status of wives and mothers, protected by a patriarchal family, to independent but subordinated members of the secondary work force. Along with the demands for rights in the workplace, they are looking for support among women to protest the increasing violence against women and children. In the fifth annual "Take Back the Night" march in 1984, women spoke out for the right to walk without fear after dark without requiring a protector. AWARE, the All Women's Advocacy, Relief and Empowerment project, works with the Battered Women's Task Force and the Women's Services Center to ensure legal support for women who have experienced assault.

Retirees and the Aging Population

Retirees are probably the most politically active people in the city. With a great deal more leisure time, and with several active centers and clubs where they congregate, the retirees are learning to make demands on the system through their elected representatives.

The most significant legislation regarding redistribution to the older population was Social Security. The Social Security Act was the keystone for the construction of the welfare state when it was passed in 1935, and, along with the Fair Labor Standards Act of 1938, established the minimum wage and institutionalized the eight-hour work day. In addition to these regulations of the labor market, it moved retired workers from the ranks of welfare recipients to pensioners, as well as transforming disabled workers from beggers to independent status. Wives and widows were added only after 1939. The system has grown from a limited insurance plan to a "gigantic tax system aimed at redistribution of current income from workers to retirees and other beneficiaries" (Mait 1978:35). The passage of the Social Security bill was clearly related to the growing awareness of "the mounting human problems of dependent old age in an industrial urban economy" when, Mait goes on to say (1978:43), "People could not go back to the security of the farm life, nor could they rely on the income from the recently laid off son. The loss of savings through bank failures and depreciated investments had reduced many self-reliant old people to dependence on relief."

The increasing numbers covered currently upsets the reciprocal balance of employed workers putting in portions of their wage for redistribution to the retired. In 1940, there were 145.8 workers for each beneficiary, and by 1972 there were only 2.9 workers per beneficiary, an increase from three million to thirty million recipients. Those increases have risen to thirty-four million people receiving benefits directly and as beneficiaries. These represented one-seventh of the working population.

These issues have stimulated political activism of the retired working population of Pittsfield. One of the most active groups is that of the General Electric retirees associated with the IUE. The group meets once a month in an open session planned by a board that meets weekly in the union hall. They tend to focus on reinforcing their pension and medical benefits from the corporation, but they are actively tuned in to state and national programs that relate to their concerns as pensioners trying to maintain a decent standard of living in an inflationary situation. Periodically they invite congressional representatives at the state and local level to explain what they are doing and respond to their questions. At each of the meetings, participants are given a postcard on the issue the executive board has earmarked as their current drive. After explaining the issue, sometimes with an outside speaker to respond to questions, the members have the choice of sending the card to their representatives with a personal message.

Most of the action taken has a direct cost benefit for the retired. Anticipating a vote on Reagan's attempted cuts on Medicare benefits, Al Litano, who serves as vice president for the retirees' club, said:

> This meeting coming up on September 26 in Washington, D. C. with Congress, we will have a helluva vote if it is run right. Reagan spoke to the American Medical Association proposing that the first sixty days in the hospital you would pick up the whole bill. The government will pay only for terminal illness with Medicare. Last October, my wife was in for four months. If I had to pick up the first sixty days, I would be on welfare. As president, Reagan has free access to any hospital. They have the best welfare program for themselves.

The message is always couched in personal, concrete terms that communicate effectively to the group. Sometimes those who have served in the union and other public positions draw wider political conclusions, as Al did that same morning:

> We've got to get a president in office who's interested in retirees since we are almost a majority of the country. Reagan will probably

be a candidate, but he is not for us. When he went in, he said he would not touch Social Secuirty and welfare. But now we see such delays in meeting the cost-of-living increases for retirees, but there are billions for foreign countries. If that guy gets away with this, we're going to go for broke. The next card we get out should go to Reagan before he goes on his trip to the Far East.

Al spoke in the election year of 1984 when the IUE was trying to get support for Mondale on the Democratic ticket. Sentiment was strongly against the Reagan domestic and foreign policy, but the only step the union took was backing a protectionist bill requiring a set proportion of parts in any automobile sold in the U. S. to be made in the country. Whether the discussion relates to foreign trade or the attack on welfare, leaders in the IUE Retirees' Club try to ground the issues in the direct concerns of their constituency. Most of them were concerned with unemployment because it affected whether their children could find jobs in the city and remain near them.

Linking the problems of unemployment, robotization and the attack on Social Security, the retirees started a campaign for making robots pay taxes. In June 1982, when retired workers of IUE Locals 254 and 255 went out on their annual picket line at the main gate of Pittsfield's GE plant, the messages on their signs could teach plant managers, government representatives and the public in general a lesson in redistributive economics. One read, MUST WE BEG FOR THE GOOD THINGS? A DECENT MEDICAL PLAN IS NOT A LUXURY, another said. But the statement that went beyond what we see in the media or business journals was Guy Pelegrinelli's sign, ROBOTS SHOULD PAY SOCIAL SECURITY. The proposition was elegant in its simplicity and ability to capture an American idiom of appropriate behavior. By paying taxes for each robot, corporations would compensate for the losses in income to the Social Security rolls resulting from their policies of automation. Indeed, it would serve to curb the process at the same time that it would activate the redistributive processes, circulating the gains from production as wages once did.

These signs show that workers have a more profound sense of the implications of technological change and its link with the redistributive system essential for maintaining the social system intact than the hired economists of business or government. While management specialists in the burgeoning field of automation worry about the competitive market in gearing up plants for robots, workers in industry and those who are retired are concerned with the fundamental problems that threaten our society. These are, first and foremost, jobs. Without wages and income, who can consume the flow of products that robots are capable of producing? But no less important are the taxes needed to pay for basic social services won over the years by organized labor — pensions, Social Security, medical insurance, education for children and retraining workers displaced by automation.

Retirees have more immediate goals regarding their pensions from the General Electric Company. In 1984, the fund had an annual interest return of $800,000,000 with only $400,000,000 disbursed to living workers. Leo ''Bus'' Rodgers, president of the retirees' club, presented the case for increasing pensions at a meeting of the IUE conference board during national negotiations. He pointed out that those who retired prior to 1970 averaged about $100 per month from their GE pensions. This added to $230 per month from Social Security did not cover normal expenditures in the year 1979. Comparing the pensions GE workers receive, which have been adjusted periodically to inflation amounting to 40 percent, compared to a cost-of-living increase of 115 percent, he urged that, ''The working people who produced goods for the world market, enabled the existence and the flow of profits for whomever they worked, should be recognized with increased pensions and improved medical care insurance plan.''

The retirees meet with state and federal congressmen in each election year. They let them know what they want and hear them defend their records in office. The retirees are completely pragmatic in choosing the candidates they back, considering only their voting records, their power in committees to get legislation through and eschewing ideological debates. They are far more active in community outreach than the Local 255, yet they are not officially recognized by the national or local units. A representative from the club was asked to attend the negotiations of the 1984 contract with the corporation, and this may be a move toward greater recognition.

While these claims are made in reference to workers' past contributions to the industry, another area of redistribution pools funds from state and private sources to attend to the needs of the elderly in home care and in centers provided for them. The Berkshire Home Care service enables older people to remain in their own homes when they are unable to do all the self-care themselves, by providing strategic services with a staff of paid and volunteer workers. Since 1974 when the service was begun, they have had a 90 percent increase in their casework, operating with a budget of $48,000 initially and now with $2,500,000. The homemaker volunteers work with the elderly doing light cooking and housework. They also provide bus service and health services as well as nutritional centers where advice on diets and instruction in food preparation is given.

Many of the general welfare aids such as assistance in paying energy bills and housing are directly or indirectly aimed at the senior citizens. Over 1200 volunteers put in many hours working for the elderly throughout the county: in hospitals, as drivers giving rides for elderly and handicapped, and providing "meals on wheels" — low-priced, hot meals for elderly who are confined to their homes. Mental health counseling and a program called "Good Grief" help the elderly to relate to death and dying. A hot line telephone service enables the sick to summon aid immediately. Legal services, occupational therapy and free recreational trips enable the elderly to live active lives. An inter-generational child care service promotes the extended ties missing in many American homes. Congregate housing and sharing home arrangements are made in both publicly- and privately-owned homes, overcoming the isolation many senior citizens face.

This extraordinary level of activity shows a remarkably successful fusion of the community concerns typical of a small town combined with the know-how and practiced administration of a bigger city. According to the director, the subtle balance of private and public funding and the mix of volunteer and professional help will go down the drain if federal funding is reduced, since they need stable input to build programs. Formerly CETA workers mixed with the volunteers, "helping like one of the family." Reaganomics has destroyed this and crippled the rest of the program as well. The specious call for turning such public activities back to charities does not take into account that well over 50 percent of these programs are already financed by private funds from United Way and volunteer work, but that the core payments from regular government sources sustain the whole structure.

This complex network of service organizations, with board members drawn from industry and labor, is a complementary part of an anarchic mode of production in which workers and their families bear the brunt of shifts in the business cycle. These agencies contrast with the state welfare agencies wherein you become a category excluded from the hard-working, sports-loving, privatized family mode of living that characterizes the citizens of the city. Even now, with many forced to go on welfare, some members of the community would endure deprivation rather than check out a grocery cart using food stamps. As these numbers increase, the onus on relief will shift from the recipients to the system for failing to provide employment. Even when the Reagan government was proclaiming an end to the recession of 1982, there was an increase in the claims on emergency centers in Pittsfield. The Salvation Army provided 4,848 nights' residence to the homeless in the fiscal yar 1985, and it was projected at 6,325 from 1986

(*The Berkshire Eagle* December 6, 1985). The average of 602 vouchers for shelter each month of the third quarter of 1985 represented an increase of 576 percent over vouchers given in the same period in 1983. An average of seventy-five restaurant meals per month were underwritten in 1985, up 316 percent from 1983, along with 3,588 meals from the food pantry, up 30 percent over 1983. The emergency meal centers provide about 375 families with food each month, and the State Department of Public Health found malnutrition affecting 2 to 4 percent of the children in the state (*The Berkshire Eagle* March 26, 1985). In December, the local press (*The Berkshire Eagle* January 25, 1985) estimated that there were ten to twenty street people in Pittsfield. Although most economic indicators were looking good at the end of 1985, with real estate sales up $19 million dollars over the same period in 1984 and unemployment rates down to 4 percent, 1.2 percent lower than in 1984, it was clear that the gap between rich and poor was growing.

These figures show that the safety net of welfare is inadequate in the face of a growing cohort of people who are not earning enough for their own or their family's subsistence in the current economy. The welfare system is asked to bear a greater burden precisely at the moment that funds are being cut.

The Interdependence of Industry and Community

Conrad Arensberg wrote over forty years ago (1942): "The form of the community and its established behaviors in many cases exert as strong an influence on organization in industry as do the newer technological innovations upon social structure. The relationship between industry and community is one of 'mutual dependence'." In the half century of change that has intervened, the balance in this relationship has changed. If we look at the first side of this equation, it is clear that the ability to absorb a given labor force and the attraction of immigrants depends upon the jobs available in a community. In advanced industrial locations, the Massachusetts Department of Labor and Industry (quoted in Bacon 1969:18) calculates that for every job in production, two service jobs are supported. The community with its infrastructure of shops, schools, hospitals, municipal maintenance systems and consumer services, clearly depends on income generated by primary production enterprises.

The other side of the dependency equation, that of corporations on community, is diminishing in importance. In the nineteenth and early twentieth centuries, factories were more tied to investments in a plant and to the work force residing in a particular place. The development of corporations with several plants located in different regions gave management greater flexibility to operate throughout the nation prior to World War I and throughout the inter-war period. This process was encouraged with tax policies in the late sixties that promoted investments in new plants by providing major tax write-offs. Nationally integrated industrial unions organized in the thirties were able to make demands on major national firms in the early post–World War II period. However, with the increase of investments overseas, especially since the middle of the 1960s when the investments were channeled into offshore plants in low-wage areas, the power of management has increased. Workers in the U. S. are in effect competing with workers throughout the world, with the lower wage-earning areas attracting capital investment.

The resulting imbalance has weakened the process of redistribution at the workplace. The diminution of wages as a portion of the gross earnings from production reduces government income from payroll taxes and consequently redistribution through governement channels. This is another way of stating that the number of the retired population is growing at a greater rate than that of the prime working-age cohort, but it demonstrates the political economic issues of the changing relations in industry as production work is eliminated from U. S. industry. Guy Pelegrinelli recognized the loss of revenues for the redistribution process with automation and capital-intensive investments in his slogan "Let robots pay taxes."

The complete turnabout from "Welfare Capitalism" in the early part of the twentieth century to welfare for capitalism in the eighties coincides with the incorporation of workers as a-political dependents of large-scale corporations, protecting the privileges of the primary work force against the unorganized secondary work force and the unemployed. The major drive of organized labor for protective tariff reflects the position of nineteenth-century capitalists rather than labor in a capitalist world. This is a measure of the incorporation of organized labor in the hegemonic control. Change will come from the segments of the society that lie outside the institutions organized within and through the corporations, as women heads of families, youths who can no longer gain access to primary work force jobs and the retired assert the need for changes to ensure redistribution in production, at home and in government.

Chapter 11

The Restructuring of American Industry and the Threat to Community and Family

Pittsfield is a city where all of the major transformations in the industrialization of America have left their mark. Almost as in a time capsule, we can see the new plastics industries taking over in the nineteenth century brick factories. They in turn took over the water privileges that powered the early grist mills and iron forges. From the beginning of industry at the turn of the nineteenth century, as Smith (1876) said over a century ago, "love of country and patriotic zeal" combined private enterprise with government initiatives to spur industrialization. Pittsfield's growth as a city was directly correlated with the stimulus provided by U. S. army contracts for blankets, uniforms and muskets in the War of 1812 spurring production in the fulling and dyeing works and iron forges that were formerly an adjunct to domestic production. The growth of its textile industries following the Tariff Act of 1824 reached a limit after the Civil War as competition throughout the United States negated the advantage it held in superior water power. Its survival as an industrial base after textiles moved to the south was predicated on the growth of the electrical machinery industry. At the turn of the twentieth century, Pittsfield opened its gates to receive immigrants from Europe who are now the natives that are concerned with the survival of the community and the industries that once thrived there.

Pittsfield is now experiencing the restructuring of basic industry as the movement from basic production of consumer goods to research and development in high-tech industries and a service and sales economy transforms American corporate development. This began with General Electric's withdrawal from their northeastern plants of production of consumer goods such as radio bases, electric bulbs, plastic casings for electric appliances after industrial unions began to form in the during the inter-war periods. The remaining specialized production of electrical power equipment was threatened when they moved small and medium transformers to the south after the big post-World War II strikes, and this policy was accelerated in the early

315

seventies after the 101-day strike against Boulwarism with the removal of all but larger transformer production. Later, in 1986 with the Power Transformer Division completely shut down after a decade of demands by management to raise productivity on the threat of going out of town, most of the blue-collar work force is retiring, or being forced to take lower-paid jobs in service industries. Throughout the 1980s General Electric's corporate leaders in Fairfield, Connecticut emphasized high-tech defense work in their Pittsfield plant with the production of naval missile systems and an automated gear shift for the Bradley fighting tank. With Ordnance now threatened by the drying up of military contracts and with immediate more than 900 layoffs in 1988, research and development in the Plastics Division is the only growth pole, but even here there will be few jobs for the laid-off production workers.

Pittsfield is losing the owner-operated shops remaining from the nineteenth century or springing up in the wake of General Electric's plastic production in the merger wave beginning in the 1960s. Controlled by conglomerates that invest in them speculatively and write them off when the profit levels dip below the highest return they can expect from the wide variety of industries they enter, the new merger ownership has increased the vulnerability of small firms to shutdowns. Sheaffer Eaton paper plant closed in the last months of the writing of this book, and the largest of the new plastics firms, has passed over to two successive conglomerates, the last of which then transferred its operations to New Hampshire. The only remaining firm from the nineteenth century has been purchased by a multinational corporation that so far has left this older plant intact. The reduction of 10,000 in the work force in industrial production is correlated with the decline from 57,000 to 49,000 in the population from 1970 to 1987. The entry of hundreds of engineers and technicians has changed the consumption patterns, but the thousands of laid-off workers have either migrated or turned to low-paid jobs in the sales and service sectors.

The transformation in Pittsfield provides a context for questioning the premises of corporate hegemonic control in American life. The framework for this control was the incorporation of workers' struggles in a structure in which the organization of production and decision-making in investment was dominated by the corporations, with the government ensuring the social contract between labor and management and providing the welfare programs to rescue those who fell out of the preferred sectors of the employed work force. Trade union participation in the Cold War during the 1950s, their tacit permission of private disinvestment in the United States and runaway shops in the Third World mitigated an independent stance for labor in the 1980s (Howe 1986). The reformist roles of government defined during President Roosevelt's presidency in the 1930s and 1940s, and expanded by President Johnson in the War on Poverty, declined as the constructive policies that characterized labor's position in the preceding decades gave way to increasing dominance by the corporations and rejection on their part of class collaboration. With vast numbers of Third World workers at their disposal, the corporation no longer needed to sustain its end of the social contract. The growing disparity in wages of organized sectors of industry and the declining percentage of trade union organization further weakened the basis for class solidarity in the emerging society.

Some of the propositions regarding the evolution of the labor control system and the deindustrialization of America can be tested in Pittsfield. The ways in which workers in Pittsfield interpret the changes that are affecting their lives are considered within the logic of corporate hegemonic control. The trends in Pittsfield provide a basis for assessing whether a new social contract between labor and capital can emerge within the context of corporate hegemony or whether labor must forge new links with government in developing a democratic industrial base that no longer gives priority to initiatives from the private capitalist sector.

Macro-Economic Trends and the Labor Process

Gordon, Edwards and Reich (1982) provide a comprehensive framework relating capitalist accumulation to changes in the work process that I have modified to include local developments in Table 11.1. In their analysis they maintain that the concentration of capital and the consolidation of the market for goods provided the base for each transformation in the relations of production. Control over the labor process engendered opposition from workers as they resisted labor discipline and depression of wages. The following table draws upon Clawson (1980), Montgomery (1987), Edwards (1979) and Gordon, Edwards and Reich (1982) and Burawoy (1984;1985) to define the macro trends in which Pittsfield's development is analyzed.

Table 11-1

Periods of Capitalist Accumulation and the Labor Process
in the U. S. and Pittsfield

Types of Enterprise in U. S. Capitalism	*Trends in Pittsfield*
I A) 1790–1820 small crafts shops and mills; minimal class differences and easy entry into ownership of mills and workshops	1772–1812 water powered flour and saw mills, fulling and dyeing works and forges under public control. With the onset of the War 1812 and government orders, small factories producing military goods, rifles, textiles
B) 1820–1840 growth industrialization and size of enterprise.	1824 Tariff Act encouraged growth of textile mills Decline of public responsibility for corporations and emphasis of private rights of ownership.
II A) Mid–1840s to 1873 Rapid growth of domestic industries and size Repressive or "patriarchal" control over labor.	Intensive concentration of ownership in a few family-owned textile companies with a variety of industries including paper mills, shoe and machinery firms.
B) 1873–1890 Recession followed by consolidation of corporations and financial institutions. "paternalistic" labor control system.	1890 formation of William Stanley company and growth with Roebling investments at end of decade; persistence of textile companies and a variety of small industries.
III A) Late 1890s to World War I Merger movements and oligopolies	General Electric purchase of Stanley Company in 1903 forced by patent suits brought by Westinghouse
B) World War I to World War II Period of prosperity and "Welfare capitalism" followed by severe depression. Technical and bureaucratic control of the labor process with government intervention.	Employment dominated by General Electric with 60 percent of work force in period of expansion of consumer goods production followed by extreme collapse. Government intervention in support of unions, welfare, job promotion reversed in 1937. Recessionary tendencies reversed by war buildup

| IV A) World War II to early 1970s Expansion of large corporations at home and abroad | Shutdown of remaining textile firms; movement of product lines from Pittsfield GE to south and overseas. |
| B) Early 1970s to present Accelerated investment overseas | Contraction in Power Transformer Division; Buildup of Defense production; Absorption of most small industries in conglomerates. Declining role of government in welfare. |

In tracing the development of capital accumulation and the labor process in Pittsfield, a definitive periodization of labor control processes with capital accumulation such as that proposed by Gordon, Edwards and Reich (1982) and Burawoy (1984) overlooks the uneven development of U. S. industry. Within a community such as Pittsfield with a multiplicity of industries revealing different levels of organization, there is a great deal of diversity in the labor control systems operating at any one time. Paternalistic and arbitrary management policies persisted in some of the textile and paper plants long after General Electric had developed complex bureaucratic procedures in personnel policies. Repressive controls on the order of mid-nineteenth century practices emerged during the strike that took place in 1982 in the only remaining garment factory where the predominantly female work force had none of the protection that evolved in male-dominant industries. These contrasting yet coexisting labor control systems relate to distinct accumulation processes in firms that are differentially integrated in the capitalist system. As a result, they do not conform to a single overriding model of historical change.

Managerial practices often contain contradictary tendencies that do not conform to specific processes of accumulation and labor control systems. In the same period that management moved against craft autonomy from the 1870s to 1920s leading to the debasement of labor, corporations developed some of the policies that Burawoy calls ''paternalism'' in contrast to an earlier stage of ''patriarchy''. This was an attempt to minimize turnover in employment and overcome the alienation to the monotonous work routines introduced by management. In some cases this involved improvement of company housing, as in the Amoskeag plant (Hareven 1982; 1987), development of leisure time activities sponsored by the corporation as in the General Electric Athletic Association in Pittsfield, and in the Elfun Association of managers to improve the community image of General Electric plants throughout the nation. This did not, however, involve a total break with the past ''patriarchal'' arrangements, as Buroway (1984) argues, since repressive labor tactics continued throughout the early decades of the twentieth century. General Electric used goon squads, private detectives and metropolitan police to counter the 1916 strike, and blacklisted workers who tried to organize independent unions on into the Depression years. The company accepted independent labor organization only after the National Labor Relations Board became an effective deterrent to unfair labor standards laid out by federal law.

Similarly the periodization of labor control processes minimizes the persistence of some elements of nineteenth century work organization because of specific characteristics of the job. The reason that General Electric toolmakers and machinists could evade the control exercised through the piecework system was that their tasks involved long cycles and constantly changing specifications. As a result, skills requiring long-term training persisted in the power transformer division of the Pittsfield General Electric plant long after concerted efforts at debasement of the work force took place in the early decades of the century (Leahey 1985–6:39; Nash 1984).

Segmentation of the work force, even in the specific terms in which Gordon, Edwards and Reich present it (1982:165) as "structured labor processes in a 'primary' sector [that] diverged from labor processes in 'secondary' sectors" aimed at controlling the work force, prevailed in many shops in the nineteenth century as well as today. John Stewart Mills discovered these non-competing groups in the labor movement in his day, and Marx envisioned the development of bureaucratic controls in the first volume of *Capital* (cited in Clawson 1980). In Pittsfield's textile mills, machinists in charge of installing, repairing and maintaining the machinery, enjoyed privileged status and pay over machine operatives, and workers were channeled in rigid gender and ethnically defined job categories. Throughout the 150 years of the textile industry's rise and decline, men constituted the long-term, higher paid segment of the work force, whether as operatives in the woolen mills or as supervisors and foremen who exerted control over the women, youths, and recently arrived immigrants on the shop floor.

To present the current exploitation of a segmented job structure as a recent and strictly managerial innovation is impractical if not theoretically indefensible. Management has improved on earlier techniques of labor segmentation, often absorbing rank-and-file or union inputs in structuring the work force. An important change in the segmentation of labor in the twentieth century was, as Gordon, Edwards and Reich point out (1982:174), the development of private vocational training within the plant and the divorce of supervisory functions from foremen who rose form the ranks of production workers to supervisors.

Along with these earlier tactics that became highly organized in the General Electric firm nationally, we found an evolving mechanism of managerial control over a segmented job structure in the allocation of jobs as union eligible or non-eligible based on new computer technology. Relatively unskilled computer operators are classified as non-eligible on the basis of their access to classified information through terminals. The rising numbers of technical and professional employees categorized as "exempt" are excluded from union ranks through managerial control of job descriptions and hiring and firing. This is the group that Gordon, Edwards and Reich call the "independent primary segment." When the IUE attempted to organize these employees at the Raytheon plant the company conceded salary and benefits gains that defeated the organization of a local (interview with Peter De Cico, President of IUE District Council November 22, 1986). Thus the union has effectively been sidestepped in precisely the areas of increasing employment, and as yet the cooptive measures taken by the company to integrate these employees in the hierarchy have counterbalanced efforts to form professional organizations.

The union has also lost ground in shoring up the position of the "subordinate primary" group of semiskilled production jobs by the corporations' increased use of temporary employees and subcontracting. The local plant hires "Kelly Girls" at half the pay the union has won for organized employees, and management subcontracts increasing amounts of production work to small, often unorganized plants. This became a major issue in the 1988 negotiations over the IUE contract. The union was not in a position to threaten a strike over this and other issues related to job security because of the high number of layoffs in the subordinate primary work force where its strength once lay.

Another innovation in labor management in the General Electric plant was the category of "labor relations" people distinct from the personnel department, who were drawn from the union ranks to serve as an interface in negotiations. Their knowledge of the job from the inside enabled them to communicate more effectively with workers and overcome antipathies between labor and management. At the same time, it reduced the mediation of working class organization within the workplace in defining the goals of workers and developing a strategy to attain them.

Some of the techniques developed by management to control the work force became the basis for working class struggle. This was the outcome of the labor control system that Gordon Edwards and Reich (1982) term "homogenization" and the Braverman calls "debasement" of craft skills. Working within the parameters of a homogenized work force, trade unions developed a counterplot in the solidarity of the working class that became a powerful tool in organizing industry-wide organizations and overcoming the parochialism of the craft unions. This fictive unity of members in industrial unions became ever more difficult to maintain in contract negotiations following World War II as job and skill diversity were increasingly manifest. Draftsmen were among the first to break away from the IUE when the wage gains in contracts were translated into cents per hour based on the average workers' pay and unions have as yet been unable to organize the engineering and technical staff that are replacing production workers in the new high-tech production.

The other side of the dialectic in which management transforms elements contained within working class culture and social movements and makes them part of a control system is not as often recognized. Workers and trade union leaders interviewed in the Pittsfield plant uniformly claimed as their own victory the "bureaucratic" organization of production, applauding the move from arbitrary authority of foremen to negotiated rules and regulations contained in union-mediated shop floor practice. Women in particular were able to avoid the sexual harassment that prevailed before the union. Seniority rights, definition of jobs and bumping rights are principles that bind management to trade union proscriptions just as the unions are bound by prescription of strikes during a contract period and other company prerogatives. Even piecework, one of the most notorious attempts to instigate worker compliance to production schedules, was turned to their advantage by General Electric workers until management withdrew it as an incentive system (Chapter 5).

A focus on workplace struggles ignores the more pervasive issues of job security and mobility (Vallas 1987) that influence class consciousness and struggle. Community responses to the strikes that occurred in General Electric in 1916, 1918, 1946, and 1969 reveal dramatic changes in attitudes that affected the power struggle. In 1916 state and local police were mobilized to defend company property against strikers. Strikers failed to coordinate their action with workers in Schenectady and Lynn General Electric plants, and the corporation was able to parcel out work among these competing sites in a way that defeated labor. With this position of power, the plant supervisor refused even to give an audience to the leaders of the strike. In 1918 the National War Labor Board intervened to force wage concessions and other conditions by the corporation. By 1946, the police force, still headed by the same chief of police, responded to the rights of strikers as well as company officials.

The local press and the business community clearly championed the cause of the workers. Democratic and Republican political representatives at state and national levels backed labor's demand for arbitration of the 1969 strike in General Electric plants across the nation. This led to the dispersion of production throughout its U. S. plants immediately after the strike to avoid future action by government officials and community leaders in what had been company dominated towns. It certainly contributed to the flight overseas in the 1970s as company officials recognized the challenge to corporate hegemony in U. S. communities.

Holistic studies of communities enable one to go beyond the unilineal evolutionary model of the labor process that emphasizes managerial initiatives over labor strategies in structuring the work place.[1] Throughout the decades of capital flight following World War II, the very embeddedness of labor in the operation of the corporation and the lack of an alternative vision posed by left-wing militants after the purge of "communists", inhibited an independent stand in the wider society. Leaders in the trade union movement in Pittsfield became active promoters of General Electric contracts in the public arena. They accompanied General Electric sales engineers in their trips to Boston to get state utility contracts and to Washington to secure Pentagon defense contracts, using their voting power as a constituency to persuade state and national representatives to allocate public spending on local production. One business agent explained that he accepted a congressman's explanation for his vote in favor of federal anti-labor legislation when the latter said that he did it because General Electric threatened to withdraw a contract from the Pittsfield plant if he did not do so.

These actions reveal the central role played by labor within corporate hegemony in the prosperous decades of the 1950s and 1960s when trade unions gained concessions from the corporations that ensured a higher standard of living and greater mobility for their children than labor had ever enjoyed in history. The ability to buy back the goods that they produced encouraged future growth in the economy and support for the institutions that reproduced the system. The fact that it was a conciliatory role that did not challenge the premises of corporate power ensured labor a position so long as they were necessary to the accumulation of capital. Even as their position within the corporation has eroded, workers adhere to the rules of the game within the hegemonic alliance. When General Electric announced the closing of Pittsfield's Power Transformer Division, some of the delegates were more outraged with the company's violation of competitive norms in forming a power transformer production plant with

Westinghouse in Canada than they were with a managerial decision that left workers and the entire community divested.

This behavior does not fit a cooptation model since the motivations are not personal gain through bribery, but, rather, commitment that comes from hegemonic construction that involves both corporate and worker input. The distinction between "them" and "us" that once drew the lines of combat between capital and labor (cf. Matles and Higgins 1974) was increasingly obliterated as workers became committed to the system. Corporate hegemony operates by coopting the broader issues, goals and values of workers, not the individuals or even the labor organizations for narrowly defined advancement. Hegemony is, as Mike Davis (1984:7) argues, "a dynamic system which unifies accumulation, legitimation and repression on a world scale."

In the century of concentration and growth of corporations from 1878 to the mid-1960s, the compromises that ensued from the struggle between owners and/or managers of corporations and workers strengthened corporate hegemony. Since that time, the major tactic in labor control has been to withdraw production. As a result of the failure of the union or the government to counter overseas flight, labor has no longer served as a counterweight to corporate power. Union organization is at the lowest point since the Depression, with less than two thousand of the six thousand employees in the Pittsfield plant in the membership rolls of the IUE. The lack of alternative political channels for both employed and unemployed workers is a serious deterrent to democracy in the workplace discussed below.

U. S. Disinvestment and the Acceleration of Commercialization

The analysis of deindustrialization in the United States points to the most important control mechanism, almost overlooked in an approach that focuses on workplace struggles.[2] General Electric consciously used the threat and actual practice of moving production elsewhere when they recognized the strength of nationally organized unions after the 1946 strike. Their growing global investments were as much an attempt to control the labor movement in their domestic plants as to take advantage of cheap labor in export processing plants or branches within low-wage countries. In the favorable environment for overseas investment following World War II, General Electric increased its overseas capacity fourfold, from twenty-one foreign plants in 1949 to eighty-two in 1969 (Bluestone and Harrison 1982:171-2). Their investment in Japanese firms such as Toshiba Electronics Systems Co.,

Ltd., of which they own a 40 percent chunk (Bluestone and Harrison 1982:143) makes them less concerned with foreign competition than workers in their domestic plants.

Deindustrialization theory poses a nationalistic model of change that, from a Third World perspective, involves industrial growth. Bluestone and Harrison (1982) attack both sides of this global transformation, although their policy concerns are primarily with the impact of "widespread systematic disinvestment of the nation's productive capacity." They show how government policies in the 1960s and 1970s encouraged investment abroad through changes in the laws allowing the re-entry of products made in overseas branches of industries with tariffs only on the value added. Tax write-offs for losses in old firms encouraged the abandonment of factories in older industrial areas. These laws were not the reason for the deinvestment but part of a process encouraged by corporate influence in government as corporations pursued profits in an international setting.

Anthropological inquiry into deindustrialization is as much concerned with the local and particular interpretation of these processes as with the dimension of global accumulation itself. Katherine Newman edited a volume of *Urban Anthropology* (1985a) devoted to analyses of the local impact of corporate disinvestment policies that reveal the devastating effects on families and communities. She found in her own study (1985b; 1988) of laid-off Singer sewing machine workers in Elizabeth, New Jersey a tendency towards self-criticism that we observed in Pittsfield. Singer workers appeared to accept the explanation of U. S. industries' inability to compete with Japanese goods as a result of the inferiority of American workers. Although the loss of skill and commitment to work was frequently based on U. S. managerial tactics stressing speedup and task debasement, their guilt derived from their sense of having abandoned traditions of craftsmanship and quality. This choice was often forced upon them by management.

Pittsfield workers were more prone than Singer workers to criticize management directly. "Too many chiefs and not enough Indians," was a frequent refrain in our interviews with 100 General Electric workers on the active and laid-off list of the IUE. The survey was done in 1982 during the recession that followed Reagan's first year in office and before the development of the Plastics Research Center or the marked increases in Ordnance, and thus reflect a pessimistic outlook on the part of blue collar workers who were the most severely affected by this first phase of restructuring. One of our respondents in the survey, a 44-year-old man, pinpointed the problem:

This is the trouble — GE is making all of its products overseas that it once made here. There won't be any jobs for anyone. Toyota, Honda, Suzuki — we never knew those names when I was growing up. It's crazy the way things are. Unemployment is 10.9 percent (1982 figure) and they still send work out. I blame American industry and our government. In the 5 and 10 cent stores they used to have articles made overseas, but cars and electrical products were made here. Now whatever is made is made overseas. The bottom could drop out of the economy any day. American business owns a lot overseas and they don't care. I would probably do the same if I had a business. I could open a shop overseas. I'm not an economist, but I can see what that does to the economy.

Another man commented that GE as a company is "empowered — they empower themselves to move industry out because of the high costs of operation here." The resulting unemployement, hovering around 7 percent from the mid-seventies to the mid-eighties, has meant the loss of the young workers who want to remain active in the workforce.

Table 11–2 indicates the categorized respones.

Table 11–2

Production Workers' Solutions for Unemployment

Don't know		16
No answer		9
Hopeless		6
Things are ok		1
Increase government intervention		29
more unemployment compensation	3	
more government initiated programs	6	
more welfare	1	
more defense contracts	1	
lower inflation	2	
restrict foreign imports	8	
restrict overseas investment	1	
lower interest rates	3	
more CETA or CCC type programs	3	
work on environmental problems	1	
Decrease government intervention		2
lower taxes	1	
cut government spending	1	
Municipal solutions		2

bring in by-pass	1	
increase local control	1	
Corporate solutions		10
reduce management	6	
broaden business base	3	
prevent moonlighting	1	
cut down the work week	1	
TOTAL		75

These answers to the question, "What do you think should be done to improve the present situation?" were freely offered, and not checked off a proposed list. The high proportion of people who expressed a "don't know" attitude reflects the depoliticization of workers. Politics is something for the experts, and people express some irritation when asked what they think. "If I knew that, I would be president," one said. And another responded, "I don't know what to think any more. Everything is in a turmoil. As an individual like myself, I can't do anything." Yet the fact that 29 proposed more government regulation, in a climate of deregulation, is doubly significant. The most frequently voiced solution was foreign tariffs and protection of the U. S. market, a proposal offered by the union. One man suggested,

"You know that you have to sell all over the world, but we don't have the same protections that other countries have overseas. Japan specifically. They have all kinds of laws. We should have more of that. Especially when it is a government contract. GE lost that contract in Utah to a Swedish company. GE has tried, but it didn't help. ...We are the direct current leaders of the world. There isn't any reason why those contracts should go to other countries.

None offered, even in the few cases when pressed, suggestions for an increased role for unions. The image of the union is that of a "business agent", dealing within the constraints of the market for labor and accepting the prerogatives of corporate inititative in bringing in or reducing employment opportunities. With the union-eligible work force down to less than 2000, and further layoffs expected, the business agent characterized himself as a begger when he went into negotiations with General Electric.

Labor unions, particularly the IUE following in the tracks of the garment and shoe workers unions, have called for trade quotas, tariffs and protected markets that were the demand of the early industrialists in the nineteenth century. The labor movement continues to respect the rights of the corporation to make the major decisions affecting the life and death of industry, but the drive for controls on management prerogatives portends a new labor strategy although existing legislation does not as yet pose a major threat to corporate control. When Power Transformer was shut down in 1986, the Massachusetts law on plant closings requiring prior notification on planned closings, extension of unemployment and medical benefits a few weeks beyond existing provisions, and retraining programs did not apply since General Electric still had a presence in Ordnance and Plastics. The recent passage of a national shutdown law in 1988 overcomes the competitive disadvantage in attracting new investment when it is posed state by state, but the law does not challenge the company's right to make decisions regarding production level.

The growing indignation of the union members at the arbitrary exercise of power by the corporation was expressed by the business agent for the Local 255 of the IUE, Bruce Farren, in his address to District Council representatives of the IUE on November 21, 1986, when General Electric announced its intention to shut down Power Transformer:

> It's just a shame brothers and sisters, and I'll just give you my opinion now, being a past vice president of the AFL/CIO and a past chairman of the negotiating committee with GE, that I don't know what's happening in this country. The textile industry is extinct, that's gone and all the buildings around that area have been demolished; the shipbuilding is now overseas; the radar is being made in England; the Bradley Fighting Vehicle could be sent to Israel — we're already buying foreign parts for the transmission. What the hell do we have left? The power transmission system is going offshore. Steam turbines as well. God forbid if anything happens to us and we have to go to war. With our textiles gone, we're going to have to buy our uniforms overseas, our weapons overseas, our boats are being made overseas. Quincy shipyard is closed. It's just atrocious that we're allowing this to happen. We try to vote in the people we think will represent us. We have suggested at the national negotiating committee to ask the General Electric that one of these days we have a big meeting in Washington, that we make our concerns known. How much good it's going to do, I don't know, but certainly it's a step in the right direction.

Workers and the union leaders clearly recognize the paradox of billions of dollars spent in an arms buildup while basic industry is destroyed by the very corporations earning super profits from defense contracts.

As the union began to adjust to the reality of the shut down of Power Transformer Division, they worked in cooperation with management to set up a counciling and retraining center for the laid-off workers. Management tried to present themselves as initiators of the program, but union officials advised me that it had already been mandated in contract negotiations. Union officials had filed for Title 3 money coming from trade assistance legislation to assist workers laid off because of foreign competition, and when the company tried to take over the operation to "polish their logo", the union demanded equal participation.

As the union became involved in bumping rights and early retirement benefits, the larger issues that loomed in the crisis period faded into the background. Only two months later, when the General Electric Company announced that it would coordinate its defense systems division with plants located in Burlington, Vermont, Philadelphia and the newly acquired RCA plants making similar products in their Pittsfield headquarters, the union business agent looked forward hopefully to new defense contracts (*The Berkshire Eagle* January 24, 1987:A1). The acceptance of dependency on the Ordnance plant obliterates the subconscious awareness that it poses a danger for the community with little chance of positive growth. As a result, the conversion to peace production movement has gained few supporters in the ranks of labor or technical and professsional staff at the local plant, and it was not picked up as an issue by the AFL/CIO national headquarters.

The proliferation of commercial activities parallels the decline in productive enterprises. Consumerism that was the drive of early twentieth century industry threatens to turn inward as industries consume the potential of labor to produce while manufacturing missiles and war machinery. In the emerging logic of corporate hegemony sales promotion of a product, whether it is made for consumption or destruction, at home or abroad, is justified in terms of profits. Sales promotion of the city itself is the major strategy of development committees as they try to attract new enterprises to overcome the economic decline in the wake of disinvestment. The "mall wars" often result in redundant commercial outlets where the new jobs created in the sales and service sector do not provide the security, mobility or rising standards of living that industries provided in the past. What Mike Davis (1984:7) calls "the new regime of accumulation based on 'over-consumptionism' and expanded low wage employment" is beginning to undermine the support for the system in the political social arenas.

A full understanding of workers' struggles must put together the conflicting demands of work, family and community (Lamphere 1987:

327). Consciousness of exploitation is conditioned by the needs and satisfactions assessed in these contexts. This often differs for men and women, and it was single female household heads who expressed the most militant consciousness in words and actions during our research. Redistribution of income in the family may cushion the sense of deprivation experienced by a laid-off worker, yet the inabilty to meet the needs of dependent members of a family may also sharpen a workers' awareness of the inadequacy of his or her wages. Since family members often work in firms that are differently integrated in the structures of accumulation, they frequently do not share a unitary view of the systems in which they live and work (Nash 1985).[3]

Corporate Responsibility and Community Welfare

The failure on the part of the corporation to take responsibility for the chaos in U. S. industrial production is paralleled by a consistent, conscientious withdrawal of government programs to redress the families and communities destroyed by disinvestment. In the past half century there has been a shift from welfare capitalism of the 1920s to a demand for welfare for the corporation. Corporate leaders of earlier decades such as Gerard Swope were concerned with stimulating consumer demand for electrical machinery by providing security to workers in wage payments and pensions. During the Depression the corporation personnel retention plan giving priority to heads of households with dependent children. Given that this policy allowed the company to retain a cohort of preferred male workers in their most productive years, it was necessary to phrase their moves in terms of concern with family and community. During World War II the country appealed to patriotism to gain the commitment of the work force. Throughout the first half century of its presence in the city, the corporation successfully coopted the real commitments to country and community that workers and their families experienced.

The uneasy balance between the corporation and the community was totally upset in the 1980s. The breakdown occurred in three arenas: (1) at the site of production there are fewer workers producing higher returns for the corporation; (2) the wage returns for workers are declining in real terms and there is a widening gap between wages for production workers, salaries for managers and directors at the top level and profits; and (3) the corporation is returning less revenues in the form of taxes at the state and local level.

(1) *The Decline in Wage Disbursements.* Gainful employment is the

principle basis for claims on the social surplus in corporate America, yet the number of jobs that can support a family are declining nation-wide. Workers in Pittsfield are so committed to this principle that they try to avoid going on welfare even at extreme personal sacrifice. The corporation has pursued a policy, particularly from 1976 to 1986, to reduce their operations in enterprises that emphasize production jobs while buying up enterprises and expanding their own operations in defense and finance. In the period from 1976 to 1986, the total number of workers declined from 380,000 to 359,000 (after a slight rise recorded in the years 1978 to 1981). This trend culminated in the period 1884 to 1986 when there was a rise in net profits of 11 percent and in profits per worker of 23 percent (Table 11.3a).

Table 11–3a

Sales, Revenues, and Profits in General Electric

Year	Sales	Total Revenue	Net Profits	Workers	Sales per Worker	Profits per Worker
		(millions of dollars)			*(millions of dollars)*	
1976	15,697	15,972	930.60	380,000	41,307.89	2448.95
1980	24,959	25,523	1,514.00	402,000	62,087.06	3766.17
1984	27,947	28,936	2,280.00	330,000	84,687.88	6909.09
1985	28,245	29,272	2,336.00	304,000	93,042.76	7684.21

Source: United Electric Radio and Machine Workers of America, "General Electric Business Segment Information," in *Fight Back Package*, 1986

The major change is from a consumer goods industry to defense communications, and financial services industry. This can be seen in the following table:

Table 11–3b

Revenues for Each Segment of General Electric Operations, 1986–1982 Compared

	1986		1982	
	(in millions of dollars)			
Aerospace	4,318	11.8%	1,935	7.0%
Aircraft Engines	5,977	16.3%	3,140	11.6%
Consumer Products	4,654	12.7%	3,558	13.1%

Financial	585	1.6%	286	1.0%
Industrial	4,711	12.8%	4,949	18.2%
Major Appliances	4,107	11.2%	2,751	10.2%
Materials	2,331	6.4%	1,593	5.9%
NBC	1,817	5.0%	—	—
Power Systems	5,262	14.3%	6,229	22.9%
Technical Services	3,266	8.9%	2,086	7.7%
Other	774	2.1%	1,410	5.19%
Eliminations	1,077		748	
TOTAL	36,725	100.0%	27,189	100.0%

Source: United Electric Radio and Machine Workers of America, 1987. Ibid.

The changing proportions of investments show a movement from high employment to low employment, high revenue industries, particularly notable in power systems, industrial production, and major appliances to aerospace, aircraft engines and communications. In Pittsfield, 50 percent of the company's revenues were from old traditional core manufacturing while in 1986 this constituted only 20 percent. With the current purchases of 338 businesses in a variety of communications and services fields for $11.1 billion and its divestment of 232 businesses in traditional manufacturing between 1980 and 1986, General Electric is beginning to approximate a conglomerate.

President Reagan commented on the national changes reflecting this trend in the U.S. in his report to Congress in 1987:

> The move from an industrial society toward a post-industrial service economy has been one of the greatest changes to affect the developed world since the Industrial Revolution. The progression of the economy such as America's from agricultural to manufacturing is a natural change.

The tactic of making change appear part of a natural and hence inevitable progression is the essence of an ideological control system that attempts to depoliticize the population.

Employment in the Pittsfield plant relates to the long trends in the U. S. economy but shows particular variation around military engagements with the Korean War and the arms buildup reflected in upswings or absorption of declining power production in the 1980s (See Chart 11.3c). The current decline to 5,000 is the lowest since the Depression.

**Loss of Jobs
GE**

Source: UE "Fight Book Package" 1986 GE and Westinghouse Information

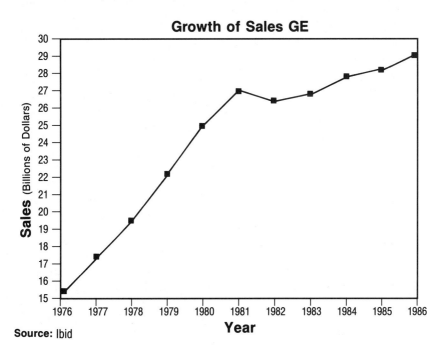

Growth of Sales GE

Source: Ibid

(2) *The Growing Gap between Wages and Revenues.* Top directors of the General Electric Corporation receive six digit salaries while workers are having a hard time keeping up with inflation. John F. Welch, Jr. received $1,687.617 in total cash compensation in 1986 (*Wall Street Journal* March 16, 1987), a figure that is frequently cited in union negotiations. The averge GE worker makes in Pittsfield won an increase of 4.5 percent, bringing their wage from $12.02 per hour to $13.40 in July 1988 negotiations. What minimized the sense of victory was the knowledge that in the same period the corporation had a 17 percent increase in earnings (*The Berkshire Eagle* July 3, 1988). When the company purchased RCA, workers learned that the former directors would receive as much money for attending a two-hour board meeting as they would get working a hundred hours. The vast differences in power and wealth affecting the country as a whole are shaking the confidence of people in the equity of the system when they compare their position with that of leaders in the corporation they work for, and the growing squeeze between profits and wages.

(3) *Corporate Taxes.* In the past, the company felt it was necessary to justify their position with some reciprocal benefits, even if only in the form of public relations releases. Yet from 1981 to 1984, the corporation paid no income taxes during a period when it reported earning $9.5 billion. In October 1985 John F. Welch made a speech to the Commercial Club in Cincinnati in which he asserted that the corporation invested $18 billion and created or preserved 250,000 jobs. He claimed that the only way to maintain U. S. competitiveness in the world market is by retaining tax writeoffs on investments and research and development. The local press editorialized on the speech with the title "What's good for GE....," satirically invoking the early post-World War II maxim of Charles Wilson of General Motors that what was good for his corporation was good for the country:

> If every company were able to take advantage of the tax code as aggressively as GE, it would mean the country would in effect have no corporate income tax. That may not be such a bad thing, but it would lead either to a worse budget deficit than Washington already has or to a substantial increase in personal taxes — something neither Congress nor Mr. Reagan has any stomach for.

Robert S. McIntyre, director of federal tax policy at Citizens for Tax Justice, was even more outspoken in his criticism of the tax incentives for corporations, which he says have actually killed GE's appetite for investment (*The Berkshire Eagle* February 21, 1985). Contrasting Whirlpool, a maker of consumer products, with General Electric,

McIntyre states that Whirlpool pays the highest federal income tax rate among major corporations and has increased investment in new plant and equipment while General Electric has been the nation's top tax refund recipient while at the same time cutting back on investment. Whirlpool paid $297 million to the U. S. Treasury between 1981 through 1983, they were able to increase capital spending by 7 percent. General Electric, on the other hand, paid no income taxes on the $6.5 billion earned and cut purchases of plant and equipment by 15 percent in the same period. He further asserted that his Whirlpool washer was a far better product than the General Electric dryer he bought at the same time. Summing up the General Electric fortunes in the first Reagan Term, Philip M. Stern (*New York Times* March 17, 1986) stated that the corporation made nearly ten billion in profits but paid not a penny of tax. Shareholders received a 30 percent dividend increase and the chief executive officer got a 141 percent pay incrase, but there were 18 percent fewer jobs.

Corporate responsibility is conditioned by the level of commitment to an area and to the workers in industry. The decline in interest in its Pittsfield plant is illustrated by General Electric's policies regarding potentially hazardous substances. Since 1934 General Electric used Pyranol, an oil containing polychlorinated biphenyls (PCBs), as an insulator in its power transformers. Despite evidence for the dangers associated with contact with the substance from 1968 when rice contaminated with PCBs caused eye discharges, severe skin eruptions, neurological disorders and reproductive problems, the General Electric Company continued to use the insulant and to discharge effluxes containing it into Silver Lake until 1978.

In Pittsfield, the city became aware of the danger in the mid-seventies when fish taken out of the Housatonic River were tested and found to have dangerous levels of PCB (*The Berkshire Eagle* August 8, 1975). Workers and managers in the Power Transformer Division were even more concerned as they saw dozens of their fellow workers succumbing to cancer. Edward L. Bates, Jr., a retired manager in the testing department, said in a talk to the retirees of General Electric, "In the seventies it seemed to me that I was going to a wake or a funeral every other week of people who worked with me, especially in the testing laboratories where they worked with pyranol." Ed and a colleague have challenged the results of an epidemiological study begun in 1979 that was not made public until 1987. The results, that denied a scientifically verifiable correlation between cancer and PCB exposure, are being questioned on the grounds of adulterated samples in crucial buildings (Nash and Kirsch 1986; 1988). The demands of the employees who were in high exposure areas are simple: a medical monitoring of the people exposed at the expense of the General Electric; medical insurance for all workers past the present cut-off age of 65; and compensation to families of General Electric workers. The corporation has been accused of denying growing evidence for a linkage between contact with Pyranol and cancer, and with avoiding responsibility to its employees.

The difference in the way the corporation related to its community and work force emerged after the post- World War II strikes. Ed Bates was one of the few managers from that period who refused to leave the Pittsfield plant in order to gain mobility in the corporate hierarchy. He noted that when he first went to work at the Pittsfield GE plant in the late thirties, he had a general manager who was in the plant until he died, and the manager who followed him remained until he became president of the corporation. There were managers under him who would be in the position ten, fifteen or maybe twenty years. After the sixties, they started to move their managers around "like chess pieces," he said. As a result, Ed commented, "They've lost a lot of the closeness that they used to have with the workers and with their own people." He reasoned that the policy started when the corporation expanded rapidly after the war in different places around the country where they didn't have manager trained that could go in and so they used those from older plants. When the decentralization move began with Ralph Cordiner, managers were expected to move around or lose posibility for advancement. Ed Bates lost several promotions because he chose to stay in Pittsfield where he was born and to raise his five children there.

The corollary of the corporation's policy to move managers around was to minimize the commitment of managers to the area and to the workers in the particular plant. This, in turn, strengthened the control by central headquarters since they were less likely to encounter the resistance of local plant managers to closing down a division or entire works.

The emphasis on short term profitability affects the way in which management perceives information on environmental hazards and how they respond to laws regarding the use of hazardous substances. The differential power and resources of corporate interests from those of workers and residents in a community channel the diffusion of scientific information. The first community relations director to whom I spoke had resisted offers to move up and out of the city. When he was confronted with the growing awareness of the dangers of PCBs, he did everything in his power to get the corporation to compensate homeowners whose property was affected. He was among the first high level managers to be replaced in 1982 when the Division was reduced in size.

The infrastructural costs that were borne by nineteenth century industrialists extended to the financing of educational and cultural institutions that are the inheritance of contemporary industry. The mutual dependence of industry and community that once encouraged redistribution of at least some of the profits in the interest of the locality through charity and taxes is no longer experienced as the greater mobility of the corporation enables them to escape such obligations in the right to work states in the U. S. and overseas.

Throughout the century of corporate hegemonic control, the costs of the mobility of plant and personnel have been borne by the families and community. The present structure of industry is no longer synchronized with community and family organization. Corporate private enterprise fails to meet minimal standards of continuity in employment that would permit raising a family, staying in one's home, and retiring in the community. The corporations have polluted the waters and consumed most of the resources that once attracted industry to the Berkshires. The unique response to critics in the government or in labor unions is to threaten or actually to withdraw production sites. The corporate side of the social contract with communities has been abrogated as investors have sought more profitable ventures abroad (Bluestone and Harrison 1982). Those who are upholding corporate hegemony in the U. S. are workers and local politicians who are offering welfare to the corporations in the form of takebacks in wages and benefits, tax rebates, and public funds for capital investment. If their efforts fail, U. S. corporations will be the losers along with communities.

The breakdown of the old social contract, measured in terms of economic waste, unemployment, dislocations of families and communities, military waste, crime and health (Bowles, Gordon and Weiskop 1983), signals the need for a new social contract (Carnoy, Shearer and Rumberger (1983:6). The basis for this exists in Pittsfield and elsewhere in groups that were only marginally integrated in corporate hegemony. These include the unions that have tried to organize the minimum wage earners in sales and service work; women's organizations that have addressed the needs of home workers, battered wives and abused children; the peace movement; Vietnam veterans whose claims have been ignored more than those of servicemen from any previous wars; and public interest groups that mobilized around issues of environmental contamination, the homeless and other welfare issues. The future struggles of American workers are more likely to be organized outside of the workplace and in neighborhoods and communities where the unemployed and homeless meet with the poorly paid underclass of workers and heavily mortgaged homeowners to work out a new social contract.

Notes

Chapter 1

1. Natalie Sokoloff (1980) summarizes the evidence from studies indicating that education and skill are not attuned to reward.

2. Heidi Hartmann (1976) summarizes the evidence for segregation by sex stimulated by trade unions and professional associations.

3. Throughout the four volumes of *Professional Management in General Electric* the authors maintain the fiction that wages are direct payments for the individual contribution of each employee.

4. Robert Asher (personal communication) has interviewed displaced employees of the International Silverwork Company in Meriden, Connecticut, who maintain that the company also followed similar policies of excluding industries that would compete for the labor force in the fear that it would drive up wages.

5. This does not mean that *all* women accept layoffs with equanimity. Women who are single heads of families as well as women with unemployed or intermittently employed spouses require the certainty of full-time work. They are among the most militant workers, as I show in Chapter 6. Yet employers perceived a greater compliance to layoffs among spouses of employed General Electric that influenced their employment preferences.

6. Preference for male workers was not true in all General Electric plants, as Milkman demonstrates (1976). The Pittsfield plant had already shifted production to power transformers which employed principally a male work force by the time of the Depression.

Chapter 2

1. David Montgomery (1979) found a stratified labor force in place in many production shops at the end of the nineteenth century. Richard Price (1986:99), in his thoughtful review essay of Gordon, Edwards Reich and others, criticizes their failure to recognize ''prior structures of segmentation''.

2. Marjorie Able (1987) shows the significant number of women employed in western Massachusetts in the nineteenth century.

3. Able (1987) cites Massachusetts Bureau of Labor Statistics showing that

a family of four spent $649 a year, far more than a man's earnings in Pittsfield. Clearly it was a necessity for women to enter the paid work force.

Chapter 3

1. The date of purchase was 1903, but the name Stanley Company was retained and the firm enjoyed a certain amount of autonomy until 1907 which may account for the confusion.

Chapter 4

1. In 1971, J. Stanford Smith, the head of General Electric's International group, said that "60 percent of the total market for General Electric products is outside of the United States, and it is a market that's not only larger but growing faster than the U. S. market." General Electric Investor, Fall, 1971, p. 3, cited in Woodmansee (1975:14). In the mid-seventies, General Electric employed 404,000 employees in more than 240 plants and 100 laboratories around the world. 307,000 of them worked in the 111 major General Electric locations in 32 states of the U. S. The rest worked in 80 overseas plants found in 23 countries (General Electric Management 1973:12; General Electric Corporations Education Services 1972).

Chapter 5

1. Engineer William Ginn was involved in the communication with rival firms to set bids in the late 1940s and 1950s. His success with this officially uncondoned practice caused him to be promoted to division manager in 1952. Then he decided to turn over a new leaf, but sales representatives and marketing managers under him continued to discuss prices with competitors, for which he was held responsible (Walton and Cleaveland 1964:80 et seq.)

2. Montgomery (1987) calls the Bedaux system the "Taylorism of the Great Depression and GE its managerial vanguard".

Chapter 6

1. Figures are not available for General Electric personnel, but I am going by unofficial comments by people in managerial positions.

Chapter 9

1. Sennet (1970) demonstrates the importance of familial aid in allowing mobility for children in his book on Chicago immigrant families in the late nineteenth century.

2. Jane Humphries (1977) analysis of redistribution in British working class families indicates the material basis for family support of corporate hegemonic structures. She states (1977:25) that "family ties, vitalized by ideologies, bind together labouring and non-labouring members and secure for the latter a share in the former. The historical basis for such a network of definite relationships is kinship. So family ties provide a basic element in this mode of appropriation, the social significance of these ties constituting the basis of redistribution through which the surplus is appropriated."

3. Blau and Ferber (1986) summarize data from sequential studies of housework in the following table:

4. Although the Equal Employment Opportunity Act may be considered a minor piece of legislation compared with Title VII of the Civil Rights, it generated more affirmative action in the Pittsfield General Electric plant because non-compliance threatened the military contracts in the growing Ordnance division.

Chapter 10

1. Some aspects of this chapter are touched on at Bellagio in 1985 in a paper given at a Wennergren Converence (Nash 1989).

Chapter 11

1. Among the cultural historians and anthropologists who provide a broad context in which to analyze working class formation are Cumbler (1979); Frisch (1972); Gutman (1975); Hareven 1978; 1982; Lamphere (1979; 1987) David Montgomery (1979;1987); Newman (1985; 1988); Rosenzweig (1983); Wallace (1978).

2. John P. Zipp and Katherine E. Lane (1987) note the failure for many labor analysts to see offshore processing and deindustrialization as a labor control system. The literature on global integration of industry is, however, replete with such analysis (cf. bibliography in Nash and Fernandez-Kelly 1984).

3. Tamara Hareven (1982) found distinct differences in the response of Amoskeag workers to the plant shutdown based on age, marital status and gender. Older workers were more defeated, females were able to get comparable jobs more easily, and marriage dampened militance.

References Cited

Able, Marge. 1987. "Gender, Ethnicity and Industrial Labor." Paper prepared for the 86th Annual Meeting of the American Anthropological Association, Chicago, IL November 18–22, 1987.

Adams, Leonard and Robert L. Aronson. 1977. *Workers and Industrial Change: A Case Study of Labor Mobility.* Ithaca, NY: Cornell University Press.

Allen, William. 1845. *The Berkshire Jubilee Celebrated at Pittsfield, Massachusetts.* Albany: Weare C. Little.

Arensberg, Conrad W. 1942. "Industry and Community." *American Journal of Sociology* 48, 1:1–12.

Backman, Jules. 1962. *The Economics of the Electrical Machinery Industry.* New York: New York University Press.

Bacon, George Fox. 1969. *Background to Planning for Franklyn County Technical Report,* Massachusetts Department of Industry and Department of Commerce. A. D. Little Projective Economic Studies of New England, Associated Industries of Massachusetts. Boston.

Baer, Walter E. 1975. *Strikes.* New York: American Management Association.

Berkshire County Development Commission. n.d. *Business Opportunities in the Berkshires.*

Birdsall, Richard D. 1959. *Berkshire County: A Cultural History.* New Haven: Yale University Press.

Blau, Francine D. and Marianne A. Ferber. 1986. *The Economics of Women, Men, and Work.* Englewood Cliffs, N.J.: Prentice Hall. Bluestone, Barry and Bennett Harrison. 1982. *The Deindustrialization of America.* New York: Basic Books.

Bluestone, Barry and Bennett Harrison. 1982. The Deindustrialization of America. New York: Basic Books.

Boltwood, E. 1916. *The History of Pittsfield Massachusetts from the Year 1876 to the Year 1916.* Pittsfield: Eagle Printing Co.

Boulding, Elise. 1976. "Family Constraints on Women's Work Roles." in Martha Blaxall and Barbara Reagan, eds., *Women and the Workplace; The Implications of Occupational Segregation.* Chicago: University of Chicago Press.

Boulware, Lemuel R. 1969. *The Truth about Boulwarism: Trying to do Right Voluntarily.* Washington, D. C.: Bureau of National Affairs.

Bowles, Samuel, David M. Gordon and Thomas E. Weiskop. 1983. *Beyond the Wasteland: A Democratic Alternative to Economic Decline.* Garden City: Doubleday Anchor.

Braverman, Harry. 1974. *Labor and Monopoly Capital.* New York: Monthly Review Press.

Brecher, Jeremy. 1972. *Strike!.* San Francisco.

————. 1984. "Crisis Economy: Born Again Labor Movement?" *Monthly Review.* 35, 10:1–17.

Burawoy, Michael. 1979. *Manufacturing Consent: Changes in the Labor Process under Monopoly Capitalism.* Chicago: University of Chicago Press.

————. 1984. "Karl Marx and the Satanic Mills; Factory Politics under Early Capitalism in England, the United States, and Russia." *American Journal of Sociology.* 90,2 (Sept.): 247–287.

————. 1985. *The Politics of Production: Factory Regimes under Capitalism and Socialism.* London: Verso.

Carnegie, William and Carol Hill. n.d. *A Berkshire Sourcebook: The History. Geography and Major Landmarks of Berkshire County, Mass.* Pittsfield: Junior League of Berkshire County.

Carnoy, Martin, Derek Shearer, and Russell Rumberger. 1983. *A New Social Contract: The Economy and Government after Reagan.* New York: Harper and Row.

Carr, L. J. and J. E. Stermer. 1952. *Willow Run: A Study in Industrialization and Cultural Inadequacy.* New York: Harper and Brothers.

Clague, E. and W. J. Couper. 1934. *After the Shutdown.* New Haven: Yale University Press.

Clawson, Dan. 1980. *Bureaucracy and the Labor Process: The Transformation of U. S. Industry, 1860–1920.* New York: Monthly Review Press.

Clowes, Florence W. 1981. *Pol–Am: A History of the Polish Americans in Pittsfield, Massachusetts 1862–1945.* Webster, MA: Economy Press.

Cordiner, Ralph L. 1957. in *General Electric Professional Management.* Vol. II. New York.

Cowan, Ruth S. 1987. "Women's Work, Housework, and History: The Historical Roots of Inequality in the Workforce Participation." in Naomi Gerstel and Harriet E. Gross, eds., *Family and Work.* Temple University Press.

Cumbler, J. T. 1979. *Working Class Community in Industrial America; Work, Leisure and Struggle in Two Industrial Cities, 1881–1930.* Westport, Conn.: Greenwoo Press.

Davis, Mike. 1984. "The Political Economy of Late Imperial America." *New Left Review.* 143 (Jan Feb): 6–38.

DeGrasse, Robert M. Jr. 1984. *The Military is Shortchanging the Economy.* Council on Economic Priorities.

Doeringer, Peter B. and Michael J. Piore. 1971. *Internal Labor Markets and Manpower Analysis.* Lexington, MA: D. C. Heath and Co.

Drucker, Peter. 1953. *The Practice of Management.* New York: Harper and Brothers.

Edwards, Richard. 1979. *Contested Terrain: The Transformation of the Workplace in the Twentieth Century.* New York: Basic Books.

Erie, Steven P., Martin Rein, and Barbara Wiget. 1982. "Women and the Reagan Revolution: Thermidor for the Social Welfare Economy." Paper given at the Annual Meeting of the Western Political Science Association, San Diego, CA.

Federal Writers' Project. 1938. *The Berkshire Hills.* New York: Duell, Sloan and Pierce.

First Gazeteer, Berkshire County, Massachusetts 1725–1885. 1885. Syracuse.

Frisch, Michael H. 1972. *Town into City: Springfield, Massachusetts and the Meaning of Community 1840–1880.* New York: Cambridge University Press.

Galbraith, John Kenneth and Paul W. McCracken. 1983. *Reaganomics: Meaning, Means and Ends.* New York: The Free Press.

General Electric. 1953–1959. Professional Management in General Electric. New York. 4 volumes.

Gladden, Washington. 1897. *Social Facts and Forces: The Factory, the Labor Union, the Corporation, the Railway, the City, the Church.* New York: G. P. Putnam Sons.

Gluckman, Max. 1968. "The Utility of the Equilibrium Model in the Study of Social Change." *American Anthropologist.* 70, 2:219–237.

Gordon, D. and R.C. Edwards and M. Reich. 1982. *Segmented Work, Divided Workers; The Historical Transformation of Labor in the United States.* Cambridge: Cambridge University Press.

Gorz, A. 1982. *Farewell to the Working Class.* London: Pluto Press.

Gouldner, Alvin. 1954. *Wildcat Strike.* Yellow Springs, Ohio: Antioch Press.

Gramsci, Antonio. 1973. *Selections from the Prison Notebooks of Antonio Gramsci,* edited and translated by Quintin Hoare and Geoffrey Nowell Smith. New York: International Publishers.

The Great Barrington Historical Society. 1986. "An Interview with William Stanley." *The Great Barrington Historical Society Newsletter.* 8 (Special Issue.)

Greenwood, R. G. 1974. *Managerial Decentralization.* Lexington, MA: D. C. Heath Co.

Gutman, Herbert. 1975. "Work, Culture, and Society in Industrializing America 1815–1919." *American Historical Review* 78,3 (June): 531–89.

Hall, Stuart and Tony Jefferson. 1983. *Resistance through Rituals: Youth Subcultures in Post-War Britain.* London: Hutchinson and Company. First published 1975.

Halle, David. 1984. *America's Working Man: Home and Politics among Blue-Collar Property Owners*. Chicago: University of Chicago Press.

Hareven, Tamara K. 1975. "Family Time and Industrial Time; Family and Work in a Planned Corporation Town 1900–1924." *Journal of Urban History* 1:365–8.

———, 1978. *Amoskeag: Life and Work in an American Factory City*. New York: Pantheon Books.

———. 1982. *Family and Industry in New England*. New York: Cambridge University Press.

———. 1987. "The Dynamics of Kin in an Industrial Community," in Naomi Gerstel and Harriet Engel Gross, eds., *Families and Work*. Temple University Press.

Hartman, Heidi. 1976. "Capitalism, Patriarchy and Job Segregation by Sex." *Signs* 1 (Spring): 137–169.

———. 1981. "The Family as Locus of Gender, Class and Political Struggle; The Example of Housework." *Signs*. 6,3:366–394.

Herman, Edward. 1981. *Corporate Control, Corporate Power*, Cambridge, England.

Horowitz, Morton J. 1977. *The Transformation of American Law 1780–1860*. Cambridge, MA: Harvard University Press.

Housing and Urban Development (HUD). 1984. *Community Planning and Development: Urban Conditions and Trends. The President's National Urban Policy Report*. Washington, D. C.: Government Printing Office.

Howe, Carol. 1986. "The Politics of Class Compromise." *Review of Radical Political Economy. Review of Radical Political Economics*. 18.

Humphries, Jane. 1977. "The Working Class Family, Women's Liberation and Class Struggle; The Case of Nineteenth Century British History." Review of Radical Political Economics. 9 (Fall): 25–41.

Hunter, Louis C. 1979. *A History of Industrial Power in the United States 1780–1930*. Charlottsville, Va.: University Press of Virginia.

Jacobs, Barry. 1980. "The Poisoned Land; PCBs: Deadly Footprints of the Chemical Industry," *The Progressive*, 6,44:43–47.

Jahoda, M., P. Lazarsfeld, and H. Zeisel. 1971. *Marienthal; The Sociography of an Unemployed Community*. Chicago: Aldine. First published 1937.

Kornblum, William. 1974. *Blue Collar Community*. Chicago: University of Chicago Press.

Kuhn, James. 1980. "Electrical Products," in Gerald C. Somers, ed. *Collective Bargaining, Contemporary American Experiences*. Madison, WI: Industrial Relations Research Association Series, University of Wisconsin.

Kuhn, James W. and Ivar Berg. 1968. *Values in a Business Society; Issues and Analyses*. New York: Harcourt, Brace and World.

Kusterer, Kenneth. 1978. *Know How on the Job: The Important Working Knowledge of the Unskilled*. Boulder, Colo. Westwood Press.

Lamphere, Louise. 1979. "Fighting the Piece Rate: New Dimensions of an Old Struggle in the Apparel Industry." in Andrew Zimbalist, ed., *Case Studies in the Labor Process*. New York: Monthly Review Press.

———. 1986. "From Working Daughters to Working Mothers: Production and Reproduction in an Industrial Community." *American Ethnologist.* 13,1:118–30.

———. 1987 *From Working Daughters to Working Mothers: Immigrant Women in a New England Industrial Community.* Ithaca, N.Y.: Cornell University Press.

Landis, Paul H. 1934. *Three Ironmining Communities.* Ann Arbor, Mich.: Edwards Bros.

Leahy, Philip J. 1985–81. "Skilled Labor Another Ruse of the Modern Corporation: The Case of the Electrical Industry, Labor History 27, 1: 31–53.

Littler, Craig R. 1982. *The Development of the Labour Process in Capitalist Society: A Comparative Study of the Transformation of Work Organization in Britain, and the U.S.A.* London: Heinemann Educational Books Inc.

Lynd, Robert and Helen Lynd. 1929. *Middletown; A Study in Contemporary American Culture.* New York: Harcourt, Brace.

———. 1937. *Middletown in Transition: A Study in Cultural Conflicts.* New York: Harcourt, Brace, and World.

Mait, Stephen H. 1978. "Social Security: A Program to Prevent Poverty." in Herman Berliner, ed., *Programs to Prevent or Alleviate Poverty.* New York: Hofstra University Yearbook of Business Series 12, Vol. 2, pp. 32–113.

Maret, Elizabeth and Barbara Finlay. 1984. "The Distribution of Household Labor among Women in Dual-earner Families." *Journal of Marriage and the Family,* 46:357–360.

Massachusetts Division of Employment Security. 1982. *Employment and Wages Report.* ES202. Boston.

Matles, James J. and James Higgins. 1974. *Them and Us: Struggles of a Rank and File Union.* Englewood Cliffs, New Jersey: Prentice.

Mayor's Office of Community and Economic Development, Charles L. Smith, Mayor, Janet L. Goldberg, Commissioner. n.d. *The Pittsfield Economic Revitalization Plan: An Industrial Development Agenda for the 80's.* Mimeo.

Melman, Seymore. 1979. "Inflation and the Pentagon's Budget," *America* 140 (June 30):532–4.

———. 1983. "How the Yankees Lost their Know-how." *Technological Review.* 86 (Oct): 56–8.

Milkman, Ruth. 1976. "Women's Work and the Economic Crisis: Some Lessons of the Great Depression." *Review of Radical Political Economics.* 8,1 (Spring): 73–97.

———. 1982. "Female Factory Labor and Industrial Structure; Control and Conflict over 'Woman's Place' in Auto and Electrical Manufacturing." Paper read at the colloquium for Social History, City University of New York Graduate Center.

————. 1985. *Women, Work and Protest: A century of U. S. Woman's Labor History.* Boston: Routlege and Kegan Paul.

Miller, J. A. 1948. *Men and Volts at War.* New York: McGraw Hill Book Co.

Montgomery, David. 1979. *Workers' Control in America: Studies in the History of Work, Technology and Labor Struggles.* New York: Cambridge University Press.

————. 1987. *The Fall of the House of Labor.* New York: Cambridge University Press.

Mullany, Katherine. 1895. *Catholic Pittsfield.* Pittsfield Eagle Publishing Company. Volume 1.

————. 1924 *Catholic Pittsfield.* Pittsfield Eagle Publishing Company. Volume 2.

Nash, June. 1984. "The Impact of Industrial Restructuring on a World Scale on a New England Industrial Community," in C. Bergquist, ed. *Labor in the Capitalist World-System.* Berkeley, CA: Sage.

————. 1985. "Deindustrialization and Economic Restructuring in a New England City," *Urban Anthropology* 14, 1-3: 31-82.

————. 1989. "A Redistributive Model of the Evolution of Law," in June Starr and Jane Collier, eds., History and Power in the Study of Law. Ithaca: Cornell University Press.

Nash, June and Max Kirsch. 1986. "Polychlorinated Biphenyls in the Electrical Machinery Industry: An Ethnological Study of Community Action and Corporate Responsibility." *Social Science and Medicine.* 2,1:131#138.

————. 1988. *"The Discourse of Science: Corporation and Community in the Construction of Consensus." Medical Anthropology Quarterly* June issue forthcoming.

———— and M. Patricia Fernandez-Kelly. 1984. Women, Men and the International Division of Labor. Albany: SUNY Press.

Newman, Katherine S. 1985. "Urban Anthropology and the Deindustrialization Paradigm." *Urban Anthropology and Studies of Cultural Systems and World Economic Development.* 14, 1-3 (Spring-Summer-Fall): 5-19.

————. 1985. "Turning your Back on Tradition: Symbolic Analysis and Moral Critique in a Plant Shutdown." ibid.: 109-150.

————. 1988. *Falling from Grace: The Meaning of Downward Mobility in American Culture.* New York: Free Press.

History and Power in the Study of Law. Ithaca: Cornell University Press.

Northrup, Herbert R. 1964. Boulwarism: The Labor Relations Policies of the General Electric Company, their Implications for the Public Policy and Management Action. Ann Arbor: Bureau of Industrial Relations, Graduate School of Business Administration, University of Michigan.

Passer, Harold. 1953. *The Electrical Manufacturers 1875-1900: A Study in*

Competition, Entrepreneurship, Technical Change, and Economic Growth. Cambridge: Harvard University Press.

Peattie, Lisa and M. Rein. 1983. *Women's Claims.* Cambridge, Mass.: MIT Press.

Piven, Frances Fox and Michael Cloward. 1982. *The New Class War.* New York: Pantheon Books.

Polanyi, Karl. 1947. *The Great Transformation.* Boston: Beacon Press.

Polanyi, Karl, Conrad M. Arensberg, and Harry W. Pearson. 1957. *Trade and Market in the Early Empires.* New York: The Free Press.

Prew, Bertha E. 1983. "World War II: A Berkshire Housewife's Chronicle." *Berkshire History.* (Spring) 3,2.

Price, Richard. 198. "Review Article." *Journal of Social Research.* 91–110.

Rosen, Ellen Israel. 1987. *Bitter Choices: Blue Collar Women In and Out of Work.* Chicago: University of Chicago Press.

Rosenzweig, Roy. 1983. *Eight Hours for What We Will: Workers and Leisure in an Industrial City 1870–1920. Cambridge, England: Cambridge University Press.*

Schatz, Ronald W. 1983. *The Electrical Workers: A History of Labor at General Electric and Westinghouse 1923–1960.* Urbana and Chicago: University of Illinois Press.

Searlemen, Bruce E. 1979. *Paper and Allied Products in Massachusetts.* Massachusetts Department of Economic Statistics.

Sennet, Richard. 1970. *Families against the City: Middle Class Homes of Industrial Chicago 1872–1890.* Cambridge, MA: Harvard University Press.

Smith, E. A. 1869. *The History of Pittsfield, Berkshire County, Massachusetts from the Year 1734 to the Year 1800.* Boston: Lee and Shepard.

———. 1876. *The History of Pittsfield, Berkshire County, Massachusetts from the Year 1800 to the Year 1876.* Springfield: C. W. Bryan and Co.

Smith, Chard Powers. 1946. *The Housatonic, Puritan River.* New York: Rinehart and Co.

Sokoloff, Natalie J. 1980. Between Money and Love: *The Dialectics of Women's Home and Market Work.* New York: Praeger Pbls.

Steiner, P.O. 1975. *Mergers: Motives, Effects.* Ann Arbor: University of Michigan.

Sundquist, James L. ed. 1969. *On Fighting Poverty; Perspectives from Experience.* New York: Basic Books.

Tarbell, Ida. 1927. *The Nationalizing of Business 1878–1898.* New York: Macmillan.

Trachtenberg, Alan. 1982. *The Incorporation of America: Culture and Society in the Gilded Age.* New York: Hill and Wang.

United States Department of Labor, Bureau of Labor Statistics. 1982. *Monthly Labor Review Bulletin.* 105 (September).

United States Security and Exchange Commision. 1982. *110 Report.* Washington, D.C.: Government Printing Office.

Vallas, Steven Peter. 1987. *The Labor Process as a Source of Class Consciousness: A Critical Examination."* Sociological Forum 2,2:237:256.

————. 1950. *Steeltown: An Industrial Case History of the Conflict between Progress and Security*. New York: Harper

Walker, C. R. 1937. *American City: A Rank and File History*. New York: Farrar and Rinehart.

Wallace, Anthony. 1978. *Rockdale. The Growth of an American Village in the Early Industrial Revolution*. New York: Knopf.

Walton, Clarence C. and Frederick W. Cleveland, Jr. 1964. *Corporations on Trail: The Electric Cases*. Belmont, CA: Wadsowrth Pbls. Co., Inc.

Warner, William Lloyd. 1953. "An American Sacred Ceremony," *American Life, Dream and Reality*. Chicago: University of Chicago Press, pp. 1–26.

———— and J. O. Low. 1937. *The Social System of a Modern Factory*. New Haven: Yale University Press.

———— and P. S. Lunt. 1941. *The Social Life of a Modern Community*. New Haven: Yale University Press.

———— and P. S. Lunt. 1942. *The Status System of a Modern Community*. New Haven: Yale University Press.

———— and L. Srole. 1945. *The Social System of American Ethnic Groups*. New Haven: Yale University Press.

Weiss, Robert S. 1984. "The Impact of Marital Dissolution on Income and Consumption in Single Parent Households." *Journal of Marriage and the Family*. 46:115–27.

Westwood, Sallie. 1984. *All Day Every Day: Factory and Family in the Making of Women's Lives*. Urbana: University of Illinois Press.

Wickman, W. C. C. 1969. "The Product Division General Manager Responsibilities and Role in Planning and Control." in *A Case Study of Management Planning and Control at General Electric Company*, New York: Controlership Foundation, Inc. pp. 23–28.

Wilensky, Harold. 1975. *The Welfare State and Equality: Structural and Ideological Roots of Public Expenditures*. Berkeley: University of California Press.

Williams, Gwynn A. 1960. "Gramsci's Concept of Hegemony." *Journal of the History of Ideas*. 21:586–99.

Willison, George F. 1957. *The History of Pittsfield, Massachusetts 1916–1955*. Pittsfield: The Sun Printing Co.

Woodmansee, John et al. 1975. "Our World and Welcome to It," in *The World of a Giant Corporation*. Seattle, Washington: North County Press.

Zalch, M. and M. Berger. 1978. "Social Movements in Organization," *American Journal of Sociology*. 83.

Zipp, John F. and Katherine E. Lane. 1987. "Plant Closings and Control over the Workplace: A Case Study." *Work and Occupations* 14,1 (Feb):62–87.

Index